CLASSIC CAR

CLASSIC CAR

THE DEFINITIVE VISUAL HISTORY

Penguin Random House

DORLING KINDERSLEY

Senior Editor Chauney Dunford

Senior Art Editor Saffron Stocker

Editors Natasha Kahn, Sam Kennedy, Constance Novis, Marianne Petrou, Steve Stetford

Designers Steve Bere, Shahid Mahmood, Simon Murrell

US Editors Christy Lusiak, Margaret Parrish

Photographers Deepak Aggarwal, James Mann, Gary Ombler

Picture Researchers Nic Dean, Roland Smithies, Sarah Smithies

DK Picture Library Laura Evans, Romaine Werblow

Jacket Designer Mark Cavanagh, Saffron Stocker

Jacket Editor Claire Gell

Jacket Design Development Manager Sophia MTT

Producer, Pre-Producer Jacqueline Street-Elkayam

Producer Luca Bazzoli

Managing Editor Gareth Jones

Managing Art Editor Lee Griffiths

Art Director Karen Self

Publisher Liz Wheeler

Publishing Director Jonathan Metcalf

DK INDIA

Senior Editor Anita Kakar

Project Art Editor Vaibhav Rastogi

Editor Sneha Sunder Benjamin

Assistant Art Editors Yashashvi Choudhary, Anusri Saha

Managing Editor Rohan Sinha

Managing Art Editor Anjana Nair

Jacket Designer Suhita Dharamjit

Managing Jackets Editor Saloni Singh

Picture Researcher Nishwan Rasool

Managing Picture Researcher Taiyaba Khatoon

DTP Designer Sachin Gupta

Senior DTP Designers Harish Aggarwal, Sachin Singh

Pre-Production Manager Balwant Singh

Production Manager Pankaj Sharma

Editor-in-Chief Giles Chapman

Writers Martin Gurdon, David Long, Andrew Noakes, Chris Quiller-Rees

US Consultant Lawrence Ulrich

First American Edition, 2016
Published in the United States by DK Publishing
345 Hudson Street, New York, New York 10014

Copyright © 2016 Dorling Kindersley Limited
DK, a Division of Penguin Random House LLC
16 17 18 19 20 10 9 8 7 6 5 4 3 2 1
001–289028–Sept/2015

A catalog record for this book is available from the Library of Congress.
ISBN 978-1-4654-5339-6

DK books are available at special discounts when purchased in bulk for sales promotions, premiums, fundraising, or educational use. For details, contact DK Publishing Special Markets, 345 Hudson Street, New York, New York 10014 or specialsales@dk.com

Printed in China

A WORLD OF IDEAS:
SEE ALL THERE IS TO KNOW
www.dk.com

Contents

THE 1940s: REVVING UP AGAIN

Car manufacturers worldwide faced tough times after World War II, but huge demand for new models meant an exciting future was on the horizon. While the US led the world in automotive style, the UK chased the 120 mph (193 km/h) sports-car dream, and Europe created innovative small cars that everyone could afford. Gasoline supplies eased and auto shows returned after a long absence. From here, it was foot down to the future.

THE 1950s: WORLD ON WHEELS

Rapidly improving road networks in many parts of the world opened countries up for exploration, and what better way to enjoy this new-found freedom than in a car? The choice of cars available was now enormous. Detroit went crazy with chrome plating and jet-age imagery, and all manufacturers sought to make their cars go faster and farther. Only the bubble car, with its birdlike appetite for fuel, put rationality first and foremost in this age of motoring excitement.

THE 1960s:
INNOVATION AND ENERGY

This was the decade when new technology led the way—everything from front-wheel drive to the rotary engine. Executive sedans and two-seat roadsters put the accent on swift acceleration and high-speed handling prowess. The Ford Mustang gave suburbia its own sports car—with Toyota's trusty Corolla to do the shopping—while the E-type and Cobra were race-bred firebrands.

THE 1970s:
A CLEANER STYLE

After the party of the '60s came the hangover of the '70s, with valid concerns about air pollution halting the muscle car, and the convertible almost killed off by road safety fears. Yet hatchbacks made family cars so much more versatile, while motoring fantasies were fueled by wedge-shaped, mid-engined supercars. Four-wheel drive was a new leisure buzz phrase, and crucial new cars abounded.

THE 1980s: ADVANCING TECHNOLOGY

There had never been such an exciting time to buy your ultimate car, as top speeds smashed through the 200 mph (322 km/h) barrier. But at every level, electronic wizardry boosted performance and comfort in everything from engine management to CD players. Even ordinary sedans received turbochargers and four-wheel drive. Meanwhile, lead-free gasoline and catalytic converters cleaned up the typical car's act enormously.

Preface

When I was young, I could gaze at a beautiful image like the one opposite, of the Mercedes-Benz 300SL "Gullwing," and only hazard at how such a spectacular car came to be. Certainly, it was nothing like the humdrum vehicles I saw in everyday life. Even so, occasionally a car that was manifestly old or unusual would clatter past our house or the playground. And, once again, I would turn to wondering why modern equivalents—with their drab plastics, uninspiring sounds, and bewildering logos with combinations of letters and numbers —seemed so much less appealing. The fascination slowly took hold and, before long, I was covertly reading car magazines under the chemistry lab benches when I should have been writing down methods and conclusions. I never did learn much about chemistry, but what I did discover then is that if the classic car knowledge bug gets you, it bites, and I was bitten really hard.

My destiny was to work on a classic car magazine myself, and that is what I did for several years. Along the way, of course, I have owned a few dozen classic cars. They have ranged from a Cadillac DeVille all the way down to a Reliant Robin, with hot hatchbacks and sports cars in between. I have had plenty of adventures, and learned even more over time about what makes old cars tick. As well as writing about great cars for magazines and newspapers, I have also authored about 40 different books on classics of all types. However, when the opportunity arose to be Editor-in-Chief of this, *Classic Car*, I knew it would be something unique.

Over several months, I have been able to look again at the whole spectrum of classic cars from every part of the world, and bring together the most significant, interesting, memorable, and downright beautiful. I have also had the chance to pick some classics of the future—the cars which, in my long experience of watching values hurtle ever upward, will be the ones to cherish. And some of them, such as the Fiat Barchetta, are currently bargains. (Incidentally, the Barchetta is the only brand-new car I have ever bought, and as many other enthusiasts will know about their own "lost loves", it is one that I wish I had not sold.)

But as to my favorites, the process of curating *Classic Car* has left me just as perplexed as ever. There is as much to love about a humble Austin A40 Somerset as there is a sublime Maserati Mistral. I would like to have a Porsche 911 behind my garage door, just as much as a Corvette.

Few of us have the money and time to own and enjoy every classic car that strikes our fancy. Instead, most of us will just be looking at pictures and daydreaming when we should be doing something else. But if you *are* one of the fortunate few —someone who can use this fantastic book as a menu, and plan epic journeys in the cars of your dreams—then do the rest of us a favor: just make sure that you relish every moment!

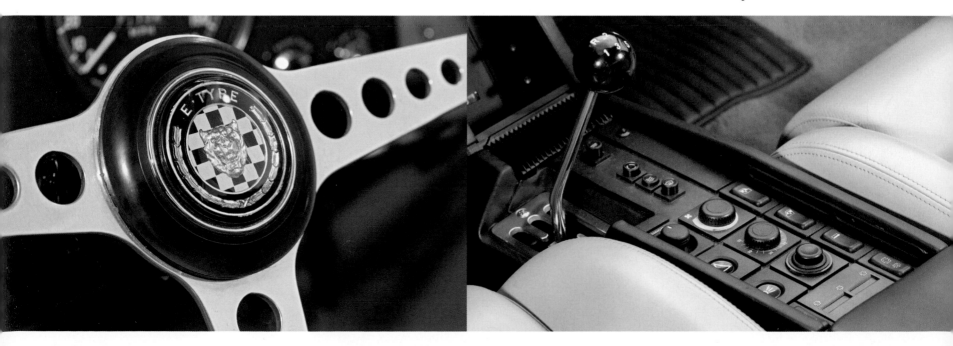

A World of Classics

The closest thing to an "official" description of a classic car probably comes from the venerable Classic Car Club of America. For many years, this organization has insisted that only "distinctive" or "fine" cars manufactured between 1915 and 1948 qualify for the title of classic car, with the Lincoln Continental often acting as the closing bracket for the genre.

In the UK–arguably the European birthplace of old vehicle preservation–traditional authorities such as the Royal Automobile Club have planted their own markers in the sand. According to these bodies, "veteran" cars–such as the aged machines that take part in the famous annual London-Brighton run–are defined as those built from 1885 to 1903. "Edwardian" cars are those made from 1904 to 1914, while "vintage" cars hail only from the period between 1919 to 1930. Following the Wall Street Crash of 1929, the bankruptcy of Bentley, and the demise of several other great marques, a golden era is seen to have ended. According to these categories, any worthwhile car built from 1931 to 1939 is classified, perhaps derisively, as a "Post-Vintage Thoroughbred."

Yet most of these decrees already seemed dated in the 1970s and '80s, when awareness of the value of a greater range of older cars was rising rapidly. Hand-built, pioneering, and expensive road and racing cars would always be collected and cherished, but enthusiasts were now banding together simply to save the few remaining cars that had populated their own childhoods. A new-found nostalgia meant that the humblest of Dodges, Morrises, Renaults, or Fiats now had a value. Clubs were formed, magazines published, histories written, memorabilia sought and saved, all in the name of preserving a bygone era of motoring.

And as time marched forward, so new waves of cars entered the classic vista, and had to be accommodated. Japanese cars for example, once the source of prejudice among long-time enthusiasts, became antiquated and scarce, and it was agreed that some of them really did stand the test of time.

For the purposes of this book, "classic" means cars made in the period after World War II until the beginning of the 1990s– which itself is more than a quarter of a century ago. Beyond that, extraordinary lengths of research have brought every type of roadgoing car together within these pages. They range from the most economical to the most powerful, popular family sedans to esoteric indulgences, ugly brutes to unrivaled beauties, and from the utterly conventional to the technically adventurous.

This breadth belies the truth behind the "classic" label. Besides the unmistakable fact that a car needs to be old and rare enough to evoke surprise and reawakened affection, what makes a classic is ultimately subjective. The criteria are different in the minds of each and every car enthusiast; as personal as their taste in music, food, art, or partner. This fact is reflected in the extent and scope of this book. There is not a car here that someone, somewhere, would not want to own and drive, or simply to possess, perhaps restore, and feel proud of its historical significance. Of course, there are many more that would cause frenzied bidding among collectors at an auction. There are cars that, perhaps, you have owned yourself, or wanted to own, or which still resonate for their looks, their features, their performance, or their ability to sum up a time, a place, a journey. All of them have their place in the classic car firmament–they have played their individual parts in the long and complicated evolution of the car.

"Everyone **dreams** of driving a **Ferrari**; it was my **intent** from the **start**"

ENZO FERRARI

The classic car world is enormously wide and varied. At its heart are owners who have made it their passionate business to preserve cars that might otherwise have long ago been destroyed, once their usable life had petered out. All over the globe, there are hundreds—if not many, many hundreds—of individual owners' clubs, each catering to a single marque—sometimes, even, a single model. The clubs provide the support, camaraderie, and expertise that make the labor of love required to restore and run a classic car a realistic prospect.

The restoration process usually begins when a car reaches the end of its useful life. Most cars, after several owners and maybe more than 100,000 traveled miles, are sold at their scrap values. The good news for the environment is that about 85 percent of a typical car can be recycled. But for a car with classic status—by dint of age or merit, or both—this is just the beginning of a new, regenerative process. Life is about to start again.

Every enthusiast dreams of stumbling across a classic in a barn or garage. Yet most will come from ads online or in the back of the many classic car periodicals that continue to defy the decline of print media. Dealers and auctions are also key sources. Locating all the necessary spare parts is another matter entirely. They will usually need to be sourced through a mixture of personal contacts, autojumbles (fleamarkets of used car material), and tips from the wider community.

For very old cars, or specialty sporting models, the road to recovery is relatively simple. The cars should—in theory at least—come apart easily because the body panels are bolted to the separate chassis frame. There is usually still plenty of corrosion to repair, among a hundred other tasks, but it will be relatively

logical. For a car with unibody construction—where there is no separate frame as the structure of the car is welded into one piece—things are harder, but still possible with skill and patience. The rebuilding of an engine and gearbox is often a trickier activity. Technically minded owners relish taking such tasks on themselves; for others, there is an entire industry devoted to painstaking mechanical refurbishing. In many cases, highly experienced specialists have had to learn how to remanufacture long-obsolete parts—originally turned out in their thousands by thundering machinery—by hand and eye.

Repainting a car demands an entirely different skill set, as does working with wood and leather to recreate period interiors with all the attention to detail of the best antique restorers. Fortunately, many of the oldest cars carry exemptions from emissions rules and regulatory inspection, which mean they can still be used on today's roads, often with zero-rated levels of tax. Coverage against loss or accident can be very cheap, as insurers know that classic car owners are the drivers least likely to be reckless with their precious possessions.

Once the work is complete, the rewards are there for the taking. Classic car owners love to show off the fruits of their labors and share the joy. Devotees make the pilgrimage to classic car shows where debate over a car's finer points is likely to be fierce and forceful. Other events include race meetings, *concours d'élégance*—essentially, a beauty pageant for old metal—and road trips that sometimes run through several countries.

GILES CHAPMAN, EDITOR IN CHIEF

The 1940s
REVVING UP AGAIN

FUTURAMIC STYLING!

FUTURAMIC DRIVING!

OLDSMOBILE

A Product of General Motors

*Hydra-Matic Drive standard equipment on Series "88" models, optional at extra cost on "76".

REVVING UP AGAIN

The 1930s had proved a tough decade for the world's automakers, with the Great Depression following the Wall Street Crash of 1929, making it hard to sell cars built around luxury, performance, or excitement. Then, just as prosperity had returned, the world was plunged into war in 1939.

Car production around the world slowly ground to a halt as hostilities intensified, with Detroit succumbing in 1942. As an engineering-heavy industry, its car factories were repurposed for weapons, aircraft, and armaments manufacture. Development of the motor vehicle itself—except for rugged military trucks and four-wheel-drive systems—all but ceased.

Getting started again in 1945 was slow and laborious. Many car factories had to be completely rebuilt after taking direct hits from enemy bombs, and it was mostly prewar designs that made their way down rejuvenated production lines.

The US motor industry, mostly unscathed, was quick to embrace new styling and technology that would make its Cadillacs, Buicks, Fords, and Hudsons the envy of the world. In Europe, punishing tax regimes favored small cars, and designers made a variety of "people's cars" from scratch. By the end of the 1940s the choice was wide, with the UK's Morris Minor, France's Renault 4CV and Citroën 2CV, the Italian Fiat 500C, and Sweden's Saab 92 all vowing for attention.

The UK's new high-performance cars set the pace. First the Healey 2.4 lit and then the Jaguar XK120 was vaunted as the world's fastest production car. Meanwhile, four-wheel-drive Land Rover challenged the battle-won, off-road reputation of the US's Jeep.

> "Study **all the possibilities**, including **the impossible.**"
>
> PIERRE-JULES BOULANGER, VICE PRESIDENT OF CITROËN, 1938

◁ **US magazine ad** for Oldsmobile cars, 1949

△ **American motors lead the way**
While European car manufacturers struggled to rebuild after World War II, US automakers, such as Cadillac launched a string of highly desirable new models.

Key events

▷ **1945** The first batch of Volkswagen sedans is completed under British Army supervision.

▷ **1945** Renault was nationalized by the French government after founder Louis Renault is jailed for collaborating with the Nazis.

▷ **1946** The British motor industry celebrates its 50th birthday with a parade in London, and Austin builds its one-millionth car.

▷ **1946** The first call is made on an in-car radio-telephone, made by Motorola.

▷ **1946** Mercedes-Benz receives permission from US Army occupational forces to restart vehicle manufacture.

▷ **1947** Motor industry legends Henry Ford, Ettore Bugatti, and General Motors founder William C. Durant die.

▷ **1947** Donald Healey launches his Healey 2.4 liter—at 110 mph (177 km/h), it is the world's fastest production car.

▷ **1948** The Land Rover is unveiled at the Amsterdam motor show.

▷ **1948** Citroën's 2CV brings radical new meaning to economy motoring.

▷ **1949** Cadillac builds its 1-millionth car.

▷ **1949** Jaguar's new XK120 sports car reaches 152 mph (245 km/h) in Belgium.

▷ **1949** Saab's first car, the 92, is released for sale to the public.

△ **Streamlined Swede**
Saab launches its first car, the 92, in 1949. Highly aerodynamic for its time, the body was stamped from a single piece of steel to reduce wind resistance.

Prewar Designs

During World War II, automakers turned their mass-production expertise over to manufacturing essentials for the war effort, producing everything from tin hats to fighter planes and tanks. After the war, the factories had to be reorganized and retooled, and returning them to their prewar levels of car production took time. The simplest and quickest way for companies to do that was to reintroduce the models built in the late 1930s—occasionally with some minor updates. Some of these cars, or the engines and running gear underpinning them, would soldier on in restyled models for years to come.

FRONT VIEW

REAR VIEW

External spare wheels

Flat face
The Morgan three-wheelers usually hid behind their big, exposed, air-cooled V-twin engines, which were mounted at the front of the car, but the 4/4's engine was fitted under a conventional hood, fronted by this flat radiator grille.

Desirable convertible
Morgan built the 4/4 as an open two-seater, a four-seater, or this convertible coupe. The convertible offered a higher standard of weather protection and a better class of luxury than the other cars, but only 41 were built.

Lightweight, thin tires

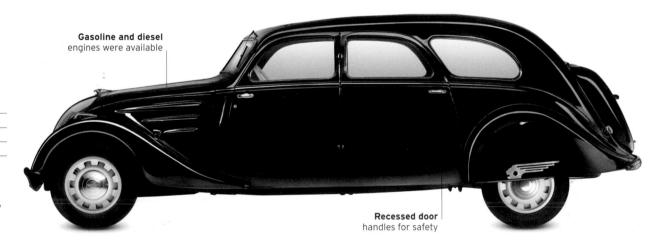

Gasoline and diesel engines were available

Recessed door handles for safety

▷ **Peugeot 402 1935**

Origin	France
Engine	1,991cc, straight-four
Top speed	75mph (121km/h)

The 402 was far more successful than most streamlined cars of the 1930s, mainly due to its low price–75,000 were sold. Retaining a separate chassis allowed Peugeot to offer 16 body styles. It was still produced during the war, particularly in van and utility versions.

Hood flutes–a Vauxhall trademark

Unibody construction

◁ **Vauxhall H-type Ten-Four 1937**

Origin	UK
Engine	1,203cc, straight-four
Top speed	60mph (96km/h)

Vauxhall's entry-level car was a little bigger than its rivals and boasted a unitary construction body, independent front suspension, and hydraulic brakes. A new grille was the most noticeable change when it reappeared in 1946, but it barely lasted a year as Vauxhall's focus turned to larger cars.

▽ **Morgan 4/4 1938**

Origin UK

Engine 1,122 cc, straight-four

Top speed 80 mph (129 km/h)

After 27 years of building three-wheeled vehicles, Morgan launched its first four-wheeler in 1936—the 4/4. This entry-level sports car was reintroduced in 1946, by which time the Coventry-Climax engine had been swapped for a Standard unit. In 1955, a 1,172 cc Ford engine was introduced. Morgan still makes a 4/4 today.

Foldaway roof

Simple, ladder-frame chassis

Front-opening doors

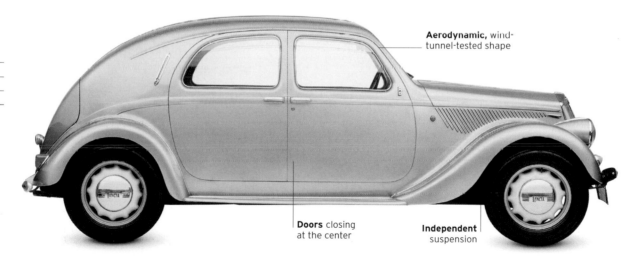

▷ **Lancia Aprilia 1937**

Origin Italy

Engine 1,352 cc, V4

Top speed 80 mph (129 km/h)

Probably the most advanced prewar sedan, the unibody Aprilia had all-independent suspension, a narrow-angle V4 engine with overhead cam, hydraulic brakes, and pillarless doors. A larger 1,486 cc engine was introduced in 1939 and retained after the war. The Aprilia continued until 1949 with more than 27,000 built.

Aerodynamic, wind-tunnel-tested shape

Doors closing at the center

Independent suspension

Side-valve four-cylinder engine

Spare wheel concealed

◁ **Ford Prefect E93A 1938**

Origin UK

Engine 1,172 cc, straight-four

Top speed 60 mph (96 km/h)

Descended from the 1932 Model Y, and big brother to the Anglia E04a, the Prefect had an all-new body and larger engine. Reintroduced in 1949 as the E439A, with headlights moved to the fenders, it was the cheapest four-door car in the UK.

Impressive British Sedans

Britain has always been able to make elegant, formal sedans that other countries simply cannot match. After World War II, the premium British car companies rebuilt and reorganized factories that had been previously turned over to war production, where they blended together the best of new and old. They maintained the traditional allure of fine wood and leather interiors, but updated exterior styling to appeal to modern taste. Straight-six and even straight-eight power units—mostly developments of their prewar products—provided effortless smoothness and refinement, while modern technology such as power steering and automatic transmission made these cars easier and more rewarding to drive than ever before.

Traditional values
The interior had an "old world" charm. The dashboard and door cappings were veneered wood, and square instruments were set into the center of the fascia. The seat facings were leather, with full-width front seats (despite the floor-mounted gear lever) and plenty of space for passengers at the rear.

▷ **Austin Sheerline 1947**

Origin	UK
Engine	3,993 cc, straight-six
Top speed	83 mph (134 km/h)

Austin's vast and regal-looking Sheerline had hints of the "razor-edge" styling that was in vogue at the time, and an interior swathed in traditional wood and leather. The straight-six engine was a prewar truck unit, bored out for more power, which drove through a 4-speed manual transmission.

Split windshield reflects prewar style

Razor-edge design influenced the sharper styling

Engine is adapted from a truck unit

Huge Lucas P100 headlights

LLD 273

Six-cylinder smoothness
Early Sheerlines (A110) used a 3,460 cc, six-cylinder engine, but only a dozen were built before the engine was expanded to 3,395 cc (A125). The later engine produced a smooth 130 bhp, and was incorporated into Austin's Princess model, built by Vanden Plas, as well as Jensen's Interceptor and 541.

Cheaper luxury
Marketed as an alternative to a Daimler or a Bentley, the Sheerline had all the luxurious features, but at a considerably lower cost.

Fully equipped interior blends wood and leather

Sweeping styling evokes Rolls-Royce

SIDE VIEW

"Landaulet" style body offers
open air for rear passengers only

Partition behind
driver's seat for
passenger privacy

▷ **Daimler DE36 1946**

Origin UK

Engine 5,460 cc, straight-eight

Top speed 83 mph (134 km/h)

This huge, postwar Daimler was supplied to seven
royal families around the world, including the
Windsors, but only 205 were built in eight years.
It had immense presence and refinement, and
weighed more than two tons. The DE36 contained
the UK's last production straight-eight engine.

Four-door sedan
body type

External spare wheel
is an elegant touch

Distinctive body
built by hand

Sweeping front
fenders give
clean lines

Spirit of Ecstacy
ornament tops
Rolls-Royce grille

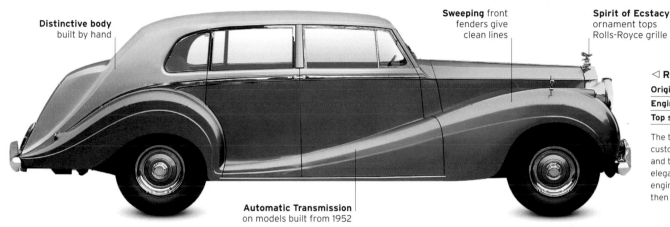

◁ **Rolls-Royce Silver Wraith 1946**

Origin UK

Engine 4,257 cc, straight-six

Top speed 85 mph (137 km/h)

The top UK postwar, luxury car had its body
custom-made, generally paneled in aluminum,
and the best styles were supremely imposing and
elegant. Its smooth, and virtually silent, six-cylinder
engine grew in size over the years, first to 4,566 cc,
then to 4,887 cc by 1959.

Automatic Transmission
on models built from 1952

Interior is a mix of plush
leather and fine wood

Unibody cabin same
as Morris Six

Hood opens
sideways revealing
smooth straight-six

▷ **Wolseley 6/00 1940**

Origin UK

Engine 2,215 cc, straight-six

Top speed 79 mph (127 km/h)

This reliable sedan, based on the Morris Six,
became the standard police car in the UK in the
1940s, used for both patrol and pursuit duties. It
had a factory-supplied, heavy-duty specification,
while a modern overhead-cam engine gave it
faster than average performance.

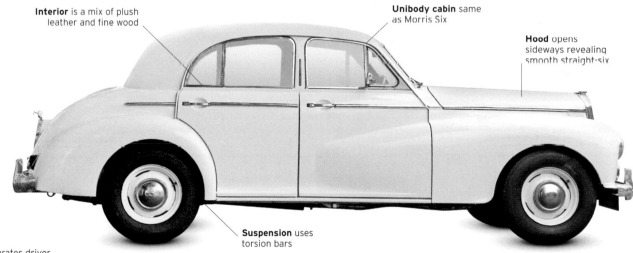

Suspension uses
torsion bars

Partition separates driver
from rear-seat passengers

Smooth, quiet,
straight-six engine

Headlights
on the fender

◁ **Humber Pullman II 1948**

Origin UK

Engine 4,086 cc, straight-six

Top speed 75 mph (121 km/h)

A favorite with government ministers, the revised
version of the prewar, seven-seat Pullman limousine
was launched in 1948, and featured a longer chassis.
Humber also produced the same car without a rear
partition, designed for owner-drivers. The car was
continued in Mk III and Mk IV forms until 1954.

Longer chassis means
room for seven inside

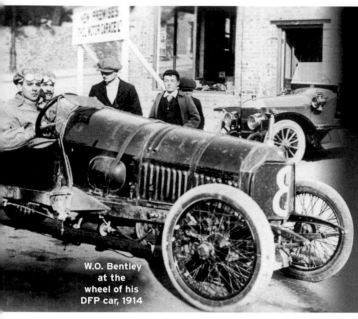

W.O. Bentley at the wheel of his DFP car, 1914

Great Marques
The Bentley Story

Today's Bentleys are some of the most lavish cars available, with a decades-long reputation as the pinnacle of the British motor car. The company's founder, Walter Owen Bentley (known as "W.O."), was an engineer who was concerned about engine performance and reliability when he began his own company in London in 1919.

BORN IN 1888, W.O. BENTLEY was apprenticed in building locomotives for the Great Northern Railway. He joined his brother in importing DFP cars from France in 1912, and his engineering background led him to modify the engines with aluminum pistons and a modified crankshaft. This made them race winners, and inspired Bentley to become an automaker himself in 1919.

By 1921 the first car, costing $1,500 (£1,050), was delivered. It was the first of the 3 liters, proving a revelation in performance and mechanical refinement at a time when the typical rival was noisy and crude. It developed 80bhp and could sustain speeds of 80mph (129km/h), which was quite amazing for the time in a production vehicle.

Not surprisingly, it was among Europe's most desirable sports cars. Bentleys set speed records from Brooklands to Indianapolis and were raced widely, culminating in five outright victories in the Le Mans 24-hour race in 1924, 1927, 1928, 1929, and 1930. Many of the wealthy racing drivers who loved Bentleys were part of a social set known as the "Bentley Boys." One of these, Woolf Barnato,

took control of the struggling Bentley Motors in 1926, and sanctioned a supercharged model. W.O. did not approve of it but, as he was now merely an employee, he was unable to veto the move.

Barnato was deeply involved in everything Bentley, and personally won at Le Mans in 1928 and 1929. Driving a Bentley Speed Six, he famously raced the "Blue Train" express between Cannes and Calais in 1930, easily beating his track-bound competitor to win a $150 (£100) bet.

The "vintage" era of Bentleys was finished by the aftereffects of the Wall Street Crash in 1929, and in 1931 the bankrupt company was bought by Rolls-Royce. Manufacturing was shifted to Derby, and the new Rolls-based Bentley 3.5 liter was sold as the "Silent Sports Car." In 1939, the marque moved to the Rolls-Royce plant in Cheshire, England launching the Bentley Mk VI, the new mainstay of Rolls-Royce's output, in 1946. It was the first model to have a "standard steel" body (all cars up to that time had been clothed by outside coachbuilders, as were all expensive cars) on its separate chassis.

In 1952 came the return of a really sporting Bentley, the R-type

Advertising for the 1955 Bentley S-Series

Continental. With speeds of 120mph (193km/h), it had a special chassis and ultramodern aerodynamic bodywork. After that, however, Bentleys entered a very long period in which they were merely Rolls-Royces by another name, which was the case with the S series (Rolls-Royce Silver Cloud), T series (Silver Shadow), Mulsanne (Silver Spirit), and Arnage (Silver Seraph).

W.O. Bentley himself died in 1971, but the first stirrings of a Bentley revival came in 1982, when the Mulsanne received a performance-boosting turbocharger. Then came the Continental R coupe of 1991, the first Bentley for decades for which there was no Rolls version.

Bentley S2 Continental, 1959
The svelte and imposing lines of Bentley's Continental were the work of the English coachbuilder H.J. Mulliner of London, where the car's bodywork was handcrafted. The S2 designation signified the car's improved V8 engine.

Bentley MkVI, 1946
Staff at the Rolls-Royce/Bentley factory in Cheshire, England give a Bentley MkVI the finishing touch; it was the first car to carry uniform "standard" coachwork.

134 HLH

"I wanted to make a fast car, a good car: **the best in its class.**"

W.O. BENTLEY, TALKING ABOUT THE DESIGN OF HIS FIRST CAR, THE 3-LITER

Bentley R-type Continental, 1952
At the time of its launch, the Bentley Continental was probably the most desirable car on the planet due to its lightweight, aerodynamic coachwork and 120 mph (193 km/h) top speed.

In 1998, Bentley and Rolls-Royce were split up and sold off, with Volkswagen paying $712 million (£500 million) to obtain control of Bentley and the historic Crewe factory. Volkswagen wasted little time in rejuvenating its new subsidiary, taking advantage of shared technology that was available from its other divisions, including Audi.

As a result, a new Le Mans team scored a third overall place at Le Mans in 2001, and yet another breakthrough came when the company created a custom State Limousine for ceremonial use by Queen Elizabeth II.

Bentley's image received another boost two years later. A sophisticated new Continental GT model, with an unusual, 6-liter, W12-arrangement engine with twin turbochargers, was launched into the market. This model massively increased sales around the world; it is the mainstay of the marque in a plethora of different versions.

CLASSICS OF THE FUTURE

Mulsanne This ultra-luxury sedan was named after a stretch of the Le Mans race circuit. The accomplished design mixed elements of Bentley's 1950s S-type with today's contemporary Continental GT style, with each of the sculptural front-fender shapes made possible using advanced aluminum superforming techniques. The engine was virtually an all-new, all-aluminum unit with 505 bhp of power and 752 lb-ft (1,019 Nm) of torque. The automatic transmission was an eight-speeder.

△ **Bentley Mulsanne 2010**

Origin UK	Each Mulsanne takes 15 weeks to build: the body is spot-welded and brazed by hand; 170 hours alone are devoted to the interior.
Engine 6,750 cc, V8	
Top speed 184 mph (296 km/h)	

Bentayga No luxury car marque could ignore the success of the Porsche Cayenne and the Range Rover, but Bentley reached a new pinnacle, creating an off-roader with sumptuous appointments and astonishing pulling power. The W12 engine offers 531 lb-ft (720 Nm) of torque through its four-wheel-drive system, making it unstoppable on rough terrain. The enormous wheels measure 22 in (56 cm) in diameter. Bentley claims no other SUV has such a range of colors, leathers, and wood veneers for configuration to suit individual tastes.

△ **Bentley Bentayga 2015**

Origin UK	Bentley described this as a "crossover vehicle." It even included a towbar, electrically deployed, for pulling a horse trailer.
Engine 5,950 cc, W12	
Top speed 170 mph (274 km/h)	

Sporting Beauties

With the motor industry hitting its stride again after the war, thoughts could turn to sports cars once again. Jaguar introduced the XK120, the fastest production car of the era, which went on to set speed records and sire successful racing machines. Ferrari, a company set up to build racing cars, turned its attention to fast road cars for the first time. Sedan mechanicals were adapted for sports cars with traditional open-top bodies or new-era, fixed-roof bodywork. There were also elegant, grand touring cars designed for long-distance travel that offered speed and comfort.

▽ **Jaguar XK120 1948**

Origin	UK
Engine	3,442 cc, straight-six
Top speed	125 mph (201 km/h)

William Lyons' XK120 was the star of the 1948 Earls Court Motor Show in London. It was planned as a short production-run and prestige show-stopper, but overwhelming interest meant it went into series production in 1950. Like all the best Jaguars, the XK120 combined speed, beauty, and charm.

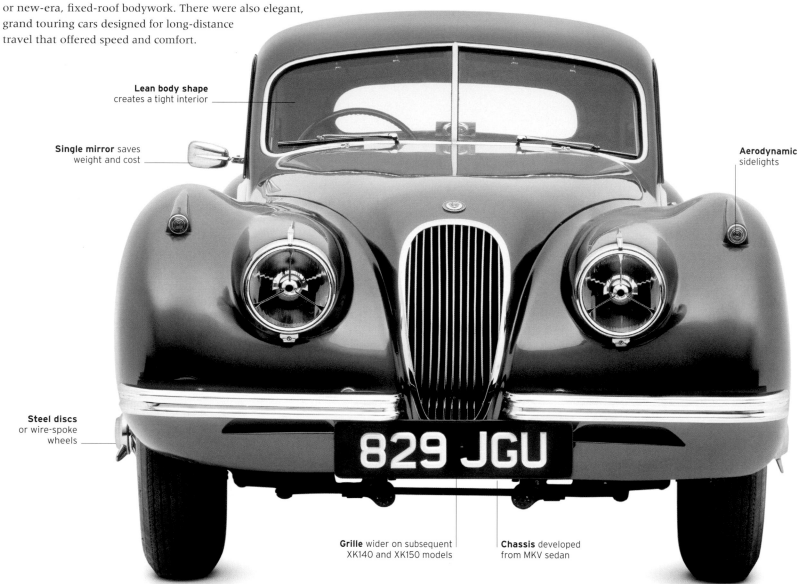

Lean body shape creates a tight interior

Single mirror saves weight and cost

Aerodynamic sidelights

Steel discs or wire-spoke wheels

Grille wider on subsequent XK140 and XK150 models

Chassis developed from MKV sedan

Production in steel
Early XK120s were made in small numbers with aluminum bodies, but in 1950 Jaguar started full production using steel panels.

- **XK120** has curvaceous roofline

Bodywork designed by company founder William Lyons

Terrific twin-cam
Design of the XK twin-cam engine began during WWII. The 3.4-liter, six-cylinder unit was fitted with two SU carburetors and developed around 160 bhp in its production form. It also proved to have plenty of potential for future tuning.

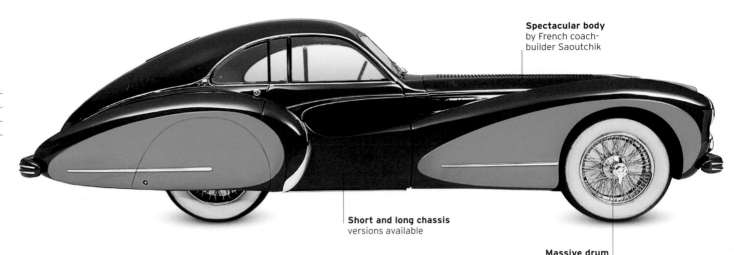

Spectacular body
by French coach-builder Saoutchik

▷ **Talbot-Lago T26 Grand Sport 1947**

Origin France

Engine 4,482 cc, straight-six

Top speed 120 mph (193 km/h)

The ultimate Grand Tourer of the 1940s enjoyed a wide range of fabulous coach-built bodies, with none finer than this model by Saoutchik. A lighter version won Le Mans 1950, Louis Rosier driving all but 45 minutes of the 24 hours.

Short and long chassis
versions available

Massive drum brakes fill the wheels

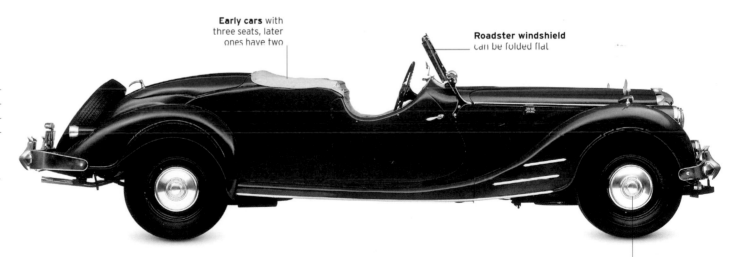

Rear window is the only curved glass on the car

Radio aerial still a rarity in this era

Engine has novel, "cross push-rod" valve gear

◁ **Bristol 400 1947**

Origin UK

Engine 1,971 cc, straight-six

Top speed 94 mph (152 km/h)

Bristol Aeroplanes entered the car market with a repackaged prewar BMW design, brought back to the UK as "war reparations." The efficient engine design gave it good performance and Bristol's standards of construction—based on aircraft engineering practice—were second to none.

Early cars with three seats, later ones have two

Roadster windshield
can be folded flat

▷ **Riley RMC Roadster 1948**

Origin UK

Engine 2,443 cc, straight-four

Top speed 100 mph (161 km/h)

This two-door version of the 1945 RM sedan had traditional good looks and a twin-cam engine with enough power for it to hit "the ton." The Roadster had a single row of three seats and a very long tail. In total, 507 cars were made.

Front brakes
are hydraulic; rear ones mechanical

High-revving
V12 engine

Short windshield
on Barchetta body

Competition numbers
added on cars for racing

◁ **Ferrari 166 MM Barchetta 1949**

Origin Italy

Engine 1,995 cc, V12

Top speed 125 mph (201 km/h)

This was the first true production Ferrari sports car, powered by a high-revving V12 engine and usually fitted with a fabulous Touring Barchetta body. Ferrari was essentially a racing car manufacturer, and racing versions of the 166 won the Mille Miglia, Spa, and Le Mans races in 1949.

MG TC

Produced from 1935–55, the MG T series was a popular range of small, convertible sports cars, mostly steel-bodied on a wooden frame, and capable of around 80 mph (129 km/h). The postwar TC enjoyed particular success with sales of more than 10,000, in large part because of the car's achievements on the export market. It did especially well in the US, the open-bodied two-seater being widely credited with introducing American drivers to the concept of the small sports car.

PRODUCTION AT MG was interrupted by World War II, when the factory at Abingdon stopped making cars and switched instead to the manufacture and repair of military equipment. When peace was declared in 1945, the company moved swiftly back to car production. With the government warning companies to "export or die," there was a particular focus on overseas sales and a new TC model was hastily developed.

The basic format was carried over from prewar models, including the ash frame, compact two-seater body, and the 1,250 cc four-cylinder engine. Although dated, the cutaway doors, swept wings, a slab-type fuel tank, and a trunk-mounted spare wheel gave the MG a sporty appearance. With little in the way of competition, the car sold well, particularly for something the factory regarded as little more than a stopgap model.

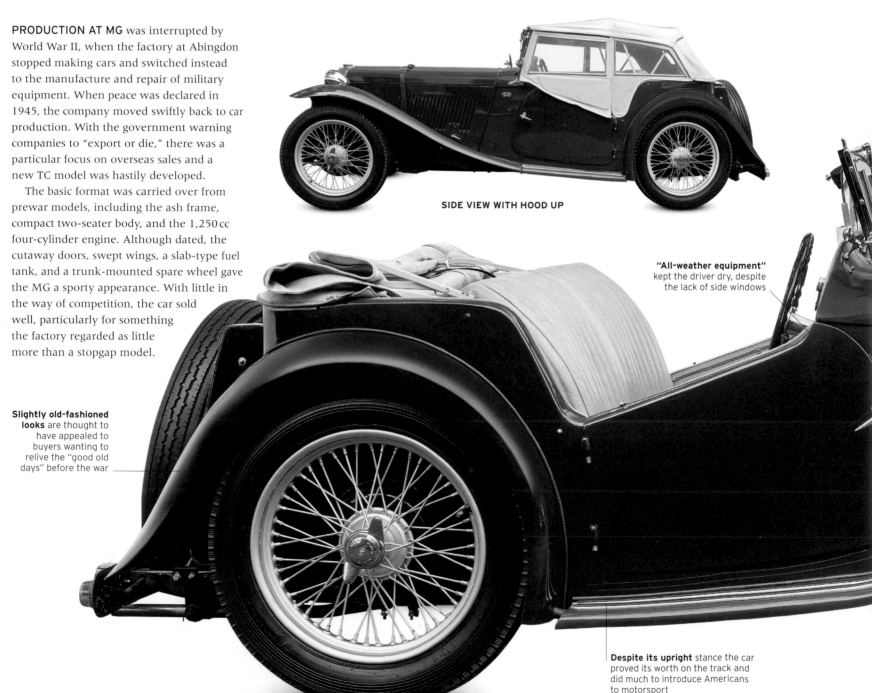

SIDE VIEW WITH HOOD UP

"All-weather equipment" kept the driver dry, despite the lack of side windows

Slightly old-fashioned looks are thought to have appealed to buyers wanting to relive the "good old days" before the war

Despite its upright stance the car proved its worth on the track and did much to introduce Americans to motorsport

FRONT VIEW

REAR VIEW

MG badge
Short for Morris Garages, the name MG was chosen by founder Cecil Kimber whose early cars were modified Morris Cowleys. By 1924 the octagonal logo appeared on all cars, and many also had eight-sided dials in the cockpit.

SPECIFICATIONS	
Model	MG TC (1947-49)
Assembly	Abingdon, UK
Production	10,000
Construction	Steel chassis, ash-framed steel body
Engine	1,255 cc, straight-four
Power output	54 bhp
Transmission	4-speed manual
Suspension	Front and rear leaf springs
Brakes	Four-wheel drums
Maximum speed	73 mph (118 km/h)

Relatively simple engineering
meant the TC was easy for amateurs to tune and repair

Styling
Although similar in appearance to its predecessor, the TB, the TC was actually 4 in (10 cm) wider. This improved its stance and allowed for a slightly roomier interior. Cutaway doors gave it a sporty look and provided extra elbow room for the driver.

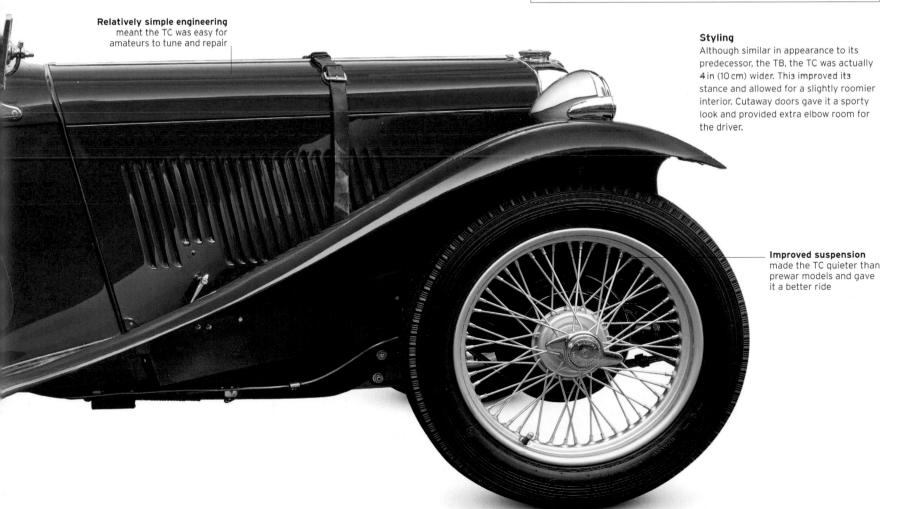

Improved suspension
made the TC quieter than prewar models and gave it a better ride

ON THE ROAD

The fact that it was essentially a postwar machine with prewar looks did little to dent MG sales when it was new, and decades later it serves only to enhance the already considerable appeal of the sprightly TC.

It may not be a vintage car but it certainly looks like one, and perhaps that is the point. The performance of these little MGs was always modest, but even now they cry out to be driven. Most at home cruising leisurely along country two-laners, it's not hard to see why people flocked to buy them in the 1940s. Seeing one now—parked outside a New England bed-and-breakfast or on a leafy campus—its simple but stylish shape is still pretty hard to resist.

1. Lights only 6-volt not 12 **2.** Engine bay louvers provide additional cooling **3.** Wing mirror is an essential modern addition **4.** Leather strap secures the hood closed **5.** Rear spare mounted on slab-type fuel tank **6.** Improvised fuel gauge—the TC only had a low fuel warning light **7.** Adjustable mount for fold-flat windshield **8.** Beautiful art deco-style dashboard **9.** Passenger grab handle—the TC had no seat belts **10.** Easy access to engine

5

6

7

8

9

10

Dante Giacosa
with a Fiat 600

Great Marques
The Fiat Story

Fiat (*Fabbrica Italiana di Automobili Torino*, or the Italian Car Factory of Turin) was founded on July 11, 1899, by Giovanni Agnelli, and quickly established itself in almost every automotive sector. Its specialty in small cars began in the 1930s, and continues today. The company has owned Ferrari and Lancia since 1969, Alfa Romeo since 1984, and Maserati since 1993.

FIAT BUILT ITS FIRST CAR, the 4 hp, in 1900, and in that year production averaged one car every two weeks. The impetus for growth came in 1903, however, when the company joined the Italian stock market and began manufacturing commercial vehicles. These found a ready market.

By 1906, Fiat's car range encompassed models extending from a modest 8 hp to a powerful 130 hp. Before long, its output was to include trams and marine engines.

Well before the outbreak of World War I (for which it produced aero engines and 20,000 lorries) Fiat was chasing the middle-class buyer with its affordable Zero model. In 1916, the company began construction of its enormous Lingotto plant outside Turin. With its rooftop test track (made internationally famous in the 1969 film *The Italian Job*), the Lingotto plant was the source of the big-selling 501 economy model, which was introduced in 1919.

**Poster advertising
the Fiat 1400**

In the 1920s Fiat launched the 519 luxury car, and broke new technical ground by pioneering mass-produced, aluminum cylinder heads. Starting in 1927, the company began switching all of its cars from right- to left-hand steering, and in 1929 the 514 became Fiat's mainstream model.

Following on from many cars launched during the early 1930s, including the 508 Balila family car and the aerodynamic 1500 sedan, Fiat introduced its baby 500 Topolino in 1936. It was designed by Dr. Dante Giacosa and had a tiny, four-cylinder engine at the front. Its playful character earned it the nickname "Mickey Mouse."

With two large factories at Lingotto and the newly built Mirafiori assembly site, Fiat was swiftly able to rebound after World War II, with a revised 500, the 1100, and 1500. With the debut in 1953 of the new, overhead-camshaft engine in the accomplished 1100 sedan, everyday Fiats gained a reputation for responsiveness (it also briefly made a super-sports car, the 8V of 1952).

Such responsiveness was less notable in the ponderous 1400, Italy's first diesel-powered passenger car. Nonetheless it formed the basis of the Seat 1400, built under license in Spain by automaker SEAT (Sociedad Española de Automóviles de Turismo), helping Spain join the list of major automaking nations.

In 1955, once the Italian government had committed to a major road-building program, Fiat launched the 600 economy car, with its engine at the back. It was followed in 1957 by the immortal Nuova 500 city car, which also had its engine—an air-cooled twin—mounted in the rear. These vehicles would prove hugely popular throughout the 1960s, raising annual output from 425,000 to 1.7 million cars. Many small Italian sporting marques, especially Abarth, relied on Fiat for hardware, and this boosted the zesty reputation of Fiat's cars still further.

The 1966 Fiat 124 sedan was a popular model and sold strongly. It formed the basis of the first VAZ/Lada in Russia, while in 1968 the 128 was the

**Six people aboard a
Fiat 600 Multipla, 1957**
This versatile version of the 600 was designed principally as a taxi, pioneering the concept of a compact, multi-passenger vehicle (MPV).

"A design of **considerable flair** offering good economy and performance at a **sensible price.**"

AUTOCAR MAGAZINE IN MARCH 1977 ON THE FIAT X1/9.

Fiat 124 Spider, 1966
This gorgeous, two-seat roadster, with Pininfarina styling, was in production for almost 20 years in various forms.

company's first front-wheel-drive model; the spin-off 127 was among the first hatchback "superminis." All three garnered European Car Of The Year awards. Meanwhile, the Fiat Dino sports cars used Ferrari engines, and the Fiat 130 was a new, large executive sedan and coupe.

In 1976, Fiat opened a major new research center, and in 1978 introduced robotized manufacture to build the Ruitmo/Strada, which was intended as a rival for the Volkswagen Golf. As ever, though, it was in small cars that Fiat excelled. The box-shaped

Panda of 1980 was followed by the '83 Uno—a superlative family hatchback with global sales that exceeded 8 million. The car was later succeeded by the Cinquecento and Punto, while Fiat introduced the first direct-injection diesel engines (1987), first common rail diesel (1997), and first automated manual transmission (1999).

After almost 50 years at Fiat's helm, Giovanni Agnelli died in 2003, his brother Umberto a year later. Then, in 2009, by signing a strategic alliance, Fiat became an unlikely savior of the American automaker Chrysler. The two companies had both withstood rollercoaster fortunes, but their futures were fused together in 2014 when Fiat-Chrysler Automobiles was formed, with the Agnelli family owning almost one-third of the merged automaking giant, the world's seventh largest.

Fiat Panda Mk 1, 1980
With styling input from automotive design and engineering company Italdesign, the Panda actually made boxy practicality desirable, and was very economical to drive.

CLASSICS OF THE FUTURE

Barchetta Fiat's 1200, 1500, 124, and 850 Spiders from the 1950s–70s with this mainstream marque had a solid reputation as being delightful sports cars. From 1972 they were boosted by the mid-engined X1/9. The company returned to the genre with this beautifully styled roadster, only this time it was given a front-wheel-drive Punto chassis. As with other Fiat sports cars, the assembly was carried out by a coachbuilder, in this case Maggiora, but it was always a much rarer car than either the market-leading MX-5 Miata or the MGF.

△ **Fiat Barchetta 1995**

Origin Italy	
Engine 1,747cc, straight-four	
Top speed 124 mph (200 km/h)	

Barchetta means "little boat" in Italian. This open-top two-seater offered excellent handling on all types of road surface.

Abarth 500 Fiat belatedly followed the new Volkswagen Beetle and BMW-sponsored Mini in the trend for classic revivals, turning its Trepiùno Concept car into the New 500 in 2007. Based on the Fiat Panda/Ford Ka platform, it was instantly successful, with its compact dimensions, "wheel at each corner," painted-metal interior, and stubby charm. A year later, Fiat re-established Abarth as a separate marque, making this the home of sports-orientated 500 models.

△ **Abarth 500 2008**

Origin Italy/Poland	
Engine 1,368cc, straight-four	
Top speed 127 mph (205 km/h)	

The turbocharged engine, five-speed transmission, lowered suspension, and four-wheel disc brakes make this car a true pocket rocket.

American Trendsetters

US automakers big and small kept buyers interested in the latest models by accelerating the introduction of bold, new, full-width styling and by updating designs annually as the 1940s wore on. Pioneering technical advances, such as automatic transmission, made American cars easier to drive, while big six-cylinder and V8 engines used ever greater quantities of fuel, which was cheap and abundant, to provide more power and refinement than ever before. This was an era of change in the industry, with big conglomerates increasingly dominating the market and selling cars for prices that smaller companies were unable to match.

▽ **Cadillac Series 62 Club Coupe 1949**

Origin	USA
Engine	5,424 cc, V8
Top speed	92 mph (148 km/h)

General Motors' 1948 body design featured tailfins inspired by the Lockheed P38 Lightning fighter plane. After ten years in the making, 1949 saw the introduction of a sophisticated new OHV engine. Smaller and lighter than its predecessor, it delivered more power and achieved better fuel economy.

FRONT VIEW

REAR VIEW

Beautiful chromed hood ornament

Cadillac crest
The Cadillac company was named after Frenchman Antoine Lamet de La Mothe, sieur de Cadillac, the founder of the city of Detroit. The imposing emblem on the front of the car was based on his coat of arms.

Fantastic fins
The subtle fins of the Series 62's were merely the beginning. Fins grew and grew over the next few years, reaching their maximum at the end of the 1950s.

"Fastback" design means roof slopes toward rear

High waistline gives a solid appearance

▷ **Hudson Super Six 1948**

Origin	USA
Engine	4,293 cc, straight-six
Top speed	90 mph (145 km/h)

One of the few small firms in postwar US car production, Hudson excelled with its low-built "step down" 1948 models and powerful new Super Six engine. In 1951, the Super Six evolved into the Hudson Hornet, which dominated American stock car racing from 1951–54.

Step-down design with a low floor

Boxier style comes to Ford in 1949

Optional external sun visor fitted

Streamlined wheel arches give smoother appearance

◁ **Ford Custom V8 1949**

Origin	USA
Engine	3,917 cc, V8
Top speed	85 mph (137 km/h)

Ford's new styling arrived in 1949. It was clean, low, modern, and boxy—features that were soon seen on European Fords, too. Power came from developments of two prewar engines: an L-head straight-six, and the famous Flathead V8.

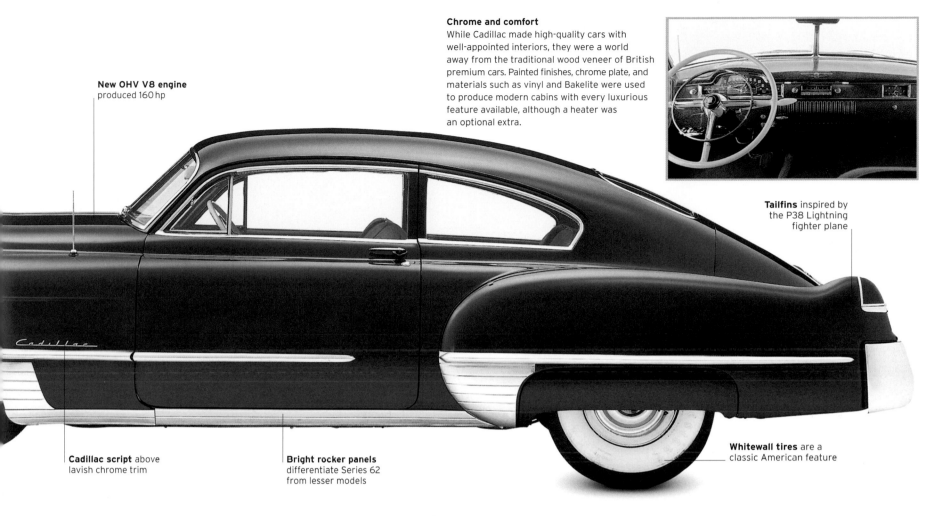

Chrome and comfort
While Cadillac made high-quality cars with well-appointed interiors, they were a world away from the traditional wood veneer of British premium cars. Painted finishes, chrome plate, and materials such as vinyl and Bakelite were used to produce modern cabins with every luxurious feature available, although a heater was an optional extra.

New OHV V8 engine
produced 160 hp

Tailfins inspired by the P38 Lightning fighter plane

Cadillac script above lavish chrome trim

Bright rocker panels
differentiate Series 62 from lesser models

Whitewall tires are a classic American feature

Covered fuel filler
for a sleek look

▷ **Pontiac Chieftain Convertible 1949**

Origin	USA
Engine	4,079 cc, straight-eight
Top speed	85 mph (137 km/h)

Low, sleek, full-width bodies were the hit of 1949 at Pontiac. Chieftains could be customized with a long list of extras, including a valve radio, seat heaters, and even a Remington shaver. Power brakes and air conditioning were available later. The model continued until 1954.

Streamlined spats
can be removed

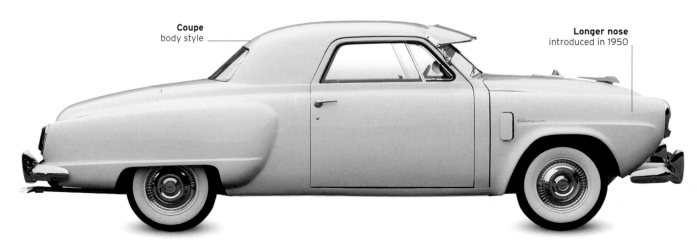

Coupe
body style

Longer nose
introduced in 1950

◁ **Studebaker Champion 1947**

Origin	USA
Engine	2,779 cc, straight-six
Top speed	82 mph (132 km/h)

In 1947 Studebaker was the first big name to introduce postwar styling. By 1950, the Champion was on to its first major revision, with a longer nose, a more powerful engine, and automatic transmission. Two-door and four-door sedans, station wagons, coupes, and even convertible models were available.

Great Designers
Harley J. Earl

Bombastic, chintzy, overblown—these are some of the criticisms regularly leveled at the designs of Harley J. Earl. But this undoubted overlord of 1950s' American auto styling certainly knew how to design cars that the public craved. In doing so, he created some of the most iconic models of all time, and helped turn General Motors (GM) into the world's largest corporation.

Career highlights

▷ **1927** Harley J. Earl designs the 1927 LaSalle for Cadillac—a huge sales success

▷ **1927** Earl gets his first big job, leading GM's Art and Color Section

▷ **1930** The Cadillac V16 supercar is styled by Earl and Larry Fisher. It is the first production car with a 16-cylinder engine

▷ **1933** Earl's first "show car," the Cadillac Aerodynamic Coupe, debuts in Chicago

▷ **1938** The era of the dream car is launched with the Buick Y-Job

△ **Buick Y-Job, 1938**
One of the auto industry's very first concept car, the Y-Job, established several styling cues that would be used by Buick until the 1950s. The vertical waterfall grille still appears on the company's cars today.

▷ **1945** Earl sets up his own independent design firm, the Harley Earl Corporation

▷ **1948** Inspired by jet fighters, the '48 Cadillac becomes the first car with tailfins

▷ **1953** The Corvette sports car, conceived by Earl, reaches production

▷ **1954** At GM's snazzy Motorama roadshow, the era of jet design truly takes off with the XP-21 Firebird

▷ **1959** Earl retires just as the extravagance of Cadillac tailfins reaches its heady peak

▷ **1969** Earl dies at age 75

YOU COULD ARGUE that car "styling" as such did not exist before Harley J. Earl. But this talented craftsman did more than merely invent the role of car stylist—he was a true pioneer whose influence can still be felt today.

The son of a coachbuilder who had made a success of producing one-off, custom-made car bodies for Hollywood stars such as Fatty Arbuckle, Harley J. Earl learned his craft at a young age, working alongside his father at Earl Automotive Works. Indeed, he was one of the first people to use modeling clay to give physical form to his ideas.

When Cadillac's manager, Larry Fisher, saw Earl at work, he knew instantly that he was the right man to lead the new Art and Color Section at GM in 1927. Within a decade, Earl had been promoted to vice president, and his department renamed the Styling Section.

DREAMS INTO REALITY

Earl had the brilliant idea of changing styling on an annual basis—a totally new concept at the time, but quickly adopted by the whole car industry. This significantly boosted new car sales at GM, further endearing Earl to the management.

Then, in 1938, Earl's experimental Buick Y-Job effectively gave birth to the "concept car." It set an auto-industry trend for show cars that exhibit new styling and technology. The Y-Job (Earl's personal car for more than a decade) had long, sleek lines, concealed headlights, and an electric folding roof.

But Earl's most famous idea was the tailfin, inspired by a Lockheed P-38 Lightning fighter plane. When fins first appeared on Earl's 1948 Cadillacs, the "jet-age" of car design had truly begun. Earl's 1951 Buick LeSabre dream car bristled with jet-age innovation—cast magnesium bodywork, heated seats, and a roof that raised itself when a sensor detected rain. Taking the aircraft theme literally, the 1954 Pontiac Bonneville Special even used genuine Lockheed P-38 seat belts.

Chevrolet Corvette C1 publicity drawing, 1953
This sketch, showing the rear of a Corvette C1, not only gives a sense of the car's smooth, sleek appearance, but also an implied feeling of speed as it accelerates away. Just 300 Corvettes were made in the first year of production.

But for jet-age fantasy, nothing beat the XP-21 Firebird of 1954. It was powered by a jet turbine and even looked the part with its plane-inspired fenders. By 1958 the Firebird III had evolved into NASA-rocket territory, with out-of-this-world fins, astronaut-style bubble canopies, and "electroluminescent" instruments.

PROLIFIC OUTPUT

This was an era of pure showmanship, embraced by GM in rolling carnivals called Motorama that toured the whole of the US. The centerpieces of these extravaganzas were always futuristic visions of a brighter, faster, bigger age. In the peak Motorama year (1956), GM spent $10 million on the shows and attracted 2 million visitors.

Earl's output was prolific. In just one year

Earl's GM LeSabre, 1951
Designed as a concept car for GM, Earl's LeSabre inspired a fashion for jet-age styling.

CHEVROLET CORVETTE 1953

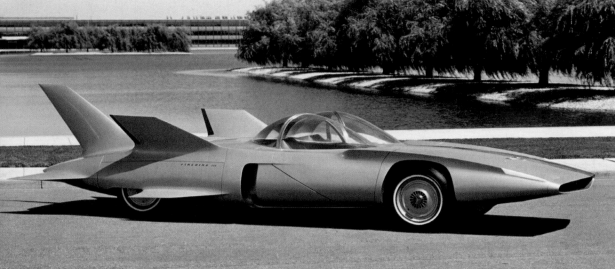

GM FIREBIRD III 1958

(1954) no fewer than 12 different dream cars were paraded in front of the public. Highlights included the Buick Centurion, Oldsmobile Golden Rocket, the knee-high Pontiac Club de Mer, Chevrolet Corvette SS, and jet-inspired Cadillac Cyclone.

Some of these Motorama "concepts" actually reached production, most famously the Chevrolet Corvette, which was an Earl product from conception to realization. America's first real sports car in the European idiom, the 1953 Corvette, was also the world's first mass-produced, fiberglass-bodied car. Many of Earl's pioneering style ideas, such as two-tone paint, wraparound windshields, and quad headlights, appeared on GM cars before any other manufacturers'.

EARL'S LEGACY

The excesses of the tailfin era—when Earl did battle with Chrysler's Virgil Exner to see who could push things the furthest—reached their peak

> # "Design and beauty not only command attention, but they are the very foundation of living."
>
> HARLEY EARL

with the 1959 Cadillac. The '59's towering tailfins were punctuated by sci-fi rear lights and rich swathes of chrome, while at the front, the wraparound windshield and double grille completed the car's flamboyant look.

But the excess could not last. The '59 Caddy was Harley Earl's last design for GM. He promptly retired, and handed the reins of the styling department he had built over to Bill Mitchell. With immediate effect, the era of excessive ornamentation was over.

Earl died in 1969 and his legacy cannot be overstated. Among his many achievements, he was a pioneer of promoting female stylists (his so-called "Damsels of Design"), he championed the use of crash-test dummies, and he established the Auto Design Scholarship program. Above all, he gave cars soul, turning design into the single most important factor within the auto industry. He proved, with the numbers of vehicles he sold, that cars were not just functional transport but were also about style, passion, and aspiration.

Motoring in Miniature

Motorsports were too frivolous a hobby in occupied France, but at least these adults could enjoy the spectacle of children racing in pedal cars. Like toy cars, pedal cars had been around since the early days of motoring. They reached their height of popularity in the interwar years. Some were generic in design, but many closely mirrored real road cars of the time.

TOYS TO PROMOTE SALES

Automakers soon realized they could exploit children's enthusiasm for cars to boost sales. In the US during the 1930s, Graham-Paige used diecast Tootsietoy models to promote the life-size cars in its showrooms. Even before that, Citroën had commissioned

a range of tinplate models of its cars to sell to the offspring of customers. Bugatti went a step further and built an electric-powered child's car, the Bébé, that was a half-scale version of its Type-35 racer. In 1949, Britain's Austin Motor Company launched a pedal-powered junior machine called the J40. Based on the design of its real-life A40, it was intended to generate interest in everything Austin sales. But there was also altruistic thinking behind the venture: it was made by disabled ex-miners, at a special factory in South Wales, on a not-for-profit basis.

A pedal car Grand Prix on the Esplanade Des Invalides, Paris, in October 1941. The cars are from the 1930s, made before wartime metal shortages.

Austerity Motoring

Low-cost motoring had been popularized in the 1920s and 1930s by the Ford Model T in the US and the Austin Seven in the UK. In the 1940s, many more small economical cars arrived to provide motoring for the masses—often using tiny, two-cylinder engines. While larger, conventional cars usually had the engine at the front driving the rear wheels, in these minicars the engine and drive-wheels were at the same end, so the transmission required less space. Although these cars served a humble purpose, their design was clever and characterful.

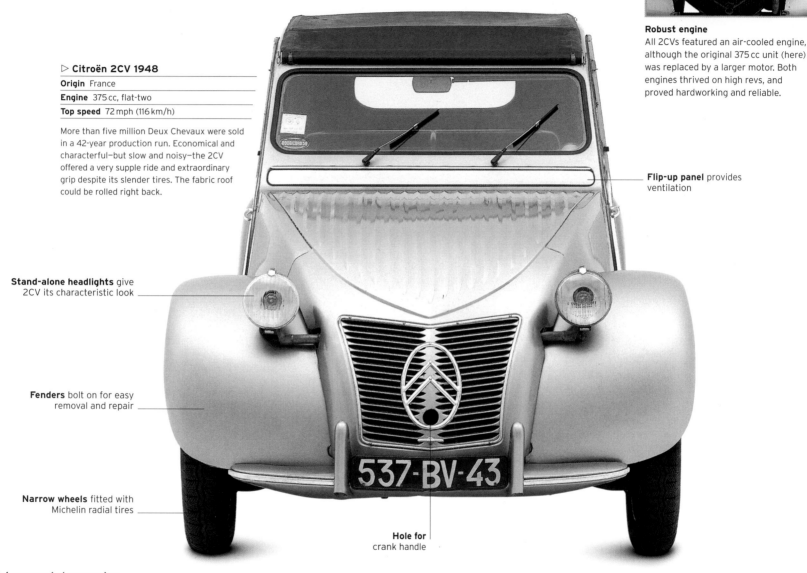

▷ **Citroën 2CV 1948**

Origin	France
Engine	375 cc, flat-two
Top speed	72 mph (116 km/h)

More than five million Deux Chevaux were sold in a 42-year production run. Economical and characterful—but slow and noisy—the 2CV offered a very supple ride and extraordinary grip despite its slender tires. The fabric roof could be rolled right back.

Robust engine
All 2CVs featured an air-cooled engine, although the original 375 cc unit (here) was replaced by a larger motor. Both engines thrived on high revs, and proved hardworking and reliable.

Flip-up panel provides ventilation

Stand-alone headlights give 2CV its characteristic look

Fenders bolt on for easy removal and repair

Narrow wheels fitted with Michelin radial tires

Hole for crank handle

537-BV-43

Interconnected suspension
The long-travel suspension was linked front to back, and allowed the 2CV to travel smoothly over rough surfaces.

Air-cooled two-cylinder engine unit, initially 375 cc

Fold-back roof allows large items to be carried and provides ventilation

SIDE VIEW

Simple signaling
Indicators were added to the rear pillars in the 1950s. An ingenious innovation, they could be seen from the front and the rear in this position, which meant that only two were needed. Simplicity was key to the design of the 2CV.

External headlights show the design's age

Small rear trunk offers little space

Rear-hinged "suicide" door

▷ Standard 8HP 1945

Origin UK

Engine 1,009 cc, straight-four

Top speed 60 mph (96 km/h)

Standard rushed its prewar 8HP back into production in 1945, having improved it with a four-speed gearbox. The 8HP designation referred to its RAC horsepower rating, which determined its rate of road tax (the engine actually produced 28 bhp). Standard sold 53,099 examples of this model in three years.

Indicator and side lights

Front and rear doors hang on same pillar

◁ Renault 4CV 1946

Origin France

Engine 760 cc, straight-four

Top speed 57 mph (92 km/h)

Renault's small car, the 4CV, looked similar to its British rival, the Morris Minor. However, with an all-independent suspension and a rear-mounted engine under the skin, it had more in common with the German Volkswagen. It was the first French car to sell more than a million.

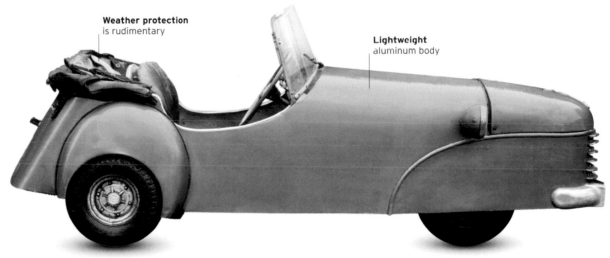

Weather protection is rudimentary

Lightweight aluminum body

▷ Bond Minicar 1948

Origin UK

Engine 122 cc, one-cylinder

Top speed 38 mph (61 km/h)

Bond's three-wheeler Minicar was cheap to run, inexpensive to tax, and could be driven by anyone who had a motorcycle licence. The simple design featured an air-cooled motorbike engine that pivoted with the front wheel and had no reverse gear.

Cabriolet roof rolled back

Snug cabin has room for a driver and passenger

Front end was restyled in 1949

◁ Fiat 500C 1949

Origin Italy

Engine 569 cc, straight-four

Top speed 60 mph (96 km/h)

This was the final version of Dante Giacosa's brilliant 1937 "Topolino" (Little Mouse), which mobilized the population of Italy in the 1930s. Like the earlier cars, the 500C of 1949 had only two seats, and a front-mounted, four-cylinder engine. Coupe, cabriolet, estate, and van versions were made.

Gallic Charm

In the 1930s, the French auto industry was one of the most vibrant on the planet, but after the war, in the mid- to late 1940s, it struggled to regain its momentum. Peugeot had dabbled in electric cars before production was stopped by occupying German forces. Now, like its rivals Citroën and Renault, Peugeot simply restarted manufacture of prewar models. Luxury cars, though, were hard to find buyers for, as Talbot and the like discovered. Yet all 1940s' French cars today are desirable for their character and venerability.

Cream wheels with black coachwork are standard livery

Welded unibody construction

Low-built body has no need for running boards

Straight-six engine offering 170 bhp

Design features sweeping lines

Wire spoke wheels with "knock-off" hubs

Chrome finish to end of tapered mudguard

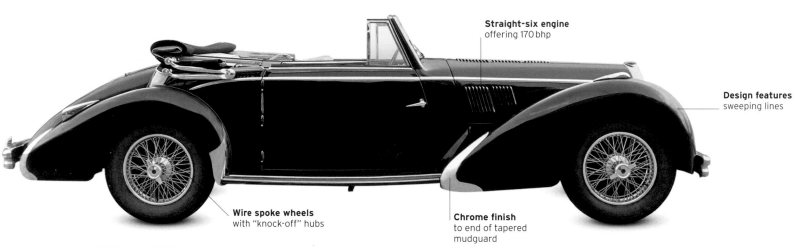

△ **Talbot Lago T26 Record 1946**

Origin France

Engine 4,482 cc, straight-six

Top speed 105 mph (169 km/h)

Company owner Antonio Lago was quick to launch a new postwar Talbot, although it was similar in concept to prewar models. A powerful luxury touring car, the large engine incurred high taxation in France, and sales were slow.

▷ **Renault Juvaquatre 1945**

Origin France

Engine 1,003 cc, straight-four

Top speed 60 mph (96 km/h)

This was the wagon version of Renault's first unibody-construction, mass-market model. It was conventional and basic, with only three gears and mechanical brakes. The wagon and sedan were dropped in 1948, but a van was still on sale as late as 1960.

Small and thrifty four-cylinder engine

Extended station wagon model popular with French buyers

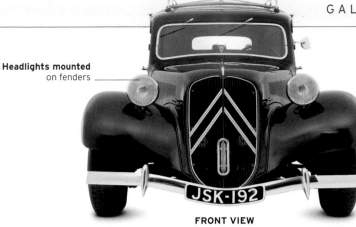

Headlights mounted on fenders

FRONT VIEW

Brilliantly packaged
The Citroën's front-wheel drive gave a new dimension to roadholding for 1930s', '40s', and '50s' drivers. The advanced front suspension, with a torsion bar and wishbone arrangement, helped make the driving experience both safe and smooth.

▽ **Citroën Traction Avant 15CV 1938**

Origin	France
Engine	1,911 cc, straight-four
Top speed	73 mph (118 km/h)

Citroën shook up the motoring world with its Traction Avant or "front-wheel drive" range in 1934, with the cars still setting the standard for roadholding, comfort, and driving enjoyment more than a decade later. The car designer W.O. Bentley was an ardent fan. Indeed, in various forms, the 15CVs were on sale until 1957.

Attractive styling by Italian designer Flaminio Bertoni

Accommodating car
Traction Avants were spacious inside, but trunk space on standard sedans was restricted, especially with the spare wheel stored in the trunk lid. Models manufactured for British buyers came with larger luggage space.

Freestanding number plate on rear fender

REAR VIEW

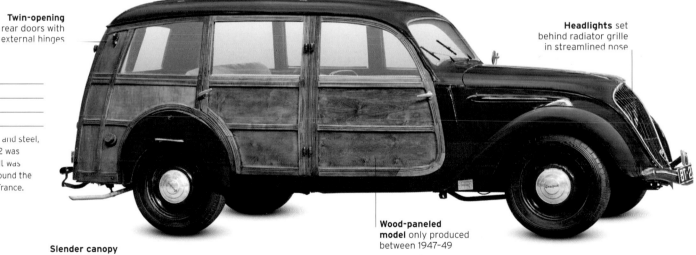

Twin-opening rear doors with external hinges

Headlights set behind radiator grille in streamlined nose

▷ **Peugeot 202 1947**

Origin	France
Engine	1,133 cc, straight-four
Top speed	62 mph (100 km/h)

Made from a combination of timber and steel, this wagon version of the trusty 202 was practical, elegant, and economical. It was also an ingenious way of getting around the shortage of sheet steel in postwar France.

Wood-paneled model only produced between 1947–49

Slender canopy supports keep weight low

Four 12-volt batteries power electric motor

Sturdy convertible roof

◁ **Peugeot VLV 1942**

Origin	France
Engine	Electric motor
Top speed	22 mph (35 km/h)

Peugeot designed this tiny, battery-powered *Voiture Légere de Ville* or "light city car" as a response to France's gasoline rationing. However, Nazi forces closed down production after only 377 had been built.

Great Marques
The Citroën Story

Parisian André Citroën started business life in the gear-making industry (this is obvious in the double chevrons of the helical gears in the marque's logo). He amassed a fortune manufacturing shells in World War I and, having studied Henry Ford's car-making methods, decided to spend his earnings setting up a car company.

Citroën cars under construction in the busy Paris factory in the 1920s

ALTHOUGH LATER CITROËNS would eventually develop into some of the most adventurous cars ever conceived for public sale, the original aim was a complete car at a low price.

In 1919, the Type A 10CV prototype elicited 16,000 orders because it had such an extensive specification and yet was less expensive than what most of the competition was offering. The Paris factory could barely cope with demand.

In 1922, Citroën unveiled the tiny 5CV three-seater, with its 856 cc engine, aimed at the female driver on a limited budget. It was very user-friendly, the need for a starting handle obviated by an electric starter motor, and came in vivid colors. Sales took off. André Citroën's genius as a marketer was confirmed and enhanced even further by selling toy Citroën cars, and lighting up the Eiffel Tower with 25,000 light bulbs. In a publicity stunt, the Citroën-Kegresse exploration vehicles crossed the Sahara Desert in 1922, gaining enormous attention.

Before long there was a huge and complex range of Citroëns. However, the company decided to hit the technical innovation trail in 1934 by launching the 7CV. It had front-wheel drive, an integrated body/chassis structure, and daring styling by a sculptor named Flaminio Bertoni—the soon-to-be-world-famous Traction Avant. The cost of bringing the car to market almost bankrupted the firm, and probably hastened André Citroën's death in 1935. Had he survived, he would have learned that the car drove wonderfully. And, once some of its teething troubles had been ironed out, the Traction Avant proved to be enduringly

Citroën Traction Avant
The brilliant front-wheel-drive range was in production from 1934 until 1957 in various versions. The vehicle helped establish Citroën's reputation for innovation.

popular, remaining on sale in various forms until 1957.

Citroën's next surprise was a car of its austere times, the 1948 2CV. This supremely basic, four-door sedan had suspension so forgiving that farmers could allegedly drive their eggs to market across plowed fields and arrive with them undamaged. The 2CV's twin-cylinder, air-cooled engine and front-wheel drive was unchanged throughout the car's incredible 42-year lifespan.

By contrast, the DS19 of 1955 was as daring as the Space Age itself, again the visionary work of Flaminio Bertoni. It offered both self-leveling suspension and hydraulic actuation for everything from the steering to the clutch, all in a shark-like, streamlined body unlike anything seen before.

The Ami of 1962 was an amalgam of 2CV economy and sharp DS styling. There were also further developments on the 2CV theme, including the 1967 Dyane with its hatchback rear, and the Mehari of 1968, an open utility vehicle with all-plastic bodywork. In 1970, Citroën broke new ground with two new cars: the air-cooled, flat-four GS family

Poster, c.1927
This vivid poster extolling the virtues of properly servicing a car was typical of Citroën's enthusiastic use of marketing to promote its products.

car—1971 European Car of the Year—and the futuristic SM with its 2.7-liter Maserati engine.

The 1960s and '70s were a difficult time for Citroën, which, since the 1930s, had been owned by the tire-maker Michelin. It acquired first Panhard, the cornerstone of the French motor industry, and then five years later Maserati. But by 1974, Citroën was nearly insolvent after ploughing money in an abandoned rotary-engine venture, which saw an undignified emergency takeover by Peugeot.

The CX, replacement for the DS, was felt to be the last "proper" Citroën. After its launch in 1974, much of the hardware inside models like the

Citroën DS23, 1973
The ultimate version of the car, the DS23 had a 2.3-liter engine that, with fuel injection, was—at 141 bhp—the most powerful.

"The ultimate in cars ... becomes at once more **spiritual.**"

PHILOSOPHER AND WRITER ROLAND BARTHES ON THE CITROËN DS IN HIS BOOK *MYTHOLOGIES*, 1957

LN, Visa, BX, and AX was shared with equivalent Peugeot models. And that, of course, meant conventionality. However, the little AX set new standards for economy, and the XM and Xantia still exuded some of that characteristic Citroën "different-ness," with their hydropneumatic suspension systems.

After some years of marketing rather bland products, Citroën went its own way with the 2009 DS3, and has since used the old DS name to launch a string of new models offering arch alternatives to other mainstream family cars.

Citroën Mehari, 1968
This plastic-bodied, open utility vehicle using 2CV mechanical parts was as chic as it was practical. Here, the advertising associated it with a relaxed, youthful lifestyle.

CLASSICS OF THE FUTURE

C6 Big, comfortable, and very different than its rivals, this was the first large Citroën since the XM vanished in 2000. The concave rear window was novel, and the profile suggested a tailgate, although the C6 had a conventional trunk. It was notable for its rich package of safety features, including a lane-departure warning system, one of the first "pop-up" hoods to help cushion a pedestrian in an impact, and a head-up instrument display. It came as a diesel as well as a 3-liter gasoline engine.

△ **Citroën C6 2005**

Origin	France
Engine	2,720 cc, V6
Top speed	143 mph (230 km/h)

Citroën boldly decided to offer an idiosyncratic French alternative to German executive cars; those who owned one loved it, but less than 24,000 were sold over seven years.

C4 Cactus For many years, Citroën devotees had bemoaned the loss of the quirky character that defined the company's cars. However, this entry into the compact SUV sector was satisfyingly original, with its simple interior, digital read-outs, and chunky looks thanks to a bluff nose and "Airbump" plastic panels on the sides and corners. There was nothing else quite like it on the road.

△ **Citroën C4 Cactus 2014**

Origin	France/Spain
Engine	1199 cc, straight-three
Top speed	117 mph (188 km/h)

The figures were for the turbocharged version of the small gasoline engine. Thanks to its 108 bhp, this basic but charismatic family car had verve to match its thrift.

International Auto Shows

In bygone times of limited media communications, auto shows gave a unique opportunity to admire and compare the newest models and learn of the latest developments in automotive design. Events in Paris, Turin, Geneva, Detroit, and London attracted many thousands of visitors. Car manufacturers used these extravaganzas as public relations exercises, promoting their brands to dealers, journalists, and the public. Auto shows were often the favored venues for important car launches.

POSTWAR ENTHUSIASM

The London Motor Show of 1948, the first in the city since the outbreak of World War II, was an unparalleled success, drawing in more than 560,000 car enthusiasts. Held at the Earls Court exhibition center, the show saw the launch of several auto legends, including the Jaguar XK120, Morris Minor, and Bristol 401; the Morris stand is just visible at the rear of the hall. While American marques appear prominent, few of these impressive, powerful cars would be sold in Britain. There were much better prospects in store for the country's caravan-makers (some can be seen at the very back), as improved roads and greater prosperity triggered a new wanderlust in European drivers.

After the austerity of the war years, the British public relished the chance to get up close to the finest cars of the day at the 1948 London Motor Show. The London show ran from 1903 until 2008, and was revived in 2016.

Land Rover Series 1

The opening chapter of a very long success story began with a British attempt to replicate the success of the wartime Willys Jeep. Seeking to offer a similar mix of simple, bulletproof engineering and genuine go-anywhere capability, the original Land Rover proved wildly popular with farmers, emergency services, and off-road enthusiasts, and has become one of the most widely recognized classic vehicles on the road today.

THE BASIC SHAPE of the Land Rover has changed little since the vehicle's inception in 1948, and that was just one of the reasons enthusiasts loved their "Landies." For hardcore fans, the Series 1 was the go-to model. Nothing else came close to its simple, wholly practical design.

These early vehicles were as tough as they were uncomplicated. The first boxy shape was made from an aluminum/magnesium alloy, left over from wartime aircraft production. Built with engineering technology that was designed to be easily fixed if something went wrong, its resilience made it invaluable to both the armed forces and off-road devotees.

The stark interior betrayed the marque's origins as a utility vehicle

SIDE VIEW

Land Rover badge
Barely changed in decades, the oval-shaped badge was thought to have been based on a sardine can out of which the designer had eaten his lunch. The name, a reminder of the brand's origins as part of Rover cars, could not be more appropriate.

All-wheel drive with only minimal modifications meant the Series 1 could go anywhere, even crossing small rivers safely

FRONT VIEW

REAR VIEW

The steering wheel was located centrally on the prototype; production vehicles offered right- or left-hand drive

A low center of gravity meant the vehicle could lean 30 degrees from the vertical without fear of rolling over

SPECIFICATIONS	
Model	Land Rover Series 1, 1948–58
Assembly	Solihull, UK
Production	212,685
Construction	Steel chassis, aluminum body
Engine	1,595 cc, straight-four
Power output	50 bhp
Transmission	4-speed manual
Suspension	Front and rear leaf springs
Brakes	Four-wheel drum
Maximum speed	55 mph (88 km/h)

Styling
A near-perfect triumph of function over form, the Land Rover "look" has remained similar since the first of 48 prototypes rolled out in 1948. Later models were larger and offered (marginally) more comfort, but their DNA was obvious and none could be mistaken for anything but a descendent of the first Series 1 prototype.

Good ground clearance and minimal front and rear overhangs were essential for crossing rough territory

ON THE ROAD

The nearest the UK ever got to matching the brilliantly robust simplicity of the World War II Jeep, the Series 1 represented a complete departure for the Rover Car Company when chief designer Maurice Wilks built the first prototype on his Welsh farm in 1947. Wilks salvaged parts from an old US Army jeep, but what he saw as a new kind of small agricultural vehicle has come to be deemed a quintessentially British icon. It is this that accounts for much of its appeal to collectors. Its basic construction and deliberate lack of frills also help to make it one of the easiest machines that could be restored at home.

1. Robust hood latch typifies functional approach to design   **2.** Door handles fitted only on later models   **3.** Indicators are a later, regulatory addition **4.** Centrally-mounted headlights on early cars   **5.** Simple, three-spoke wheel **6.** Sparse instrumentation—earlier cars had only two gauges   **7.** Gear lever, four-wheel-drive selector, and low-ratio lever   **8.** Two-liter engine replaced 1.6-liter unit in 1950–51

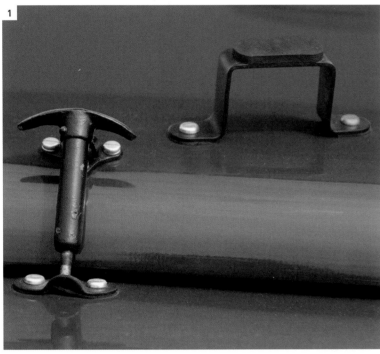

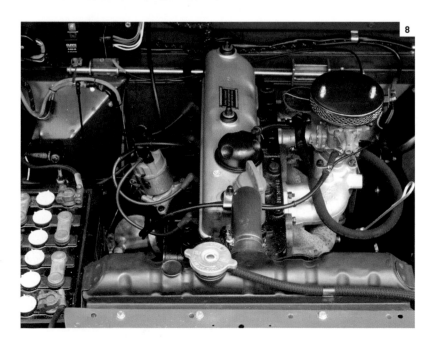

Hardworking Vehicles

Versatile, go-anywhere vehicles, such as the US military's Jeep, were initially developed for wartime use. After the end of hostilities, the Jeep found a ready civilian market in agriculture, construction, and emergency services, and some people even drove them just for fun. At the same time, the pickup emerged as a new class of strong and adaptable purpose-built vehicle. It became a familiar part of the US automotive scene that is still very much with us today. Sedans were being made more practical, too, with extra seats and conversions to station wagons that offered plenty of space for passengers and luggage.

Folding roof is a luxury

▷ Willys MB "Jeep" 1943

Origin	USA
Engine	2,199 cc, straight-four
Top speed	60 mph (96 km/h)

Willys, Ford, and Bantam competed for the US Army contract to build a light, four-wheel-drive reconnaissance vehicle. Willys won with the MB, and Ford also built it as the Ford GPW. More than 600,000 were made, and the US military continued to use them well into the 1960s.

Leaf springs, fitted front and rear, are simple but robust

Extended trunk increases luggage capacity

Three side windows denote nine-seat Familiale version

◁ Citroën 11 Familiale 1935

Origin	France
Engine	1,911 cc, straight-four
Top speed	65 mph (105 km/h)

The longest of the innovative front-wheel-drive Citroëns was over 15 ft (4.5 m) long with a huge turning circle. Ideal for the larger family, or as a taxi, it had three side windows and three rows of seats, and it could carry nine people.

Front-wheel drive ensures safer cornering

Front-mounted spare wheel easily accessible

▷ Volkswagen Kübelwagen 1940

Origin	Germany
Engine	985 cc, flat-four
Top speed	50 mph (80 km/h)

Ferdinand Porsche's Beetle-based military transport served in all land-based fields of war, despite being only two-wheel drive. The flat underside slid over tough terrain and the engine, located over the driving wheels, aided traction. A remarkable 50,435 of these were built from 1940–45.

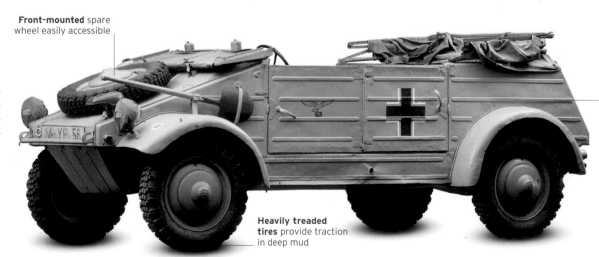

Stamped ribs increase body strength

Heavily treaded tires provide traction in deep mud

Load area can be adapted to carry people or cargo

Spare wheel hangs off the back to avoid taking up payload space

Vital information
The dashboard was strictly rudimentary, but it gave the driver all of the information needed to ensure that the vehicle was running properly. In addition to a speedometer, instruments included an ammeter, a fuel gauge, and engine oil level and temperature gauges.

All action, all terrain
True to its military purpose, the Jeep's interior was functional. Doors were superfluous and the windshield could be removed. An instruction panel explained how to use the gear-shift and transfer box, and a rifle holder sat prominently behind the steering wheel.

Straight-six and V8 engines were used

Two sizes of load bay are available

Ford offered a choice of eight colors

◁ **Ford F-Series Pickup 1948**

Origin USA

Engine 3,916 cc, V8

Top speed 70 mph (113 km/h)

Ford's first all-new, postwar product was a purpose-designed pickup that was "Built Stronger to Last Longer." Proving an instant success, the 1948 F-Series powered Ford truck sales to their best year for almost two decades. The F-Series' descendants have become America's most popular vehicle, outselling every car or truck for 34 straight years.

Front end shows clear likeness to the Jeep

▷ **Willys Jeep Jeepster 1948**

Origin USA

Engine 2,199 cc, straight-four

Top speed 60 mph (96 km/h)

Designed by Brooks Stevens, the Jeepster was an attempt to create a fun sports car from the basic wartime Jeep idea. It was available as rear-wheel drive only, with more equipment and chrome decoration to distance it from its utilitarian forebear. It was on sale for only three years.

Chrome trim brightens up the Jeepster

Improving Car Quality

Intensified rivalry, the rising demands of export markets, and, of course, ever more discerning customers all forced the postwar car industry into upping its game. Motoring had taken on a practical new aspect as car ownership became more affordable and so more widespread. Automobiles were no longer amusing playthings but serious consumer products. Gradually, car manufacturers adopted a scientific approach to perfecting their vehicles, and that meant endless prelaunch testing.

RIGOROUS TESTING

Endurance runs helped to identify structural and mechanical flaws, while road testing in hot and cold climates was essential to see if a vehicle could withstand extremes of weather. Innovative factory techniques were also devised to assess the durability of new models. Specially designed rigs subjected components to weeks of continuous durability simulation tests. Keeping dust, fumes, and water out of a car was important to protect its interior and prolong its life. This Russian ZIS 110—similar to the limousine used by Russian leader Joseph Stalin—is here being deluged with dozens of high pressure water jets to check for leaks. Perhaps not surprisingly, Stalin's own modified ZIS, which weighed more than 4 tons, was completely impregnable, since it was fully armor-plated.

An example of the ZIS 110 limousine, possibly a prototype, undergoing painstaking water-ingress tests at the Moscow factory, c.1949. The ZIS was based on the design of the Packard Super Eight.

Karl Benz, with his commercial clerk in the patent motor car, 1887

Great Marques
The Mercedes Story

The two founding fathers of the motor car industry came together when Daimler and Benz merged in 1926–the two companies' founders had effectively invented the automobile. In addition to being a luxury marque, Mercedes-Benz, the company formed by the merger, has since laid a trail of industry-leading innovation.

THERE IS NO RECORD OF KARL BENZ (1844–1929) and Gottlieb Daimler (1834–1900) ever having met while they were independently developing their first cars. Benz's three-wheeled "Motorwagen" was patented in Mannheim, on January 29, 1896. Its single-cylinder, four-stroke internal combustion engine ran on gas.

Cannstatt engineer, Gottlieb Daimler's, gasoline-powered engine was running in 1883. He initially installed his invention in a primitive motorcycle (demonstrated for the first time in 1885) and then in an adapted carriage a year later. Benz was the first to sell cars to the public, in 1888, with Daimler following in 1892. A year later, the all-new Benz Velo became the

Mercedes 220
This example of the popular "Ponton" series is shown on the runway at Frankfurt Airport in 1958.

world's first production car, offering pivoting axles, two seats, and four wheels. However, it was the 1901 Daimler 35 hp that truly set the pattern most successful automakers copied: a pressed steel chassis frame; occupants behind the engine (a four-cylinder unit, under a hood with a honeycomb radiator ahead of it) rather than sitting above it;

an aluminum crankcase set in line; a gate gear-shift mechanism; foot throttle; and a steering wheel on a raked column. Thanks to its lowered center of gravity, the vehicle was a revelation in roadholding. Moreover, the car was marketed under the Mercedes brand, and was named after the daughter of Emil Jellinek, the brilliant sales agent who had exclusive rights to sell Daimler's cars, including the 60 hp model of 1903, with its advanced overhead-valve engine. Benz's Blitzen racing car, designed by Ferdinand Porsche

"It is a **temple** to mankind's **power** to think and imagine and **strive** for progress."

KARL BENZ, WRITING ABOUT A DISPLAY OF BENZ CARS IN THE DEUTSCHES MUSEUM, 1925

Mercedes-Benz S-Class, 1979
This version of the long-lived S-Class, codenamed the W126, was a paragon of both aerodynamic efficiency and occupant safety.

(see pp. 56–57), held the world land speed record from 1909 to 1924, reaching 141 mph (228 km/h). Benz and Porsche also pioneered supercharging (1927's Mercedes-Benz SSK was the most formidable sports car available). Meanwhile, Mercedes created a range of cars in several sizes.

The merged partners complemented each other well. Car manufacturing took place in Stuttgart, and Mercedes-Benz in Nazi-ruled 1930s' Germany built mostly large, powerful cars, such as the 540K roadster and the "Grosser Limousine."

Recovery from World War II was slow. The prewar 170V was back in production in 1946, followed by the luxurious 300 series in 1951.

1953's W120 series, known as the Ponton for its full-width styling, was an

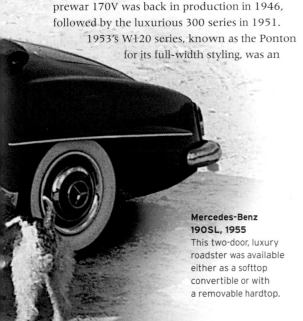

Mercedes-Benz 190SL, 1955
This two-door, luxury roadster was available either as a softtop convertible or with a removable hardtop.

all-new, four-cylinder sedan with unitary construction and, soon, diesel and six-cylinder gasoline options. By 1958, the firm was making 100,000 cars a year.

With its W125, the company dominated European car racing in the 1930s. The W154 of the 1950s picked up this winning streak, giving Juan Manuel Fangio his second World Championship in 1954. The 300 SL, which won the 1952 Le Mans race, went on to become the ultimate roadgoing sports car, the first car ever with gullwing doors and standard fuel injection. By 1955, however, Mercedes had axed its racing program after crash debris killed 83 spectators at Le Mans. Mercedes' driver Pierre Levegh (in a 300 SLR) was also killed.

In 1959, the Fintail 200/300 series, the first car to have scientifically designed crumple zones, replaced the Ponton. This standard mid-range Mercedes would be replaced in 1967, 1976, and 1985 in steady evolution.

The 190 SL roadster arrived in 1955 and was popular despite its leisurely performance. Fuel injection, used in its 1963 replacement, the 230 SL, made for a feistier performer. Along with timelessly broad styling, the model had a dished hardtop roof.

Highlights of the 1980s included the world-first fitment of airbags to the aerodynamic S-Class in 1981. A new SL in 1989 was the first car with an innovative pop-up rollover bar.

Between 1998 and 2007, Mercedes-Benz had an ill-fated alliance with Chrysler. It also acquired the Smart city car venture, brought out the A-Class Golf-size family hatchback, and revived the Maybach marque. AMG was recently absorbed into Mercedes as their in-house high performance division.

CLASSICS OF THE FUTURE

SLK 230 Kompressor For Mercedes-Benz, the SLK roadster was a radical departure. It was, at the time, the shortest car the company had made, and it was built around a supercharged 2.3-liter, four-cylinder engine, with drive to the rear wheels. Automatic transmission was popular, but the car's main feature was its Vario roof, an electronic two-piece hardtop that folded into the trunk, yet left a useful amount of luggage space.

△ **Mercedes-Benz SLK 230 Kompressor 1996**

Origin	Germany
Engine	2,295 cc, straight-four
Top speed	145 mph (233 km/h)

The 1990s saw renewed interest in two-seat sports cars, and Mercedes countered BMW's Z3 with this luxury model. A 3.2-liter AMG model followed.

SLR McLaren The SLR was conceived and styled by Mercedes-Benz as a powerful touring sports car before being handed over to McLaren Automotive to engineer, develop, and manufacture; unlike other high-performance Mercedes-Benz cars, it was built in the UK. The SLR was prodigiously fast, with a 208-mph (335-km/h) top speed. A technological tour de force, with 2,252 examples produced up to 2009, the SLR proved to be an outstandingly lucrative supercar.

△ **Mercedes-Benz SLR McLaren 2003**

Origin	UK/Germany
Engine	5,439 cc, V8
Top speed	203 mph (326 km/h)

With 617 bhp, this was one of the most powerful production cars ever. The "butterfly" doors were an homage to the gullwing doors of the 1950s' 300 SL.

Small Family Cars

With money short and fuel still rationed in many countries, long after the War was over, the focus was very much on small, economical cars. Most famous of them all was the Volkswagen, designed in the 1930s and put into full production by the British in 1945. It became a massive world-wide best-seller that remained in production for decades. But there were many more small cars, from across Europe and even in the relatively affluent US. Each one had its own approach to providing affordable family motoring, often based on novel engineering.

Ribbed bumpers on early models

Running boards show the aging roots of the original design

Front and rear fenders are detachable

Turn signals incorporated into pillar

Dummy "waterfall" design grille

▷ **Morris Eight Series E 1945**

Origin UK

Engine 918 cc, straight-four

Top speed 58 mph (93 km/h)

A revamp of the previous model, the Series E gained an upgraded engine, a new radiator grille, and headlamps. It also lost its running boards, giving it a modern enough appearance to continue in production until being replaced by the popular Morris Minor.

Steep fastback rear end

◁ **Ford Taunus G93A 1948**

Origin Germany

Engine 1,172 cc, straight-four

Top speed 60 mph (96 km/h)

Ford of Germany built this compact family car using the same engine, chassis, and suspension as Britain's E93A Ford Prefect. They fitted their own bodies, which looked more modern and were inspired by the American Lincoln Zephyr. The car reappeared after the war, in mildly modified form, as the G73A.

Body welded to chassis, rather than bolted on

Rear-hinged "suicide" doors

Split rear
windshield

◁ **Volkswagen Beetle 1945**

Origin	Germany
Engine	1,131 cc, flat-four
Top speed	63 mph (101 km/h)

Adolf Hitler commissioned engineer
Ferdinand Porsche to design this low-cost
vehicle for the German people. The rear-
mounted engine was durable and air-cooled
so it couldn't boil over. Production began
after World War II and continued, latterly
in Mexico, until 2003. A remarkable 21
million were sold over seven decades.

FRONT VIEW

REAR VIEW

Guards on
bumpers give
minimal protection

Comfort not speed
Despite its modest engine, good aerodynamics and
simple, lightweight construction ensured the Beetle
was a capable cruiser. Four-wheel independent
suspension also gave a comfortable ride and
reasonable handling for the day.

Compact design
An advantage of positioning the engine at the back
of the car was that it eliminated the need for a
heavy rear axle, reducing weight, and helping to
keep the design simple. Trunk space was provided
at the front of the car, but was limited.

Hood ornament
unique to 1948
model

Light-weight,
copper-brazed
engine is noisy

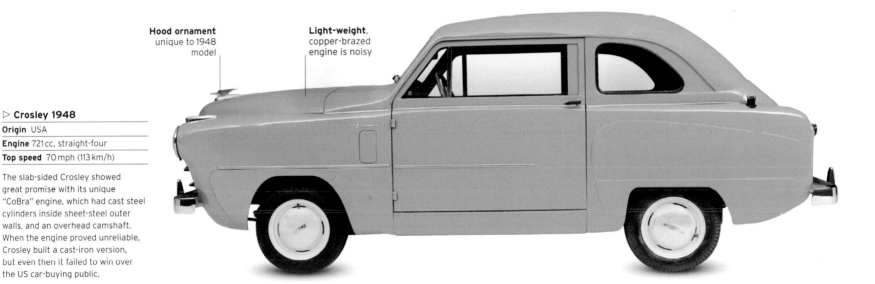

▷ **Crosley 1948**

Origin	USA
Engine	721 cc, straight-four
Top speed	70 mph (113 km/h)

The slab-sided Crosley showed
great promise with its unique
"CoBra" engine, which had cast steel
cylinders inside sheet-steel outer
walls, and an overhead camshaft.
When the engine proved unreliable,
Crosley built a cast-iron version,
but even then it failed to win over
the US car-buying public.

Body stamped
from a single
piece of steel

Green paint was army
surplus on early cars

◁ **Saab 92 1949**

Origin	Sweden
Engine	764 cc, straight-two
Top speed	65 mph (105 km/h)

Aircraft maker Saab gave its 92 a radical
low-drag body shape and a two-cylinder,
two-stroke engine, with front-wheel drive,
a 3-speed manual gearbox, and a free-wheel
device. The 92 and its successors, the 93
and 96, proved to be successful rally cars.

Torsion bar suspension

Great Designers
Dr. Ferdinand Porsche

Porsche is a name ingrained in sports car enthusiasts. Yet its founder, Ferdinand Porsche, was so much more than the creator of one of the world's most recognizable marques. A man of inventiveness and rare skill, he designed the Volkswagen Beetle, pioneered hybrid vehicles, and was the brains behind some of the most successful racing cars. He even chauffeured for Archduke Franz Ferdinand.

Career highlights

▷ **1897** Porsche designs and builds a pioneering wheel-hub motor that is powered by electricity

▷ **1900** The Lohner-Porsche is launched at the Paris World Fair. It is the world's first hybrid gasoline/electric road car

▷ **1928** The Porsche-designed Mercedes-Benz SSK instantly becomes one of the world's greatest sports cars

▷ **1933** Porsche engineers the hugely successful Auto Union racing car

▷ **1934** Adolf Hitler's "people's car" program is awarded to Porsche, who designs the Volkswagen Beetle

▷ **1948** With the Porsche 356, Ferdinand Porsche creates a new sports car dynasty under his own marque

△ Porsche 356, 1948
The first production vehicle to be built by the Porsche company, the 356 sports car was so named to indicate that it was the 356th project on which Ferdinand Porsche had worked.

▷ **1949** Porsche relocates to Stuttgart with his family

▷ **1999** Porsche is posthumously awarded the title of "Car Engineer of the Century"

DR. FERDINAND PORSCHE was born in 1875 in the village of Maffersdorf, in what was then the Austro-Hungarian Empire. Even at a very young age, he was fascinated by engineering, and especially the exciting new field of electricity.

At 18, he decided to forego a full-time university opportunity in order to pursue a career in electrical engineering. He joined the company Béla Egger and in 1897, despite having no formal training, built a pioneering, electric wheel-hub motor. The concept was highly advanced and provided an energy-efficient propulsion system.

In 1898, Porsche began working at Jakob Lohner, a Vienna-based company owned by the Austro-Hungarian Army. Soon afterward, his wheel-hub design was installed into the Lohner-Porsche—quite possibly the world's first front-wheel drive car. Exhibited at the 1900 Paris World Fair, it was an immediate success and hailed by the press as an "epoch-making innovation."

Porsche then built a second car for Lohner—the world's first true hybrid vehicle. It not only had a battery pack, but also an internal combustion engine powering a generator, which in turn fed the electric hub motors. Since there

Mercedes-Benz SSK, 1929
Capable of speeds up to 120 mph (193 km/h), the last car that Ferdinand Porsche worked on at Mercedes-Benz was also the fastest vehicle of its day, a status that guaranteed it several racetrack victories.

was a motor in each of the four wheel hubs, this amazingly advanced machine also qualifies as the world's first four-wheel drive car. However, it weighed more than four tons (4,000 kg); it was simply too large to have a viable future.

However, Porsche entered races with this car and scored several victories. His skill as a driver was recognized when he was appointed as Archduke Franz Ferdinand's chauffeur. Luckily, Porsche was not driving the car in which the crown prince was assassinated in 1914.

Porsche had recently moved to Austro-Daimler in 1906, where he was appointed technical manager. In 1923, he made the bold decision to emigrate to Germany, working in Daimler's head office. It was here that he oversaw the famous Mercedes supercharged engine program, which culminated in probably the world's highest-performing car of its age—the formidable Mercedes-Benz SSK sports car.

Porsche left Daimler for Steyr in 1929, only to form a new consulting company in 1931 under his own name in Stuttgart. With financial backing from the Austrian government, he designed new cars for Wanderer and Zündapp.

A CAR FOR THE PEOPLE

In 1933, the German Chancellor, Adolf Hitler, instigated two projects, both of which would involve Porsche. The first was a state-sponsored

AUTO UNION TYPE A 1933/34

HEADLIGHT, VW BEETLE 1938

"If one does not **fail** at times, then one has not **challenged himself.**"

DR. FERDINAND PORSCHE

racing car, which resulted in the Auto Union that Porsche designed. This featured a very powerful V16 engine and such Porsche innovations as a limited-slip differential.

The second project was a new German "people's car" or *volkswagen*, and it was Porsche to whom Hitler turned to lead the car's development, which he did, together with his son, Ferry. They produced a simple but effective design using a separate chassis, an air-cooled, rear-mounted engine, and a distinctively curvaceous body that would give the car its nickname (and eventual title)—"Beetle."

WAR PROJECTS

In 1938, again at the instruction of the Nazi government, Porsche designed a streamlined racing car based on the VW chassis—the Type 64— with a tuned VW engine. This was undoubtedly a precursor to the Porsche sports car that would make the marque famous.

A legacy continues
Ferdinand Alexander Porsche, grandson of the company's founder, is best known for designing Porsche's celebrated 911. It is testament to Ferdinand's vision that the company has built so many iconic cars.

However, World War II intervened in 1939, hindering progress of the VW Beetle. Porsche was diverted onto military projects, adapting the Beetle to create the jeeplike Kübelwagen and the amphibious Schwimmwagen. He also designed several tanks for the Nazis, and contributed to numerous aircraft projects.

When the war ended in 1945, Porsche was requested to relocate to France, along with his factory equipment, as part of the war reparations. However, this met with several objections from the French auto industry, and Porsche was instead arrested alongside Ferry because of his Nazi affiliations. Ferry was released in six months and worked to keep the company in business. While Ferdinand was in prison, Ferry created a new

racing car, the Cisitalia, which greatly impressed his father on his release. Encouraged, the pair decided to create their own sports-car marque with a car that used the Beetle's format of a rear-mounted, air-cooled engine set-up that would not change for decades. Production of the 356 started in late 1948 in a small factory in Gmünd, Austria, but Porsche soon relocated to Stuttgart, where his empire continues to flourish today.

Ferdinand Porsche died in 1951 at age 75 before he could see the true glory years of his company, which he left in the very safe hands of his son, Ferry. Porsche senior's legacy has been widely recognized, not least by his 1999 posthumous award of the accolade, "Car Engineer of the Century." And it is hard to argue that he does not deserve it.

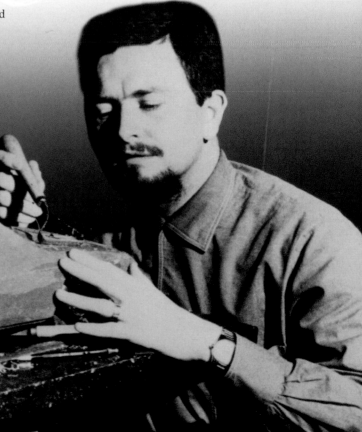

Vincenzo Lancia at the wheel of a Fiat in the 1907 Targa Florio race

Great Marques
The Lancia Story

Now reduced to a subsidiary of Fiat Chrysler, Lancia's long history blended engineering innovation with style in a manner that few companies could rival. Since its creation in 1906, the Turin-based company, its cars, and drivers have enjoyed a glittering career in motorsports, particularly in recent years in international rallying.

ORIGINALLY TRAINED AS A BOOKKEEPER, Vincenzo Lancia was a restless autodidact who quickly rose to become a chief engineer and test driver at Fiat. His driving was so impressive, in fact, that he was invited to race for the company, and soon earned a reputation for speed. His most notable victory came in 1904, when he thundered across the line of the 230-mile (370-km) Coppa Florio in a 10.5-liter Fiat.

With backing from friends, Lancia became an automaker in his own right in 1906 after buying a factory from Itala and hiring about 20 staff. In less than a year, their first car was up and running; but almost immediately the car and the blueprints needed to build it were destroyed in a disastrous fire. It took seven months to ready a replacement, powered by a 2.5-liter, four-cylinder engine of a novel, two-stage design.

More than a dozen of these replacement cars were built and sold; a second production model followed and by 1911, with export sales to the UK and the US on the rise, a much larger factory was needed. Unusual for the time, the company not only built bodies for its own cars, but also supplied engine and chassis assemblies to coachbuilders, such as Locati e Torretta, Farina, and (in the UK), Maythorn.

Lancia Fulvia HF, 1966
The HF was the most responsive version of the pretty Fulvia Coupe, with up to 132 bhp available from its 1.6-liter, flat-four engine; its lightweight body panels and glass also made for excellent handling.

Successive vehicle types in those early days were simply called Beta, Gamma, Delta, all the way through to Zeta. When the company had exhausted the Greek alphabet, a long line of cars, from the 1931 Artena to the 1972 Fulvia, then took their names from the daughters of the rulers of Ancient Rome.

Some of Lancia's best designs were among them and included several highly significant cars, such as the 1922 Trikappa with its narrow-angle V8, and a year later the Lambda, which introduced unibody construction. Another star was the 1937 Aprilia, launched shortly after Vincenzo Lancia's death, which scored various victories, including taking five of the top six places for its class in the 1938 Monte Carlo Rally.

Vincenzo Lancia's passion for technical innovation meant that, in the early years, his cars tended to be costly and upmarket. It was 1930 before the factory addressed the issue of mass transportation, which it first did with the little Augusta. This model had a V engine, but with four cylinders rather than eight. It sold more than 14,000, an impressive total helped in no small part by its perhaps surprising popularity among racing drivers of the day.

Augusta owners included some of racing's most heroic figures such as Tazio Nuvolari and Achille Varzi, something which helped to build Lancia's reputation as a marque for enthusiasts and the cognoscenti. This reputation was to last far longer than warranted for many of its later cars, perhaps

sustaining the company through some tricky times. Further class wins followed in major events such as the Spa 24 Hour and the Alpine Rally, and did so even though the factory lacked a dedicated competition department until well into the 1950s. The establishment of one led the company into a brief flirtation with Formula 1 before it was decided to leave single-seater racing to the likes of Cooper, Lotus, and Ferrari.

The other big news in the mid-1950s was the decision of Lancia's widow and son to sell the firm to the millionaire, Carlo Pesenti. Having made his money in cement, Pesenti spent much of it on a wide-ranging

Lancia Flavia Sport Zagato, 1963
Quirky or futuristic, depending on your viewpoint, this two-door version offered lightweight coachwork and an electrically operated rear window for ventilation. Extra power came from twin carburetors.

Lancia Flaminia Sport Zagato, 1958
Just under 600 of these GTs were made, with a choice of V6 engines; "double bubble" twin humps in the roof profile were a signature feature.

"A large, glossy car of **supreme elegance**, most probably drawn up outside a **palatial entrance**. In simple terms that is the legacy of **Vincenzo Lancia.**"

EARLY ADVERTISEMENT FOR LANCIA

program of modernization and expansion. For many Lancia diehards, the new company lost part of its soul at this point, but cars such as the Flavia Zagato Coupe and the Fulvia HF showed it still had plenty to offer.

Compact, light, and stylistically distinctive, these cars are now very desirable and, while always much cheaper than the Stratos, they are also becoming increasingly valuable as collectors' cars. Throughout the same period, financial imperatives required the

Lancia Delta Integrale, 1987
With its 165 bhp, turbocharged, 2-liter engine and four-wheel drive, this practical, five-door hatchback lived a double life as a rally car firebrand.

company to produce many more unremarkable machines, as well (family cars such as the Beta, Thema, and poorly named Dedra), but marque enthusiasts are happy to forget these and to concentrate instead on what Lancia did best.

CLASSICS OF THE FUTURE

Delta Integrale Evoluzione II Lancia was sold to Fiat in 1969, and it was hoped a high-performance hot hatch would recapture Lancia's earlier glory. The specialized S4 took second place in the 1986 World Championship and, eager to capitalize on this success, Lancia built a range of turbo-powered, all wheel drive models. The Evoluzione was fast and boxy, with widened arches and prominent spoilers. The cars did well and today find ready buyers.

△ **Lancia Delta Integrale Evoluzione II 1993**

Origin Italy	
Engine 1,995 cc, four-cylinder	
Top speed 137 mph (220 km/h)	

Introduced in 1993, the Evoluzione II had a more powerful engine than the previous model, producing a blistering 215 bhp. It also sported cosmetic changes.

Kappa Coupe A shortened wheelbase, wider track, and frameless doors served to distinguish the coupe from its sedan sibling, but sales were slow, making this a rare beast for any would-be Lancia collector. Offered only in left-hand drive, the car used an engine from its Alfa Romeo stablemate and was styled in-house. It failed to reignite interest however, although this was as much to do with its high price as with any specific shortcomings.

△ **Lancia Kappa Coupe 1997**

Origin Italy	
Engine 2,955 cc, V6	
Top speed 137 mph (220 km/h)	

Based on the executive Kappa sedan, this model was Lancia's first coupe since 1984. While praised for its sporty engine range, the styling was not popular.

Mid-Range Family Sedans

Family cars went through enormous changes in the 1940s. Separate fenders, running boards, and stand-up headlamps were out, and modern, full-width styling was in. Inspiration came from the design leaders in the US auto industry, which meant car companies across Europe increasingly used chrome trim and innovated with man-made materials. Underneath, these cars varied a lot as each manufacturer aimed to produce cars best suited to their home markets. Toughness and reliability were common aims, but while some concentrated on low cost, others opted for comfortable ride quality or nimble handling.

▽ **Peugeot 203 1948**

Origin France

Engine 1,290 cc, straight-four

Top speed 73 mph (118 km/h)

The 203 was state-of-the-art. The tough unibody construction had been wind-tunnel tested to reduce drag, and the fluid suspension could smooth out the bumpiest of roads. The engine had an aluminum cylinder head with overhead valves and hemispherical combustion chambers. Almost 700,000 were sold by 1960.

FRONT VIEW

REAR VIEW

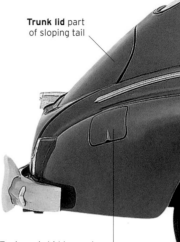

Trunk lid part of sloping tail

Fuel cap is hidden under a cover set flush to body

Period styling
Many of the 203's design elements were typical of sedans of the era. Its headlights, which were incorporated into the bodywork not mounted externally, were just such an example.

Slender but spacious
Although tapered, the rear end of the 203 nonetheless included a wide-opening trunk. It had large bumpers but absurdly small taillamps by today's standards.

Spacious trunk has a drop-down lid

Front ornament completes "razor-edge" design

▷ **Triumph 1800 1946**

Origin UK

Engine 1,776 cc, straight-four

Top speed 75 mph (121 km/h)

Standard bought Triumph in 1945, and relaunched it as an upmarket marque with sharp styling by Mulliners of Birmingham. The engine was enlarged to 2,088 cc in 1949, and a new chassis introduced when the model became the Triumph Renown in 1950. Production lasted until 1954.

Steel body new to Swedish market

Laminated windshield for safety and security

Prominent hood established styling "shoulder"

◁ **Volvo PV444 1947**

Origin Sweden

Engine 1,414 cc, straight-four

Top speed 76 mph (122 km/h)

With unibody construction and a new overhead-valve engine, the Volvo was ahead of its time. The prototype had first been revealed three years earlier, in 1944. In 1956, the PV444 became the first Volvo to be sold in the US, in a more responsive, twin-carburetor form.

Rack-and-pinion steering

Simple sedan
The interior of the 203 was simple and straightforward. Initially, the speedometer was centrally mounted in the painted metal dashboard, but later in 1952 it was moved in front of the driver, when quarter windows were also added to the front doors and the rear window was enlarged. The front seats were moved to fill the entire width of the cabin and the gear lever was on the steering column.

Headlights faired to the fenders

Live-axle, coil spring rear suspension

High-gloss finish to paintwork

Fastback profile still allows for roomy cabin

Engine mounted forward of front axle

◁ **Jowett Javelin 1947**

Origin UK

Engine 1,486 cc, flat-four

Top speed 78 mph (126 km/h)

The small Yorkshire company, Jowett, created the Javelin in a brave attempt to build a postwar car that was almost entirely new. It had an advanced flat-four engine that resulted in a low center of gravity, giving it excellent handling.

Rear-wheel drive, as were all mainstream family cars of the era

"Suicide" doors at front

Aerodynamic "teardrop" shape

▷ **Tatra T600 Tatraplan 1948**

Origin Czechoslovakia

Engine 1,952 cc, flat-four

Top speed 80 mph (129 km/h)

The brilliant T600 had a strikingly modern body with unibody construction and a very low drag coefficient of just 0.32. Power came from an air-cooled, flat-four engine that was mounted at the rear, giving enough space inside to seat up to six people in comfort.

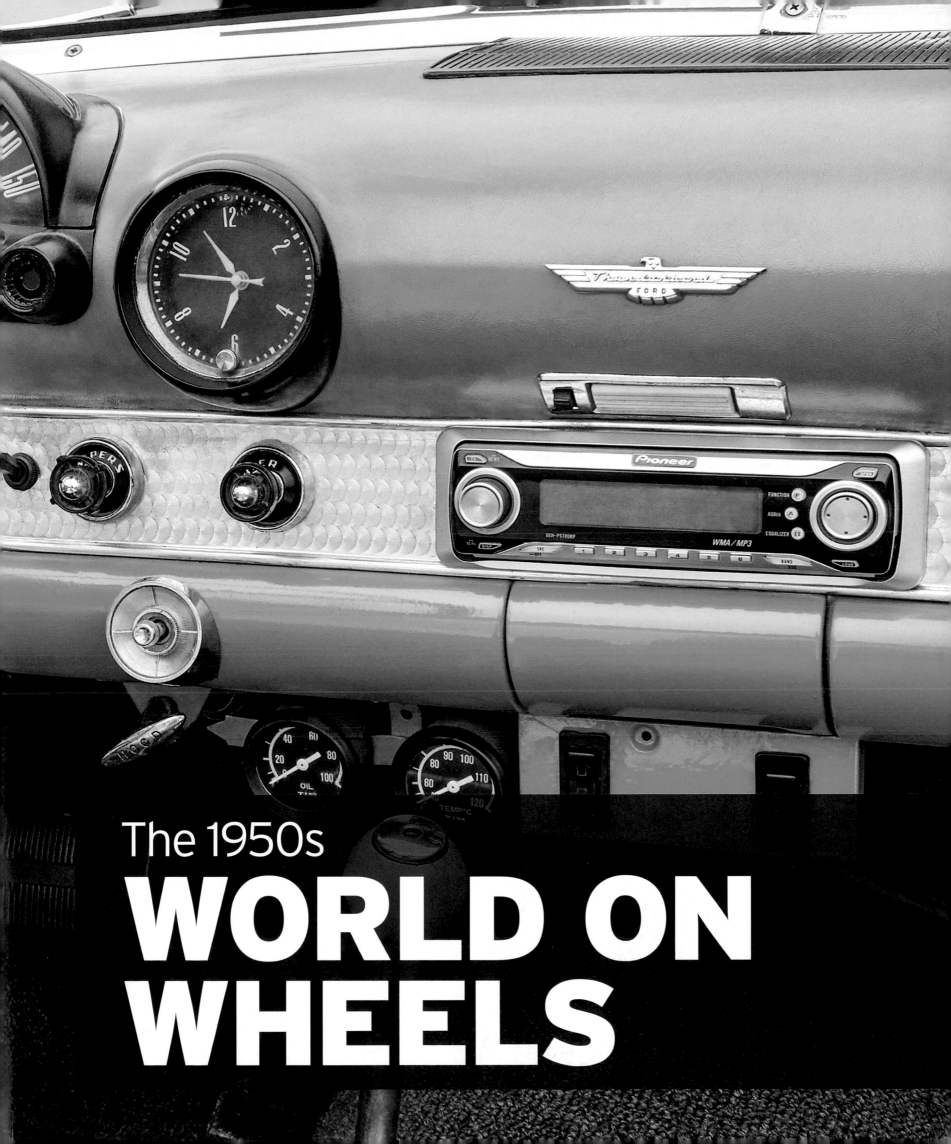

The 1950s
WORLD ON WHEELS

WORLD ON WHEELS

In the 1950s, the car took center stage in daily life. Ownership was still by no means universal, but many millions of people could now realistically aspire to driving on the world's still relatively uncrowded roads, in a car they could call their own.

American automakers embraced new technologies, unveiling cars that emphasized power, luxury, and elongated glamour. Stylists produced innovative designs that adopted aerospace imagery and chromium-plated decor in equal measure, heightening public desire in their products. Their engineering efforts focused on combining smooth operation with abundant power. The horsepower race had started with a vengeance.

In Europe, with resources still scarce and—in 1956—the shock of a fuel crisis sparked by rising tensions in the Middle East, the emphasis was on attractive economy cars. Larger models, aimed at bigger families, were often also working vehicles, serving taxi drivers or police forces. Luxury sedans were the reserve of business leaders and government officials.

But stirring and efficient racing machines from Italy, Germany, and the UK also led to great sports cars that fused science with style. The Japanese car industry, meanwhile, was in its infancy, struggling to meet Western standards. Korea had only just got off the starting blocks; China was still predominately a land of bicycles.

Multilane highways around the world were shrinking travel times, but with higher-sustained driving speeds came a new concern—safety. Crash protection, braking, driver attitudes, and the cars' mechanical stamina all had some way to go to catch up with the new pace of on-road life.

△ **Safety measures**
Launched in 1959, the Mercedes-Benz W111 was the first car introduced with front and rear crumple safety zones, here being tested using a rocket-propelled sled.

" The fact is, I don't drive **just to get from A to B**. I enjoy feeling the car's reactions, **becoming part of it**."

ENZO FERRARI, LEGENDARY RACE AND ROAD CAR CONSTRUCTOR

◁ **Poster advertising** the Messerschmitt KR200, 1955

Key events

▷ **1950** Rover unveils the world's first turbine-engined car, and demonstrates its jet-propelled performance.

▷ **1952** Lotus Engineering Company is started by Colin Chapman; Austin and Morris merge to form the British Motor Corporation.

▷ **1953** Chevrolet builds the first of its long-lived Corvette line of powerful sports cars.

▷ **1954** The age of the supercar dawns with the Mercedes-Benz 300SL, boasting gullwing doors and the world's first standard fuel injection.

▷ **1954** The first of Ford's Thunderbird luxury sports cruisers comes off the Detroit production line.

△ **US auto manufacturing might**
During the 1950s, car manufacturing became the largest industrial segment in the US, with sales reaching almost 60 million cars during the decade.

▷ **1955** RCA and Philco offer transistor radios in US cars for the first time.

▷ **1955** Film heartthrob James Dean is killed in his Porsche in California.

▷ **1956** 20,000 people attend the launch of the Renault Dauphine in Paris.

▷ **1957** Fiat introduces its tiny Nuova 500 economy car.

▷ **1958** Aston Martin's DB4 is a beautiful and powerful new GT.

▷ **1959** The Mini is unveiled as the first transverse-engined, front-wheel-drive economy car.

▷ **1959** Jaguar launches the iconic Mk 2 sedan.

A Volvo PV51 and 52 bodywork inspection, in the late 1930s

Great Marques
The Volvo Story

As Swedish as Abba, despite being foreign-owned since 1999, Volvo has a reputation for safety. A century ago, the original company made ball bearings and took its name from the Latin for "I roll." Its first cars were not built until 1926, a series of 10 pre-production models, one of which had a fabric-covered body on a wooden frame.

THE FIRST TRUE PRODUCTION Volvo appeared in April 1927, a 2-liter car of undistinguished appearance, but one that the company hoped would make 1,000 sales. To begin with, engines and transmissions were brought in from outside suppliers and sales remained modest at just a few hundred a year until a decision was made to design a new six-cylinder engine. Unique to Volvo, this entered production in 1929.

With their slightly derivative American styling, Volvos were largely restricted to the domestic market until 1947, when the launch of the streamlined PV444, two-door sedan saw it combine American glamour with smaller European proportion. By January 1956, more than 100,000 of these cars had been built, and a visit to the US by one of the founders, Assar Gabrielsson, encouraged the idea that Volvo should build a sports roadster expressly for the American market. Unfortunately, the entire project was abandoned when Gabrielsson retired, by which time fewer than 70 of the P1900 had been produced.

Instead, success in the increasingly important export market had to wait for the 120 series Amazon. This model shared the underpinnings of the PV444 but had more up-to-date styling and revised rear suspension. The car also pioneered three-point front seatbelts, a hugely important life-saving advance, and the start of a commitment to driver and passenger safety that has never abated.

The car went on to be assembled in Belgium, Chile, South Africa, and Canada as well as at home in Sweden, and as a strong, handsome machine it set the template for future Volvo cars. Selling more than 660,000 in all, the wagon version of the car proved particularly popular.

From the mid-1970s onward, much larger wagons, such as the 200, 700, and 900 series cars, became something of a trademark for Volvo. When the company decided again to try its hand with a sports car (the 1961 P1800), it even went so far as to produce a wagon version, badged the P1800ES.

With a tendency to keep cars in production for many years, Volvo has sometimes risked looking a little staid. The last PV rolled off the factory line as late as 1965, while the Amazon remained on sale

Volvo PV444, 1947
Designed during World War II, delays in production meant that the PV444 was considered dated from the beginning. It still proved a sales success for Volvo.

until 1970, and although sales were modest, the P1800 enjoyed a 12-year run.

The fact that Simon Templar drove a Volvo P1800 in *The Saint* television series brought a little glamour to the brand (The Who's Roger Daltrey owned one as well). Occasional forays into motorsports also succeeded in whipping up interest, although the almost van-like 850 wagon could manage only eighth place in the British Touring Car Championships in the mid-1990s.

The company also had a go at producing a coupe, the slightly odd-looking 262C Bertone, but family cars and ample cargo haulers were what it did best and for years the Volvo Car Corporation built little else.

In 1999, the parent company, AB Volvo, decided to focus on trucks and therefore sold the automotive division to Ford. The news stunned many Swedes, but it would bring the

Volvo 221/222 Amazon Wagon, 1962
This rugged family hauler brought the Swedes a well-deserved reputation as a leading maker of the roomiest station wagons, for both family and business life.

"I'll keep driving my Volvo P1800. Not much will **change**. But whether I drive **four million miles** is more up to me than it is the car."

IRV GORDON

company useful economies of scale by enabling it to share components and new model development costs. In 2010, ownership switched to China's Geely.

Since then the company has gone some way toward widening its portfolio, with cars like the XC90, a luxury sport-utility vehicle. The square-back Volvos of old have long gone and new cars sport a more streamlined appearance. Sales have risen accordingly, although it is probable that where Volvo owners were once among the most brand-loyal drivers anywhere, today they are more willing to consider models from Audi and BMW.

Volvo can at least lay claim to building the car with the highest mileage in the world: American Irv Gordon owns a 1966 Volvo P1800S with over 3 million miles (4.8 million km) on the clock.

Volvo P1800S, 1963
The actor, Roger Moore, as lead character Simon Templar on the set of British TV adventure series, *The Saint*.

CLASSICS OF THE FUTURE

C70 Convertible Clearly an attempt to echo the success of the P1800, the sleek C70 was available as both a coupe and a convertible, with the latter selling an impressive 50,000 units prior to the model's overhaul in 2006. A range of economical gasoline and diesel engines were offered, too. Today the rarest C70s are those with Volvo's "signature" saffron pearl metallic paint, of which fewer than 150 were produced.

△ **Volvo C70 Convertible 1997**

Origin	Sweden
Engine	2,319 cc, five-cylinder
Top speed	155 mph (250 km/h)

The C70 offered family-friendly performance driving, combined with style and comfort. Its Roll-Over Protection System (ROPS), provided enhanced safety.

C30 T5 A further attempt at producing a compact sport wagon, the two-door C30 could be viewed as a successor to Volvo's earlier 1800ES and 480ES, but was far superior to both. This was In large part this was due to the multiplicity of parts and the know-how brought across from the high-performance versions of the Ford Focus, whose platform it shared. Agile with rapid acceleration, it gave other Volvos a run for their money.

△ **Volvo C30 T5 2006**

Origin	Belgium
Engine	2,435 cc, five-cylinder
Top speed	149 mph (240 km/h)

Volvo's entry-level coupe was compact, sleek, and nimble. With 220 bhp and three suspension settings, it was a joy to drive.

Family Cars

These bigger sedans were the sort of cars people aspired to, purchasing them as their children grew and their careers progressed. They were cars driven by managers rather than their staff. Rarely the most exciting models in their makers' lineups, they were often big enough sellers and commanded a high enough price to be the first cars in their ranges to have design sophistications such as independent suspensions or all-in-one-piece bodies that did away with separate chassis frames. They were often among the first truly new vehicles produced after World War II, taking over from designs that dated back to the 1930s.

Dashboard style
With its ribbon speedometer, large steering wheel with chrome ring horn push, and column gear lever, the Zephyr had a typical 1950s dashboard.

▷ **Ford Zephyr Mk II 1956**

Origin	UK
Engine	2,553 cc, straight-six
Top speed	90 mph (145 km/h)

Replacing the slab-sided 1951 Zephyr, the British Mk II gained a stylish unibody with strong American overtones, column gear levers, umbrella handbrakes, and strip speedometers. Soon these cars were available with overdrive and automatic transmissions, but still retained vacuum wipers that slowed down as the car sped up.

Front bench
could seat three

Chrome
headlamp surround

Extra driving lights
were popular options

Long and low
The longer wheelbase of Britain's Mk II Consul, Zephyr, and Zodiac models permitted sleeker looks with a lower stance; the wraparound rear window greatly increased visibility.

Body shared by Consuls, Zephyrs, and Zodiacs

Generous trunk
space

SIDE VIEW

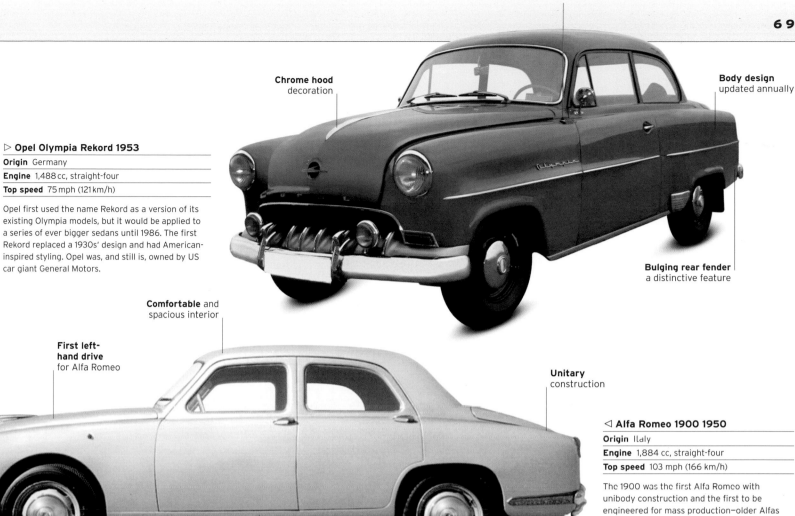

Chrome hood decoration

Body design updated annually

Bulging rear fender a distinctive feature

▷ Opel Olympia Rekord 1953

Origin Germany

Engine 1,488 cc, straight-four

Top speed 75 mph (121 km/h)

Opel first used the name Rekord as a version of its existing Olympia models, but it would be applied to a series of ever bigger sedans until 1986. The first Rekord replaced a 1930s' design and had American-inspired styling. Opel was, and still is, owned by US car giant General Motors.

Comfortable and spacious interior

First left-hand drive for Alfa Romeo

Unitary construction

Unitary frame

◁ Alfa Romeo 1900 1950

Origin Italy

Engine 1,884 cc, straight-four

Top speed 103 mph (166 km/h)

The 1900 was the first Alfa Romeo with unibody construction and the first to be engineered for mass production—older Alfas were low volume and many parts were made and built by hand. With its twin-cam engine and full-width, aerodynamic body, the 1900 was a truly modern car.

▷ Mercedes-Benz 220 1954

Origin Germany

Engine 2,195 cc, straight-six

Top speed 101 mph (162 km/h)

The first Mercedes to forego a traditional steel frame, the 1953-launched 220 was still a solid and well-made car whose body found a ready market. It was popular with everyone from affluent businessmen to taxi drivers who liked the diesel versions. Six-cylinder gasoline versions arrived in 1954, and the car sold well.

Gas and diesel versions available

Famous three-pointed star hood ornament

Fastback body carried over from earlier PV444

Rounded body styled in the 1940s

Powerful straight-four engine

◁ Volvo PV544 1958

Origin Sweden

Engine 1,583 cc, straight-four

Top speed 95 mph (153 km/h)

The first Volvo to sell in quantity outside Scandinavia, the PV544 quickly established a reputation for and robust toughness. With its unibody construction, independent front and coil spring suspension, it handled well too. The PV544 continued in production until 1965.

Cars from the Jet Age

The 1950s were exciting times in the US. Jets and space rockets fired the public imagination, and car manufacturers did their utmost to link their products with these new technologies in order to capitalize on the positive mood. The less-than-subtle placement of a fighter plane in the background of this 1956 Chrysler magazine advertisement emphasizes that these cars are at the forefront of developments in the modern jet age.

BORROWING FROM TOMORROW

As the great marques of Detroit sought to outdo each other in terms of style and power, their publicity material often made questionable and exaggerated claims for new models.

For Chrysler, its dramatic 1956 range spoke for itself, with its stunning color palette and bold "Forward Look" design. The text accompanying this advertisement simply asserted: "From jutting headlights to crisply upswept tail, this simple clean line says *action*! This is a design that borrows from tomorrow." The hint of a more rational future was almost lost at the end of the hyperbole: "Safety Seat Belts, if you wish." However, for now the optimism could not help but be totally infectious.

A lineup of models from Chrysler's various marques, including Chrysler itself, Dodge, DeSoto, Imperial, and Plymouth–plus a jet fighter aircraft–adorn this photograph from a 1956 magazine advertisement.

Exotic High-Performers

Many of the most iconic names in motoring came of age in the 1950s, producing cars that in some cases are still closely associated with their makers' images today. In Europe, where the hardships of World War II were still a recent memory and many ordinary cars struggled to get beyond 70 mph (110 km/h), the latest Ferraris and Jaguars with their voluptuous bodies and high-speed performance seemed impossibly exotic. Cars like this brought film-star glamour to an often gray world. Some were synonymous with sporting success on the road and racetracks too, becoming symbols of national identity—and national pride.

Light yet powerful
The 2,953 cc, overhead camshaft V12 engine fitted to the 250 GT SWB was lighter than many rival power plants and enabled this car to reach speeds of 168 mph (270 km/h).

▷ **Ferrari 250 GT SWB 1959**

Origin	Italy
Engine	2,953 cc, V12
Top speed	168 mph (270 km/h)

Revealed at the 1959 Paris Motor Show, the V12-engined 250 GT SWB was intended as a serious competition car that could also be used on the open road. Its flowing bodywork, styled by Italian design house Pininfarina, became a template for the look of many future Ferraris.

Roll cage fitted for racing

Body made from steel and aluminum

V12 engine used in many Ferraris

Utilitarian interior
The 250 GT SWB's elegantly functional, gimmick-free cabin was designed for the driver, with all the major controls within easy reach of the steering wheel.

Built for pace
Early road-going 250 GT SWBs had hand-beaten, lightweight aluminum bodies, but this material was later reserved for pure racing versions. The Ferrari proved to be formidable on the track.

Distinctive sleek profile

Vent helps to keep brakes cool

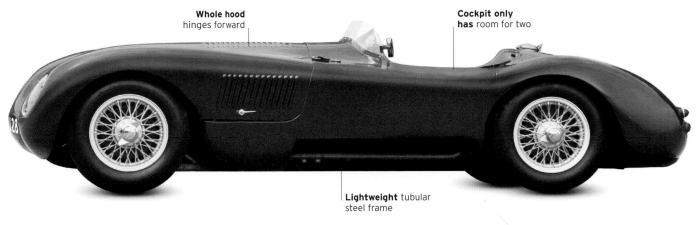

Whole hood hinges forward

Cockpit only has room for two

Lightweight tubular steel frame

◁ **Jaguar C-type 1951**

Origin UK

Engine 3,442 cc, straight-six

Top speed 144 mph (232 km/h)

A racing car that could also be driven on the road, the sinuous C-type was the XK120's competition cousin, and featured a lightweight tubular chassis. The C-type won the Le Mans 24-hour race at its debut in 1951, and won again two years later when equipped for the first time with innovative disc brakes.

Rear hatch gives access to trunk

Air scoop for cooling engine

▷ **Aston Martin DB2/4 1952**

Origin UK

Engine 2,580 cc, straight-six

Top speed 116 mph (187 km/h)

Based on the DB2, this grand tourer was offered in a range of body styles. All featured W.O. Bentley's Lagonda twin-overhead-camshaft engine and a tubular steel chassis. Competing in the 1955 Monte Carlo Rally, the DB2/4 had genuine racing pedigree.

Quick-release "knock-off" wire wheels

Interior has room for a driver and three passengers

Body built by Pinin Farina

◁ **Lancia Aurelia B20 GT 1953**

Origin Italy

Engine 2,451 cc, V6

Top speed 112 mph (180 km/h)

This clever, four-seat coupe served as a template for the modern compact grand tourer. The car's sharp handling, thanks to independent suspension, rear-mounted "transaxle" gearbox, and then-revolutionary radial tires, was aided by strong performance from the world's first production V6 engine. It also featured a strong, lightweight monocoque steel body.

Twin aerials add style

Curved windshield takes inspiration from American cars

▷ **Facel Vega FVS 1954**

Origin France

Engine 2,528 cc, V8

Top speed 115 mph (185 km/h)

Facel Vega made bodies for vehicle producers such as Ford before launching its own supercar in 1954. The FVSs, with their light aircraft-like instruments and sharp coachwork, mixed French style with American power, since they had Chrysler V8 motors. Using big American engines was an idea other European high-performance vehicle-makers would adopt.

Italian Flair

Italy combined art and engineering to produce stylish cars that were fun to drive—and they came in all sizes and price ranges. Innovations such as V engines, overhead camshafts, disc brakes, independent suspension, and unibody construction put Italian models way ahead of the humdrum machinery and prewar engineering that was prevalent in most of Europe at the time. The success of these new cars established the motor industry in Italy as one of the country's biggest and most successful exporters, and it is no wonder that Italian car production boomed, quadrupling during the 1950s.

Canvas roof folds down

De Dion or "dead axle" rear suspension

Tiny doors with removable side screens

Body designed by Pinin Farina

Narrow-angle V8 engine

Four-wheel drum brakes

Four-wheel independent suspension

▷ **Fiat 8V 1952**

Origin Italy

Engine 1,996 cc, V8

Top speed 118 mph (190 km/h)

This rare sports coupe features a 70-degree V8 engine, with 105 bhp from 2 liters, that was originally intended for a luxury sedan. Only 114 were made between 1952 and 1954, but it was a successful racing car, dominating the Italian 2-liter GT Championship.

Body style more rounded than 1959 cars

Engine carried over from prewar 1100E model

◁ **Fiat 1100 1953**

Origin Italy

Engine 1,089 cc, straight-four

Top speed 75 mph (121 km/h)

The long-running 1100 combined a prewar engine with a new unibody shell. Sedan, wagon, and rare convertible versions were available, and in 1959 there was a 1,221 cc engine option. Production kept going until 1969, when it was replaced by the front-wheel drive 128.

▽ **Lancia Aurelia B24 Spider 1954**

Origin Italy

Engine 2,451 cc, V6

Top speed 115 mph (185 km/h)

The B24 Spider put the revolutionary production V6 engine and independent rear suspension that Lancia had first developed for its first Aurelias in 1950 into a gorgeous Pinin Farina-designed, open two-seater body with a wraparound windshield and distinctive rear arch haunches. Just 240 were built from 1954 to 1955.

De Virgilio's V6

The Aurelia's V6 engine was designed by Francesco de Virgilio, an engineer who worked for Lancia's brilliant technical chief, Vittorio Jano, in the 1940s. There was a 60-degree angle between the cylinder banks, and the valves were operated by a single camshaft running down the V of the engine.

Left or right?

Italy had switched to driving on the right by the middle of the 1920s, and Aurelias were all manufactured in right-hand drive, as was Lancia's usual practice. In 1954, the fourth series sedans and the B24 Spider were offered with the option of left-hand drive. Of the 240 Spiders that were built, 181 were left-hand drive cars.

▷ **Alfa Romeo Giulietta Sedan 1954**

Origin Italy

Engine 1,290 cc, straight-four

Top speed 88 mph (142 km/h)

This little brother to Alfa's 1900 sedan was a long time coming, but worth the wait. It had unibody construction, all-alloy engine with twin overhead camshafts, and superb handling from independent front suspension and a live rear axle. Rust destroyed them quickly, but it was a delightful car when performing well.

Twin-overhead cam engine

Unibody construction

Live axle with coil springs

Lancia "shield" grille

Aluminum panels used on early models

◁ **Lancia Appia 1953**

Origin Italy

Engine 1,089 cc, V4

Top speed 75 mph (121 km/h)

Lancia's small car of 1953 copied the style of the bigger Aurelia. Its sliding pillar front suspension harked back to Lancias of old, and there was a live axle at the back, but the engine was a new, narrow-angle V4. Its high price meant sales were limited.

Great designers
Zagato

Over three generations, the Zagato family has forged a coachbuilding dynasty with a century-long history. A Zagato design is utterly unmistakable, characterized by extremes of shape, construction, and performance. Today the Milanese company's work–especially with prestige marques such as Alfa Romeo, Maserati, Ferrari, Aston Martin, Bristol, and Lancia–still sits in the very top flight.

Career Highlights

▷ **1929** The Alfa Romeo 6C 1750 is transformed into a mercurial and race-winning roadster by Ugo Zagato

▷ **1957** Zagato's ingenious signature "double-bubble" roof first appears

▷ **1962** A new factory opens in the shadow of the Alfa Romeo plant in Milan

▷ **1962** Zagato's new design guru, Ercole Spada, creates the utterly individual– and controversial–Lancia Flavia Sport

△ **Alfa Romeo TZ2, 1965**
Zagato collaborated with the Italian team Autodelta to refine the Alfa Romeo TZ into this model, which was only used for racing competition. It had a purpose-built spaceframe chassis and a lightweight fiber glass body.

▷ **1974** With the release of the Zele, Zagato becomes a pioneer of electric cars

▷ **1989** The Zagato factory gets into full swing making the Alfa Romeo SZ

▷ **1996** Zagato's Lamborghini Diablo-based Raptor concept car is almost put into production as a new Lamborghini but is ultimately rejected

▷ **2000** Zagato enters its "neoclassical" era, rejecting mass-produced cars in favor of more "emotional" one-offs

▷ **2013** Zagato designs a series of iconic cars for Aston Martin's centenary year

UGO ZAGATO WAS ONE of the first designers to apply aeronautical science to motor cars when, in 1919, he left the aircraft company he was working for to set up his own coachbuilding firm. Ugo proved a design pioneer, his cars scoring a string of racetrack victories for Alfa Romeo and, later in the 1920s, Scuderia Ferrari. His strength was his application of airplane construction techniques to sports cars, creating smooth, aerodynamic, low-weight bodies, wind-cheating wheel covers, tilting grilles, and convex trunk lids. One such design was the Panoramico body, which utilized plexiglass to maximize visibility and minimize weight.

It was Ugo's son, Elio, who truly brought the Zagato name to prominence. Having graduated from college in 1947, he immediately joined the family business as a racing driver. He built his own Gran Turismo cars and drove them to victory against the likes of Juan-Manuel Fangio and Tazio Nuvolari. Elio won 83 of the 160 races he entered and was GT series champion five times.

Zagato designed many standout cars in its glorious 1950s "GT" period, but its most distinctive innovation at this time was the "double-bubble" roof, developed jointly by Ugo and Elio, and applied to the Abarth 750 GT. This curved roof, which arched over the individual occupant's head, had a clear structural benefit: it boosted torsional rigidity. The design went on to grace dozens of Zagato's cars.

Aston Martin V8 Vantage Zagato design sketch
In 1985, this tantalizing drawing was enough to make all 50 examples of this limited edition Aston Martin sell out in mere days. The revenue helped both Aston and Zagato survive and helped establish Zagato's limited-edition business model.

Zagato produced a string of aerodynamic and elegantly lightweight coupes throughout the 1960s. Perhaps the most special of these was the Alfa Romeo Giulietta SZ. Built on the Alfa Sprint Speciale chassis and designed for competition use, it was 265 lb (120 kg) lighter than the base car and it debuted another Zagato hallmark— the "coda tronca" (cut-off tail)—which offered proven aerodynamic benefits. The TZ version that followed in 1962 was even more highly regarded.

UNMISTAKABLE SHAPES
The commercial and competition successes of the SZ and TZ, as well as Zagato-designed versions of the Lancia Appia and Flaminia, encouraged Elio

> **"You see that car? Is it different from all the others? Then it's a Zagato."**
> ELIO ZAGATO

COOLING VENT, MASERATI-A6G 1953   **ASTON MARTIN DB4 GT ZAGATO 1960**

to construct a new factory in 1962 in Rho, next to the Alfa Romeo factory northwest of Milan. Hiring Ercole Spada as a designer at the same time was another inspired decision. Highly talented and utterly original, Spada designed a series of instantly recognizable, distinctive shapes. None of his creations were more striking than the outlandish 1963 Lancia Flavia Sport. This was followed by his Lancia Fulvia Sport in 1965 and the 1969 Alfa Romeo GT Junior Zagato.

In the 1970s and '80s, the market for coachbuilt cars began to diminish, but, under the guidance of the company's new CEO, Elio's son Andrea, Zagato weathered the storm and expanded. In 1984 the marque won the contract not only to design but also to build the Maserati Biturbo Spyder. This then led to a similar arrangement with

Aston Martin for the V8 Vantage Zagato in 1986. Other limited-edition sports cars followed, such as the Alfa Romeo SZ, Lancia Hyena, and Nissan Autech Stelvio.

EXCLUSIVE DESIGNS

In the 1990s, Andrea reorganized Zagato into both a coachbuilding studio and a design center, specializing in tailor-made cars, limited-edition series, and engineering prototypes. By Elio's death in 2009, Zagato's reputation as an exclusive design house making one-off and limited-series cars was unmatched.

In recent years, the company has continued to produce collaborations with high-end marques such as Ferrari (575 GTZ), Aston Martin (DB7 Zagato), Maserati (GS Zagato), Bentley (Zagato GTZ), Alfa Romeo (TZ3,) and BMW (Zagato Coupe). However, Zagato also keeps one eye firmly on its heritage. The company lovingly creates official reconstructions of older Zagato vehicles that deserve to be remembered.

Elio at Monza
Ugo Zagato's son Elio followed his father into the family business. Thanks to his experience as a racing driver, he had an almost intuitive feeling for what made a great GT car.

Convertible Style

Convertibles added fun and a touch of glamour to the most dowdy, workaday cars and so were popular additions to many model lineups. As the 1950s progressed, automakers moved on from just chopping the roofs off their sedans to making stand-alone open models. Many were not out and out sports cars, sharing engines and many other parts with their family sedan counterparts, and providing often similarly genteel performance and handling. However they often shared some of the space and a lot of the practicality of their closed counterparts, which made them more versatile than open, two-seat sports cars.

▽ **Cadillac Eldorado 1959**

Origin USA

Engine 6,390 cc, V8

Top speed 120 mph (193 km/h)

An in-house competition was held to find a name for the Eldorado, and Mary Ann Zubosky, a secretary, won. She received a $25 "defense bond" as a prize. First launched in 1953, the car's wraparound windshield and the tailfins of its body, styled by Harley J. Earl (see pp. 32–33) were already American car design staples.

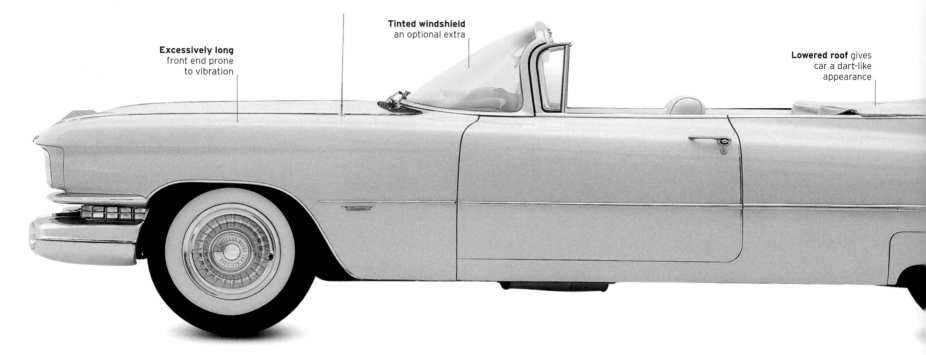

Excessively long front end prone to vibration

Tinted windshield an optional extra

Lowered roof gives car a dart-like appearance

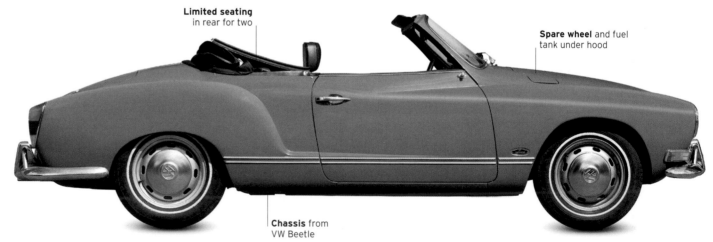

▷ **Volkswagen Karmann Ghia 1957**

Origin Germany

Engine 1,192 cc, flat-four

Top speed 77 mph (124 km/h)

Improving standards of living prompted Volkswagen to consider creating an upmarket Beetle-based car (see pp. 54–55), and the result was the Type 14 Karmann Ghia. Launched in 1955, its bodywork was styled by Italian design house Ghia, and German coachbuilder Karmann built it. A total of around 10,000 were sold in the first year.

Limited seating in rear for two

Spare wheel and fuel tank under hood

Chassis from VW Beetle

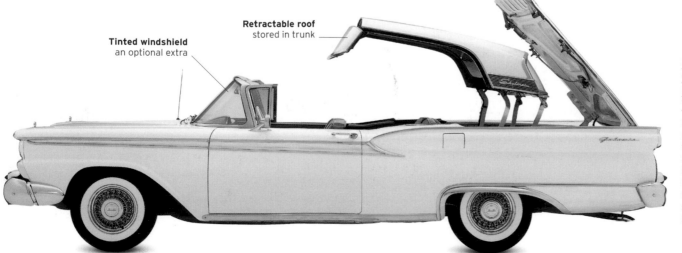

Retractable roof stored in trunk

Tinted windshield an optional extra

◁ **Ford Fairlane 500 Skyliner 1958**

Origin USA

Engine 5,440 cc, V8

Top speed 120 mph (193 km/h)

Featuring the world's first mass-produced retractable roof, the Skyliner topped the Fairlane range. It was very expensive to buy, however, and only offered limited trunk space and leg room. Sales were low and production stopped in 1960 with fewer than 50,000 cars manufactured.

Every comfort
Designed for easy cruising, this car's equipment included power brakes and steering, and an automatic gearbox. Passengers could enjoy electric windows, powered seat adjustment, and cushion-soft air suspension.

Space for all
At nearly 18 ft (5.5 m) long, the Cadillac was huge even at a time when excess was standard. The interior seated five passengers and a driver in comfort, while the cavernous trunk had space for five spare tires.

FRONT VIEW

Tailfins stand more than 3 ft (1 m) from the ground

Protruding, dome-shaped rear lights

Stellar styling
Considered garish when it was launched, the 1959 Eldorado marked a pinnacle of design exuberance. The year after its launch, Cadillac trimmed 6 in (15 cm) off the fins of the Eldorado's replacement model.

Stylized chrome ornaments evoke the jet age

Reversing light resembles jet engine

REAR VIEW

Folding fabric roof or detachable hardtop available

Car was named Floride in Europe until 1962

▷ **Renault Floride/Caravelle 1958**

Origin France

Engine 845 cc, straight-four

Top speed 76 mph (122 km/h)

The Floride/Caravelle design was inspired by American Renault dealers. Styled by Italian design house Frua and built by French coachbuilder Chausson, it used the rear-engined Renault Dauphine sedan's underpinnings. The car's limited performance improved with time. Later models even had four disc brakes.

Retractable roof folds flat

Seating for driver and passengers

American-style fins

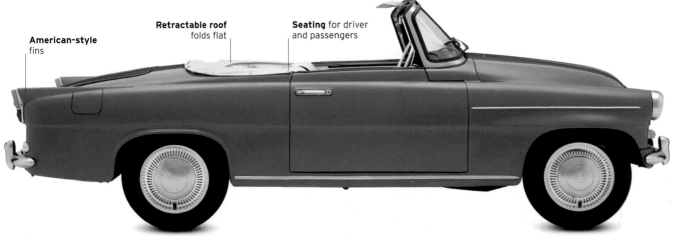

◁ **Škoda Felicia Super 1959**

Origin Czechoslovakia

Engine 1,221 cc, straight-four

Top speed 87 mph (140 km/h)

In 1959 when Škoda launched the attractive Felicia convertible, Czechoslovakia was a communist-controlled country. Cars were deemed purely functional, so this model was considered decadently subversive. Mechanically it was simple and conventional. It had a separate chassis frame and, thanks to swing-axle rear suspension, crude handling.

Ford Thunderbird

With 11 distinct generations of cars launched over a 50-year period, the Ford Thunderbird was not conceived as a sporty car like the Mustang, but rather as a personal luxury car. With an emphasis on style and sophistication for two rather than outright performance, it gave American buyers an entirely new driving experience and the company more than 4.4 million sales, outdoing its rival Chevrolet Corvette.

THE THUNDERBIRD made its debut in 1954, initially as a two-seat convertible that Ford hoped would rival Chevrolet's racy Corvette. With its scooped hood, covered, rear-mounted spare tire, and (somewhat optimistic) 150 mph (241 km/h) speedometer, the car undoubtably had upmarket credentials, but like the early Corvettes it was never meant to be overtly sporty. While striking to look at, it used the same conventional 4.8-liter V8 as several other cars in Ford's Mercury stable.

By emphasizing the Thunderbird's comfort and luxury, Ford sold more than 16,000 Thunderbirds in the first year, while Chevrolet managed to move only about 700 Corvettes.

SIDE VIEW

Mounting the spare tire on a Continental-style bumper left more room for storage in the trunk

Stylish fiberglass hardtop with optional porthole windows concealed a folding fabric roof

FRONT VIEW

REAR VIEW

Ford badge
Originating in the deserts of the southwest, the name "Thunderbird" came from Native American legends and was proposed to Ford by young car stylist Alden Giberson, in 1954. Giberson purportedly won a $95 suit from Saks Fifth Avenue for suggesting the name.

SPECIFICATIONS	
Model	Ford Thunderbird, 1954–57
Assembly	USA
Production	53,116
Construction	Steel body and chassis
Engine	4,785 cc, V8
Power output	193 bhp
Transmission	3-speed manual or automatic
Suspension	Front coil springs, rear leaf springs
Brakes	Four-wheel drums
Maximum speed	115 mph (185 km/h)

The telescopic steering column was innovative at the time

Clean lines concealed what was actually fairly conventional engineering

Styling
Although not the fastest Ford, appearance came first for many Thunderbird buyers. By making it relatively large for a two-seater, the company was able to create a sleek, low-riding shape with high levels of interior comfort. With its single headlamps and small rear fins, it was instantly recognizable as a Ford.

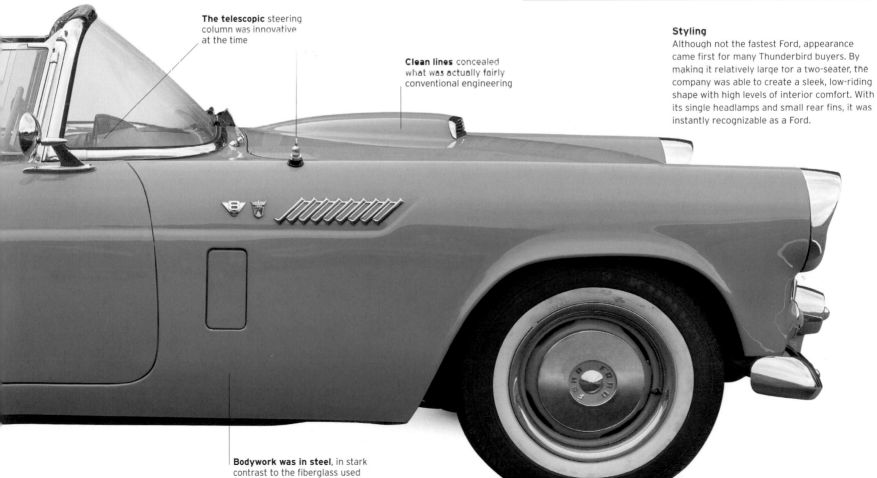

Bodywork was in steel, in stark contrast to the fiberglass used for the rival Corvette

ON THE ROAD

Looking back over a distance of 60 years or so, this huge car with its fins, chrome, and circular "opera" windows could scarcely look more American or be more redolent of the 1950s.

This accounts for much of its charm. As a lazy, luxurious boulevard cruiser, it makes little sense anywhere except on the wide open roads of the US, but that too enhances its appeal. It suggests the owner can afford what he wants whereas the rest of us must be content with what we can afford.

Most European cars handled better, and domestic rivals such as the Corvette were markedly faster. The Thunderbird name remains highly evocative, however, and these early models still look every inch the Hollywood star.

1. Iconic Thunderbird name **2.** Chromed hood scoop hints at its V8 power **3.** Tiny rear-view mirrors mounted on doors **4.** Deep, chromed eyebrows over headlights **5.** V8 was always the US engine of choice **6.** Louvers provide a sporting accent to the sleek shape **7.** Lights echo period fashion for fins **8.** Rear-mounted "Continental" spare **9.** Superb period interior **10.** Heater controls **11.** Sweeping speedometer **12.** Bench seat built for two

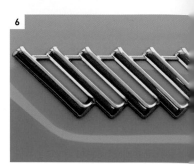

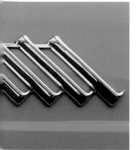

Economical Cars

The 1950s was a decade when a lot of people who had only dreamt of owning a car actually managed to do so for the first time. For some, economy was important, so they either bought something second-hand, or even ultra-frugal microcars, such as the Heinkel three-wheeled "bubble car." For most, however, a small sedan with more space for people and luggage was needed. Many of the decade's most popular small cars were rear-engined, made in their millions by the likes of VW, Fiat, and Renault, who offered their customers plenty of models and designs to choose from.

Split windshield
was later replaced
by one-piece design

▷ **Morris Minor 1948**

Origin	UK
Engine	918 cc, straight-four
Top speed	62 mph (100 km/h)

The Morris Minor has a raised area in the middle of its hood as the design was changed before production, making the car shorter and wider. Designed by Mini creator, Alec Issigonis (see pp. 146–47), the Minor mixed practicality with good handling. It saw massive success throughout the 1950s.

Front fenders
rubberized in
some Minor vans

**Bigger raised
headlights** featured
on later Minors

LGO 786

Timeless design
During the Morris Minor's 23-year production run, its distinctive shape remained little altered. Its look was influenced by 1940's car styling trends, and because rounded panels were often stronger than flat ones.

Flathead engine
Early Morris Minors were powered by "flathead" engines, which dated from the 1930s. They were replaced by the Austin-designed A Series engine, which remained with the car until 1971.

Basic body is 1930s design

Old-fashioned stand-alone headlights

▷ **Ford Popular 103E 1953**

Origin UK

Engine 1,172 cc, straight-four

Top speed 60 mph (96 km/h)

By 1953 the Ford Popular 103E was an antique, the basic design of which dated back to the 1930s, as demonstrated by its separate fenders, rod brakes, three-speed gearbox, and side-valve engine. This did not stop Ford from selling it until 1959 to buyers for whom affordability mattered more than fashion.

Spare wheel mounted on trunk

American styling and British mechanicals

◁ **Nash Metropolitan 1954**

Origin UK/USA

Engine 1,489 cc, straight-four

Top speed 75 mph (121 km/h)

A joint venture between Britain's Austin and America's Nash, the Metropolitan was designed to combine transatlantic style and British engineering in a compact form intended to appeal to wealthy women. To make it cost-effective, it was built using a large number of existing Austin parts.

▷ **Renault Dauphine 1956**

Origin France

Engine 845 cc, straight-four

Top speed 66 mph (106 km/h)

A development of the tiny, rear-engined Renault 4CV sedan, the Dauphine kept that vehicle's mechanical layout, but put it into a larger, stylish body that resembled Renault's conventional Fregate big sedans. Despite sometimes wayward handling and rust problems, more than two million Dauphines were sold in 12 years.

Luggage storage in front of car

Air intake for rear engine

High-seated driver position similar to a van

Three rows of seats

Engine behind rear seats

◁ **Fiat 600 Multipla 1956**

Origin Italy

Engine 633 cc, straight-four

Top speed 55 mph (88 km/h)

This box-shaped car could hold six people, even though its body was just 11½ ft (3.5 m) long. The engine was located at the back, and the car's front occupants sat above the front axle. A very early people carrier, it was originally conceived as a taxi.

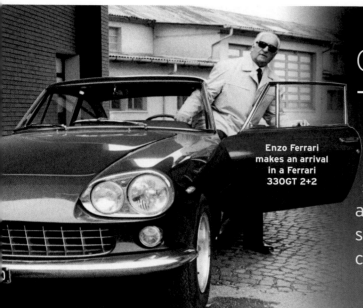

Enzo Ferrari makes an arrival in a Ferrari 330GT 2+2

Great Marques
The Ferrari Story

The prancing horse of Ferrari has become a fixture at the very summit of automotive achievement. Enzo Ferrari's steadfast approach to speed ensured that his team became the most successful of them all in Formula 1 racing, and his company has created some of the fastest and most desirable cars ever made.

ENZO FERRARI WAS A RACING DRIVER from Modena in northern Italy. He became a works driver for Alfa Romeo in 1920, then ran Alfa's official racing team under his Scuderia Ferrari banner from 1933. When Alfa decided to bring its racing back in-house, Ferrari was appointed racing manager, but he left instead to found his own company, Auto Avio Costruzione, which soon established itself in Maranello, where Ferrari is still based today.

After some success with Fiat-based racing cars, Ferrari launched the first car under his own name, the 125S, which went on sale in 1947. Ferrari's cars won the Mille Miglia and Targa Florio in 1948, and the prestigious Le Mans 24-hour race in 1949. Their first win in Formula 1 Grand Prix racing came in 1951, and Alberto Ascari won the F1 World Championship for Ferrari in 1952 and 1953. From there, Ferrari became a fixture in F1 racing, winning two more World Championship titles in the 1950s

with Juan-Manuel Fangio and Mike Hawthorn, and another in 1961 with American driver Phil Hill. At the same time, Ferrari won at Le Mans six times in a row to seal its place as the greatest racing team motorsport had ever seen.

But success did not come easily. Ferrari was driven by winning and did not tolerate failure.

Ferrari 275GTB4, 1966
All-independent suspension, four camshafts, and six Weber carburetors helped to make this model a fearsome road/race machine.

Detailed debriefs in the company boardroom followed every lost race, and often saw Ferrari hurl broken components across the table at startled team members. Key engineers and star drivers were often treated with arrogant disregard. Paying customers were often treated with similar disdain. Ferruccio Lamborghini, legendarily, was so incensed by Ferrari's dismissive attitude that he started his own car company, which became one of Ferrari's biggest road car rivals. True or not, it all added to the mystique of the company and the man behind it.

Dino (Ferrari) 246GT, 1968
Notionally, Dino was a separate, junior Ferrari marque, but this delectable V6, mid-engined two-seater was every inch the thoroughbred, with superb handling.

"The **most exciting** projectile we have **ever been fortunate** enough to handle."

AUTOCAR MAGAZINE ON THE FERRARI 365GTB/4 DAYTONA IN SEPTEMBER 1971

Ferrari 365GTS/4 Daytona Spyder
Fewer than 130 Daytona Spyders were ever produced by Ferrari, and are highly prized by enthusiasts. Cashing in on this, many hardtop 365GTBs have since been modified like this one, with the roof removed to give the appearance of a Spyder.

While Enzo Ferrari's real interest was racing, his company constructed an extraordinary reputation for its road cars. The 250 family encompassed everything from race winners to civilized GT cars, and later models, such as the 275GTB and 365GTB/4 Daytona had unmatched speed and glamour. Even then, Ferrari was too small a company to survive as an independent and an approach from the US giant Ford very nearly led to a takeover, but Ferrari pulled out at the last minute and eventually did a deal with Fiat, which took a 50 percent shareholding in 1969.

This gave Ferrari the stability to branch out into a wider range of road cars, building on the success of the delectable 206/246 Dino to produce a profitable line of middleweight, mid-engined sports cars, beginning with the 308GTB in 1975. The top-end, high-performance machines also adopted mid-engined layouts in the 1970s 365BB and 512BB supercars, and later in their successors, the Testarossa and 512TR.

On the race track, Ferrari's force had waned, but it returned to the front of the Formula 1 grids with Austrian driver Niki Lauda, who won F1 world titles in 1975 and 1977, and there was another title for Ferrari in 1979 with South African Jody Scheckter.

After Enzo Ferrari's death in 1988, Fiat took a 90 percent shareholding in the company, and Ferrari produced more cars to higher levels of quality than ever before. But the prancing horse would suffer another lean spell in Formula 1, until the arrival of driver Michael Schumacher and engineer Ross Brawn in 1996. They secured five driver's titles and six constructor's championships between 1999 and 2004, before Kimi Räikkönen added another driver's title to Ferrari's record in 2007.

In 2015, Ferrari was separated from its Fiat parent, and now faces the future as an independent company with what is said to be the world's strongest sports-car brand, valued at a staggering $9.8 billion.

CLASSICS OF THE FUTURE

LaFerrari The ultimate Ferrari, and some would say it was the ultimate hypercar of its era. Together with the Porsche 911 Spyder and McLaren P1, LaFerrari marked the arrival of hybrid powertrain technology in supercars, delivering 789 bhp from its 6.3-liter, V12 engine and adding another 161 bhp from an electric motor, with all power transmitted to rear wheels through a seven-speed, dual-clutch transmission. Only 499 were built between 2013 and 2015, and you had to be a long-standing Ferrari customer even to be invited to buy one.

△ **LaFerrari 2013**

Origin	Italy
Engine	6,262 cc, V12
Top speed	217 mph (348 km/h)

The ultimate Ferrari—at least until the next ultimate Ferrari—combined a V12 and electric motor for exhilarating performance.

458 Speciale A The last of the V8-powered 458 family, and of Ferrari's "mainstream" naturally aspirated cars, the Speciale might one day be regarded as the last "old school" car from Maranello. The 4.5-liter engine revved to a spine-tingling 9,000 rpm and generates 597 bhp, giving extraordinary performance: 0–60 mph 0–96 km/h) in three seconds with the top speed nudging 200 mph (322 km/h). The Speciale A adds a retractable hard top and was built as a limited edition of just 499 cars.

△ **Ferrari 458 Speciale A 2015**

Origin	Italy
Engine	4,499 cc, V8
Top speed	199 mph (320 km/h)

The naturally aspirated engine of the 458 offered a thrilling performance. The folding roof added another touch of glamour to the car's striking looks.

Great Designers
Pininfarina

Pininfarina is one of Italy's towering giants of car design, but it was founded by someone very short—being only 5 ft (152 cm) tall, Battista Farina's nickname of Pinin, or "tiny," was apt. His design empire became a hallmark of quality and genius, as well as a significant manufacturing business—Pininfarina's Turin factory gave birth to many classic Fiat, Lancia, and Alfa Romeo sports cars.

Career highlights

▷ **1930** Battista "Pinin" Farina founds Carrozzeria Pinin Farina in Turin, Italy

▷ **1946** Designs and builds the single-shelled Cisitalia, exhibited in New York's Museum of Modern Art in 1951

▷ **1951** A meeting with Enzo Ferrari establishes Pinin Farina as the sports car company's principal design partner

▷ **1958** Pinin Farina's new factory opens at Grugliasco, producing the Farina-designed Alfa Romeo Giulietta Spider

▷ **1961** Pinin hands over the company reins to his son, Sergio; the family name is officially changed to Pininfarina

▷ **1966** Pinin dies at age 73

△ **Ferrari 512S Modulo, 1970**
With its sleek, canopy-style roof, low, aerodynamic body, and partly covered wheels, the 512S Modulo had a futuristic look that still retained the purity of line and proportional harmony for which Pininfarina was famous.

▷ **1978** The company constructs a new design facility in Cambiano

▷ **1995** Sergio Pininfarina wins the *Compasso d'Oro* industrial design award

▷ **2010** Pininfarina manufactures its very last cars at Grugliasco—the Alfa Romeo Brera and Spider—before its factory closes down

▷ **2012** Sergio Pininfarina dies

CARS IN THE EARLY DAYS were mechanical marvels, pure and simple, and engineers left the matter of the bodywork to independent coachbuilders. In Italy, one of the most famous of these was Giovanni Farina, who set up shop in Turin in 1906 expressly to coachbuild wood-framed, metal-paneled car bodies.

The firm's early reputation for excellent design came to the attention of Giovanni Agnelli, founder of Fiat, who in 1911 wanted to build a mass-market car in the idiom of Henry Ford's Model T. He asked Giovanni to give the new Fiat Zero a distinctive radiator grille, and from a dozen proposals, Agnelli chose one that had been created by Giovanni's 18-year-old brother, Battista "Pinin."

In 1930 Battista established Pinin Farina in rivalry with his brother, and by 1931 he had designed the first car under his own name, the distinctive Fiat 525 SS coupe. By 1939 the company employed 500 workers building 800 car bodies a year.

After World War II, Pinin realized the days of one-off, coachbuilt cars were all but over. His 1946 Cisitalia 202 design therefore marked an absolute revolution. With the world's very first "full-width"

Cisitalia 202
Described by Arthur Drexler as "rolling sculpture," this car revolutionized postwar design by incorporating elements such as headlights, hood, and bumpers into the body shell.

body, a single shell without separate fenders, the car was even displayed at the Museum of Modern Art in New York in 1951.

LASTING LINKS
By 1947, the factory was humming with the construction of stylish Fiat 1100 cabriolets, Maserati roadsters, and Cisitalia GT coupes, and in 1952 the Nash-Healey (designed and built by Farina) marked a new era of cooperation with foreign marques. Many long-lasting relationships were forged, including France's Peugeot, General Motors in the US, and the British Motor Corporation.

However, one company stands out—Ferrari. It was in 1951 that Farina signed an agreement with Enzo Ferrari to design his cars and, following the debut of the 250 series in 1952, almost every road-going Ferrari since has been the work of Farina. The relationship became so successful that Pinin was appointed a vice-president of Ferrari, while his son Sergio joined Ferrari's board of directors. Innumerable classic Ferraris—250s, 500s, the Dino 246, Daytona, 512 BB, Testarossa—bore Farina's famous blue "F" badge.

> **"Purity of line** and harmony of proportion. If they are **good,** they are **good forever."**
> SERGIO PININFARINA

FERRARI 365GTB/4 DAYTONA 1968

SIDE STRAKES, FERRARI TESTAROSSA 1984

The frenzy of activity in the 1950s continued with a contract to design the Lancia Aurelia B20 GT, an object of fastback purity and simplicity. And when Alfa Romeo commissioned Pinin to style and manufacture a two-seat roadster version of its Giulietta, a large, new factory was opened in Grugliasco, near Turin, turning the designer into a fully fledged, production-line manufacturer.

NEW ERA, NEW NAME

In 1961, the Italian president authorized Pinin to create a new family surname and business trademark—Pininfarina. At this point, Pinin handed the reins of the business to his son, Sergio; the old master died in April 1966 at the age of 72.

Pininfarina became a real nursery for emerging talent, nurturing brilliant designers such as Aldo Brovarone (Ferrari Superfast, Dino 206 GT, Lancia Gamma Coupe), Leonardo Fioravanti (BMC 1800, Ferrari 512 BB, Ferrari F40), and Paolo Martin (Ferrari Modulo, Rolls-Royce Camargue, Fiat 130 Coupe).

The Grugliasco plant, meanwhile, was a full-on, automated car factory, with thousands of Fiat 124 Spiders, Alfa Romeo Duettos, and Peugeot 504 convertibles rolling off the production line. In 1972, Pininfarina also opened its own full-sized wind tunnel, the very first in Italy.

The company's pure show cars were united by their flowing lines and perfect proportions. Pininfarina declared its inspiration came from wind-formed Alpine snowscapes. One of the most influential designs was the Dino 206, which led directly to the Dino production car, while the later Ferrari 512 prototype also led to the wedge-shaped Berlinetta Boxer of 1973, perhaps the greatest sports car form of all time.

Pininfarina was always more interested in classical design qualities than pure fantasy, but some concept cars did push the outer limits. The futuristic Ferrari Modulo of 1970, for example, explored the extremes of sports-car design.

Its low, sculptural shape consisted of a flat, almost symmetrical arc, and it eschewed conventional doors in favor of a canopy that slid forward over the hood, while the Studio CNR of 1978 was an exercise in pure aerodynamics, winning the Compasso d'Oro Award in 1979 for The Ideal Aerodynamic Shape.

The Pininfarina name is a true survivor. Despite an economic climate that has swept aside almost every other design house, Pininfarina's balance of design, taste, technical research, and innovation mean the company continues to flourish today, with offices in Italy, Germany, China, and the US.

Family business
Sergio Pininfarina (right) discusses sketches for the Ferrari 240 P5 with his brother-in-law, Renzo Carlo. Although not universally loved, the car pioneered the mounting of glass screens above Ferrari's engines.

American Exuberance

For many Americans, the 1950s was a time of increased wealth and prosperity, and this was reflected in the cars they drove, which got bigger and more powerful. They had styling influenced by everything from science fiction films to rockets and jet fighters, with extravagant wraparound windshields and tailfins that grew bigger each year. Annual model changes used styling and spec upgrades to keep customers buying, and chrome detailing, whitewall tires, and two-tone paint were employed to sell cars that were often mechanically simple, despite their futuristic looks. In 1950s America new cars were big, bold statements of success.

▽ **Hudson Hornet 1954**

Origin USA

Engine 5,047 cc, straight-six

Top speed 106 mph (171 km/h)

Large and aerodynamic, this sedan sat so low to the road that occupants had to lower themselves in, hence being known as "Step-down." Despite its size, it offered good handling and power, although poor fuel economy. The car was available with two or four doors.

Optional sun visor

Hudson never offered a V8 engine

Poor fuel economy at 17mpg/13.8L/100km

Enclosed rear wheels give an aerodynamic appearance

▷ **Oldsmobile Super 88 1955**

Origin USA

Engine 5,309 cc, V8

Top speed 101 mph (162 km/h)

First introduced in 1949, the range was revised in 1954, giving it a longer, lower body with distinctive detailing, and an enlarged Rocket V8 engine. Well-equipped, the Super 88 was a mid-range model, with two- and four-door options available.

Two-tone paint in 18 options

Wraparound front and rear windows

Rocket hood ornament

Twin ornaments mounted on hood

Chrome appears heavily on Limited versions

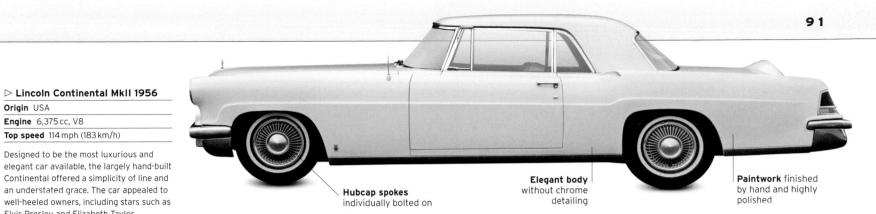

▷ **Lincoln Continental MkII 1956**

Origin	USA
Engine	6,375 cc, V8
Top speed	114 mph (183 km/h)

Designed to be the most luxurious and elegant car available, the largely hand-built Continental offered a simplicity of line and an understated grace. The car appealed to well-heeled owners, including stars such as Elvis Presley and Elizabeth Taylor.

Hubcap spokes
individually bolted on

Elegant body
without chrome
detailing

Paintwork finished
by hand and highly
polished

V8 engine was
available with
fuel injection

◁ **Chevrolet Bel Air Nomad 1956**

Origin	USA
Engine	4,343 cc, V8
Top speed	108 mph (174 km/h)

This model's styling, with sloping rear roofline, was inspired by a Chevrolet Corvette-based show car. The two-door Nomad was compact compared to many American cars of the period, and its sporting looks were a big departure from most utilitarian station wagons.

Styling influenced
by Corvette Nomad
show car

Fins made
from fiberglass

Interior provides
room for four adults

▷ **Studebaker Silver Hawk 1957**

Origin	USA
Engine	4,736 cc, V8
Top speed	115 mph (185 km/h)

The Silver Hawk offered a more restrained design than many contemporary models, with less chrome and fewer details, and sold well. It was available in two engine sizes, both offering lively performance.

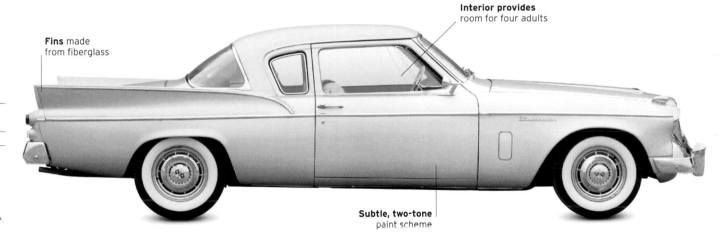

Subtle, two-tone
paint scheme

15 chrome flashes
unique to the
Limited Riviera

◁ **Buick Limited Riviera 1958**

Origin	USA
Engine	5,965 cc, V8
Top speed	115 mph (185 km/h)

Buick first used the Riviera name in 1949. By 1958 the model had become big, broad, and brash. Sedans were the first four-door "hardtop" Buicks with no central door pillars, and the model had features including air-assisted suspension, self-dipping headlamps, electric aerial, and power seats.

Limited badge
used on Buick's
top model

Luxury and Power

By the start of the 1950s, Europe's most prestigious automakers were unveiling new, range-topping models. Firms such as Mercedes-Benz were well-known, but others, including British aircraft-maker Bristol, were new to the market. With a lot to prove, they were quickly demonstrating that they could make cars every bit as good as their established rivals' models. In a world still ravaged by six years of war, where food and fuel were often rationed and streets still scarred with bomb damage, these exotic models, bought by an elite number of film stars, tycoons, and statesmen, seemed impossibly glamorous, and also hinted at future prosperity for everyone else.

▽ **Bentley R-type Continental 1952**

Origin UK

Engine 4,566 cc, straight-six

Top speed 115 mph (186 km/h)

Bentley was owned by Rolls-Royce, and the R-type Continental started as an unofficial project designed to reclaim Bentley as a maker of high-speed grand tourers. Its lightweight, streamlined aluminum body was wind-tunnel tested, and the car could cruise at 100 mph (161 km/h) for hours. Just 208 were made.

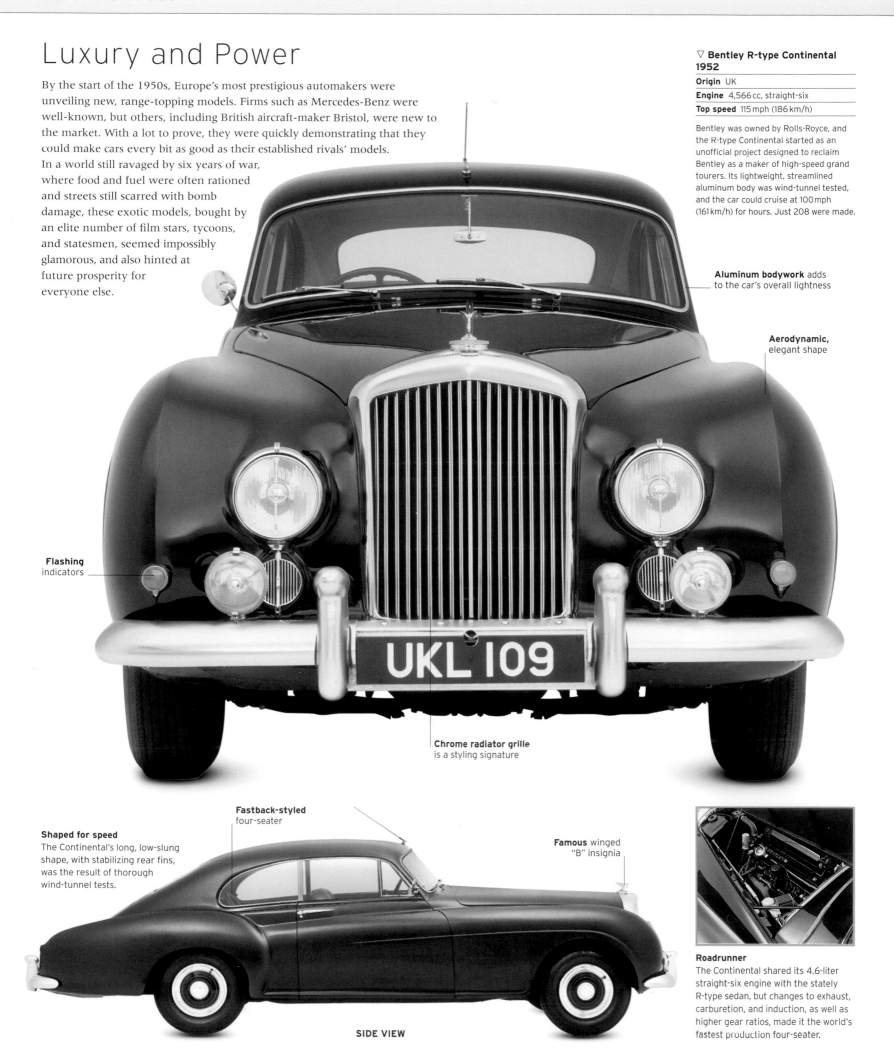

Aluminum bodywork adds to the car's overall lightness

Aerodynamic, elegant shape

Flashing indicators

Chrome radiator grille is a styling signature

Shaped for speed
The Continental's long, low-slung shape, with stabilizing rear fins, was the result of thorough wind-tunnel tests.

Fastback-styled four-seater

Famous winged "B" insignia

SIDE VIEW

Roadrunner
The Continental shared its 4.6-liter straight-six engine with the stately R-type sedan, but changes to exhaust, carburetion, and induction, as well as higher gear ratios, made it the world's fastest production four-seater.

▷ Mercedes-Benz 300 1951

Origin Germany

Engine 2,996 cc, straight-six

Top speed 103 mph (166 km/h)

Launched in 1951, the 300 was a serious Rolls-Royce and Cadillac rival, championed by the likes of actor Errol Flynn, and Germany's first post-World War II leader, Konrad Adenauer. As fast as a Porsche, later 300s had fuel injection, like their iconic 300 SL coupe stablemates.

Rear indicators mounted high on bodywork

Straight-six engine with overhead cam

Body made from hand-worked aluminum

Low-drag shape is aerodynamically efficient

Hood can open either left or right

◁ Bristol 403 1953

Origin UK

Engine 1,971 cc, straight-six

Top speed 104 mph (167 km/h)

This luxury grand tourer was virtually handmade. Its hand-beaten, aluminum body clothed suspension, transmission, and 100 bhp engine derived from 1930s' BMW technology, which the Bristol acknowledged with a BMW-like grille. The 403's wind-tunnel tested body was more aerodynamic than cars made decades later.

Curved rear window gives all-around vision

V8 engine produces 100 bhp

▷ BMW 502 1955

Origin Germany

Engine 3,168 cc, V8

Top speed 105 mph (169 km/h)

The first new BMWs since the 1930s, 502s were known as "Baroque Angels" for their distinctive shape. Transmissions were mounted separately from engines, under cabin floors. Innovations included a fully independent suspension. The BMW was also the first German car with an aluminum-block V8.

Chrome trim adds a touch of style

Rear-wheel skirts can be removed

Jaguar's leaping cat mascot

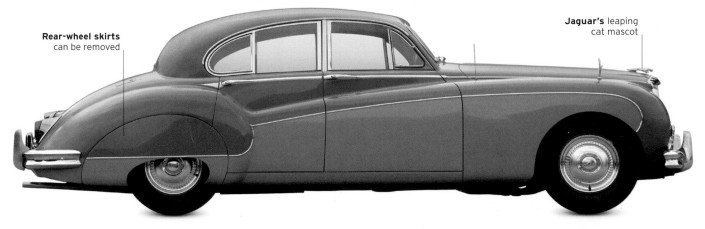

◁ Jaguar Mk IX 1958

Origin UK

Engine 3,781 cc, straight-six

Top speed 114 mph (183 km/h)

Jaguar dropped in its fabulous twin-cam, XK engine from its sports-car line to power this big sedan. Despite its American-friendly bulk, the fast, fine handling Mk IX became a successful sedan and road rally racer. Cheaper than many rivals, it lived up to Jaguar's marketing boast of "space, grace, pace."

Mass-Production Boom

Every major European country saw a huge growth in demand for small family cars during the 1950s. Each nation had its own "champion," and for France it was Renault. Nationalized in 1945, the state-owned company soon became the leading automaker in Europe, and so rapid expansion was inevitable. In 1952, Renault opened a major new plant in Flins, 25 miles (40 km) from its Paris base, and production began on a new economy car to succeed the profitable 4CV of 1946.

The state-of-the-art Dauphine marked the start of a new era for Renault, and continued the trend for rear-mounted engines that had been set by Volkswagen. The Dauphine was modern and inexpensive, and came in a range of pastel colors, with heating and adjustable seats available as standard. When it was launched in 1956, it became the star of the Paris Motor Show—a worthy successor to the 4CV.

EVER-GREATER VOLUMES

Booming sales saw production numbers increase, with a new Dauphine rolling off assembly lines every 30 seconds. Factory staff worked hard, installing parts necessary to unite the painted, trimmed, and glazed bodyshells with their drivetrain components.

Dauphine body shells travel along overhead tracks at Renault's Flins plant, being made ready to accept their engines and gearboxes.

Peter Morgan with one of his family company's distinctive cars.

Great Marques
The Morgan Story

The Morgan Motor Company, based in the English county of Worcestershire, has turned old-fashioned quirkiness into an art form. Still independently owned, the firm continues to build sports cars with a heritage dating back to the 1930s, in a factory complex that opened in 1914.

MORGAN FOUNDER HARRY "H.F.S." Morgan started his engineering career working for the Great Western Railway before setting up a garage selling and repairing cars. In 1909, he built his first car, a single seater with one wheel at the back, tiller steering, and a V-twin Peugeot engine. This basic, but carefully engineered little vehicle was one of the first "Cyclecars."

Morgan launched a production version with limited sales success, thanks to the tiller and single seat, but the car's performance and toughness won praise, and when two-seater versions with steering wheels appeared, demand grew quickly. In fact, his design template was widely copied, but rivals generally struggled to meet his cars' standards.

The Morgan's reliability and verve, along with handling that was safer than other three-wheelers, made this little tricycle a popular competition car, and a performance version, the Grand Prix, was built. Soon, Morgans were familiar and successful sights on racetracks such as Brooklands, where they beat much bigger, more powerful cars.

Morgan was to use a variety of engines for its three-wheelers, but had particular success with JAP, which had water-cooled V-twins. Its cars were chain-driven with two-speed transmissions, and many of the controls, including the throttle, were operated from levers on the steering wheel. Later Morgans gained refinements, such as a third gear, reverse, and front brakes, which were needed for

Morgan Plus 4 Plus 1964
An attractive plastic bodyshell brought Morgan into the modern world, but customers shunned it, and the Plus 4 Plus was a flop.

models such as the Super Sport. This could manage around 80 mph (129 km/h) in 1927.

By the 1930s, Morgan was fighting competition from four-wheeled sports cars, like the MG M-type Midget, which had more creature comforts and conventional driving controls. The advent of its new F-type three-wheeler in 1933 saw Morgan use Ford 8 hp car engines and conventional transmissions.

In 1936, Morgan built its first four-wheeler, the engaging little 4/4. With independent front suspension and a light body, the 1,100 cc car handled well and could

hit 75 mph (121 km/h). Its design template is still evident in many of today's Morgans.

World War II saw the Morgan factory making aircraft parts, but car production got underway again in 1946. The firm now concentrated on four-wheelers, which eventually featured more powerful Standard Vanguard engines that would soon be shared with rival Triumph TR sports cars.

FOR THOSE WHO TAKE A KEEN INTEREST IN MOTORING
The Morgan 4/4 completes the picture

Brochure advertising the Morgan 4/4

"It's not modern, but it's **deeply, deeply cool.**"

TOP GEAR MAGAZINE WEBSITE, 2016

Morgan Plus 8, 1968
Rover's all-aluminum V8 engine was installed in a widened Morgan in 1968, and an exciting new performance car was created, boasting fierce acceleration.

Morgans won the 1951 and '52 RAC Rally team awards with Harry Morgan's son Peter at the wheel. Peter eventually took over the company in 1959.

In 1963, Morgan tried to update its image with the Plus 4 Plus, a pretty coupe with a fiberglass body, but just 26 were ultimately made. In 1968, Morgan put Rover's high-performance 3.5-liter V8 engine into the Plus 4 and created the legendary Plus 8.

To this day, Morgan still builds modern versions of the 4/4, with its ash-framed body and separate chassis, but in 2000 it launched the Aero 8, a companion model with a 4.4-liter BMW, V8 engine, aluminum body, and modern bonded aluminum chassis. Morgan has since continued refining this design alongside the traditional models, and in 2008 revealed a fuel cell-powered one-off called the LIFE Car, propelled by four electric motors, and with 367 bhp.

The company is also building a modern interpretation of its classic three-wheeler, with a 1,983 cc, American S&S V-twin engine, mated to a five-speed Mazda transmission, so owners of these insect-like vehicles have the luxury of reverse gear. With a top speed of 115 mph (185 km/h), it continues the Morgan tradition of moving quickly on just one wheel at the back, and is a big success for the company.

Many famous, low-volume performance automakers have gone bust or been bought out, but Morgan continues to stand alone.

Morgan Plus 8, 2014
Very much in the traditional Morgan idiom, the visceral thrills include a 0–60 mph time of just 4.4 seconds, and windshield as an option.

CLASSICS OF THE FUTURE

4/4 The embodiment of Morgan tradition, the 4/4 was first produced in 1936, and some say it is the car with the word's longest production run. Customers know precisely what to expect from the car and a new model is always an instant classic. A wood-framed body with flowing mudguards and cutaway doors is mounted on a separate chassis, and Morgans with V8 engines can go very fast. However, for a more authentic period feel, the 4/4, with its 1,595 cc Ford engine, although still rapid, is a more leisurely proposition.

△ **Morgan 4/4 2009**

Origin UK

Engine 1,595 cc, straight-four

Top speed 115 mph (185 km/h)

The 4/4, which means four wheels and four cylinders, employs the latest Sigma series engine from Ford, producing 125 bhp.

Three-wheeler Morgan built its famous three-wheelers from 1910 to around 1946 (the last ones were assembled from parts in 1953), so a modern reinterpretation of the design was big news when it launched in 2011. With the engine fully exposed at the front of the car, and its explosive cylinders banging away, the driving experience feels more like a form of flight along the road.

△ **Morgan Three-wheeler 2011**

Origin UK

Engine 1,983 cc V-twin

Top speed 115 mph (185 km/h)

At 1,157 lb (525 kg), the three-wheeler's exemplary power to weight ratio gives maximum power from minimum revs. It is built for driving pleasure.

Fantastic Fins

By the late 1950s American car design had reached a new level of exuberance. The tailfins, two-tone paint schemes, whitewall tires, and wraparound winshields that typified most US models had inspired many European automakers, with the likes of sober Humber and sensible Simca producing cars that looked a bit like scaled-down Chevys and Chryslers. American cars received yearly styling makeovers so that owners of 1957 and '58 models would look covetously at the new luxury features and bigger tailfins of their 1959 replacements and trade in their old cars, a process helped by aggressive TV advertising and traveling circus-style sales roadshows.

▽ **Buick Roadmaster 1957**

Origin USA

Engine 5,965 cc, V8

Top speed 112 mph (180 km/h)

The Roadmaster was one of Buick's most luxurious models, wearing its hood ornament with pride. Buick called it the "proud choice of the man who carries success with ease." Standard features included speed-limiter buzzer, electric windows, and a foot-operated button for changing radio stations.

Chrome detailing suggests speed and movement

Contrasting, two-tone paintwork

"**Coke bottle kick**" to window line

Fuel filler-cap concealed in fin

Gun-sight hood ornament

▷ **Chevrolet Bel Air 1953**

Origin USA

Engine 3,859 cc, straight-six

Top speed 87 mph (140 km/h)

One-quarter of a million Chevrolet Bel Air sedans were sold in 1953, helped by competitive pricing and attractive styling. The iconic '57 models had new dashboards, windshields, and headlight air ducts, giving them distinctive "eyebrows." Options included dash-mounted overhead traffic light reflectors.

Interior has space for driver and five passengers

FirePower engine is largest production unit available at the time

◁ **Chrysler New Yorker 1957**

Origin USA

Engine 6,424 cc, V8

Top speed 116 mph (186 km/h)

The New Yorker, the sales of which revived Chrysler's flagging fortunes, was *Motor Trend* magazine's 1957 Car of the Year. It boasted a svelte torsion-bar front suspension, TorqueFlite automatic transmission, and sharp coachwork, thanks to the "forward look" styling of designer Virgil M. Exner (see pp. 100-01).

Captive-Aire tires are guaranteed not to deflate

Fin detail
By 1957, the Roadmaster had joined the ranks of American cars bearing tailfins, although compared to some rivals these were quite restrained. By making copycat models, however, Buick sacrificed its reputation for building high-quality conservative cars, and sales fell by almost one-quarter in 1957.

FRONT VIEW

Height of fashion
Like many cars of the era, the Roadmaster featured a wraparound windshield, endowing it with a modern, space-age appearance. Adding to the impression of speed, power, and excess, the oversized chrome bumper had jet engine-like protrusions, although these were purely decorative.

Tailfins house rear light cluster

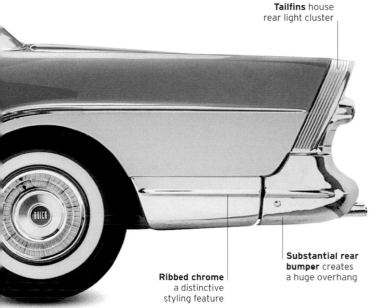

Ribbed chrome a distinctive styling feature

Substantial rear bumper creates a huge overhang

REAR VIEW

Style and substance
The wraparound rear windshield was on the small side for such a large car, and gave limited rear visibility when reversing. In contrast, the trunk was cavernous, ideal for carrying home the latest consumer products of the day.

Contrasting, red, retractable, fabric roof

▷ **Cadillac Series 62 Convertible Coupe 1959**

Origin USA

Engine 5,981cc, V8

Top speed 116mph (186km/h)

All-new styling with ever-more elaborate detailing brought Cadillac up to the minute in 1957, and the fins grew even bigger and more shark-like in 1958. The engine had grown too; it now boasted a thunderous 310bhp in standard form.

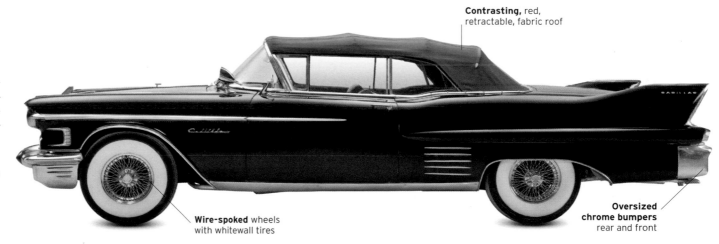

Wire-spoked wheels with whitewall tires

Oversized chrome bumpers rear and front

Hooded headlights suggest speed

Silver spears are Fury trademark

Rising tailfins give car a dart-like appearance

◁ **Plymouth Fury 1959**

Origin USA

Engine 5,205cc, V8

Top speed 105mph (169km/h)

Designed by Virgil Exner (see pp. 100-01), the Fury coupe was one of Plymouth's most stylish and rapid models to date. In unofficial speed trials following its launch, it reached 150mph (241km/h) and achieved 0-60mph (96km/h) in 7.7 seconds.

Great Designers
Virgil Exner

At his peak, Virgil Exner's influence over Detroit was as significant as any designer. A true artist endowed with an air of sophistication, he brought vision, innovation, and a much-needed sense of restraint to 1950s' American car design. Exner's ideas breathed new life into Chrysler's range and transformed the company's fortunes. His best creations are now recognized as landmarks of automotive history.

Career highlights

▷ **1947** Exner's first design to production is the striking Studebaker Champion Starlight, although Raymond Loewy is credited for it

△ **Studebaker Champion Starlight coupe, 1950**
The hugely successful, five-passenger Starlight coupe caught the eye with its long trunk cover and panoramic rear. The bullet-nose, or "spinner," front styling was a distinctive feature.

▷ **1951** The Chrysler K-310 concept car, built by Ghia in Italy, is a beacon of restraint and good proportion

▷ **1953** Exner's best-known design, the Chrysler D'Elegance, is launched, and is later bought by Volkswagen

▷ **1953** The influential Dodge Firearrow concept car mixes Italianate flavors with classic American flair

▷ **1955** Exner instigates the creation of a new luxury marque—Imperial—and invents the highly regarded "Forward Look" for Chrysler

▷ **1957** Chrysler and Imperial models feature wraparound side glass—a world first

▷ **1969** Exner revives the Stutz marque with the boldly styled, retro Blackhawk, which will remain in production until 1987

BESTRADDLED BY larger-than-life figures, such as Harley Earl and Bill Mitchell of General Motors, postwar American car design is often characterized as brash and overblown. In contrast, Virgil Exner's sensibilities were more artistic, aesthetic, and tasteful. Throughout the 1950s, his designs for both mass-production models and concept cars were notable for their understated looks and shapes that were unusually smooth by American standards.

Born in Ann Arbor, Michigan in 1909, Exner always showed a keen interest in art (which he studied while in college) and cars (he built his own Ford Model T hot rod). His first job was drawing for an advertising studio but, when Harley Earl saw some car designs he had penned for a local newspaper, Exner was offered a job in the Art & Color Section of General Motors (GM).

In 1938, Exner left GM to join Raymond Loewy's industrial design firm, where he worked on styling Studebakers. Exner even contributed to the war effort by codesigning the DUKW amphibious vehicle.

STEPPING INTO THE STARLIGHT

Exner and Loewy soon went head-to-head in competition to design Studebaker's first postwar automobile. Exner emerged victorious and the result was the striking 1947 Studebaker Champion Starlight. Loewy was publicly credited for the design however, which intensified the rivalry between the two designers.

In 1949, Exner became head of Advanced Styling at Chrysler. Here, he had the brilliant notion of teaming up with an Italian coachbuilder to realize his dream of designing cars that featured simple outlines and minimal

At the drawing board
Exner is show here in the "golden years" of his career, discussing designs for the Chrysler C-300, the first model to showcase his revolutionary "Forward Look" styling. Exner's visions were perfect for an era of excess.

embellishment. The coachbuilder was Ghia, a once-proud company that was now reduced to making bicycles in the postwar era. The first fruit of this collaboration was a landmark automobile that instantly propelled Chrysler to the forefront of the American "dream car" phenomenon: the K-310 of 1951. Chrysler trumpeted both its European influence and its distinctively American style (such as the dummy spare tire on the trunk lid). No less striking was Exner's Chrysler D'Elegance of 1953, also built by Ghia. Volkswagen stepped in the following year and bought manufacturing rights to the D'Elegance, downscaling it to become the VW Karmann-Ghia.

The American press heaped praise on Exner's designs, none more so than the elegant Firearrow concept car series of 1953–54. The tycoon Eugene Casaroll purchased the rights and produced 117 cars, renamed the Dual-Ghia, from 1956 to 1958.

CHRYSLER 300F 1960

TAILLIGHT, CHRYSLER IMPERIAL CROWN 1957

"Nothing **says style like a Virgil Exner** design."

PLYMOUTH VALIANT ADVERTISEMENT, 1962

FORWARD LOOKING

When it came to cars designed for mass-production, Exner made a huge impact with his dramatic "Forward Look" styling, which arrived with the 1955 Chrysler C-300. The low roofline, short hood, and long trunk marked a clear step into a bold new era of car design.

Exner's sleek "Forward Look" creations advanced automobile aerodynamics significantly, and the huge tailfins he espoused were said to aid stability. The 1956 Dart show car had possibly the tallest tailfins ever seen, but the claim that the Dart had just one-third the drag of a conventional car was probably a stretch.

At this stage, Exner could seemingly do no wrong, designing acclaimed models for Dodge, DeSoto, and the upmarket Imperial (a new marque that he instigated). Things quickly took a turn for the worse, however. With a fondness for caffeine, cigarettes, and alcohol, Exner suffered a heart attack in 1956. When he returned to work after surgery, other designers were in favor.

Gradually Exner was drawn into adopting the ever-increasing excesses of US styling. His late 1950s, gaping-maw grilles and contorted rear fins followed fashion, rather than setting it. By 1961, Exner had been ejected from design command at Chrysler.

Now independent, he attempted a string of abortive marque revivals: Mercer, Bugatti, Duesenberg, then Stutz (which actually saw production from 1969). It was an undistinguished end to an otherwise glittering career that set the benchmark for American car design. Virgil Exner died of heart failure in 1973, at just 64.

Design prototype
Photographed in 1954, Virgil Exner is shown here with a prototype for one of his 1955 "Forward Look" designs.

Mercedes 300SL

With its highly distinctive "Gullwing" doors, the Mercedes-Benz 300SL was the fastest production car in the world at its launch in 1954. Its name, *Sport Leicht* ("Sport Light"), denoted a sincere attempt by its creators to produce and sell a genuine racing car for the road. The decision to unveil the car at the International Motor Sports Show in New York emphasized the company's desire to win sales in the affluent American market.

THE "GULLWING" was based on the Mercedes W194 sports-racer. This legendary track car won nearly every race it entered and secured an impressive second place at its first outing, the 1952 Mille Miglia.

The new roadgoing car was very similar, but came with a number of important innovations that included fuel injection and a skeleton chassis constructed of welded aluminum tubes. This innovative "spaceframe" ruled out the use of conventional doors, so the company turned to Hans Trippel (see Amphicar, pp.152–155), who perfected the upswinging "Gullwing" design using hinges fitted to the car's roof.

The metal spaceframe was immensely strong and lightweight, but was so expensive to produce it was likely Mercedes-Benz lost money on it—despite selling 1,400 coupes and another 1,858 convertibles.

SIDE VIEW

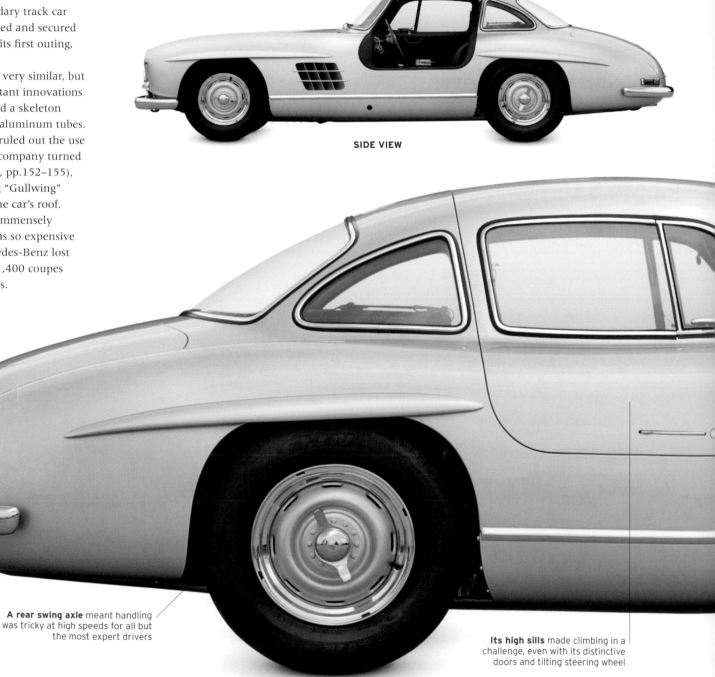

A steel body came as standard; weight-saving aluminum was an optional (expensive) extra

A rear swing axle meant handling was tricky at high speeds for all but the most expert drivers

Its high sills made climbing in a challenge, even with its distinctive doors and tilting steering wheel

FRONT VIEW

REAR VIEW

Mercedes Benz badge
Among the world's most famous emblems, the three-pointed star represented the fledgling company's ambition to succeed "on land, on water, and in the air." The name Mercedes was taken from the daughter of Emil Jellinek, an important backer of the company that became Daimler-Benz.

SPECIFICATIONS	
Model	Mercedes Benz 300SL, 1954–63
Assembly	Germany
Production	1,400
Construction	Space-frame with steel and alloy body
Engine	2,996 cc, straight-six
Power output	240 bhp
Transmission	4-speed manual
Suspension	Front and rear coil springs
Brakes	Four wheel drums
Maximum speed	129 mph (208 km/h)

At just 110 lb (50 kg), the spaceframe was extremely light, offering maximum rigidity

"Eyebrow" wheel arches improved the car's already impressive aerodynamics

Styling
The dramatic styling of the coupe closely followed the lines of its illustrious racing predecessor. Its sleek, low shape required the engine to be cleverly canted over to 45 degrees.

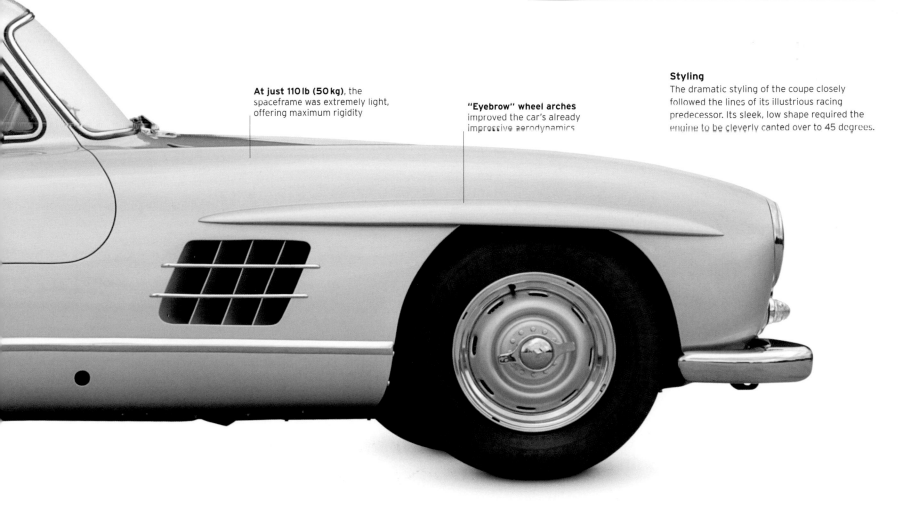

ON THE ROAD

Not to be confused with successive generations of SL sports cars—the latest iterations of which are still in production today—the original 300SL was a true technical tour de force, and one of the most outstanding machines of its day.

For the collector and enthusiast this car has everything, from a race-winning heritage, to the sort of breathtaking performance and head-turning exclusivity that only the most exceptional Italian thoroughbreds can rival. Its innovative construction, ferocious pace, superb engineering, and elegant shape have simply never lost their allure. That the car requires an expert driver to get the most out of it serves only to make it even more desirable, and those who know them well don't even blink when one of the precious survivors sells for a small fortune.

1. Iconic star emblem **2.** Subtle chrome decoration **3.** Strong pressed-steel wheels **4.** Distinctive gills cool engine bay **5.** Concealed door handles **6.** Rear lights provide a rare flash of color **7.** Restrained badge detail **8.** Comprehensive instruments **9.** Interior door handle **10.** Sculpted heater controls **11.** Engine, featuring the world's first fuel-injection system

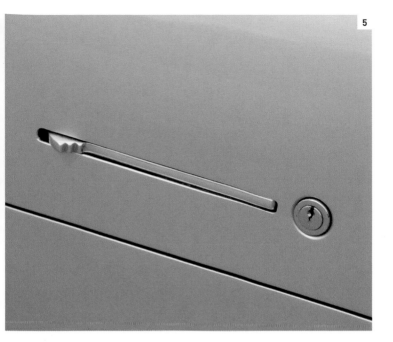

Sports Cars

Cars are complicated and expensive to design and build, so manufacturers have always tried to find ways of reusing components in as many models as possible, which meant developing new markets. In the 1950s they discovered sports cars. A new generation of drivers wanted fun and excitement, and automakers were happy to provide them with low-slung coupes and convertibles, many of which became motoring icons. Under the skin, however, most of these racy models shared engines, suspension, and other parts with sedate sedans. Americans in particular had a huge appetite for compact, European-made sports cars, and bought them by the shipload.

Style and simplicity
The simple dashboard and instrument display were in keeping with the Sprite's uncomplicated character. Some of the dials and switches were shared with Austin and Morris models.

▷ **Austin-Healey Sprite Mk I 1958**

Origin UK	
Engine 948 cc, straight-four	
Top speed 84 mph (135 km/h)	

Designed for inexpensive fun, the Sprite became known as the "Frogeye" (or "Bugeye" in the US), thanks to its distinctive inboard-mounted headlights. It is said that they were first conceived to flip up like a Porsche 928. Sprite owners had to make do without outside door handles and trunk lids.

Fenders and hood form a single unit

Flashing indicators were a modern feature

Grille shape gives car a distinctive look

GVS 668

Original windowless door design

Well-rounded ride
The Austin-Healey Sprite's characteristic, rounded appearance was dictated in part by how the car was made. There were no external door handles, so the driver and passenger had the use of interior handles.

Trunk with no lid

Economical pressed-steel wheels

SIDE VIEW

Below the hood
The one-piece hood allowed complete access to the Sprite's engine, brakes, and suspension. The car was powered by the tough A Series engine also found in the Austin A35 and Morris Minor.

Folding fabric roof
stows behind the seats
when not in use

Advanced engine
design for a small car

▷ **Alfa Romeo Giulietta Spider 1955**

Origin Italy

Engine 1,290 cc, straight-four

Top speed 112 mph (180 km/h)

This elegant sports car, styled by Italian design house Pininfarina, had performance far higher than its 1.3 liters would suggest, thanks to its superb, free-revving, alloy, twin-cam engine. Unlike its simply engineered British rivals, the sophisticated Spider was a scaled-down exotic.

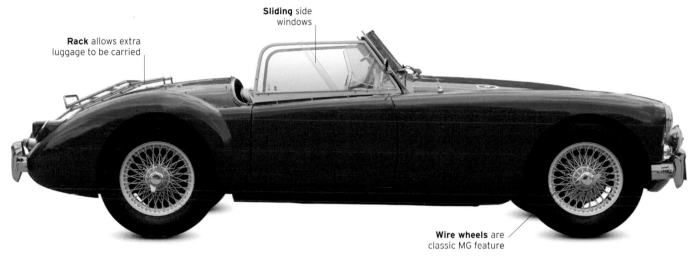

Sliding side windows

Rack allows extra luggage to be carried

Wire wheels are classic MG feature

◁ **MGA 1955**

Origin UK

Engine 1,489 cc, straight-four

Top speed 100 mph (161 km/h)

The sleek, low-slung MGA marked a big departure for its makers, which had built cars with a design template that could be traced back to the 1930s. The MGA handled nicely, could achieve 100 mph (161 km/h), and sold well in the US, though a temperamental twin-cam version proved less successful.

Small hatch gives access to engine

Body design changed little during production run

VW Beetle-style headlights

▷ **Porsche 356A 1955**

Origin Germany

Engine 1,582 cc, flat-four

Top speed 100 mph (161 km/h)

With its rear engine and swing-axle rear suspension, the 356 was essentially a high-performance VW Beetle (see pp. 54–55) with a coupe body; and both cars were designed by Ferdinand Porsche. Launched in 1950, the 356 grew ever faster, with the twin-cam Carrera version reaching a speed of 125 mph (201 km/h).

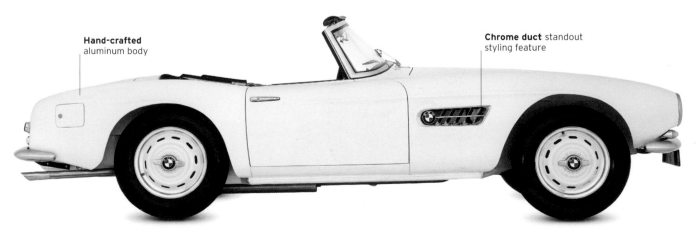

Hand-crafted aluminum body

Chrome duct standout styling feature

◁ **BMW 507 1956**

Origin Germany

Engine 3,168 cc, V8

Top speed 135 mph (217 km/h)

When the 507 was launched, BMW imagined that this beautiful V8-engined car would be a big hit in the US, but prices were virtually double those anticipated. In the event, only 250 were sold and BMW narrowly avoided bankruptcy. Despite this, the car became an instant design classic and style icon.

German Engineering

For a nation so recently devastated by wartime bombardment, Germany's automotive resurgence in the 1950s was impressive. The resurrection of the Volkswagen project, and the methodical rebuilding of the Mercedes-Benz, Opel, and German Ford marques, laid the foundations for the mighty German car industry we know today. But there was ingenuity and design innovation to be found elsewhere—from the tiny economy cars of Zündapp and BMW, to the excitement of Porsche on road and track, the return of DKW, and even the emergence of Borgward as a mainstream automaker. Germany was mobilizing again, only this time in peace and positivity.

▷ **Zündapp Janus 1957**

Origin Germany

Engine 245 cc, single-cylinder

Top speed 50 mph (80 km/h)

Developed by former aircraft company Dornier, and manufactured for just two years by the Zündapp motorcycle firm, the Janus was meant to be a cut above other "bubble" cars, with back-to-back seating and doors at each end.

Body free of side doors— entrance through front and rear panels

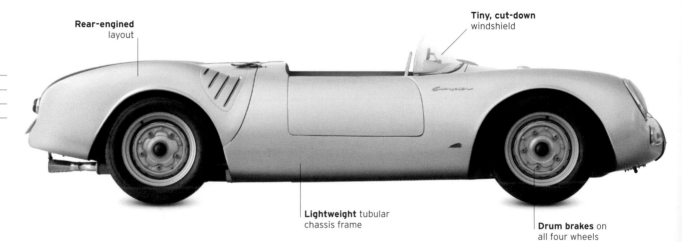

Rear-engined layout

Tiny, cut-down windshield

▷ **Porsche 550 Spyder 1953**

Origin Germany

Engine 1,498 cc, flat-four

Top speed 136 mph (219 km/h)

When Porsche designed a new engine with double overhead camshafts on each side for its 550 racer, it became a highly effective competition car. The model was made famous by the death of actor James Dean in 1955.

Lightweight tubular chassis frame

Drum brakes on all four wheels

Fabric soft top folds elegantly

Front-wheel drive was unusual for the era

◁ **DKW Sonderklasse 1953**

Origin Germany

Engine 896 cc, straight-three

Top speed 75 mph (121 km/h)

With its light, air-cooled, two-stroke engine and aerodynamic styling, the DKW was faster than its small engine size suggested. Its interior space was large, growing another 4 in (10 cm) in 1955 with the launch of the four-door version.

Separate chassis supported quality coachwork

Plexiglass sliding
windows replace
glass in 1957

Front and rear
doors styled on
BMW Isetta

Hood not required
Zündapp's own single-
cylinder, air-cooled engine
was positioned centrally
behind the seats, driving
the rear wheels. This kept
length to a minimum, while
at the same time provided
a notably spacious cabin.

FRONT VIEW

View out the back
Rear-seat passengers faced
the following traffic; indeed,
the car's "front-back" design
was named after the two-faced,
Roman God, Janus. It was a
comfortable ride, thanks to
four-wheel MacPherson
strut suspension.

REAR VIEW

Rear light clusters
following fender lines

Snug cabin
is stylish

▷ **Borgward Isabella TS Coupe 1954**

Origin Germany

Engine 1,493 cc, straight-four

Top speed 93 mph (150 km/h)

The Isabella sold over 200,000 examples in
seven years in sedan, wagon, this coupe, and
rare convertible forms. It was a fine-handling,
responsive car, but this family company from
Bremen folded in 1961.

Chrome trim follows
curvaceous lines

Vents cool
rear-mounted
engine

Front swings
open as a
single door

◁ **BMW 600 1957**

Origin Germany

Engine 582 cc, flat-twin

Top speed 62 mph (100 km/h)

This was an enlarged variation of the Isetta
microcar, featuring a larger engine from a
flat-twin BMW motorbike. The independent
rear suspension was quite sophisticated, but
the car did not sell well, and was on sale for
only two years.

Cecil Kimber
in MG "Old No. 1"

Great Marques
The MG Story

MG, the company that virtually invented affordable, fun, British sports cars – started life making stolid, unsporting Morris cars go faster – but it quickly adapted and modified them into some legendary models to produce affordable, performance cars.

THE INITIALS "MG" STAND for "Morris Garages," a Morris dealership in Oxford owned by Morris Motors founder, William Morris, and run by general manager Cecil Kimber. In 1922, Kimber began to offer racier bodies to sit on sensible, sedate Morris chassis with mechanical parts that were soon being tuned to improve performance.

Two years later he launched the MG 14/28 Super Sports, based on the 1.8-liter Morris Oxford, but with a stylish, lightweight aluminum body. The car was a success. The six-cylinder 18/80 followed, but this was more of a fast touring car than outright sports model. That came in 1929 with the M-type Midget, based on the 847cc Morris Minor, but with a pretty, open-top, two-seat body.

This 65-mph (105-km/h) machine became the UK's first truly affordable mass-market sports car, and set the mold for MG's best-known offerings, a series of open roadsters with separate fenders, cutaway doors, running boards, and often-octagonal instruments shaped like MG's famous badge. These models culminated in the TF Midget, which was built until 1955.

M-types were modified and became successful racing cars, some fitted with superchargers, and a series of competition MGs enjoyed publicity-generating attention at venues from Brooklands to Italy's Mille Miglia.

The mid-1930s saw MG give up the racetrack, when it was sold to the vehicle-making Morris Motors organization, which took over designing

MGB brochure, 1962
The MGB was a major step forward for the marque, but it had plenty of European rivals, so the advertising campaign supporting the car was constant.

MG's cars. This also meant that Cecil Kimber now had to answer to a board of directors. After a series of disputes, he left in 1941.

MG returned to car production in 1945 following the end of World War II with the Y-type sedan and the MG TC Midget sports model, which became a massive hit in America. Its 300bhp, teardrop-shaped EX181 car also grabbed headlines in the late 1950s when it reached a speed of 254mph (408km/h), to establish a land speed record.

When Morris merged with Austin in 1952 to create the British Motor Corporation (BMC),

MGB, 1962
The stylish lines hide an important change, as the B was MG's first two-seater without a separate chassis.

> "Even now, more than half a century after its launch, the MGA is **thrilling to drive**. It's hard not to **smile** as you settle into the low-slung seat."
>
> *AUTO EXPRESS* MAGAZINE, JANUARY 2014

MG TC Midget, 1945
American servicemen based in war torn Europe fell in love with the Midget, driving US export sales.

MG was part of the deal, and three years later it launched the MGA, with modern, wind-cheating bodywork. The car was another sales success, despite mechanical problems with a short-lived twin-cam version.

The early 1960s saw MG revive the Midget name for a baby sports car that was virtually identical to the Austin-Healey Sprite. In 1962, it launched the 1,800 cc MGB open two-seater, which replaced the MGA and had unibody construction. A closed GT version followed, and both sold well, unlike the short-lived, 3-liter MGC, whose heavy engine caused handling problems.

There were also MG versions of BMC sedans, such as the Morris Oxford and 1100, but by 1971, when further mergers saw MG become part of British Leyland, these were axed. Lack of funds for development saw the aging Midget and B continue until 1980. Only a short-lived, mid-'70s V8, 3.5-liter B enlivened the range. Despite an attempt by the owners of Aston Martin to buy MG, production ended, the name

was put on ice, and its famous factory in Abingdon was closed.

The MG badge returned in the early '80s on a series of sporting versions of Austin Metro, Maestro, and Montego family cars, and in 1992, the RV8, a revised B with a 3.9-liter, V8 Range Rover engine, was built to revive MG's sports car heritage. Two years later came the mid-engined MGF, which, like its classic predecessors, used many parts from sedan models, by then made by the Rover Group. This car evolved into the TF. Both vehicles sold well, having been built when BMW owned Rover and latterly, the Phoenix Group, which sold rebadged performance versions of the Rover 25, 45, and 75 sedans as MGs.

The Rover Group went bankrupt in 2005, and was bought by Chinese automaker, Nanjing Automobile. MG currently makes sedan and hatchback models in China, and has enjoyed success in the British Touring Car Championship race series.

MGA, 1955
More than 100,000 MGAs were produced at MG's bustling factory in Abingdon, Oxfordshire.

CLASSICS OF THE FUTURE

TF, 2002 A reworking of the 1995 MGF two-seater, the TF did away with its predecessor's Hydragas suspension, in favor of steel springs. It was restyled and given a variety of design upgrades. Engines ranged in power from 114 bhp 1,598 cc to 160 bhp 1,796 cc with variable valve timing. Most were five-speed manuals, but some had six-speed, CVT self-shifting transmissions. It was the UK's best-selling sports car, and to date the last open two-seater to wear an MG badge.

△ **MG TF 2002**

Origin	UK
Engine	1,796 cc, straight-four
Top speed	137 mph (-220 km/h)

The TF offered affordable open-top motoring and sporty handling. With a gutsy engine and attractive styling, it was a classy car.

ZT260 2003 Not your typical MG sports car, the ZT260 was a Rover 75-based model offered in both sedan and wagon versions. Re-engineered from front- to rear-wheel-drive, it was fitted with a Ford Mustang 4.6-liter, V8 gasoline engine and a hefty-but-effective 5-speed manual transmission (some autos were also built). The few cars that were made had instant collector appeal. Plans for an even quicker supercharged version were never realized thanks to MG Rover's collapse.

△ **MG ZT260 2003**

Origin	UK
Engine	4,600 cc, V8
Top speed	155 mph (250 km/h)

With four-wheel independent suspension and more power than any other MG, the ZT260 was a real wolf in sheep's clothing.

Driving a Nation Forward

Seeking to boost mobility and car ownership, the Italian government struck an innovative deal with the country's most important car manufacturer. Politicians pledged to invest in fast highways connecting the important cities of the long, thin country, if Fiat committed to building a new car that was affordable to almost everyone.

ITALY'S MOTORING MIRACLE

Designed by Dante Giacosa in 1957, the Nuova 500 was a tiny four-seater with an air-cooled, two-cylinder engine in its stubby tail. This compact car captured the public's imagination, and its low purchase price and operating costs meant that even those more accustomed to owning scooters finally had the realistic prospect of trading up to four wheels.

The little car was intrinsic to a consumer boom in 1960s' Italy that transformed the country, and Fiat succeeded in producing one of the first city cars able to navigate the country's narrow streets—its racing potential was later spotted by Abarth. From a slow start, the Fiat Nuova 500 became a huge success, and went on to sell more than 4 million examples.

A film crew working for Fiat attempts to portray the new-found freedom available to owners of the Nuova 500.

Solid Sedans

Sedans were the top-selling workhorses of the 1950s' car world. In an era where hatchbacks still hadn't really been invented, midsize sedans with separate trunks and four doors—or two big doors to make getting into the back a straightforward business—were in big demand. Some were solid and dependable, while others were surprisingly sporty or pioneered technical advances such as front-wheel drive and seatbelts. They were also the cars that took people to work, shopping, or on family vacations, becoming an indispensable part of their everyday lives in the process.

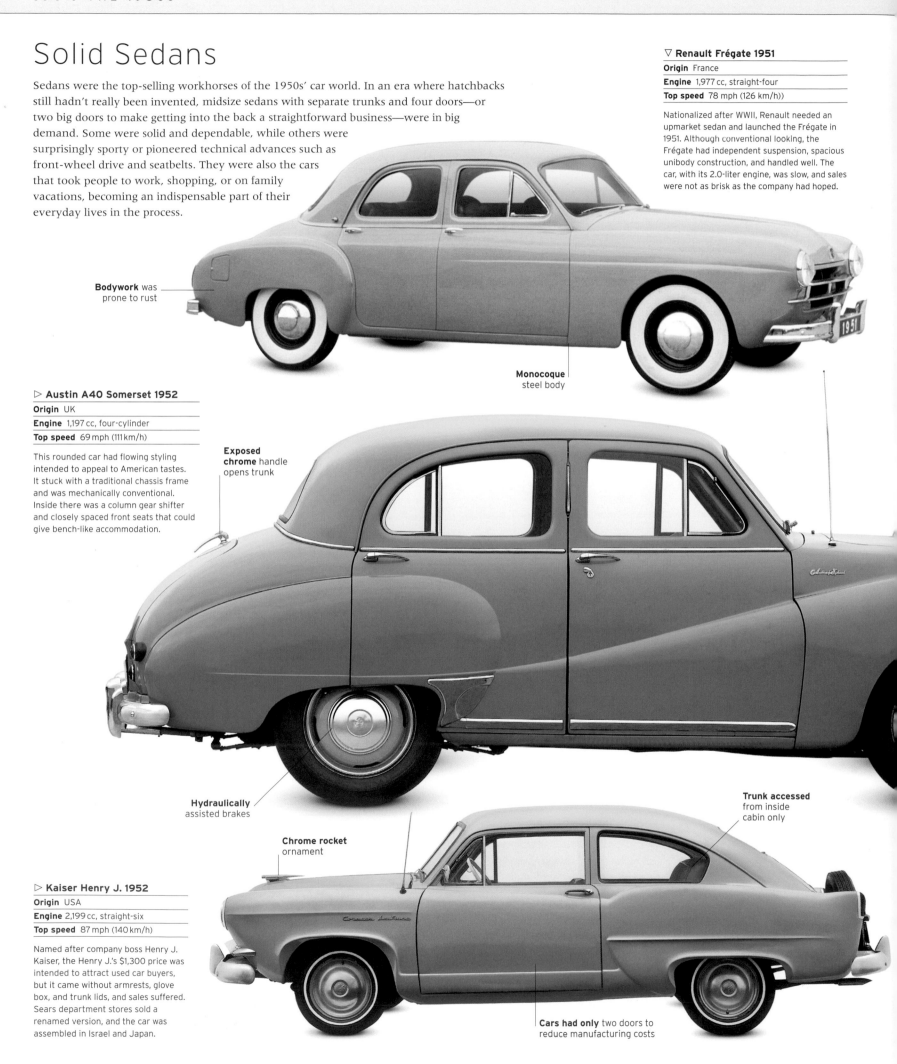

▽ **Renault Frégate 1951**

Origin France

Engine 1,977 cc, straight-four

Top speed 78 mph (126 km/h))

Nationalized after WWII, Renault needed an upmarket sedan and launched the Frégate in 1951. Although conventional looking, the Frégate had independent suspension, spacious unibody construction, and handled well. The car, with its 2.0-liter engine, was slow, and sales were not as brisk as the company had hoped.

Bodywork was prone to rust

Monocoque steel body

▷ **Austin A40 Somerset 1952**

Origin UK

Engine 1,197 cc, four-cylinder

Top speed 69 mph (111 km/h)

This rounded car had flowing styling intended to appeal to American tastes. It stuck with a traditional chassis frame and was mechanically conventional. Inside there was a column gear shifter and closely spaced front seats that could give bench-like accommodation.

Exposed chrome handle opens trunk

Hydraulically assisted brakes

Trunk accessed from inside cabin only

Chrome rocket ornament

▷ **Kaiser Henry J. 1952**

Origin USA

Engine 2,199 cc, straight-six

Top speed 87 mph (140 km/h)

Named after company boss Henry J. Kaiser, the Henry J.'s $1,300 price was intended to attract used car buyers, but it came without armrests, glove box, and trunk lids, and sales suffered. Sears department stores sold a renamed version, and the car was assembled in Israel and Japan.

Cars had only two doors to reduce manufacturing costs

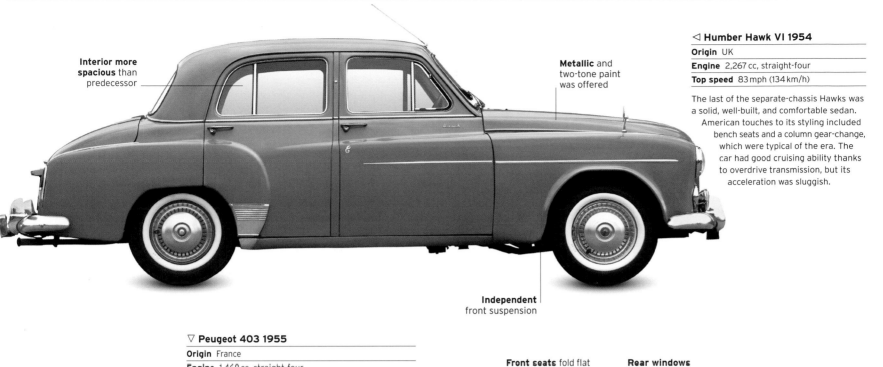

Interior more spacious than predecessor

Metallic and two-tone paint was offered

◁ **Humber Hawk VI 1954**

Origin UK

Engine 2,267 cc, straight-four

Top speed 83 mph (134 km/h)

The last of the separate-chassis Hawks was a solid, well-built, and comfortable sedan. American touches to its styling included bench seats and a column gear-change, which were typical of the era. The car had good cruising ability thanks to overdrive transmission, but its acceleration was sluggish.

Independent front suspension

▽ **Peugeot 403 1955**

Origin France

Engine 1,468 cc, straight-four

Top speed 76 mph (122 km/h)

The Peugeot 403's handsome body was designed by Italy's Pininfarina, and clothed a conventional-but-rugged mechanical set-up. The car's reliability made it popular in Africa and South America. More than 1 million sedan, estate, pickup, and convertible 403s were sold. Fictional US TV detective Columbo drove an open one.

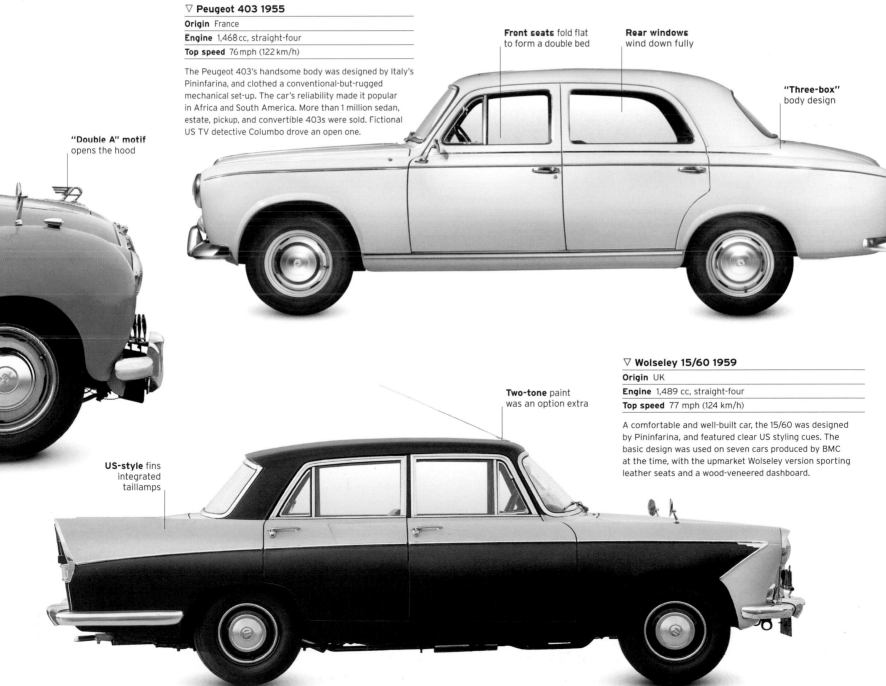

Front seats fold flat to form a double bed

Rear windows wind down fully

"Three-box" body design

"Double A" motif opens the hood

▽ **Wolseley 15/60 1959**

Origin UK

Engine 1,489 cc, straight-four

Top speed 77 mph (124 km/h)

A comfortable and well-built car, the 15/60 was designed by Pininfarina, and featured clear US styling cues. The basic design was used on seven cars produced by BMC at the time, with the upmarket Wolseley version sporting leather seats and a wood-veneered dashboard.

Two-tone paint was an option extra

US-style fins integrated taillamps

Rambler Rebel

The rare 1957 Rambler Rebel was conceived by the American Motors Corporation as a medium-sized, high-performance sedan. It has since been lauded as the first factory-produced, lightweight muscle car, and is the forerunner of icons such as the Pontiac GTO and Plymouth Road Runner, cars specifically designed in a memorable phrase for "kicking sand in the face of the 98-hp weakling."

AS THE MUSCLE CAR tag suggested, the Rambler Rebel's power and performance were somewhat at odds with its four-door configuration. Its 5.4-liter engine was by no means America's largest, but it was one of the first cars to feature electronic fuel injection and so was considerably more powerful than the V8s offered by its Chevrolet rivals.

More than 250 bhp gave the light, midsized sedan scorching performance. The company hoped this would fit well with the hot-rod craze that was sweeping America. Capable of 0–60 mph (96 km/h) in 7.5 seconds—just half a second slower than the Ferrari Dino more than a decade later—the aptly named Rebel had a top speed of around 115 mph (185 km/h).

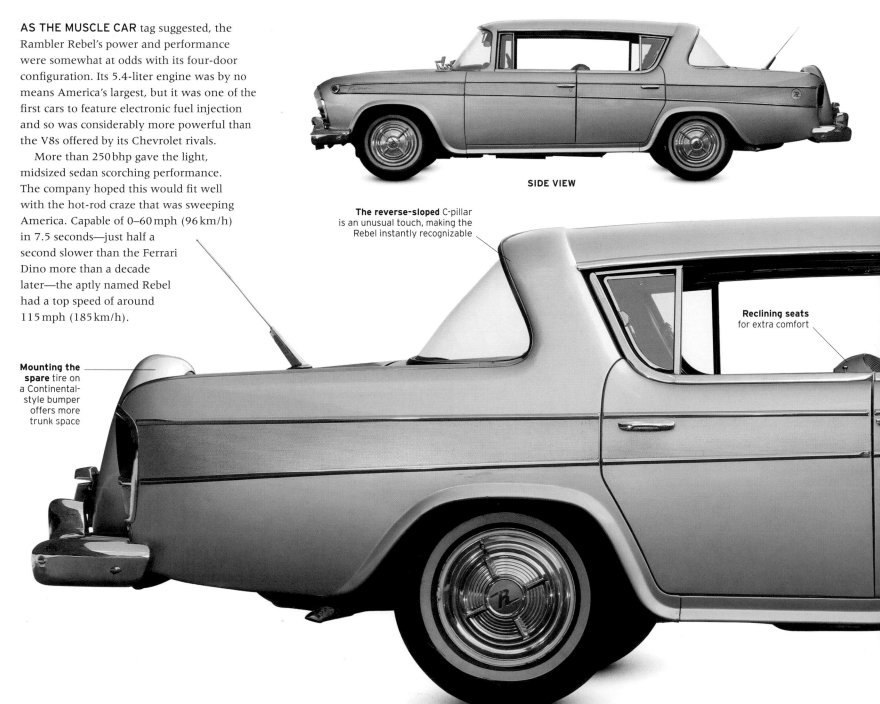

SIDE VIEW

The reverse-sloped C-pillar is an unusual touch, making the Rebel instantly recognizable

Reclining seats for extra comfort

Mounting the spare tire on a Continental-style bumper offers more trunk space

FRONT VIEW

REAR VIEW

Rebel badge
The deliberately confrontational Rebel name was carefully chosen to alert potential customers to the unusual nature of the car. Prior to this new departure, the Wisconsin-based AMC had been most closely associated with cars offering little in the way of excitement.

SPECIFICATIONS	
Model	Rambler Rebel, 1957
Assembly	Wisconsin, USA
Production	1,500
Construction	Steel monocoque
Engine	5,385 cc, V8
Power output	255 bhp
Transmission	3-speed manual or 4-speed automatic
Suspension	Front and rear coil springs
Brakes	Four wheel drums
Maximum speed	115 mph (185 km/h)

Two-tone paintwork is very much of its time

Its 5.4-liter V8 engine meant the Rebel was the first midsize car to have a large engine installed

Styling
The Rebel's high performance under the hood was matched in its exterior styling. It was only available in silver metallic paint, with gold anodized aluminum inserts along the sides. Grille-mounted headlights, padded dashboard, and visors completed the look.

ON THE ROAD

Highly unusual at the time, the Rambler's distinctive styling is still something of an acquired taste, but it is even so not hard to see why owners love their Rebels. Now genuinely rare, and almost indecently fast for a four-door sedan of this period, the Rebel badge is far from famous, but being the first ever muscle car gives the original much kudos. This obscure American sedan is an authentic automotive landmark.

Consider too the David and Goliath angle to this story: a comparative minnow taking on the might of Chrysler, Ford, and General Motors. Where David had the sling, Rambler had the grunt. Squeezing a hugely powerful V8 into an ordinary family car kicked off a revolution in performance. Before long America's Big Three were forced to retaliate with something of their own.

1. Front sidelights heavily trimmed with chrome   **2.** Wheel logo hints at racy performance   **3.** Angled wing mirror echoes car's rear pillar   **4.** Textured gold stripe runs down car   **5.** Rear light clusters resemble front sidelights   **6.** Optional Continental-style spare tire   **7.** Stylish chromed dashboard   **8.** Complex heating controls   **9.** Column-mounted gear selector   **10.** Crescent-shaped speedo   **11.** The muscle car's muscle

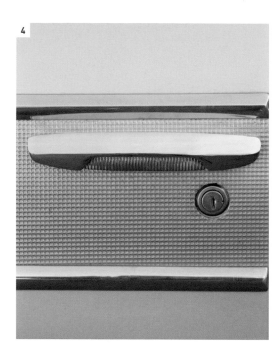

Stylish Roadsters

1950's America loved two-seat sports cars, or roadsters, and domestic automakers, as well as rivals from Europe and beyond, rushed to satisfy the endless demand. Seeing the potential of new revenue streams and fresh customers, firms such as Jowett and Triumph, traditionally makers of small vans and comfortable sedans favored by bank managers, began to manufacture sports cars. Outside America, a new generation of drivers began to find that they had more money at their disposal, and the idea of spending it on a roadster and cruising along in an open-top car seemed particularly appealing.

Plush interior rivals European models

Faired-in rear lamps

Bumper wraps around car's sides

Body made of fiberglass

▷ **Chevrolet Corvette C1 1953**

Origin USA

Engine 4,291 cc, V8

Top speed 142 mph (229 km/h)

First revealed in 1953 as a concept car, the Corvette's swooping, Harley Earl-styled fiberglass body promised speed that its six-cylinder engine could not deliver. As a result just 700 cars were sold in the first year. A beefy V8 engine, a manual gearbox, and a style makeover transformed sales and an icon was born.

Bench seat for three

Single-piece front end

Torsion bar suspension gives handling poise

▷ **Jowett Jupiter 1950**

Origin UK

Engine 1,486 cc, flat-four

Top speed 84 mph (135 km/h)

Jowett used the Javelin sedan's brilliant, flat-four engine in the Jupiter two-seater, where its low center of gravity helped the independently sprung roadster's handling. The Jupiter scored victories at Le Mans and Monte Carlo Rally, but gearbox warranty claims sank Jowett after 899 were built.

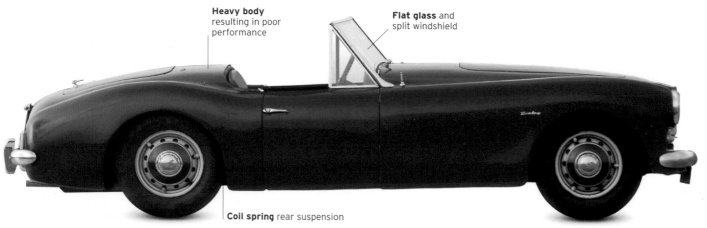

Heavy body resulting in poor performance

Flat glass and split windshield

Coil spring rear suspension

◁ **Healey G-type 1951**

Origin UK

Engine 2,993 cc, straight-six

Top speed 100 mph (161 km/h)

Before Donald Healey's Austin-Healey collaboration, the company worked with American vehicle-maker Nash to produce the Nash-Healey sports car. The G-type was basically this roadster, fitted with an Alvis engine and manual rather than automatic transmission. Only 25 cars were ever made, making it very rare.

Futuristic feel
The Corvette's designers were eager to give the car a cutting edge look, and this extended to its interior and exotically shaped instrument cluster, which grouped round dials and gauges directly in front of the driver.

FRONT VIEW

Changing times
Very early Corvettes had single, round headlamps but General Motors was quick to revise the styling. By the time V8 versions were on sale, these quad headlamps were being used.

"Flag" badges, a Corvette trademark

Back in style
The Corvette started out with fin-like, taillamp mounts, but was revised to give a more rounded look. Period road testers praised the car's roadholding.

REAR VIEW

Windowless door design

Fiberglass bodywork

▷ **Kaiser Darrin 1954**

Origin USA

Engine 2,641 cc, straight-six

Top speed 96 mph (154 km/h)

Shipbuilder Henry Kaiser began making cars after World War II. The Darrin, America's first fiberglass-bodied sports car, boasted doors that slid into the front fenders. Named after its designer, Howard "Dutch" Darrin, the car was only made after Kaiser's wife persuaded him to build it.

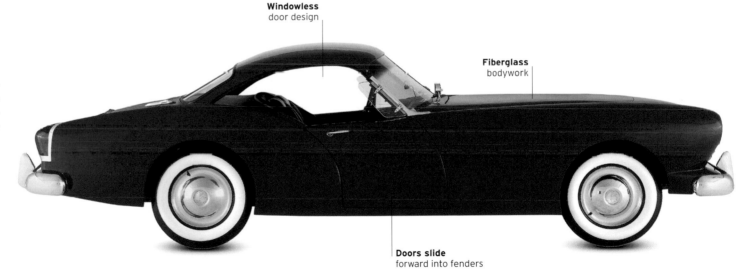

Doors slide forward into fenders

Tip-up rear seat optional

Wing "eyebrows" mimic the 300SL

◁ **Mercedes-Benz 190SL 1955**

Origin Germany

Engine 1,897 cc, straight-four

Top speed 107 mph (172 km/h)

The 190SL was the exotic, gullwing-doored 300SL's more restrained, little brother. Its convertible body shared many of the 300SL's design themes, and the 190 also had independent rear suspension. Launched in New York, the 190SL was more luxury touring two-seater than sports car.

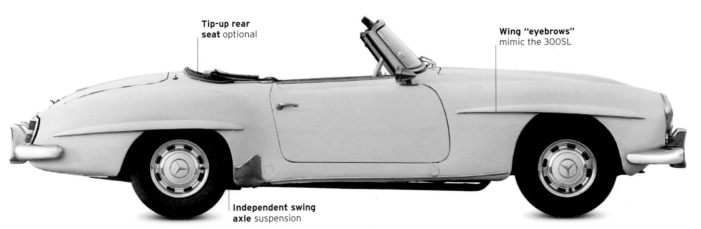

Independent swing axle suspension

Sir William Lyons, founder and chairman of Jaguar, with the E-Type in 1961

Great Marques
The Jaguar Story

In 1922, English motorcycle enthusiasts William Lyons and William Walmsley went into partnership to build sidecars. Five years later, Lyons designed a stylish body for the Austin Seven, and just one year after that his firm moved to Coventry; from these humble origins the Jaguar marque leapt into life.

THE SWALLOW SIDECAR COMPANY, run by William Lyons and William Walmsley, quickly evolved its business by offering attractive coachwork on a variety of chassis. Lyons, however, was determined to make his own cars, and in 1932 he launched the SS1, which used a modified Standard chassis that supported Swallow's rakish coupé coachwork, complete with long hood and fake hood irons. The SS1 was an immediate hit, and in 1934, when Walmsley sold out to Lyons, the company renamed itself SS Cars.

In 1935, Lyons launched his first sports car, and at the end of the year he brought out a brand-new range of Jaguar cars, including three sedans and the 100-mph (161-km/h) SS100 two-seat roadster. Buyers loved Lyons' mix of stunning line and excellent value, and SS Cars was on a roll. After World War II, the name SS Cars, with its Nazi connotations, was unacceptable, and in 1945 the company changed its name to Jaguar Cars Ltd. In quiet moments during the war, Jaguar engineers had laid plans for a superb 3.4-liter, six-cylinder twin-camshaft engine that was intended to power a new sports sedan. The engine was called the XK, and Lyons decided to build a sports car that could act as a showcase for the power unit, for display at the 1948 London Motor Show. This car, named the XK120, caused a huge stir with its 120-mph (193-km/h) performance, sub-$1,500 (£1,000) price tag, and sensational good looks. Lyons quickly turned the machine into a full production model, and it was joined in Jaguar's lineup by the handsome Mk VII sedan in 1950.

Jaguar Mk II, 1959
This is the epitome of the compact sports sedan among British classic cars, with six-cylinder engines from 2.4- to 3.8-liter.

Both cars were highly successful in motorsports. The Mk VII was an unlikely rally car, but now Jaguar set its sights on sports car racing domination with its XK120C (for Competition), or C-type. This car, which pioneered disc brakes, won the Le Mans 24-hour race in 1951, driven by Peter Walker and Peter Whitehead. Tony Rolt, Duncan Hamilton, and a C-type repeated the feat in 1953. Jaguar Cars Ltd.'s scientifically designed D-type saw Le Mans victories in 1955, 1956, and 1957—an extraordinary achievement for the small British company. Jaguar also created the first compact sports sedan in 1955—this 2.4 liter ushering in unibody construction for Jaguar cars. The year 1957 saw a 3.4-liter edition that was very fast, but the cars were transformed in 1959 when they matured to the Mk II model,

becoming one of the most universally coveted Jaguars of all time.

Feeling there was nothing more to prove in racing, Lyons shut the factory competition department, and gave his team the task of turning the D-type into a sports car. The result arrived in 1961 as the E-type—another Jaguar that made an enormous impact. Its clever, aircraft-inspired concept and aerodynamics were impressive, but it was the sleek, arrowlike profile and ability to reach 150 mph (241 km/h) that caused an instant line of impatient buyers.

Jaguar Cars Ltd., which had itself already acquired Daimler in 1960, merged with the British Motor Corporation in 1966. This in turn led to it joining British Leyland. However, the company

Advertising for the Jaguar MkVII sedan

Jaguar XK120, 1948
The sensational sports car, with its excellent straight-six engine, won itself and Jaguar instant acclaim.

"I want that car and **I want it now.**"

SINGER FRANK SINATRA, ON SEEING THE JAGUAR E-TYPE FOR THE FIRST TIME AT THE NEW YORK AUTO SHOW, APRIL 1961

clung bravely on to its independence, and in 1984 was the subject of a very successful stock market offering. The company has since been bought and sold by Ford and, today, is owned by India's Tata conglomerate. Jaguar's 1960s sport sedans included the imposing 1961 Mk X and the Mk II-based S-type/420, which adopted E-type suspension for superior roadholding and handling.

In 1968, however, all Jaguar's sedans were replaced by the XJ6, which proved to be an accomplished compromise between luxury and performance. Not long afterward, the XJ6 could also be had with Jaguar's all-new, 5.3-liter V12 engine, producing pretty much the finest car in the world.

The E-type faded by the early 1970s, replaced by the controversial XJ-S, which—despite a troubled start—met with incredible popularity throughout the 1980s. In 1986, Jaguar's venerable XJ sedans were replaced by the XJ40 series, and the decade was rounded off by the unveiling of the new mid-engined, four-wheel-drive XJ220 supercar, which eventually reached customers in 1991. The cars won glory on the racertack when Jaguar's XJR-9 and XJR-12 models saw further Le Mans victories in 1988 and 1990 respectively.

During Ford's stewardship of Jaguar, the new S-type and X-type sedans shared components with its other, more humdrum products, but since Tata has been in control the XF, XE, and XJ have all been pure Jaguar to the core.

Jaguar XJ6, 1968
The XJ6 replaced no less than four Jaguar sedans in one go, vastly upping the game for ride, handling, and performance.

CLASSICS OF THE FUTURE

XJ Some 50 per cent of the XJ's structure was made from recycled aluminum; it was about 330 lb (150 kg) lighter than conventional, steel-rich rivals, which made the car more agile as well as thriftier on fuel. This big Jaguar, codenamed X351 in development, had an all-glass roof as standard across all models. The hand-finished interior boasted chrome and piano-black detailing. British prime minister David Cameron used an armor-plated Sentinel version as his official transport.

△ **Jaguar XJ 2009**

Origin	UK
Engine	5,000 cc, V8-cylinder
Top speed	155 mph (250 km/h)

After years of the familiar XJ lines, this car was a radical departure—lower, wider, and built around an all-aluminum structure.

F-type Project 7 The F-type had a completely aluminum structure, like all modern Jaguars, and in Project 7 guise every body panel was aluminum too. The supercharged V8 engine put its power to the road through the rear wheels via an eight-speed automatic with steering-wheel paddle shifters. The so-called Aero Haunch behind the driver summoned up images of the aerodynamic stability fin on the D-type racer of the 1950s.

△ **Jaguar F-type Project 7 2013**

Origin	UK
Engine	5,000 cc, V8
Top speed	186 mph (300 km/h)

It took many decades for Jaguar to release a spiritual successor to the iconic E-type. Project 7, with 575 bhp, was Jaguar's most powerful car ever.

Microcars

After World War I a rush of very cheap, very crude, little vehicles known as "cycle cars" appeared, but these were killed off by proper cars in miniature such as the Austin Seven and Citroën 5CV. This pattern was repeated after World War II, with the appearance of tiny "microcars." Many were three-wheelers with little motorcycle engines, and they were a common feature of 1950s' roads. When more substantial compact cars, such as the Fiat 500 and original Mini, were launched, and living standards rose, microcar owners traded up and sales fell away.

▷ **Messerschmitt KR200 1956**

Origin Germany

Engine 191cc, one-cylinder

Top speed 60mph (96km/h)

In the 1940s, German aeronautical engineer Fritz Fend created a manually powered specialized car for the disabled. Powered versions followed, and Fend developed the famous tandem-seated KR200 with bubble canopy and handlebars, built by aircraft-maker Messerschmitt. Fend was working on a new microcar when he died in 2000.

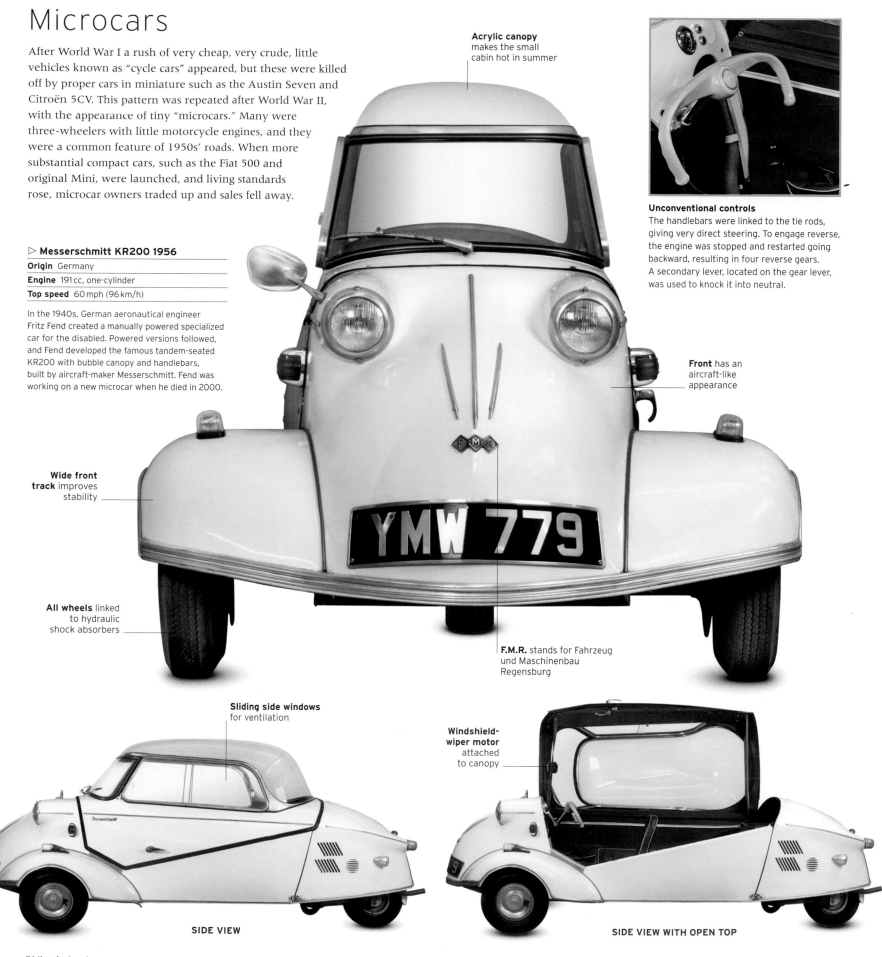

Acrylic canopy makes the small cabin hot in summer

Unconventional controls
The handlebars were linked to the tie rods, giving very direct steering. To engage reverse, the engine was stopped and restarted going backward, resulting in four reverse gears. A secondary lever, located on the gear lever, was used to knock it into neutral.

Front has an aircraft-like appearance

Wide front track improves stability

All wheels linked to hydraulic shock absorbers

F.M.R. stands for Fahrzeug und Maschinenbau Regensburg

Sliding side windows for ventilation

Windshield-wiper motor attached to canopy

SIDE VIEW

SIDE VIEW WITH OPEN TOP

Riding in tandem
With the driver at the wheel, the passengers sat directly behind. Although narrow, the rear featured seating for an adult and child. This seating pattern gave the car a low center of gravity, and with a wheel at each extreme it handled well for a three-wheeler.

Raising the roof
Hinged on the right-hand-side, the acrylic canopy was secured with a single latch. Once open, the rear bodywork could be lifted, giving access to the engine, which was located behind the rear passenger. There was also a spare wheel stowed here.

Front of car hinges outward for access

Fuel-efficient engine achieves more than 90 mpg (32 km/l)

◁ **BMW Isetta 300 1955**

Origin	Germany
Engine	298 cc, one-cylinder
Top speed	50 mph (80 km/h)

Conceived by Italian fridge-maker Iso (which later made supercars), the Isetta was later built by cash-strapped BMW, and the egg-shaped car was even assembled in an old railway workshop in Brighton in the UK. The Isetta was sold with three or close-double rear wheels.

Children can be carried at the rear

Noisy and thirsty two-stroke engine

▷ **Vespa 400 1957**

Origin	Italy/France
Engine	393 cc, straight-two
Top speed	52 mph (83 km/h)

Designed by Italian aircraft, scooter, and small truck-maker Piaggio, but built in France, this well-made two-seater had a rear engine, all-independent suspension, monocoque body, synchromesh gearbox, and hydraulic brakes. It also featured a roll-top, canvas roof, a little like the first Fiat 500.

Body constructed from fiberglass

Upright body is taller than It Is wide

Chain-driven single rear wheel

◁ **Scootacar 1958**

Origin	UK
Engine	197 cc, one-cylinder
Top speed	45 mph (72 km/h)

A British take on the bubble-car theme, the Scootacar was built in the UK, in Hunslet in Yorkshire, by a railway-locomotive-maker, apparently because a director's wife wanted something easier to park than her Jaguar. Occupants sat in tandem over the engine, and the Scootercar had one door and handlebar steering.

Air-cooled engine sits behind the seats

Chrome hubcaps add style

▷ **Frisky Family Three 1958**

Origin	UK
Engine	197 cc, one-cylinder
Top speed	44 mph (70 km/h)

English engineering firm Meadows made engines for other companies before launching the Frisky, a microcar styled by Italian designer Michelotti. The prototype had gullwing doors—production versions had normal doors and chain drive—and the engine could be started "backward" for reversing. Later Friskys were cheaper-to-tax three-wheelers.

Volkswagen Kombi

The VW Transporter T1 Microbus-based camper—often known simply as the Kombi—was much-loved when new, and is highly desirable today. The mechanical underpinnings of the Beetle were present in the Transporter (Volkswagen Types 1 and 2 respectively), but the basic van was available in a wide variety of versions to suit every need. The original split-windshield model was built from 1950 until 1967, with almost 1.5m sold.

THE IDEA FOR the Type 2 came from a Dutch VW importer who visited the Wolfsburg factory intending to place an order for Beetle cars. Instead, a prototype for a new van was produced in a matter of weeks. The Type 2 had a similar wheelbase to the Beetle, but came with a strengthened chassis for heavier loads. With its aerodynamics optimized to offset the 25 hp engine, the Kombi went into production. Rivals soon copied its "forward control" cab, in which the driver sat high above the front axle, but none could match its cool appeal.

A pop-up roof was a very popular after-market option on camper conversions, increasing headroom for daytime activities such as cooking

The high driving position improves visibility and makes the vehicle easy to maneuver on the road

The short wheelbase gives a clue as to the Kombi's Beetle origins

FRONT VIEW

REAR VIEW

Volkswagen badge
The first, prewar Beetle was known as KdF-wagen, meaning *Kraft durch Freude* or "Strength Through Joy," but Adolf Hitler's desire to build a cheap car for the masses led to it being called the Volkswagen or "People's Car," and this name was subsequently adopted.

SPECIFICATIONS	
Model	Volkswagen Transporter, 1950–67
Assembly	Germany, Brazil, and South Africa
Production	1,477,330
Construction	Steel body and chassis
Engine	1,131–1,493 cc, flat-four
Power output	25–51 bhp
Transmission	4-speed manual
Suspension	Torsion bar front and rear
Brakes	Four-wheel drums
Maximum speed	77 mph (124 km/h)

Styling
The purity of this no-nonsense design, first drawn as a doodle by Ben Pon in 1947, has always been an important part of the Kombi's charm. The first versions eschewed any ornamentation, apart from an outsized VW logo on the bull-fronted nose and the distinctive, optional two-tone paintwork.

The engine is air-cooled, like other VWs of the time

Twin barn doors give easy access to the interior, and can be thrown open for *al fresco* meals

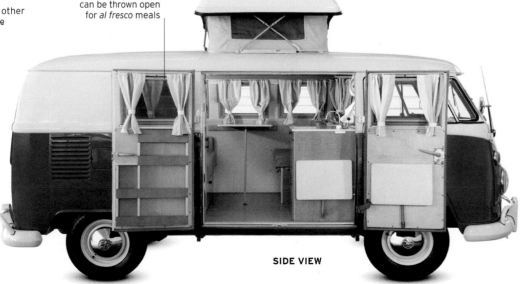

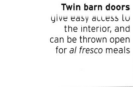

SIDE VIEW

ON THE ROAD

Still relatively inexpensive to operate and easy to work on, the friendly styling of the Kombi comes with the considerable added advantage of a plentiful supply of mechanical spares. Its close kinship with the Beetle—of which more than 21 million were built and sold—means both the panel- and camper van variants are well suited to modification by owners looking to boost the performance of the model's original 25 hp flat-four.

Like the Beetle, the Kombi has long been popular with customizers, but tastes change and many are now being converted back to near-original spec. Today the highest prices tend to be paid for mint originals, prompting a move to restore these surprisingly practical machines back to that simple, factory-fresh look.

1. Front headlight and indicator **2.** Ventilation for rear-mounted engine **3.** Louvered side window **4.** Chrome handle for sliding side door **5.** Rear lights show functional design **6.** Customized painted bumpers **7.** Cabin interior with table folded down **8.** Water tap fitted to food preparation cabinet **9.** Minimal instrumentation **10.** Compact, air-cooled engine

Charismatic Sedans

Cars such as big Opels and Vauxhalls appealed to up-and-coming consumers, who were trading up from economy-minded small sedans, but there was also a breed of large car aimed at a wealthier clientele. Just as today's Mercedes, Jaguar, and BMW models are considered a cut above mass-market cars, so too did makes such as Armstrong Siddeley and Lancia bring a certain cachet to their owners. The way many of these cars were engineered and handled was often very different. Some set store by quality construction and straightforward engineering, others found favor because of their poise and technical flair, but all of them were cars people aspired to own.

3.4-liter engine

Front doors follow fender line

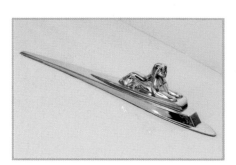

Sphinx hood mascot
Although in the 1950s Armstrong Siddeley made cars that exuded a discreet English good taste that was far from showy, its distinctive sphinx hood mascot was a small piece of chrome-plated Art Deco decadence.

Body has old-fashioned wood framing

Separate fenders give car 1930s' look

Running boards another period feature

◁ **Riley RME 1952**

Origin UK

Engine 1,496 cc, straight-four

Top speed 78 mph (126 km/h)

The Riley RME was a traditionally handsome car whose split windshield and separate fenders gave it an old-fashioned look. This extended to the way it was built, with a separate chassis and wood-framed body, but its mix of quality and sporting handling won it many friends.

Rounded shape a styling departure for MG

Engine designed by Austin

▷ **MG Magnette ZA 1954**

Origin UK

Engine 1,489 cc, straight-four

Top speed 80 mph (129 km/h)

This handsome car was an example of "badge engineering." Built by the British Motor Corporation, its body was shared with the Wolseley 4/44 and its engine came from Austin. With twin carburetors and rack-and-pinion steering, the MG was a pleasure to drive with a stylish wood and leather interior.

Unibody construction was a first for its makers

▽ Armstrong Siddeley Sapphire 346 1953

Origin UK

Engine 3,435 cc, straight-six

Top speed 100 mph (161 km/h)

Along with Rover, Armstrong Siddeley made the sort of solid, tasteful, quietly luxurious cars that British doctors and bank managers sought to own. With its distinctive sphinx hood mascot, the Sapphire came with electric pre-selector or automatic transmissions. This was to become Armstrong Siddeley's final model.

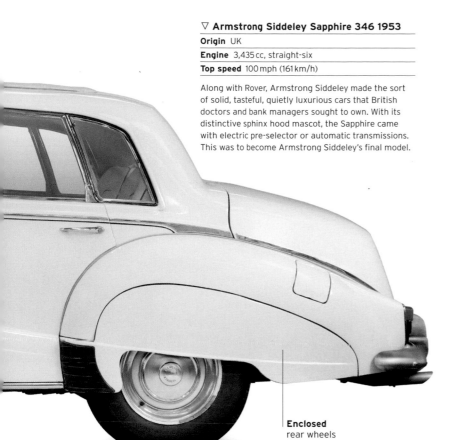

Enclosed rear wheels

FRONT VIEW

Aspirational vehicles

The Sapphire was built in an era when many families couldn't afford a car, and those who could managed with something old and secondhand. Along with the likes of Jaguar and Rover, Armstrong Siddeley made the sort of vehicles that most people could only dream of owning.

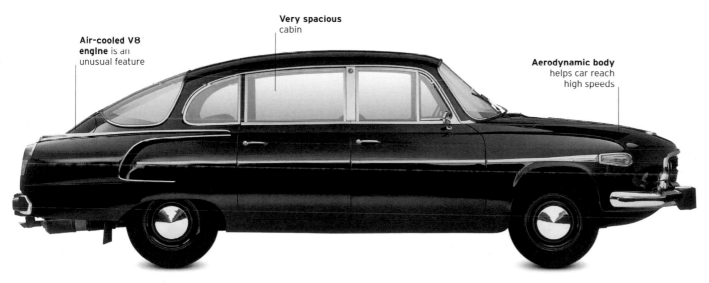

Air-cooled V8 engine is an unusual feature

Very spacious cabin

Aerodynamic body helps car reach high speeds

◁ Tatra 603 1956

Origin Czechoslovakia

Engine 2,474–2,545 cc, V8

Top speed 100 mph (161 km/h)

Czech automaker Tatra began making advanced, high-performance sedans in the 1930s. These had wind cheating bodies and rear engines, and this theme was continued with the 603, which mostly found favor with Czech diplomats. This well-made, aerodynamic car had a light, strong, air-cooled rear V8 engine and sometimes exciting handling as a result.

Convertible models produced until 1964

Engine developed from world's first production V6

▷ Lancia Flaminia 1957

Origin Italy

Engine 2,458 cc, V6

Top speed 102 mph (164 km/h)

The big, square Flaminia was styled by Italian vehicle designer Pinin Farina, which used similar visual ideas on other models including the Austin Westminster. However, unlike the British car, the Lancia, with its de Dion transaxle was technically advanced and great to drive.

Transmission at the rear

Henry M. Leland and one of the earliest Cadillacs

Great Marques
The Cadillac Story

The classic car period of 1940–1990 is the era when the Cadillac name stood for luxury, style, and power in imposingly large packages. Henry M. Leland started the company in 1902, and Cadillac became notable for its ability to manufacture high-quality cars on a large scale.

HENRY M. LELAND WAS ALREADY a veteran of the auto industry and an experienced inventor when he founded Cadillac—named after the 18th-century founder of Detroit, Antoine de la Mothe Cadillac. The initial Model A actually used an Oldsmobile engine design in a Ford-derived chassis, but it was the four-cylinder Model D three years later that propelled the marque, briefly, into the position of the world's third largest automaker.

In 1909, Cadillac was taken over by General Motors (GM), and continued to innovate with the first across-the-board use of electric starters—a complete game-changer for the marque. The V8 models were soon offered in a wide range of body styles, and in 1930 Cadillac became the first (and so far the only) manufacturer that offered V8, V12, and V16 models concurrently; meanwhile, for balance, in 1927 it also introduced the cheaper LaSalle brand, although that was axed in 1940.

During the 1930s, the name Fleetwood (after a Pennsylvania coachbuilder) was used to denote top-range Cadillacs, and the influence of youthful GM styling chief and former custom-car wizard Harley Earl began to shine through in the urbane modernity of the typical Cadillac. The 1938 Cadillac 60 Special had strikingly smooth, modern styling by another young designer, Bill Mitchell, who would head up the Cadillac styling studio on Earl's retirement in 1958.

Car production continued until 1942, when the marque built the first cars to offer air conditioning, and only the second with automatic transmission.

THE *Cadillac* ELDORADO

Cadillac poster
The first Eldorado of 1953 was a limited edition to promote Cadillac's design leadership; just 532 were built.

Cadillac then pitched in with the war effort by making tanks, staff cars, and aircraft engine parts. Production of civilian cars resumed in 1945, and in 1948 a new generation of cars featured tailfins inspired by the P38 Lightning fighter. The first Cadillac overhead-valve V8 arrived in 1949—the year the marque's millionth car was sold—enabling American driver, Briggs Cunningham, to take tenth place at Le Mans in 1950; a Cadillac-powered Allard came third.

Cadillac Eldorado Seville, 1959
The rear fins and overall proportions of the '59 Cadillac still astound for their sheer extravagance.

"Long as I was **riding in a big Cadillac** and **dressed nice** and had plenty of food, **that's all I cared about.**"

ETTA JAMES, *NME* MAGAZINE, 1978

Every Cadillac featured automatic transmission after 1950. Power steering was added in 1954, at the same time as a wraparound windshield. In 1957, the high-tech Eldorado Brougham came with air suspension and electric memory seats as standard, plus a built-in bottle of Arpège perfume.

The '59 Cadillac range sported the tallest tailfins ever to be seen on a car, and became an instant pop culture icon, but after that the cars were toned down significantly. In 1967, Cadillac's remarkable new Eldorado coupe boasted front-wheel drive and a huge 7-liter, V8 developing 440 bhp. Its capacity increased to a massive 8.2 liters by 1970.

Cadillac's new generation of cars in 1975 included the comparatively compact new Seville, and they could all now take unleaded gasoline. The car gained a controversial V8 diesel option in 1978, and retro styling inspired by classic Rolls-Royce limousines in 1980.

In stark contrast, and in the eye of a deep recession, the disastrous Cimarron of 1981 had a 1.9-liter four-cylinder engine, and also included Cadillac's first manual transmission for more than 30 years. Once prosperity returned in 1986, the marque launched its Allanté luxury two-seater, a rolling showcase for its all-new,

Cadillac Seville, 1980
The retro-style "bustle back" tail was a key design tenet for this Seville. An important departure for Cadillac was to offer this model with a diesel, V8 engine.

32-valve, aluminum Northstar V8 engine, with bodywork designed and built by Pininfarina in Italy. In 1996, Cadillac decided to stop building enormous sedans, while electing to sell European-size sedans—an experiment that failed. A renaissance began in 1998 when the marque launched its first sport-utility vehicle, the Escalade, and the sharply styled CTS compact sedan of 2002 was, finally, a genuine match for some of Europe's executive sport sedans. The 2006 Cadillac BLS sold slowly in Europe, its intended market, but the STS midsize sedan (2005), full-size DTS (2006), and second-generation CTS (2008) models all did well in the US. In 2009, Cadillac survived GM's bankruptcy and government bail-out, and its range of high-performance luxury cars is now popular in China as well as in America.

CLASSICS OF THE FUTURE

CTS-V The basic CTS sedan was considerably beefed up to cope with the huge extra power from the Corvette engine, gaining a special cradle for the engine, huge brakes, and the Corvette LS6's manual transmission. The car could do 0–60 mph (0–96 km/h) in 4.6 seconds, and the combination of excellent weight distribution, taut suspension, generous torque, and a surprisingly capable chassis meant the CTS-V could lap Germany's Nürburgring circuit in 8 minutes 19 seconds–rivaling the accomplished Mercedes-Benz C55 AMG.

△ **Cadillac CTS-V 2004**

Origin	USA
Engine	5,665 cc, V8
Top speed	163 mph (262 km/h)

The CTS-V sedan borrowed the 400 bhp, pushrod, V8 engine from the Chevrolet Corvette LS6, with a 6-speed manual transmission.

ELR The car was first seen in public as the Cadillac Converj concept in 2009, and four years later, after some prevarication, it went on sale. It was a plug-in hybrid with a drivetrain derived from the Chevrolet Volt, its small gasoline engine generating power to drive an electric motor and replenish the lithium-ion battery pack. In pure electric mode, the range was 39 miles (63 km). In 2016, the price was dropped significantly in an attempt to boost sales; the car's performance was also improved by 25 percent.

△ **Cadillac ELR 2013**

Origin	USA
Engine	Electric motor and 1,398 cc, straight-four
Top speed	106 mph (171 km/h)

An upscale alternative to the Tesla Model S, Cadillac's gasoline-electric hybrid had styling that was redolent of the marque's heavyweight traditions.

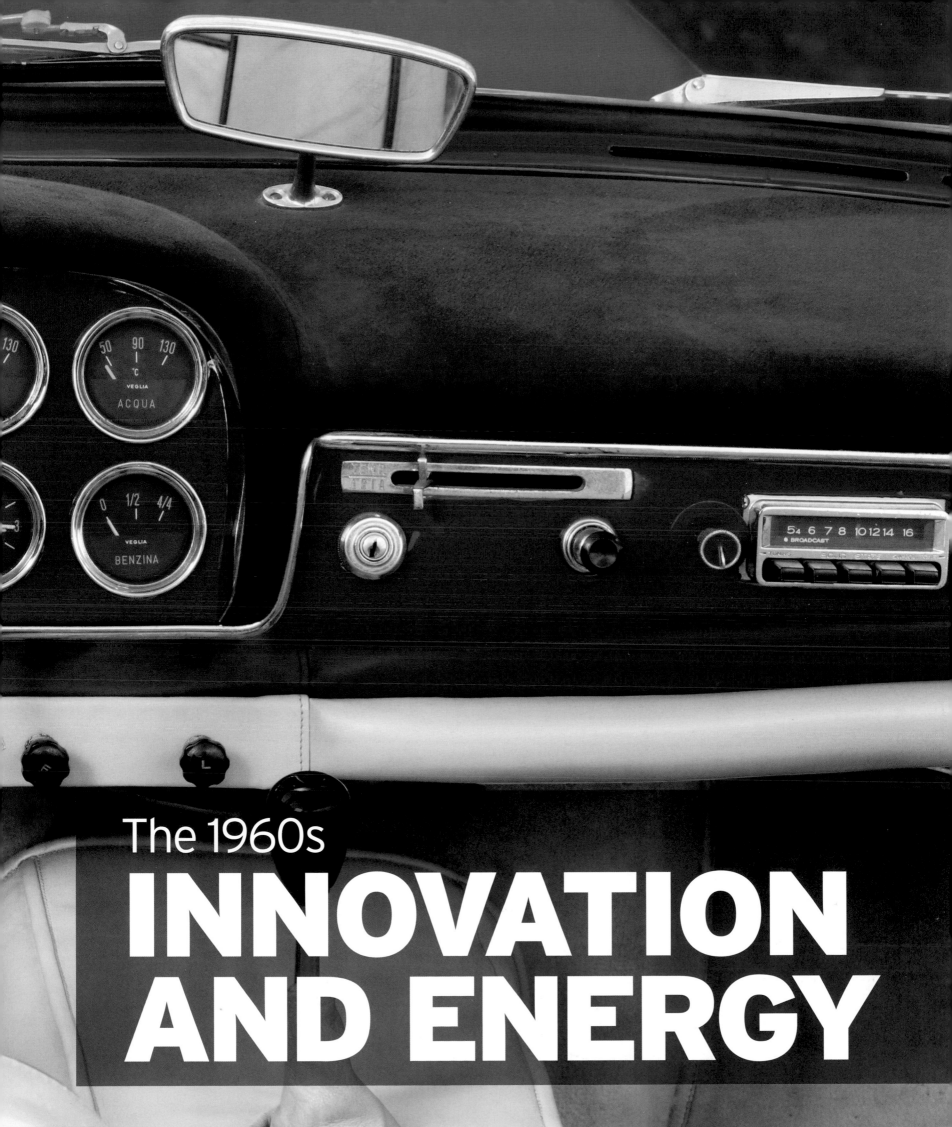

The 1960s
INNOVATION
AND ENERGY

The new AUSTIN se7en

INNOVATION AND ENERGY

The mid-1960s was probably the pinnacle of unfettered driving enjoyment. Roads worldwide were still relatively uncrowded, in many cases speed limits did not apply, and engineers—working from opposing ends of the market spectrum— devised ways to push the boundaries of handling capability.

True supercars appeared in leaps and bounds. First, Jaguar's fabulous E-type of 1961 presented a breathtaking cocktail of speed, style, science, and value. Then Lamborghini's 1966 Bertone-designed Miura introduced mid-engined racing-car style, trouncing even the beautifully honed machinery of Ferrari and Aston Martin.

It was also a golden decade for the small sports car, including the MGB, Alfa Romeo Duetto Spider, Fiat 124 Spider, and Triumph Spitfire. The genius concept of the Lotus Elan established a new paradigm in handling brilliance, while the sporty Ford Mustang ushered in the idea of unlimited buyer choices.

Innovation for everyone came as standard with the Mini. Its transverse engine and front-wheel drive delivered sure-footed control. The clever packaging started the trend for small cars that were roomy and practical.

The silken performance of the Wankel rotary engines from NSU Motorenwerke and Mazda excited technophiles. Simple, compact, and with a high power-to-weight ratio, they had many advantages, although the widespread adoption of fuel injection to bolster engine performance was of more commercial importance.

Largely unnoticed, Japanese manufacturers were learning to build cars that were not only easy to drive but also durable and reliable. Not that they yet posed a threat to the establishment in Detroit—they were still in thrall to huge horsepower, massive engine capacities, and muscular styling.

△ **Failed revolution**
The Wankel rotary engine, fitted to the NSU RO 80, promised simplicity and smooth performance. Poorly designed and built, it proved unreliable and thirsty.

> "**Adding** power makes you faster on the straights. **Subtracting** weight makes you **faster** everywhere."

COLIN CHAPMAN, FOUNDER OF LOTUS

◁ **Brochure cover** for the new Austin Seven, later known as the Austin Mini, 1959.

Key events

▷ **1960** The front-wheel drive, transverse-engined Mini draws a new template for roomy small cars, seating four adults in relative comfort.

▷ **1961** Jaguar unveils its E-type. With speeds of up to 150 mph (241 km/h), it is one-third of the price of an equivalent Ferrari.

▷ **1962** Ford produces its 30-millionth V8 engine.

▷ **1963** Elegance and performance are combined in the new Mercedes-Benz 280SL roadster.

▷ **1963** The first of Porsche's long-lived 911 coupés makes its debut, replacing the much-loved 356.

△ **A legend is born**
The first of Porsche's long-lived 911 coupes makes its debut in 1963, replacing the much-loved 356. Revised and updated many times, it is still in production.

▷ **1964** The Ford Mustang made its debut at the New York World's Fair; the Plymouth Barracuda becomes America's first "muscle car."

▷ **1965** Launch of the Rolls-Royce Silver Shadow, the first "Roller" without a separate chassis.

▷ **1966** End of the line for the Studebaker marque after 64 years.

▷ **1966** Toyota introduces the first of its hugely successful Corolla series.

▷ **1967** The NSU RO 80 is a futuristic executive sedan from Germany, complete with the first twin-rotor Wankel engine.

▷ **1968** Ferrari's 365 GTB4 Daytona is the world's most desirable supercar.

Sport Sedans

Performance had always been the preserve of open roadsters, but by the 1960s sports sedans were gaining ground. This inroad was fueled by automakers such as Ford and BMC turning out tuned versions of their family cars that made a good base for a circuit racing or rally competitor. Sedans were becoming more sophisticated, too, with disc brakes and independent suspension more common, and the adoption of light, stiff unibody structures. It was all good news for drivers who wanted not just to enjoy their motoring, but also to share it with a few friends.

Impressive instrumentation
Jaguars always blended style and substance, and the well-stocked dashboard was designed not only to look good but also to present useful information to the driver. The speedometer and tachometer were directly in front of the driver, with auxiliary gauges, light switch, accessory switches, and the ignition switch located at the center.

▷ **Jaguar Mk 2 1959**

Origin	UK
Engine	3,781 cc, straight-six
Top speed	125 mph (201 km/h)

For many, this lithe Jaguar was the epitome of the 1960s' sports sedan. The 3.4 liter was more popular on the road, but the 3.8 was a great sedan racer. It was the favorite of 1960s' getaway drivers, who would steal examples fitted with car club badges, as these were the best maintained.

Pillars are much thinner on Mk 2 than on the previous model

Door mirrors are a relatively new feature

Distinctive front-end

Big bumpers on earlier models

Larger grille required to feed six-cylinder engine

9471 CR

Versatile Monocoque
The Mk 2's monocoque body was also used for the Daimler V8-250. With the addition of independent rear suspension and some restyling, it was used yet again in the Jaguar S-type and 420.

Jaguar hood mascot known as a "leaper"

SIDE VIEW

Disc brakes on all four wheels

Smooth six
Mk 2s were available with three versions of Jaguar's smooth, twin-cam, straight-six XK engine, in 2.4-liter, 3.4-liter, and 3.8-liter guises. The 3.8 had twin SU carburetors and a gross output of 220 bhp. The more powerful car was the enthusiast's choice.

External body seams
reduce manufacturing costs

Tuned A-series engine
gives Mini Cooper a
sprightly performance

▷ **Austin/Morris Mini
Cooper 1961**

Origin	UK
Engine	1,275 cc, straight-four
Top speed	100 mph (161 km/h)

The Mini was never meant to be a
performance sedan. Formula 1 boss
John Cooper spotted its potential,
tuning the car's engines and adding
disc brakes to exploit the Mini's
fantastic roadholding abilities. A multiple Monte
Carlo Rally and British Sedan
Championship winner, it was an
exciting car for the open road.

Rugged body and
chassis built as one unit

Engine has twin SU
carburetors

◁ **Volvo 122S 1961**

Origin	Sweden
Engine	1,778 cc, straight-four
Top speed	100 mph (161 km/h)

This was a rugged yet capable sport
sedan, with a twin-carburetor engine
and 85 bhp. Later, a 123 GT with
100 bhp became available. These
were spirited performers, especially
when fitted with the optional
overdrive. Designated by numbers
in most markets, the Volvo was
known as the Amazon in Sweden.

Drum brakes all around until
front disc brakes added in 1961

Early Gordinis
finished in French
racing blue

▷ **Renault 8 Gordini 1964**

Origin	France
Engine	1,108 cc, straight-four
Top speed	106 mph (171 km/h)

The Gordini version of the R8 arrived in
1964, a restyled version of the boxy
model that had been released two years
earlier. It offered 49 bhp from its 1,108 cc
twin-carb engine, delivered through a
close-ratio manual transmission with four
speeds (the regular R8 had only three).

Four-cylinder engine
is rear-mounted

Disc brakes on
all four wheels

Mirrors follow
new fashion for
matte-black accessories

High-revving
straight-six
engine

Badge on pillar also
acts as an air vent

◁ **Nissan Skyline GT-R 1969**

Origin	Japan
Engine	1,998 cc, straight-six
Top speed	124 mph (200 km/h)

The twin-camshaft engine in the
GT-R turned the humdrum Skyline
sedan into a serious race winner that
notched up 50 race wins in its first
three years. Power was delivered to the
rear through a five-speed transmission,
and there was semi-trailing arm
independent rear suspension.

Wheel arch extensions
fitted front and rear

Austin-Healey 3000

Acclaimed former rally driver and engineer Donald Healey became a car manufacturer in his own right in 1946. He wanted to build a high-performance, inexpensive sports car, and achieved that with the Healey 100. Launched at the London Motor Show in 1952, the two-seat roadster featured a powerful 2.6-liter, four-cylinder engine from the discontinued Austin Atlantic. The Austin Motor Company was so impressed that it struck an instant deal.

LAUNCHED IN 1959, the 3000 was the third incarnation of the "Big" Healey design, following the 100 and 100-6. It adopted the British Motor Corporation's gutsy new 3.0-liter, six-cylinder engine, and had powerful front disc brakes as standard to counteract its lively acceleration. Overdrive was an optional extra on the four-speed manual gearbox.

The 3000 was the epitome of late 1950s' sports-car style, and looked especially stylish with its spoked wheels and two-tone bodywork. Yet, surprisingly, most were sold as four-seaters with two small, child-friendly seats in the back—the two-seater was a rarity even in the US, which was always seen as the car's top market.

SIDE VIEW

Levered chrome door handles sit flush with the body

The steering wheel is attached to an adjustable column

External trunk hinges used to reduce costs

FRONT VIEW

REAR VIEW

Austin-Healey badge
This badge was created after Donald Healey and Austin, part of the British Motor Corporation (BMC), joined forces. The Austin-Healey 3000 was larger and more powerful than BMC's MG TF and MGA; all three sports cars were exported in significant numbers.

SPECIFICATIONS	
Model	Austin-Healey 3000 Mk I BN7, 1959–61
Assembly	UK
Production	13,650
Construction	Ladder-type chassis, welded steel body panels
Engine	2912 cc, straight-six
Power output	124 bhp at 4,600 rpm
Transmission	4-speed manual with optional overdrive
Suspension	Front independent, rear live axle
Brakes	Front discs, rear drums
Maximum speed	114 mph (183 km/h)

Styling
Donald Healey had a brilliant instinct for "packaging" sports cars. Unlike many industry entrepreneurs, he was also design-aware, and worked closely with bodywork stylist Gerry Coker to create the 3000's harmonious profile.

Two-tone paint with a cream lower half is a characteristic feature

Wire wheels are held on with chrome spinners

The 3000 sits low to the ground, sometimes making for a bumpy ride

The chrome-plated bumper protects the body and enhances looks

ON THE ROAD

Austin-Healeys were intended for fast, open-top motoring and so, despite the beautiful exterior, they were quite basic inside to keep their weight and bulk to a minimum. With a low center of gravity—and the car's predictable road manners allied to its eager performance—this made them excellent for rallying. The model's major victories included the punishing 1960 Liege–Rome–Liege rally in the hands of Pat Moss, sister of famous racing driver Stirling Moss. The 3000 Mk II of 1961 introduced a triple-carburetor engine, while the 1963 Mk III was the most powerful of all, with 150 hp of thrust, and offered a more comfortable cockpit. The last 3000 was made in 1967, and to the dismay of enthusiasts the model was never replaced.

1. Two marques in one sports car brand 2. 3000 badge on wavy radiator grille slats
3. Wire wheel spinners carry helpful instructions 4. Headlamp with indicator light below
5. Chrome-plated overriders to ward off low-speed bumps 6. Reflector lens embedded in rear wing 7. No-frills cockpit aimed at sports-car purists; tight accommodations
8. Speedometer reads up to 120 mph (193 km/h), actual top speed was 114 mph (183 km/h) 9. 3-liter six-cylinder engine with twin carburetors (on the right)

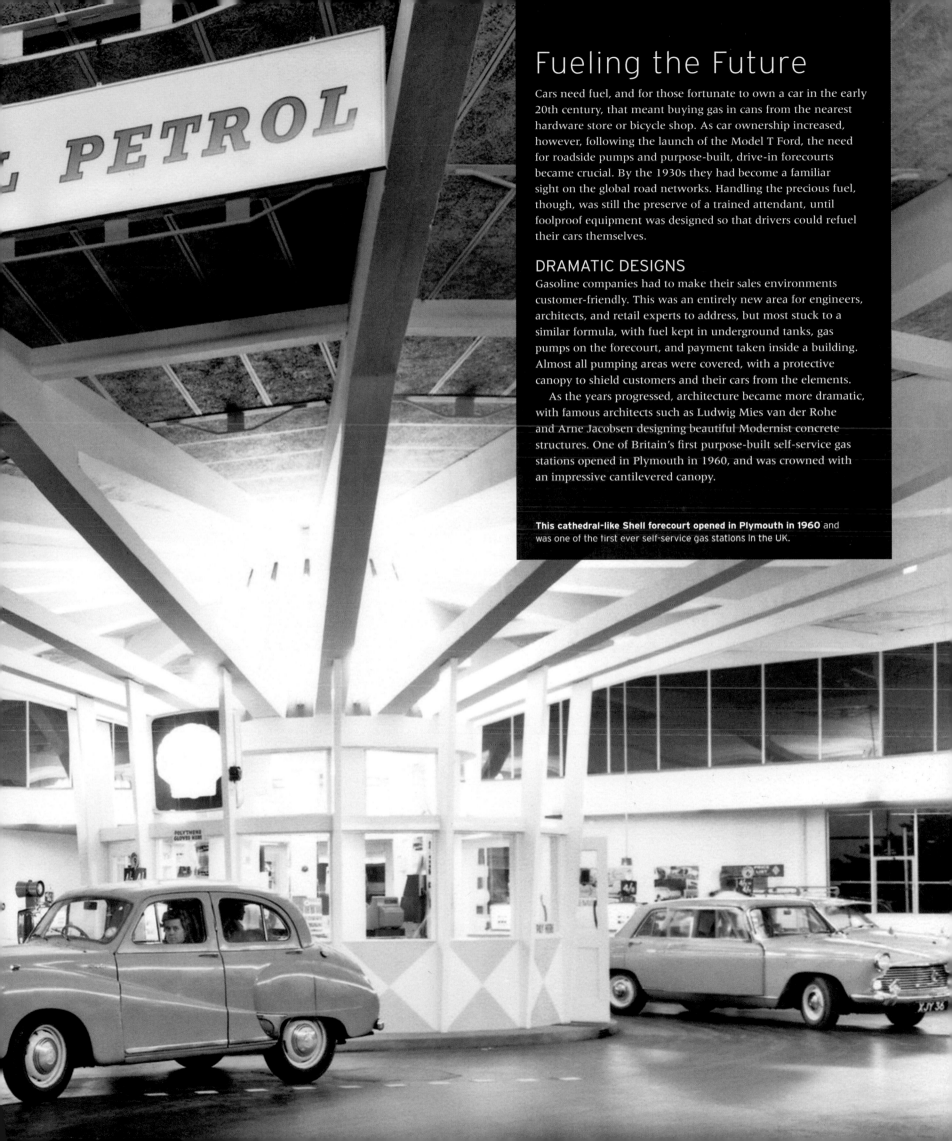

Fueling the Future

Cars need fuel, and for those fortunate to own a car in the early 20th century, that meant buying gas in cans from the nearest hardware store or bicycle shop. As car ownership increased, however, following the launch of the Model T Ford, the need for roadside pumps and purpose-built, drive-in forecourts became crucial. By the 1930s they had become a familiar sight on the global road networks. Handling the precious fuel, though, was still the preserve of a trained attendant, until foolproof equipment was designed so that drivers could refuel their cars themselves.

DRAMATIC DESIGNS

Gasoline companies had to make their sales environments customer-friendly. This was an entirely new area for engineers, architects, and retail experts to address, but most stuck to a similar formula, with fuel kept in underground tanks, gas pumps on the forecourt, and payment taken inside a building. Almost all pumping areas were covered, with a protective canopy to shield customers and their cars from the elements.

As the years progressed, architecture became more dramatic, with famous architects such as Ludwig Mies van der Rohe and Arne Jacobsen designing beautiful Modernist concrete structures. One of Britain's first purpose-built self-service gas stations opened in Plymouth in 1960, and was crowned with an impressive cantilevered canopy.

This cathedral-like Shell forecourt opened in Plymouth in 1960 and was one of the first ever self-service gas stations in the UK.

Great Designers
Sir Alec Issigonis

In Sir Alec Issigonis, the world witnessed a true genius of automotive design who single-handedly set the template for the modern small car. He was an exceptional talent with genuinely unique and radical ideas. An iconoclast and an outsider, Issigonis was also an individualist, and it is a tribute to his vision that his creations— the Morris Minor, Austin 1100, and the Mini—proved so popular.

Career highlights

▷ **1936** Issigonis joins Morris, working on suspension systems. World War II prevents his suspension for the Morris 10 from going into production. It is later used on the MG YA of 1949

▷ **1948** The first all-Issigonis design, the Morris Minor, is an instant bestseller

▷ **1959** The Mini—Issigonis's masterpiece, and quite possibly the world's most significant car—stuns the public with its debut. It sets the design pattern for the modern small car

▷ **1962** Another front-wheel drive masterpiece, the Austin/Morris 1100, is launched to huge acclaim

△ **Austin/Morris 1100, 1963**
With a surprisingly large interior considering its size, the 1100 was launched by BMC in 1962 as a four-door family sedan. It featured front disc brakes, front-wheel drive, and novel Hydrolastic fluid suspension.

▷ **1967** The Royal Society makes Issigonis a fellow, and he is knighted two years later by Queen Elizabeth II

▷ **1969** Issigonis is appointed Special Developments Director at British Leyland

▷ **1971** After retiring, Issigonis remains active, producing designs for experimental gearless transmissions and steam-powered cars

BORN IN SMYRNA (now Izmir), Turkey in 1906 to a Greek father and German mother, Alec Issigonis came to the UK with his family in 1922, when he was 15. His talent for drawing was quickly recognized, and he studied engineering at Battersea Polytechnic, but failed to pass his exams.

Issigonis became a talented racing driver, piloting his modified Austin Seven racer, and joined an engineering consultancy, working on transmissions. After spells at Humber and Austin, he was taken in by Morris in 1936, for whom he designed the independent front suspension of the MG YA.

The Morris Minor, which was produced from 1948 to 1971, was entirely Issigonis's project. It pioneered Morris's use of unitary construction and was highly space-efficient. Issigonis had wanted to use front-wheel drive; but to his disappointment, the rush to production after the war forced the company to stick with rear-wheel drive instead.

Issigonis resigned in 1952, when Morris merged with Austin to form the British Motor Corporation (BMC). He took a new position at Alvis, where he designed a V8 engine that featured the world's first hydraulic suspension with a front-to-rear interconnection. Sadly, Alvis couldn't afford to build it, so Issigonis returned to BMC in 1955 at the invitation of Sir Leonard Lord, BMC's chairman.

Sketches
These drawings, made in 1944, show Issigonis's radiator grille and headlamp ideas for the Mosquito, which would eventually enter production as the Morris Minor.

SUBSTANCE OVER STYLE

Alec Issigonis may have accepted the accolade "great designer," but he would have been horrified to have heard himself called a "stylist." The notion of "style" as propagated in America in the 1950s was the antithesis of Issigonis's approach. He preferred to describe himself as an "ironmonger."

Issigonis would sketch out ideas with striking ease, handing them to draftsmen to turn them into technical drawings. Sometimes the sketches— which bore a striking resemblance to those of Leonardo da Vinci—would be on envelopes or

"When you're designing a new car for production, never, never copy the opposition. "
ALEC ISSIGONIS

FRONT GRILLE AND NOSE, MORRIS MINOR 1949   **MINI 1959**

restaurant napkins. Issigonis's self-belief bordered on arrogance. His dislike of "luxuries" such as radios and seatbelts meant that he simply created his cars without them. He reviled the process of designing by committee, had no time for market research, and was probably the last person able to design a mass-produced car single-handedly.

MINI MAGIC

Sir Leonard Lord gave Issigonis completely free rein when designing BMC's new small car, the Mini. No car encapsulates the Issigonis ethic like this icon of motoring history. Compared to the stodgy dinosaurs of the time, the 1959 Mini was utterly revolutionary. The engine was mounted transversely to save space, powering the front

wheels. More remarkably still, the transmission was positioned under the engine to save space, and it shared the same lubricating oil as the engine. The wheels were tiny, too: at 10 in (25 cm) across, they freed up extra interior space.

Only 10 ft (305 cm) from bumper to bumper, the Mini was a miracle of packaging, able to carry four adults and luggage in relative comfort. Issigonis calculated the smallest space needed for four passengers and became obsessed with saving space in the rest of the design wherever he could. The Mini was the cheapest car on sale at launch, yet it was

quicker and more agile than many of the so-called sports cars of the day. All others eventually adopted the Mini's packaging and front-drive layout for their own small cars. As for "styling," the Mini was never styled as such: form merely followed function.

In parallel with the Mini, Issigonis worked on BMC's Austin/Morris 1100, which became Britain's best-selling car for much of the 1960s. However, the same front-wheel drive format faltered when applied to the larger Austin/Morris 1800.

Issigonis's single-minded and noncollaborative approach meant that he was gradually sidelined at BMC, and he retired in 1971. He remained a consultant to what became British Leyland almost until his death in 1988.

At the drawing board
Photographed in 1959, when he was Technical Director of BMC, Alec Issigonis is shown here in his office at the Longbridge plant in Birmingham.

Sir Alec Issigonis poses with two examples of his world-famous Mini

Great Marques
The Mini Story

Mini is now a fully fledged car brand encompassing coupes, an AWD crossover, and racing models, but at its heart lies a revolutionary small car, based on a design conceived by Sir Alec Issigonis in the mid-1950s. Now owned by BMW, the firm continues to build on the little car's success.

THE MINI WAS THE BRAINCHILD of vehicle design genius Sir Alec Issigonis, who had arrived at Morris Motors in 1932 to work on suspension systems, but went on to create the famous Morris Minor. Despite Morris founder Lord Nuffield hating its styling and likening it to a poached egg, the Minor was a massive sales success, becoming the first British car to attract 1 million buyers, partly because it was spacious in spite of its small size and handled well—things that would also make the Mini popular.

When Morris merged with archrival Austin in 1952 to form the British Motor Corporation (BMC), Issigonis left and went to work for military vehicle and luxury automaker Alvis, but BMC boss Sir Leonard Lord asked him back in 1955. The company was looking to produce a new, small, affordable sedan that was able to compete with the tiny, three-wheeled bubble cars dominating the market at the time—the German-made

Morris Mini Minor, 1959
The appeal of the Mini sprang from the highly sophisticated design it offered at an affordable price. Near-identical cars were initially sold under the Austin and Morris brands.

Messerschmitt and Heinkel. The task was made all the more urgent by soaring gasoline prices and fuel rationing following the 1956 Suez Crisis, so development on the new car was accelerated.

Rumor has it that Issigonis sketched out the basic Mini template on a tablecloth, and, to get the footprint of the 10-ft (3-m) car, he drew a chalk rectangle on the floor around four chairs. The car was known as ADO15, designed to conform to BMC's requirement that it seat four using an existing engine.

Issigonis met this challenge with an innovative car that broke the mold. His creation had a four-cylinder, water-cooled, transverse engine, front-wheel drive, and four-speed transmission. Its fabulously compact dimensions aided handling and saved space—80 percent of which was given over to passengers and their luggage.

Wizardry at work again!

THE **MORRIS** MINI-TRAVELLER

Morris Mini-Traveller brochure, 1960
For once, the BMC advertising department was not overstating the case with their publicity.

Once the Mini project was approved, Issigonis was given a year to rush the car into production. He oversaw everything, including designing the tools to make it. However, after its launch in 1959, the car revealed some teething problems, including leaking floor panel gaps due to the fact that, as Issigonis later admitted, he had designed them the wrong way around. However, the public embraced the car and the Mini was an instant hit.

Issigonis did not like compromise or taking advice. He believed cars needed to be uncomfortable to keep their drivers alert, and that radios were pointless luxuries, and so the Mini did not have space for one. What it did have though, was interior storage in its hollow doors—supposedly the right size for his favorite bottle of gin.

The Mini offered space, expert handling, and economy, became a part of the culture of the "Swinging Sixties," and was driven by everyone from the Beatles to Princess Margaret. It even had a starring role in the 1969 film *The Italian Job* with Michael Caine.

In 1961, racing car legend and automaker John Cooper put his name on performance Minis, and soon Mini Coopers became icons in their own right. The powerful S version had a racing-tuned, 1,071 cc engine, marking it out as a formidable competition car. It went on to dominate the Monte Carlo Rally in the mid-1960s, securing victories in 1964, 1965, and 1967.

The original model started life with rubber cone suspension, which was ditched in 1964 in favor of an interconnected hydrolastic system. When this was abandoned in 1971 due to unreliability and cost, the earlier, rubber suspension returned.

HJO 151

> ## "I'm the last of the **Bugattis,** a man who designed **whole cars.** Now **committees** do the work."
> **SIR ALEC ISSIGONIS, DESIGNER OF THE ORIGINAL MINI ON HIS DESIGN PHILOSOPHY**

Issigonis meanwhile started work on a replacement for the Mini. The 9X was lighter and shorter than its predecessor and looked good on paper, but this car never made it past the prototype. Instead, the Mini, which was still selling well, was given a facelift. Marketed alongside the classic "round front" model, the Clubman version launched in 1969, and featured a squared-off nose and repositioned instruments. The original car was still in production, although Minis now came with roll-down rather than sliding windows. In 1980 another replacement, the Austin Metro, was also sold alongside the Mini, which continued as a modern classic until 2000.

In 2001, Mini's new owner BMW revealed an all-new model. An immediate success, this car was bigger inside and out, had an updated design, and fun driving characteristics, without the noise, hard ride, and upright driving position of the original.

From its inception at the former Morris factory in Cowley, Oxfordshire, the Mini and its adaptations have become enormously popular worldwide. Issigonis's innovative design revolutionized the small car, and it remains one of Britain's best-loved cars.

Mini, 1999 One of the last original models built in the late 1990s shows how little this car changed.

CLASSICS OF THE FUTURE

Cooper S JCW GP This is perhaps the ultimate version of the first, 2001-launched, BMW-era Mini. Only around 2,000 of these cars were built before the Mk 2 arrived. The supercharged 1,600 cc engine pushed this car from 0–60 mph (96 km/h) in 6.5 seconds. It was robust and capable of providing enormous amounts of fun, thanks to its razor-sharp handling.

△ **Mini Cooper S JCW GP 2006**

Origin	UK
Engine	1,600 cc, four-cylinder
Top speed	149 mph (240 km/h)

The sleek, aerodynamic shape with carbon-fiber rear spoiler meant this little car could slice through the air with 218 bhp. Lack of rear seats added to its lightness.

Cooper S Coupe The Coupe was only the second Mini to have a conventional trunk lid (the original had a drop-down version), a styling tweak that provided 9.8 cubic feet (280 liters) of luggage space. This zippy two-seater promised driving enjoyment, particularly the Cooper S and JCW turbocharged versions, which produced 181 bhp and 208 bhp respectively. With a distinctive rear electric spoiler and roomy interior, the Coupe mixed fun and style with lots of practicality.

△ **Mini Cooper S Coupe 2014**

Origin	UK
Engine	1,600 cc, four-cylinder
Top speed	146 mph (235 km/h)

Greener, faster, and quieter than its predecessors, the Coupe did not scrimp on style, with a new "helmet roof," raked front headlights, and spacious interior.

Very Small, Very Cute

Small cars became big news. With more and more people living in cities, and traffic overwhelming the road networks of London, Paris, and Rome, tiny cars were one solution for beating the traffic jams—and their size made parking much easier. There was no real consensus on the best layout for a really small car. Fiat opted to place its engine at the rear, and the Rootes Group followed suit with its Imp, but Alec Issigonis went for front-wheel drive and a transverse engine for the Mini, setting a pattern for small cars everywhere that endures to this day.

Cute and compact
The Nuova 500's interior was tiny, but there was just enough room for two adults in the front and a couple of children behind. The simple dashboard included a speedometer enclosed in a pod, and very little else. The floor-mounted gear lever and small steering wheel gave a feeling of control.

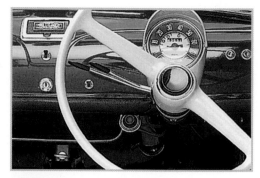

▷ **Fiat 500D 1960**

Origin	Italy
Engine	499.5 cc, straight-two
Top speed	59 mph (95 km/h)

The Nuova 500 of 1957 had a 479 cc engine, but in the 500D of 1960 that grew to 499.5 cc, making the car faster and easier to drive. More than four million 500s and derivatives were produced up to the demise of the Giardiniera wagon in 1977.

Drop-shaped indicators on side

Rounded headlights set flush with body

Wheelbase is a scrawny 72 in (1.82 m)

Drum brakes fitted front and back

Optional full-length rollback roof

Rear-hinged "suicide" doors on early models

New face
With the engine in the back, the 500 had no need for a front grille to inhale air for engine cooling or combustion. Fiat filled the space with a prominent badge instead.

Rear-mounted, two-cylinder engine unit

SIDE VIEW

Front-wheel drive
a first for Renault

**Long-travel
suspension** for
rough surfaces

△ **Renault 4 1961**

Origin France

Engine 747 cc, straight-four

Top speed 75 mph (120 km/h)

Renault's answer to the Citroën 2CV was
bigger, but no less characterful. Launched
alongside the cheaper R3, it was the R4 that
became the star. With its quirky dashboard-
mounted gear lever and lopsided wheelbase
length (its suspension meant it was shorter
on the left), production continued until 1992.

Fiberglass body
has only one door

▷ **Peel P50 1963**

Origin UK

Engine 49 cc, one-cylinder

Top speed 38 mph (61 km/h)

The culmination of the 1950s' drive
toward miniaturization, the world's
smallest production car was a city
runabout for one person and a shopping
bag or suitcase. A P50 was driven
around the top of the Blackpool Tower
in 1963 as a publicity stunt.

Tiny 50 in (1.27 m)
wheelbase

**Separate
trunk** creates a
compact sedan

Dashboard
features
wood veneer

Grille badge
lights up

◁ **Wolseley Hornet MkIII 1968**

Origin UK

Engine 848 cc, straight-four

Top speed 71 mph (114 km/h)

The Hornet added a bigger trunk, imposing
Wolseley grille, and high-class interior
materials to the Mini to make a pocket-sized
premium sedan. The 1963 Mk II had a
bigger engine, and roll-up windows arrived
with the 1966 Mk III. The Riley Elf was a
near-indentical twin.

Folding rear
bench seat

Main luggage space
under the hood

Pop-up rear
window

▷ **Hillman Imp 1963**

Origin UK

Engine 875 cc, straight-four

Top speed 78 mph (126 km/h)

The Rootes Group's small car had
a superb aluminum engine in the
back, and a pop-up rear window for
easy loading. The Imp sold around
half a million units over 13 years,
but was held back by reliability
problems and was hugely outsold
by the Mini.

Amphicar

The most successful contender in an admittedly very small field, this German-built, amphibious vehicle was exported around the world in the 1960s. This oddball car attracted a tiny cult following in the US, where around 3,000 were sold, and survivors are still highly collectible. In 1968, an attempt by two owners to cross the English Channel in a pair proved successful, although to the delight of waiting reporters, one car finished the voyage being towed by the other.

FOR ALMOST AS long as there have been automobiles, people have dreamed of cars that can fly as well as ones capable of taking to the water. German Hans Trippel had experienced amphibious models, both military and civilian, in the 1930s before unveiling one of his own, originally called the Eurocar, in 1961.

A rear-mounted Triumph Herald engine powered the back wheels, giving a top speed of 70 mph (113 km/h). Off-road, the drive switched to a pair of small propellors capable of pushing the open-topped car along at a steady 6.5 knots or about 7 mph (12 km/h). Instead of a rudder, the vehicle steered using the front wheels, a set-up that worked well in calm conditions.

SIDE VIEW

The four-cylinder, 1,147cc engine was made in the UK by Triumph Cars

Emphasizing its suitability for leisure, the car was offered only as a convertible

The car's twin propellors give away its dual-purpose character

Electrically-welded seams ensure the car remains watertight, but corrosion is still a problem

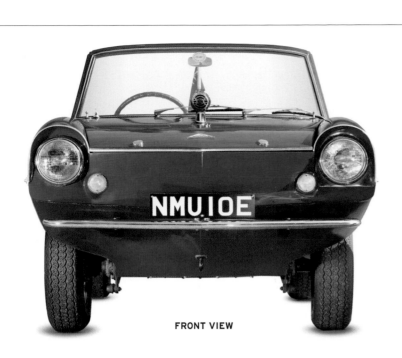

FRONT VIEW

REAR VIEW

Amphicar badge

If the name was not enough of a clue as to the car's identity, the wave pattern at the base of the A-shaped hood badge provided a clear indication of its creator's hope that adventurous owners would dive right in.

SPECIFICATIONS	
Model	Amphicar Model 770, 1961–68
Assembly	Lübeck, Germany
Production	3,878
Construction	Unitary steel construction
Engine	1,147 cc, flat-four
Power output	43 bhp at 4,750 rpm
Transmission	4-speed manual
Suspension	Coil springs front and rear
Brakes	Four-wheel drums
Maximum speed	70 mph (113 km/h) on land, 7 knots on water

NMU10E

Styling

Unlikely to win an award for its looks, the Amphicar's styling was nevertheless clean and distinctive. Small fins at the vehicle's rear looked fashionable and defended the flanks from waves, but the short wheelbase, cutaway arches, and high ground clearance could look a little strange parked alongside more conventional models.

The chassis-less body is made of steel rather than plastic like many of its amphibious descendants

ON THE ROAD

The Amphicar was a descendant of the four-wheel drive Volkswagen Schwimmwagen. Developed from the original VW Beetle, this small, amphibious, Jeep-like vehicle was used by the German army in considerable numbers from 1942 onward.

With financial backing from Deutsche Industrie-Werke, the Amphicar's designer, Hans Trippel, set out to create a vehicle based on the same principles, but intended purely for recreational purposes. The Model 770 was launched at the New York Auto Show in 1961, and despite offering only limited performance compared to most cars or boats, it became the only amphibious civilian passenger vehicle to be mass-produced. Several thousand were manufactured by the Quandt Group, but with no real attempt to develop the idea, production ceased in 1968.

1. Red and green navigation lights   **2.** Chrome cleat used for mooring
3. Externally-mounted horn   **4.** Chrome decorative detailing typical of period
5. Marine-quality hardware   **6.** Registration number repeated on bodywork   **7.** Fins contain rear light cluster   **8.** Controls for water and land use   **9.** Cream-colored throttle controls speed on water   **10.** Snug rear seating for two   **11.** Separate engine powers rear propellors   **12.** Propellors on either side of the car drive it through water

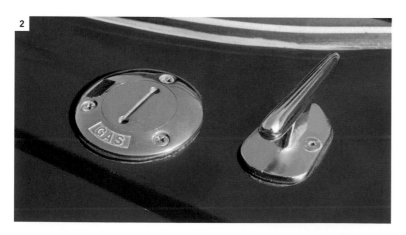

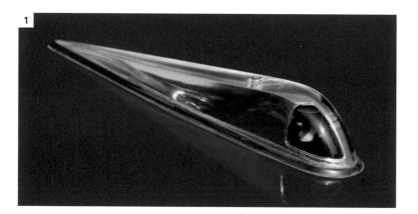

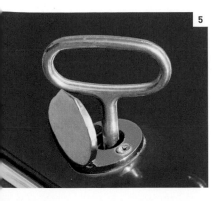

Family Cars

Mass-market cars of the 1960s were often built to template, with a four-cylinder engine at the front, driven wheels at the back, and styling that did little to excite. There were plenty of exceptions, however. The best of the family cars of the era were often clever in their design and thorough in their execution. Manufacturers such as Panhard and Lancia may have been on a downward curve, but there were new automakers to replace them—notably from the growing motor industry of Japan—and model nameplates were born that would remain familiar for decades to come.

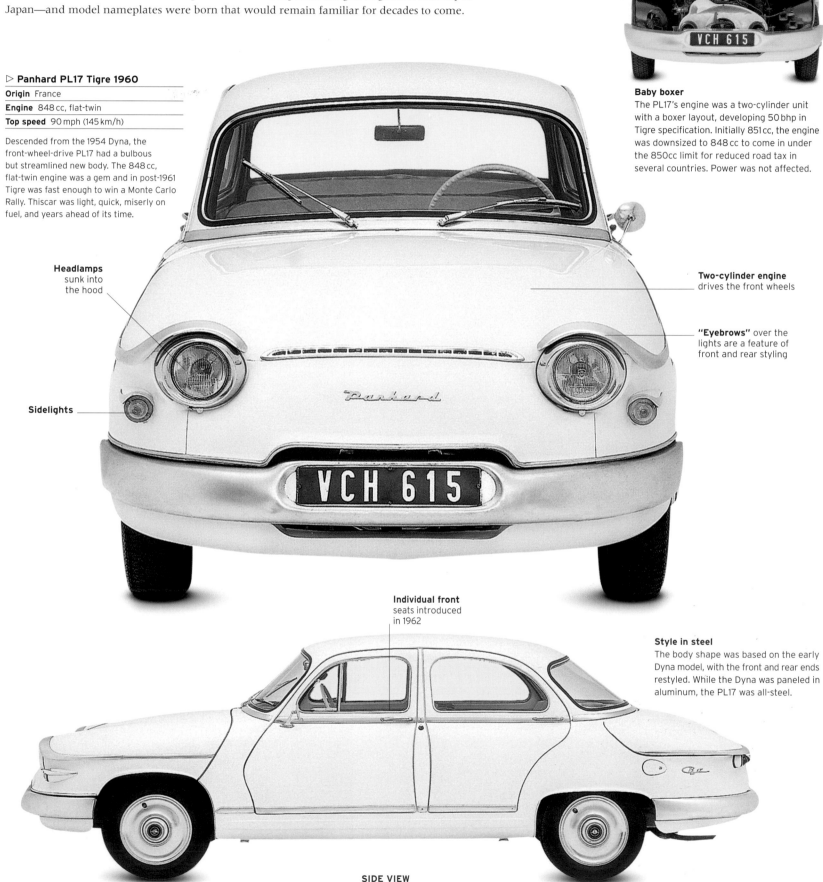

▷ Panhard PL17 Tigre 1960

Origin France

Engine 848 cc, flat-twin

Top speed 90 mph (145 km/h)

Descended from the 1954 Dyna, the front-wheel-drive PL17 had a bulbous but streamlined new body. The 848 cc, flat-twin engine was a gem and in post-1961 Tigre was fast enough to win a Monte Carlo Rally. This car was light, quick, miserly on fuel, and years ahead of its time.

Headlamps sunk into the hood

Sidelights

Baby boxer
The PL17's engine was a two-cylinder unit with a boxer layout, developing 50 bhp in Tigre specification. Initially 851 cc, the engine was downsized to 848 cc to come in under the 850cc limit for reduced road tax in several countries. Power was not affected.

Two-cylinder engine drives the front wheels

"Eyebrows" over the lights are a feature of front and rear styling

Individual front seats introduced in 1962

Style in steel
The body shape was based on the early Dyna model, with the front and rear ends restyled. While the Dyna was paneled in aluminum, the PL17 was all-steel.

SIDE VIEW

▷ Lancia Flavia 1961

Origin Italy

Engine 1,488 cc, flat-four

Top speed 93 mph (150 km/h)

This is the sort of car that made many a British sedan look impossibly old-fashioned. The Flavia had an all-aluminum, flat-four engine, front-wheel drive, dual-circuit servo disc brakes, and radial tires. In 1963 the engine became 1.8 liters, and fuel injection was added in 1965.

Fuel-injected engine available from 1965

Body is angular but stylish

Fully independent front suspension

Aeroflow ventilation introduced in 1965

Four-cylinder engine with a Weber carburetor

Automatic transmission an optional extra

◁ Ford Cortina Mk I GT 1963

Origin UK

Engine 1,498 cc, straight-four

Top speed 94 mph (152 km/h)

While Ford of Germany was innovating with the front-wheel-drive Taunus, the Cortina was clever not for its engineering but because of its focus on what real car buyers wanted. This resolutely conventional car was popular for its low-friction oversquare engine, synchromesh transmission, and spacious body.

Column-mounted gear-shift

Practical hatchback design

▷ Renault 16 1965

Origin France

Engine 1565 cc, straight-four

Top speed 100 mph (161 km/h)

Replacement for the slow-selling Frégate, the 1965 Renault 16 introduced hatchback body styles to mid-range family cars. It had a novel drivetrain, with the transmission at the front and the longitudinal engine behind it. Spacious, versatile, and comfortable, it was in production until 1980.

High roofline creates airy interior

Reliable pushrod engine

Individual bucket seats in front

◁ Toyota Corolla 1966

Origin Japan

Engine 1,077 cc, straight-four

Top speed 85 mph (137 km/h)

The best-selling car in history and the first of an incredibly successful line, the Toyota Corolla was conventional and unremarkable in its design, but was well put together and dependable. The model made an ideal family car, and exports to the US began in 1968.

A lineup of early Chevrolet Corvette production and show cars

Great Marques
The Chevrolet Story

Between 1946 and 1976, Chevrolet was the best-selling brand of car in the US. After it adopted V8 engines in the 1950s, Chevrolets, like the Bel Air, Corvette, and Camaro, became synonymous with speed and power, although the range would always be enormous and all-encompassing.

THE CHEVROLET AROSE FROM the short-lived partnership between Swiss-born racing driver Louis Chevrolet and motor industry tycoon William C. "Billy" Durant, the business brains behind General Motors (GM). In November 1911, the pair cofounded the Chevrolet Motor Car Company, and a year later they unveiled a touring car whose rapid performance and 65-mph (105-km/h) top speed came from a 4.9-liter, six-cylinder engine.

Durant was ousted from GM in 1910 and wanted to build another big corporation. But Chevrolet, whose dashing image the car carried, yearned to make high-performance machines developed with racing know-how. Their differences proved irreconcilable; Durant bought Chevrolet out in 1913, and then took GM over with it.

Louis Chevrolet
The mustachioed Swiss-born racing driver, driving goggles at the ready, is seen here in his favorite environment– behind the wheel.

Chevrolet launched its first V8 car, the Model D, in 1918, but it was actually the robust, four-cylinder Superior of 1925, with its smart disc wheels and lustrous cellulose paint, that sent sales soaring. In 1927, Chevy sales topped a million.

Throughout the 1930s Chevrolet offered an ever-broader roster of cars that, by 1941, encompassed station wagons and power-top convertibles. In 1950, automatic transmission made its Chevrolet debut. Its biggest technical milestone yet came in 1955, when the "small-block" V8 engine arrived—the most successful unit of that configuration ever, with more than 100 million

made. Used in countless Chevrolets, as well as by other GM divisions, the powerful and compact small-block V8 became the bedrock of American hot-rod culture for a generation.

The small V8, additionally, rescued the fortunes of the Chevrolet Corvette sports car. This ground-breaking roadster, introduced in 1953, pioneered fiberglass bodywork on a production car, but its straight-six cylinder engine rendered it a feeble machine. A small-block V8 transplant transformed it into a fiery performer, and the Corvette became an American institution.

In comparison, the Corvair of 1960 was a disaster. Worried by the massive US sales of Germany's Volkswagen, Chevrolet decided to imitate its concept. The Corvair had an air-cooled, flat-six engine, rear-mounted as in the Volkswagen, and clean, modern styling. But it was tail-heavy, leading to some alarming accidents and allegations from consumer groups that Chevrolet had launched the

Chevrolet Camaro RS, 1968
The Camaro was Chevrolet's sporty "pony" car to rival the Ford Mustang, becoming another US icon.

"We've always said that there's a little bit of Corvette in every Chevrolet, and that's still true."

JIM PERKINS, CORVETTE DESIGN MANAGER, SPEAKING AS THE MILLIONTH CORVETTE WAS BUILT IN 1992

car while knowing it had shortcomings. As a result, US automakers had to adopt safety measures such as seatbelts, crumple zones, and airbags.

Throughout the 1960s and 1970s Chevrolets exemplified the American car, whether it was the full-size Impala (first seen in 1958), the compact Chevelle, the stylish Monte Carlo and Camaro coupes, the El Camino pickup, or the 4x4 Blazer. And, like other US automakers, it suffered in the economic crises of the late 1970s and early 1980s. This led to moves such as the launch of the Chevette, Chevrolet's edition of the GM ultra-compact "T Car" in 1975, the Chevy Citation version of GM "X Car" front-wheel-drive platform in 1979, and the 1982 Cavalier spin-off of the GM "J Car." To offer more

Chevrolet Chevelle SS, 1970
With a huge 7.4-liter V8 engine pumping out 380 bhp, this Chevelle was a muscle car totem, perfectly suited to its era.

fuel-efficient vehicles in the 1980s, Chevrolet imported small cars from Isuzu, Toyota, and Suzuki. More recently, to boost its low-emissions credentials, Chevrolet has blazed a trail for plug-in hybrid cars with its Volt.

In 2009, GM filed for bankruptcy and secured a $49.5 billion government bailout. GM shuttered its Oldsmobile, Pontiac, and Saturn divisions, leaving Chevrolet as both its entry-level brand and, via the latest incarnations of the Camaro and Corvette, its high-performance standard-bearer.

CLASSICS OF THE FUTURE

Corvette ZO6 The most noticeable feature of the sixth-generation of America's star-spangled sports car were its headlights, under plastic fairings rather than of the pop-up variety. The ultra-high-performance Z06 had a lightweight alloy chassis, and the hand-built V8 engine was both the biggest-capacity Chevrolet small-block ever and, at 505 bhp, the most powerful non-turbo engine ever seen in a car from General Motors.

△ **Chevrolet Corvette ZO6 2005**

Origin	USA
Engine	7,011 cc, V8
Top speed	207 mph (332 km/h)

Carbonfiber and a balsa wood floor were among the lightweight materials in the Z06 edition of the Corvette C6; it could sprint from 0–60 mph (96 km/h) in 3.8 seconds.

Chevrolet Camaro The first Camaro appeared in 1967 as Chevrolet mounted a credible rival to the best-selling, sporty Ford Mustang. This 2010 model aimed to recapture much of the appeal and aura of the original, both in terms of compact good looks and surging performance. The Camaro actually shared its basic platform with several Holden models from GM's Australian division. In the same year, the Camaro began to be widely exported—a first for this Chevy.

△ **Chevrolet Camaro 2010**

Origin	USA
Engine	6,162 cc, V8
Top speed	155 mph (250 km/h)

The macho new Camaro was available with either six-speed manual or five-speed automatic transmission, the latter with 20 bhp less from the 6.2-liter V8 engine.

Chevrolet Corvette, 1953
The use of lightweight glass-reinforced plastic for the body structure of the Corvette was a car industry first.

Sporty US Coupes

Muscle cars powered onto the American motoring scene in the 1960s, driven by ever-larger and more sophisticated V8 engines. The biggest cars were well over 7.0 liters and produced around 400 bhp. Competitive racers were even more powerful. Ford's 427 cu in big-block and Chrysler's renowned 426 cu in "Street Hemi" were both used in NASCAR racing and NHRA/AHRA drag events. Insurance costs and emissions worries would spell the end for the big engines eventually, but that would be a problem for another decade—during the 1960s it was all about power.

Buick's nailhead
Renowned for their high torque output, Buick's unusually designed "Nailheads" were so named for their small, vertical valves that resembled the tops of nails. The V8 engines often idled poorly due to the race-type cam profiles they used to compensate for the small valves. The Riviera was produced in 401 cu in (6.6-liter) and 425 cu in (7.0-liter) versions, which were the last of the type before Buick replaced them with the all-alloy small block in 1963.

Razor-sharp
front end

Wheelbase
6 in (15 cm) shorter
than a Buick LeSabre

Interior features
four individual
bucket seats

Unpopular exposed
spare-wheel cover

▷ **Chrysler 300F 1960**

Origin USA

Engine 6,768 cc, V8

Top speed 120 mph (193 km/h)

The 300 Series "Letter cars" were Chrysler's most powerful machines—the 300F went to monocoque construction and ram-tuned induction, but still had 1950s-style tailfins. The spare-wheel cover in the trunk lid did not prove popular, however—its appearance was likened to a "toilet seat."

Bold badge
identifies 300F

**Swiveling bucket
seats** are standard

**Distinctive
louvered**
rear pillars

Engine ranges from a 170 cu
in V6 to a 289 cu in V8

◁ **Ford Mustang Fastback
1965**

Origin USA

Engine 4,727 cc, V8

Top speed 116 mph (186 km/h)

Its low base price, combined with a long list of optional extras available, meant more than a million Mustangs were sold in the first two years of production. The styling was so universally loved that it won the Tiffany Award for Excellence in American Design.

▽ Buick Riviera 1964

Origin USA

Engine 6,967 cc, V8

Top speed 115 mph (185 km/h)

GM's design supremo Bill Mitchell wanted "a cross between a Ferrari and a Rolls," and the handsome Riviera was the result. Prodigious, straight-line urge came from a large V8 engine, driving through a two-speed, automatic transmission. Buick capped production at 40,000 a year to maintain exclusivity.

Optional remote-control mirror

Unique proposition
Unlike most GM cars, the Riviera's body and chassis were unique. With a shorter wheelbase and overall length than the contemporary Buick LeSabre, its subtle styling set it apart.

Distinctive oversized headlights

FRONT VIEW

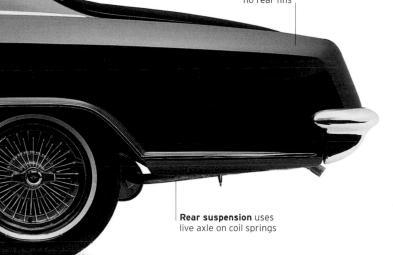

Clean styling with no rear fins

Rear suspension uses live axle on coil springs

Light fantastic
The Riviera shared its suspension layout with others in the Buick stable, but its lighter weight meant that it handled better and was quicker in a straight line, making it more of a driver's car.

REAR VIEW

▷ Oldsmobile Toronado 1967

Origin USA

Engine 6,970 cc in V8

Top speed 135 mph (217 km/h)

An automotive milestone and the most desirable Olds ever, this extraordinary Toronado had a big V8 driving through a unique chain-and-sprocket-drive automatic transmission to the front wheels. Despite its outstanding road manners and speed, it was several years before it won over conservative American car buyers.

V8 engine drives front wheels

Firestone tires designed specially for the Toronado

Roof covered with black vinyl

Bumblebee stripes only available in R/T option pack

Scallop detailing on doors

◁ Dodge Charger 1968

Origin USA

Engine 7,212 cc, V8

Top speed 120 mph (193 km/h)

"Dodge Fever" arrived in 1968 with record sales for the marque, helped by the new, super-smooth "Coke bottle-" styled Charger V8. R/T stood for Road/Track and denoted a specification that included the largest available engine (the famed 426 Hemi was an option), and "bumblebee" stripes.

The Power of Le Mans

Success at Le Mans in France virtually sealed a sports car's status as a true classic. The 24-hour race was a feat of endurance, with cars and drivers under considerable stress. For a car even to complete the arduous, around-the-clock race it had to be tough, efficient, and perform in extreme conditions. Teams of drivers worked in shifts in order to cover the most miles, and were disqualified if they did not cross the finish line after 24 hours.

WINNING QUALITIES

The 1964 24-Hours of Le Mans race was full of triumphs and disappointments. Leading the pack at the start was David Piper's Ferrari 250 LM, followed by Mike Salmon in his Aston Martin DP214, as the cars headed for the first bend. Following a dispute with race organizers, however, the Ferrari was forced to run as a prototype, while the Aston was disqualified after 235 laps and almost 18 hours for an incorrect oil change. Ford established a lap record of 131 mph (211 km/h), but its attempt at glory with its new GT40 was plagued by reliability issues—it would be back, winning four consecutive times with its GT40 from 1966–69. The race was eventually won by Jean Guichet and Nino Vaccarella, driving a Ferrari 275P.

Cars mass at the start of the 1964 24-Hours of Le Mans race, with a team's qualifying time determining its position on the grid.

Luxury Limousines

Royalty, heads of state, captains of industry, and other VIPs were well served by the most luxurious sedans of the 1960s. As was standard in the US car industry, updated versions of American limousines appeared annually. In Europe, however, cars of this class endured for many years almost unchanged. Mercedes-Benz, Rolls-Royce, and Jaguar/Daimler all made super-luxury limos that survived from the 1960s to the 1980s or 1990s. The hand-crafted wood and leather interiors of these cars assured a comfort and class that was fit for royalty: Queen Elizabeth II always ultra-luxury cloth seating for her state limousines.

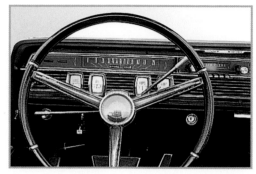

1960s splendour
The Continental's interior was all about opulence and absence of effort. The thin-rimmed steering wheel was power assisted, as were the brakes, while the mirrors had remote adjustment and the transmission was, of course, automatic. Chrome and aluminum trim together with walnut veneers (on some cars) completed a look of elegant sophistication and glamour.

▷ **Lincoln Continental 1961**

Origin	USA
Engine	7,046 cc, V8
Top speed	115 mph (185 km/h)

The Lincoln was one of the most influential and best-built American cars of the 1960s. Not only did it carry a two-year, 24,000-mile (39,000-km) warranty, but also every engine was bench-tested and each car given a 200-category shakedown. President John F. Kennedy was shot in a '61 Lincoln Continental.

Spacious interior

Power-operated door mirrors

Drum brakes on all four wheels with power assistance

"Five-bar" grille introduced in 1963

Massive chrome bumpers fitted front and rear

Suicide doors
Rear-hinged "suicide" doors were adopted to provide better access to the rear seats. They also gave the Continental an air of classic luxury. Both sedans and convertibles had four doors.

Huge V8 engine

Continental script badge hints at high status

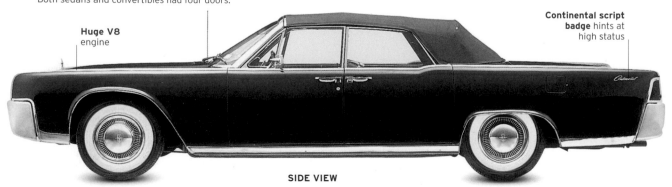

SIDE VIEW

Roof mechanism
Convertible Continentals had a complex electrohydraulic system to raise and lower the roof. The rear deck lid was hinged at the back, and opened up to allow the roof to fold down underneath before closing again.

▷ GAZ Chaika 1959

Origin	USSR
Engine	5,522 cc, V8
Top speed	99 mph (160 km/h)

A Russian-built copy of a 1955 Packard, the Chaika was built until 1981. The car was strictly for party officials, academics, scientists, and other VIPs in the 1960s who were approved by the Soviet government, and was used by Fidel Castro, Nikita Khrushchev, and the KGB.

Windshield visor is a styling throwback

Heavy chrome bumpers and adornments

Silver accents create sense of speed

Exhaust tailpipe exits through rear bumper

Coachbuilt body made of aluminum panels

Flying "B" mascot adorns distinctive Bentley grille

Running gear shared with regular S3 sedan

◁ Bentley S3 Continental 1962

Origin	UK
Engine	6,230 cc, V8
Top speed	113 mph (182 km/h)

The stately Bentley S3 sired the coachbuilt Continental, most of them bodied by H.J. Mulliner in aluminum and with sportier lines. Lighter, and with more power, these cars were quicker than the steel-bodied sedans. The four-door version was known as the Flying Spur.

M100 V8 engine was then Mercedes' biggest V8 to date

Chrome trims adorn lights

▷ Mercedes-Benz 600 1963

Origin	Germany
Engine	6,332 cc, V8
Top speed	130 mph (209 km/h)

From 1963 until as recently as 1981, Mercedes offered this large sedan for VIPs to travel in. The cabin was hushed and the car reached speeds of up to 120 mph (193 km/h). A long-wheelbase version with six doors was available, but only 2,677 Mercedes 600s were built.

Distinctive vertical rear lights

340 bhp V8 engine

◁ Cadillac Calais 1965

Origin	USA
Engine	7,030 cc, V8
Top speed	120 mph (193 km/h)

Every Cadillac was a luxury car; this model featured curved side windows, remote-controlled exterior mirrors, power brakes and steering, and, of course, automatic transmission. The similar but even more lavishly equipped De Ville model added electric windows and electric seats, with air conditioning and leather trim as optional extras.

Shelby Cobra

The AC Ace was transformed into an international star when Texan racing driver Carroll Shelby conceived the idea of installing a large American V8 engine in a small, lightweight, British sports car. Although the Anglo-American hybrid was crude, it was sleek and effective, and enjoyed success both on the track and in the showroom. As such, the car has remained in sporadic production since its first appearance in 1962.

CARROLL SHELBY WAS a past winner of the famed Le Mans 24-hour race, and his inspired creation quickly proved itself in international competition. Today, few contemporaries can touch a Cobra driven by a determined driver. Even Italian rivals Ferrari took a beating, and Argentine car maker Alejandro de Tomaso soon dubbed his own Ford-powered, Italian-bodied GT the Mangusta, or "mongoose," suggesting it was a Cobra-killer.

It never was, and in 1965 the Cobra stormed to victory in the Sports Car World Championship, putting Shelby Automotive and the car on the map for good. AC built the complete body/chassis units, ready for Shelby to install the Ford V8 engines. From the era of the so-called hairy-chested sports car, the Cobra remained the hairiest of them all.

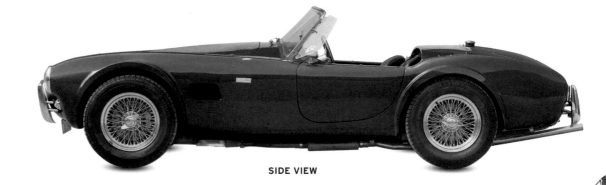

SIDE VIEW

Large, quick-release "Monza" filler cap betrays the model's racing heritage

A simple, stark interior underlines the Cobra's credentials as a driver's machine first and foremost

FRONT VIEW

REAR VIEW

Shelby Cobra badge
This image of a cobra rearing its fierce head was the emblem found on the hood of all the cars sold by Shelby in the US market. AC Cars sold a small number of the cars in the UK, but without the Cobra trademark.

SPECIFICATIONS	
Model	Shelby Cobra, 1962–67
Assembly	Thames Ditton, UK
Production	998
Construction	Aluminum body on a steel frame
Engine	4,267–6,997cc, V8
Power output	260–425 bhp, depending on engine
Transmission	4-speed manual
Suspension	Front and rear coil springs
Brakes	Four-wheel discs
Maximum speed	137–164 mph (220–264 km/h)

V8 engines originally ranged from 4.2 to 7.0 liters, with a Ford 5.0 liter considered sufficiently powerful in recent years

With its classic front-engine, rear-drive configuration, the Cobra boasts near-perfect weight distribution

Styling
The first Cobras shared the elegant simplicity of the lithe Ace. However, particularly in later, larger-engined variants, the shape gained weight visually as wheel arches expanded to accommodate the much larger tires needed to make the most of the car's formidable power.

Original cars features handmade aluminum bodywork; contemporary versions are a lighter composite

ON THE ROAD

If you see a Cobra these days, it is probably an imitation because no car before or since has captivated the attention of replica and kit car-builders quite as much as the Cobra has. The genuine model was a pleasure to behold. However, its tough stance and strong, muscular shape were as redolent of a big cat as any Jaguar—and in the wrong hands likely to be almost as dangerous.

The sleek and aggressive appearance, lightning-quick performance, responsive handling, and simple, stark cockpit underlined the Cobra's competition heritage, and its status as a driver's car first and foremost. Behind the wheel, the interior featured little in the way of creature comforts, but the forward view was spectacular—and once the Ford V8 fired up, who needed a radio?

1. Simple, circular lights **2.** Chrome overriders in place of full bumpers **3.** Wire wheels with "knock off" spinners **4.** Single aerodynamic door mirror **5.** Vents to keep brakes cool **6.** Array of dials show the car's performance **7.** Rev counter—vital when racing **8.** Stubby manual gear lever **9.** AC logo appears on steering wheel hub **10.** Famous British branding prominent on foot pedals **11.** Ford V8 engine—the heart of the Cobra

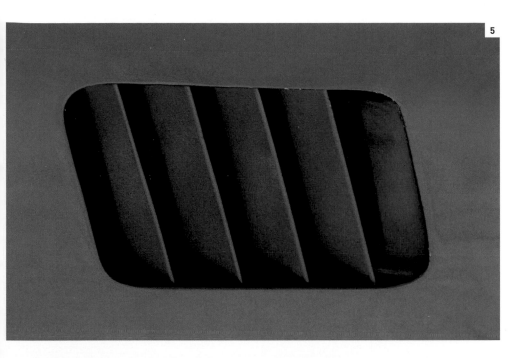

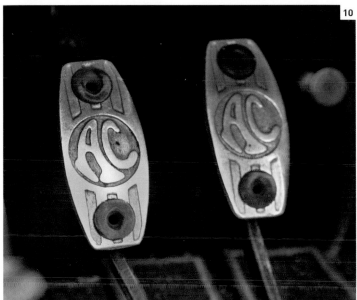

Sports Cars

The 1960s were the heyday of the sports car. Never before had there been such a choice of fast roadsters, with Europe leading the way. Alfa Romeo, MG, and Austin-Healey were the biggest names, and the sports cars they offered blended ruggedness, torquey performance, and traditional rear-drive handling that made them successful in racing and rallying, and popular all over the world. The biggest market was America, which Datsun targeted with its 240Z and successive Z-badged coupes, while the US had a sports car of its own in the shape of the fiberglass Chevrolet Corvette.

Sunvisors double as wind deflectors

Indicator lights behind the wheels on very early cars

Integrated bumpers give a smooth look

▽ Alfa Romeo Spider 1968

Origin Italy

Engine 1,570 cc, straight-four

Top speed 115 mph (185 km/h)

A gorgeous shape and accomplished handling made the Spider one of the best sports cars of its era. Launched in 1966 with a 1.6-liter engine, it was later upgraded to a 1.8-liter and joined by the 1.3-liter Spider Junior. With a five-speed gearbox and all-disc brakes, the Spider made British rivals look antiquated.

Steel body styled and built by Pininfarina

▷ MGB 1962

Origin UK

Engine 1,798 cc, straight-four

Top speed 103 mph (166 km/h)

Britain's bestselling sports car sold more than half a million between 1962 and 1980. Rugged, reliable, and long-legged, it was a perfectly proportioned, truly practical enthusiast's car. Roadsters and a useful three-door GT were available, and there was a rare V8–in GT form only.

"Packaway" hood with plastic rear windows

One-piece monocoque steel body

Hood made from lightweight aluminum

Wire-spoked wheels, a popular optional extra

Bodywork carried over from Sunbeam Alpine

Series II cars have a larger 4,736 cc V8 engine

◁ Sunbeam Tiger 1964

Origin UK

Engine 4,261 cc, V8

Top speed 117 mph (188 km/h)

Rootes commissioned Carroll Shelby, of Cobra fame, to develop its existing Sunbeam Alpine model into the Tiger. The car featured a Ford V8 engine, and uprated chassis and suspension, and was often referred to as "the poor man's Cobra."

Classy interior
The unfussy dashboard featured a painted metal finish, with many functions operated by fingertip. The windshield wipers were controlled by a button on the floor, operated by foot.

Italian Power
First introduced in 1954, and highly advanced for its time, Alfa Romeo's twin-cam engine was the first such mass-produced, water-cooled, all-aluminum unit available. Adapted and enlarged over time, it continued in service until being replaced in 1997.

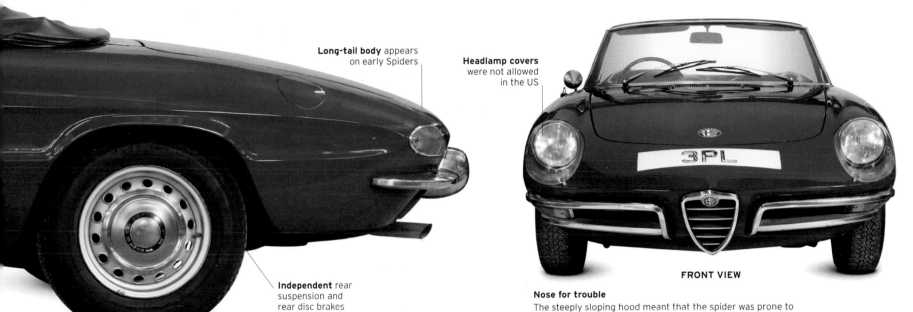

Long-tail body appears on early Spiders

Headlamp covers were not allowed in the US

FRONT VIEW

Independent rear suspension and rear disc brakes

Nose for trouble
The steeply sloping hood meant that the spider was prone to accident damage, as drivers misjudged the length of the car. The slender chrome bumpers gave little protection.

Telescopic steering wheel was an option

Pop-up headlights improved aerodynamics during the daytime

▷ **Chevrolet Corvette Sting Ray 1965**

Origin USA

Engine 5,360 cc, V8

Top speed 147 mph (237 km/h)

A stunning restyle in 1963 turned the Corvette into the Sting Ray. The lightweight, fiberglass body adopted ultramodern lines—a detachable hardtop was an optional extra. The Sting Ray oozed macho potential, which was fulfilled in the ultimate 375 bhp, fuel-injected L84 model. The Sting Ray sold well.

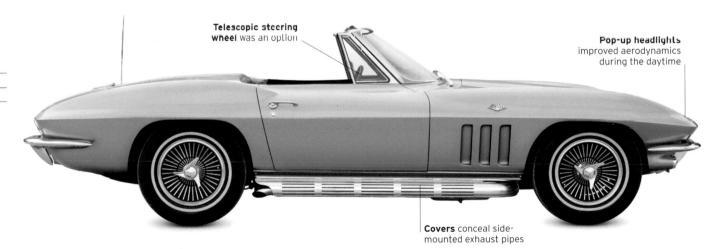

Covers conceal side-mounted exhaust pipes

Some models feature a sideways-facing rear seat

Exterior styling reminiscent of MGB

◁ **Datsun Fairlady 1965**

Origin Japan

Engine 1,595 cc, straight-four

Top speed 100 mph (161 km/h)

Fairlady 1500 of 1961 was a three-seat sports car based on a Nissan Bluebird platform. A 1.6-liter engine was fitted in 1965, and a 2.0-liter became available from 1967. This MGB-beater from Japan finally came to the US in 1969 as the redesigned Datsun 240Z, a pioneer among Japanese sports cars.

Great Marques
The Alfa Romeo Story

Italian marque Alfa Romeo is a fully paid-up member of the classic car establishment. For enthusiasts, it stands for relatively affordable sports cars and roadsters with, in the classic period, exceptional mechanical sophistication and driving pleasure. But Alfa's portfolio also includes sport sedans and historic race winners.

Roberto Bussinello in the Le Mans pits in 1964 with the Alfa Romeo Giulia TZ

THE NAME OF ALFA
ROMEO is an amalgam of the acronym for Anonima Lombarda Fabbrica Automobili (effectively, the Lombardy Car Factory) and the surname of Nicola Romeo. It was Romeo, a businessman who was leading a buyout consortium, who acquired the Milan-based company—originally, in 1906, an offshoot of the French Darracq concern—in 1915, renaming it in 1920.

Back in 1910 the first Alfa, the 24 HP with a 4,082 cc, straight-four cylinder engine, was the work of chief engineer Giuseppe Merosi. It promptly won the 1911 Targa Florio road race around Sicily, hinting at Alfa Romeo's competition penchant, and Merosi used racing-derived knowledge to develop the double-overhead-camshaft engine design.

The first car fully titled an Alfa Romeo was the G1 of 1920, a 6.3-liter straight-six in which great names such as Enzo Ferrari and Giuseppe Campari stormed racing grids. In 1923, the company's new chief engineer Vittorio Jano began work on a new straight-eight engine that was put into the P2 Grand Prix car. This swept the board in 1925, winning the first Grand Prix World Championship.

Alfa Romeo Giulietta, 1955
Under Italian state ownership after 1945, Alfa Romeo was obliged to make a sensible family car, but the Giulietta still possessed a defiantly sporting character.

In 1938, Alfa Romeo won the Mille Miglia race for the 10th time since 1928.

The other Jano-designed cars—including the P3, 6C 1750, and 8C 2300—enabled Alfa Romeo to dominate all the major theaters of motorsport, including Grands Prix and the Le Mans 24-Hours in France. Coachbuilders such as Pinin Farina (renamed Pininfarina in 1960) and Touring crafted beautiful bodies on Alfa Romeo chassis such as the 8C 2900B of 1938, in the process creating some of the most desirable road cars of the era.

After World War II, and now under Italian state ownership, the sporting exuberance of Alfa's offerings was toned down, and the firm began to concentrate on the 1900 and Giulia family sedans. However, these cars still had sporting, twin-camshaft engines, and by 1954 the delightful Giulia Spider and Sprint coupe were on sale. The highly aerodynamic Giulia Super sedan of 1962, with its five-speed transmission, brought its own spin-offs, the beautiful Duetto Spider (Pininfarina) and GT Junior/GTV (Bertone) with engines from 1.3 to 2.0 liters. It was not until 1993 that the last of these scintillating sports cars bowed out.

Advertising the Alfa Romeo Giulietta

"When I see an Alfa Romeo, I lift my hat."

HENRY FORD, TALKING TO ALFA ROMEO PRESIDENT UGO GOBBATO ON HIS VISIT TO THE US IN 1939

The company began to take things in a completely new direction in 1971 with the advent of the Alfasud. This all-new, front-wheel-drive family car set new benchmarks for handling (only surpassed by the VW Golf GTI in 1975), and provided work for a brand-new factory in Naples (hence, Alfa Sud, or Alfa South). At the other end of the scale was the 1970 Montreal, a V8-engined supercar with striking Bertone lines, while the 1972 Alfetta gave rise to a host of derivatives including the Giulietta, Alfa 6, and eventually the 75.

Back on the track, Alfa Romeo had retired from Formula 1 after 1951,

Alfa Romeo Montreal 1970
Originally a show car for Expo 67 in Canada, hence its name, the Montreal offered a V8 racing-derived engine in its Bertone-built body.

but from the 1960s it competed in the World Sportscar Championship, triumphing in 1975 and 1977. Also from the early 1960s, tuned Alfa Romeo road cars began to appear in rallying, touring car, and GT series, clinching a mass of victories.

The company struggled to make money, and Fiat stepped in in 1986. Cost savings were made by sharing components with other Fiat Group cars, but there was a return to sport sedan form in 1998 with the 156. It grabbed the European Car Of The Year award, as did the 147 of 2001. The new Spider and GTV of 1995 were well received, and highlights since then have included the sporty Brera, the compact MiTo, and the new Giulietta in 2010, the marque's centenary year.

In the 1950s, Alfa Romeo assembled the Renault Dauphine for the Italian market, and in the 1980s put its engines into a locally-made Nissan Cherry. Neither venture was lauded by fans of the marque.

Alfa Romeo Giulietta Spider, 1955
This delightful sports car, styled and built by Pininfarina, was popular in Europe and the US; the responsive engine was a 1.3-liter twin-cam.

CLASSICS OF THE FUTURE

SZ This limited edition GT was a collaboration between Fiat's styling center, where the original idea came from, Alfa Romeo, and coachbuilder Zagato, the last of which looked after construction of the 1,035 examples that were built between 1989 and 1991. Its codename was ES 30. Unlike earlier special Zagato Alfas, the body was of thermoplastics, rather than hand-beaten aluminum. There was only one color choice: red with a gray roof and a tan leather interior.

△ **Alfa Romeo SZ, 1989**

Origin	Italy
Engine	2,959 cc V6-cylinder
Top speed	152 mph (244 km/h)

The SZ took the wonderful 210 bhp, Alfa Romeo V6 engine from the 75 sedan and put it into this strangely attractive coupé.

4C The entire 2014 allocation of the delectable 4C sold out within a few days. The car's lightweight construction is built around a carbon-fiber chassis tub, aluminum subframes front and back, and tightly wrapped composite body panels; it weighs just 0.88 tons (895 kg). Its mid-mounted power unit endows it with a 0–62 mph (100 km/h) acceleration time of 4.5 seconds, and yet still returns 41 mpg (14.7 km/l). The steering is designed to give racing car-like feedback.

△ **Alfa Romeo 4C, 2013**

Origin	Italy
Engine	1,742 cc, straight-four
Top speed	160 mph (258 km/h)

Alfa Romeo stunned enthusiasts with this two-seat sports car. Just 1,000 a year would be built, by Maserati.

Baby GT Cars

While American muscle cars were trying to prove once and for all that there really was no substitute for cubic inches, in Europe there were mainstream and specialty automakers that were trying to deliver speed through efficiency and light weight. The cars were fast, fun, and better suited to roads that were narrower and more winding than most of the roads Stateside. Sadly many were cottage-industry projects that fizzled out early, like Gilbern in the UK, although a few succeeded, such as Renault-Alpine, and established enduring reputations.

Styled for purpose
Porsche interiors were functional rather than luxurious. The 356B's simple painted dashboard panel put three essential instruments right in front of the driver, the speedometer, the tachometer, and a combination oil temperature/fuel level gauge. The tachometer was in the center, a characteristic Porsche carried over to the 911. The pedals were floor-hinged, and the gear lever mounted on the floor.

▷ **Porsche 356B 1962**

Origin	Germany
Engine	1,582 cc, flat-four
Top speed	110 mph (177 km/h)

Porsche started making VW-based sports cars in 1948. By the 1960s its 356 had matured into a fast, stylish machine with more power, more equipment, and greater comfort– although its handling could still be unpredictable. The 356 continued until 1963, when the 911 took over.

Curved windshield introduced in 1955

Drum brakes all around

Bigger bumper with more substantial guards0

Volkswagen origins
Ferdinand Porsche had been in charge of the Volkswagen design, and 356 was based on the Volkswagen platform. As time went on it became more specialized, using fewer and fewer Volkswagen parts.

Folding roof stored under tonneau

Headlights raised from previous model to meet US requirements

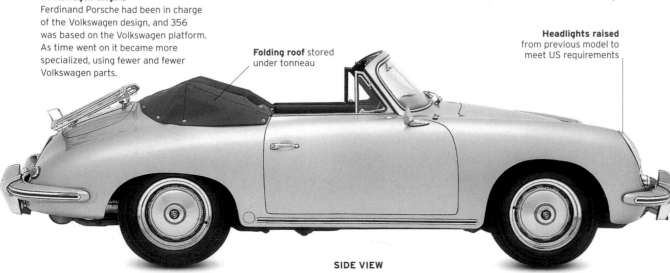

SIDE VIEW

Flat-four family
The 356B was available with the 1.6-liter 616-series engine in 1600, Super 90, and 1600S models, the 1.6-liter 692-series in the 1600 Carrera GS, and the 2.0-liter 587-series four-cam engine in the Carrera 2 GS. All were flat-four boxer engines.

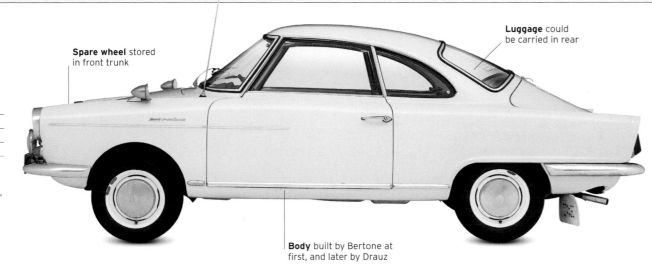

Spare wheel stored
in front trunk

Luggage could
be carried in rear

Body built by Bertone at
first, and later by Drauz

▷ NSU Sport Prinz 1959

Origin Germany

Engine 598 cc, straight-two

Top speed 76 mph (122 km/h)

Italian styling house Bertone worked
wonders to create this winsome, little
coupe for the bravely independent NSU,
based on its Prinz sedan. A light, but
tiny, two-cylinder engine meant it was
never all that fast. Even so, more than
20,000 were sold in the 1960s.

Lightweight
fiber glass body

Engine range
includes MG Midget,
MGA, and MGB units

Chassis made from
square steel tubes

◁ Gilbern GT 1959

Origin UK

Engine 1,622 cc, straight-four

Top speed 100 mph (161 km/h)

Wales's only successful car company used a
tubular steel chassis, attractive fiberglass body,
and high-quality interiors to sell this handsome
MGA and MGB-powered coupe. The Genie model
and the Invader model followed, both with Ford
V6 power. Total production of all types amounted
to only just over 1,000 cars.

Only two seats in interior

Heated rear
windshield

▷ Renault-Alpine A110 Berlinette 1963

Origin France

Engine 1108 cc, straight-four

Top speed 132 mph (212 km/h)

Jean Rédélé was a rally driver and
Renault dealer, and built his own cars
from 1956 using Renault mechanicals
inside lightweight, fiberglass bodies.
The A110 used Renault 8 or 16 engines
and was fast but hard to handle.
It made a great rally car.

Low-drag
fiberglass
body

Wraparound window
opens on later models

◁ Saab Sonett 1966

Origin Sweden

Engine 1,498 cc, V4

Top speed 100 mph (161 km/h)

Front-wheel drive, a freewheel for coasting, and a
column shifter were unusual features derived from
the Sonett's sedan parent. The first 258 built had a
peppy, three-cylinder, two-stroke engine, but most
contained larger Ford V4 engines. The neat,
low-drag body in fiberglass gained concealed
headlights on the 1970 Sonett III.

Open-Air Style

Open-top cars were a hit with pleasure-seeking motorists in the 1960s, and there was a wide range to choose from. Even drivers with limited budgets were well catered to, with beach cars like the Mini Moke, and pint-sized roadsters, such as the Austin-Healey Sprite and MG Midget, and their Italian cousin, the Innocenti Spider. Further down the line there were stylish two- and four-seat convertibles built for touring or for more sporting pursuits. Big or small, slow or fast, they all offered the extra dose of excitement that only fresh-air motoring can deliver.

FRONT VIEW

REAR VIEW

Weight-saving, fiberglass trunk lid

Sleek and space-saving
Unlike many contemporary cars, the DS did not have a conventional radiator grille. Instead it featured low-set air intakes positioned below the hood, giving it a sleek, aerodynamic profile.

Stability and structure
To provide structural rigidity, convertible DS models featured a reinforced frame beneath the body panels. Also, in order to combat understeer, the rear track was narrower than the front.

Hood can unexpectedly open when driving

Cramped rear child seat

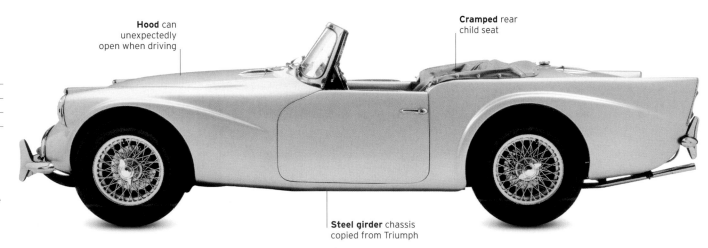

▷ **Daimler SP250 1959**

Origin UK

Engine 2,548 cc, V8

Top speed 120 mph (193 km/h)

The maker of staid luxury sedans had a new aluminum V8, and it was used in a fiberglass-bodied sports car with a chassis copied from Triumph. When Jaguar bought Daimler in 1960, the SP250 was rendered superfluous by the E-type, and production ended in 1964.

Steel girder chassis copied from Triumph

Detachable hardtop available

Body designed to suit Italian tastes

◁ **Innocenti Spider 1961**

Origin Italy

Engine 948 cc, straight-four

Top speed 86 mph (138 km/h)

Innocenti of Milan commissioned Ghia to style a more upmarket body to go with the running gear of the British Austin-Healey Sprite. New features that the British car lacked included a trunk lid, wind-up windows, and a heater. An S version with 1,098 cc engine, front disc brakes, and revised suspension was available from 1963.

▽ **Citroën DS 21 Decapotable 1961**

Origin France

Engine 2,175 cc, straight-four

Top speed 106 mph (171 km/h)

When launched in 1955, the DS was the most advanced car in the world, featuring a hydropneumatic system that powered the brakes, steering, automatic clutch, and its unique self-leveling suspension. A sleek convertible model was introduced in 1958, and with just over 1,000 sold, they are highly desirable classics.

Safe and stylish
The car's interior design reflected the futuristic appearance of the exterior, and brought all major controls within easy reach of the driver. The single-spoke steering wheel protected the driver in the event of a crash, and became a Citroën hallmark.

Re-styled front gave the DS a shark-like nose

Chrome-plated stone guard protects bodywork

Hydropneumatic suspension keeps the ride-height constant, even under load

Roof can be totally removed

Engine comes from standard Mini

◁ **Mini Moke 1964**

Origin UK

Engine 848 cc, straight-four

Top speed 84 mph (135 km/h)

The Mini Moke was originally designed for a serious purpose—as an off-road, light reconnaissance vehicle for the British Army. It eventually found popularity as a "fun" car, and was successful as a beach car, popular in Australia and Portugal. A twin-engined version with four-wheel drive was also developed.

Cabin offers a wealth of equipment

Powered hood was an option

▷ **Chevrolet Corvair Monza 1965**

Origin USA

Engine 2,687 cc, flat-six

Top speed 90 mph (145 km/h)

The rear-mounted aluminum engine and curious handling of the 1960 Corvair were too much for most Americans, but enthusiasts loved it. The second generation car of 1965 made useful improvements, but Corvair was too expensive to build and faced stiff competition from Ford's Mustang and Chevrolet's own Camaro.

National French Icons

There can be few individual cars so intrinsically linked to a country's culture than France's Citroën DS. Introduced in 1955, the DS instantly symbolized a technical adventurousness and space-age modernity that everyone could reasonably aspire to. Naturally, France's leaders were quick to adopt the car as official transport. President Charles de Gaulle is seen here being greeted by an enthusiastic French public in 1964.

LIFE-SAVING TECHNOLOGY

In 1964, De Gaulle's protection was still a major concern following the failed attempt on his life made two years previously—hence the presence of bodyguards surrounding his car. Algerian war veteran Jean-Marie Bastien-Thiry had fired on the presidential motorcade as it rolled through the Parisian suburb of Petit-Clamart on August 22. De Gaulle's car was peppered with bullets that also burst its tires. Although the car was not armored, the president was unhurt, and the damaged vehicle was still able, thanks to its hydropneumatic suspension and steering, to flee the scene safely and swiftly. The car was, of course, a Citroën DS. The failed assassination was accurately recreated for the 1973 film *The Day Of The Jackal*.

French President Charles de Gaulle on an official visit to Picardy in June 1964, being transported in a Citroën DS.

Fast Sports Tourers

When it came to engines, there were two options at the top end of the sports tourer spectrum. One of these was adopted by aristocratic names such as Bentley and Aston Martin, which built their own smooth and powerful six-cylinder and V8 engines to go into cars featuring traditional or Italian-inspired styling. The alternative approach, typified by Jensen, was to drop a big, understressed, American V8 into a stylish body. This delivered effortlessly glamorous motoring without the development costs necessary for a custom power unit. Both methods worked, and they produced some of the swiftest and most dazzling cars of the era.

Handcrafted cockpit
As a long-distance tourer, the interior was designed for comfort, with four large, leather, armchair-like seats and plush Wilton carpets. It was, however, a driver's car, with a beautifully crafted dashboard. The veneer-clad center console featured a wealth of dials and toggle switches, that some commentators compared to the flight deck of a small aircraft.

▷ **Jensen Interceptor 1966**

Origin	UK
Engine	6,276 cc, V8
Top speed	135 mph (217 km/h)

A glamorous cocktail of an Italian-styled body, American V8 engine, and genteel British craftsmanship, the Interceptor became *the* car for the successful swingers of the late 1960s and 1970s. It was handsome, fashionable, and formidably fast, and derived pioneering features from the Jensen FF, including four-wheel drive and anti lock braking.

Cabin supremely comfortable on long journeys

Chrysler V8 engine

Independent front suspension uses coil springs

Bodywork by Italian styling house Carrozzeria Touring

SIDE VIEW

Four-wheel drive wonder
The Jensen FF was launched with the Interceptor in 1966 and looked similar, though both the chassis and body were different. Underneath it had Ferguson four-wheel drive, and Dunlop Maxaret anti-lock braking, giving it extraordinary road manners for its era.

Stylish lines
by Mercedes designer Paul Bracq

Air suspension both front and back

◁ **Mercedes-Benz 300SE 1962**

Origin Germany

Engine 2996 cc, straight-six

Top speed 124 mph (200 km/h)

One of Germany's finest cars of the early 1960s, the 300SE had a race-proven, fuel-injected, six-cylinder engine, air suspension, and disc brakes to justify the substantial price jump from the 220SE. The sophisticated coupe or convertible body penned by Paul Bracq was virtually unchanged until 1971.

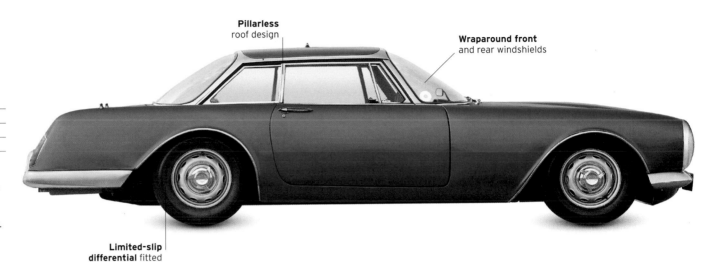

Pillarless
roof design

Wraparound front
and rear windshields

▷ **Facel Vega Facel II 1962**

Origin France

Engine 6,286 cc, V8

Top speed 133 mph (214 km/h)

Big, bold, unquestionably French, and powered by a Chrysler V8, the Facel II was firmly in the Grand Routier tradition. Sadly it was Facel's last gasp—the company shut its doors for good following production of only 180 of these expensive, exclusive cars.

Limited-slip differential fitted on later models

Supercharged V8
engine available on some models

Lightweight
fiberglass body

Front disc brakes are unusual for the time

Live axle located by trailing links

◁ **Studebaker Avanti 1962**

Origin USA

Engine 4,736 cc, V8

Top speed 120 mph (193 km/h)

The brainchild of new Studebaker boss Sherwood Egbert, the Avanti had a Raymond Loewy-styled, fiberglass sports car body married to the chassis of the compact Lark. Studebaker struggled to build it and ended production in 1963, but it was revived as the Avanti II with Chevrolet V8 power.

Bodywork designed
by Giorgetto Giugiaro

Chevrolet V8
engine

▷ **Gordon-Keeble 1964**

Origin UK

Engine 5,395 cc, V8

Top speed 136 mph (219 km/h)

British engineering, a powerful American V8 engine, and delicately beautiful Italian styling by Bertone went into creating this excellent GT. Parts supply problems hampered production and caused financial woes, eventually sinking the company. Just 100 Gordon-Keebles were built, and happily almost all of them survive.

The Maserati brothers with employees and one of their sport cars in 1930

Great Marques
The Maserati Story

The sonorous name of Maserati was, for its first two decades, chiefly associated with pure racing cars. In the 1960s, however, its various GT and luxury sedan models established the marque in the same sphere as Ferrari, Aston Martin, and Porsche. Nevertheless, plenty of ups and downs have been endured.

FIVE MASERATI BROTHERS were involved with the car company that bore their famous family name, but it was Alfieri, Ettore, and Ernesto together who first opened an engineering workshop in Bologna on December 1, 1914; the other two brothers, Bindo and Carlo, would later join them.

Within a very short time, Società Anonima Officine Alfieri Maserati had established an excellent reputation, which led to its building 2-liter Grand Prix cars for the Diatto company, and moving to bigger premises in 1919. The year 1926 proved a turning point for Maserati, which unveiled its own car, the Tipo 26. Alfieri Maserati promptly drove it to its first race victory, a class win on the 1926 Targa Florio. Simultaneously, Maserati adopted a trident logo inspired by the statue of Neptune in the fountain at the center of Bologna.

Maserati was constantly in the public eye, none more so than with the 16-cylinder V4 model that set a speed record over 6 miles (10 km) of 152 mph (245 km/h) in September 1929, driven by Baconin Borzacchini—a feat unsurpassed until 1937. In 1939 and 1940, the American Wilbur Shaw drove Maseratis to win the Indianapolis 500-mile (804-km) race in the US. In the mean time, company driving force Alfieri Maserati died in 1932, and five years later the company was bought by industrialist Adolfo Orsi, and soon after moved its premises to Modena.

In 1947, the company

Poster for 1981 *Fangio* documentary film

launched its A6 series of single-seater, sport-racing, and roadgoing sports cars, and in 1953 it entered Formula 1. Juan Manuel Fangio won the Italian Grand Prix that year—the first of 69

Maserati Formula 1 race entries (including nine wins) that gave Fangio two of his five driver World Championships, and brought two constructors' World Championships to Maserati.

However, top-level motorsports almost bankrupted the company. In 1958, with it seeming unlikely the marque could improve on its on-track achievement, the factory racing department was closed and attention turned to a new road car, the sleek and powerful 3500GT, to capitalize on the mystique of the Maserati name.

A year later, Maserati introduced the 5000GT supercar, built in strictly limited numbers for royalty and film stars. In 1963, the company launched not only the compact and stylish Mistral coupe but also the Quattroporte four-door sedan with a 4.7-liter V8 engine. It became, overnight, the world's fastest four-door sedan.

The Ghibli GT of 1966 was, at 170 mph (274 km/h), one of the fastest cars on the planet, and in 1971 Maserati followed the trend for mid-engined two-seaters with the V8 Bora, and the related six-cylinder Merak.

Citroën bought Maserati in 1968, and the Italian company built the 2.7-liter V6 engine for the Citroën SM. However, the partnership fell apart after less than a decade when Citroën hit bankruptcy and, in order to avert Maserati's liquidation, the Italian government and Alejandro de Tomaso stepped in in 1975 to save the day.

Production of the Quattroporte, by now a complex front-wheel drive car,

Maserati 450S
At the Le Mans 24-Hour race in June 1957, Juan Manuel Fangio pulls down his goggles during practice in the fearsome sports-racer. It was the driver's last appearance at Le Mans.

was axed and all effort poured into the Biturbo, a sport sedan in the BMW 3-Series mold but with a twin-turbo Maserati V6 engine. Intended as a more affordable, semi-mass-produced car, it was launched in 1981.

A huge variety of spin-off models were created from the Biturbo, including the new Ghibli and Shamal. In 1993, Fiat purchased Maserati and in 2004 began to expand Maserati's horizons

Maserati Bora, 1971
This was Maserati's contribution to the expanding world of mid-engined supercars, with a V8 engine mounted amidships. Its sister model, the Merak, had V6 engines.

> ## "**Cornering power** is at least as **breathtaking,** on first acquaintance, as the performance."
> **MOTOR SPORT MAGAZINE ON THE MASERATI BORA IN APRIL 1974**

as a sister marque to Alfa Romeo. The well-received 3200GT of 1998 became the Coupe and Spyder in 2002, and then an all-new Quattroporte luxury sedan joined them in 2003. In 2004, Maserati returned to factory-initiated motor racing with its fierce MC12 endurance GT. Team drivers Andrea Bertolini and Mika Salo delivered its first race win in September. In 2010, Andrea Bertolini and the Maserati MC12 were both declared FIA GT world champions.

The Pininfarina-designed GranTurismo arrived in 2007, followed two years later by the GranCabrio. In 2013, Quattroporte was followed by the Maserati Ghibli midsize executive sedan.

Maserati Mistral Spider, 1963
This was one of the most desirable Maseratis of the 1960s, especially coveted in this rare convertible form.

CLASSICS OF THE FUTURE

Spyder This car is sometimes referred to as the 4200GT type, to differentiate it from the earlier 3200GT model that was offered as a coupe only. The 4200GT Coupe was a four-seater, but there were only two seats in the Spyder; both cars sported handsome styling by Italdesign. The engine, indeed the whole drivetrain, was Ferrari-based, and there was a choice between six-speed regular manual transmission or an automated manual with F1-style steering-wheel paddles.

△ **Maserati Spyder 2001**

Origin	Italy
Engine	4,244 cc, V8
Top speed	176 mph (283 km/h)

Based on a shortened coupe floorplan, the Spyder was the Maserati that heralded the marque's return to the US market.

MC12 The basis for the MC12 was the Ferrari Enzo, with which it shared the mid-mounted V12 engine, and semi-automatic, six-speed transmission sending power to the rear wheels. It was a big car, and hardly practical because it lacked a rear window, spare tire, trunk space, and audio system, but the visceral thrills were huge. This was a true racing car for the road, even though many who tested it found it remarkably easy and safe to drive fast.

△ **Maserati MC12 2004**

Origin	Italy
Engine	5,998 cc, V12
Top speed	205 mph (330 km/h)

As well as the 12 racing versions that re-established Maserati as a racetrack force, the company also built 50 road car versions.

Powerful Grand Tourers

The fastest cars of the 1960s were purpose-built road machines rather than the thinly veiled racers that had gone before. Although some of them did eventually hit the tracks in stripped-down, tuned-up form, the real purpose of these cars was to provide rapid motoring and raw thrills for their drivers rather than to win races, and as the decade wore on they became further and further removed from their competition cousins. That was no bad thing: this was an era that produced some of the most spectacular and sought-after fast cars ever made.

▽ **Lamborghini Miura 1966**

Origin Italy

Engine 3,929 cc, V12

Top speed 175 mph (281 km/h)

Lamborghini invented the supercar with the Miura, launched at the 1966 Geneva Motor Show. Staggeringly beautiful, technically pre-eminent, and unbelievably quick, it was created by a triumvirate of engineering wizards all still in their twenties. Outrageously exotic colors completed a package that perfectly mirrored the mid-1960s.

Rear bodywork lifts as one piece for engine access

Very low cabin has space for two

Sills and wheels painted silver on most Miuras (gold on the SV)

Body shape is one of Giugiaro's finest designs

Old-fashioned, leaf-sprung live axle

◁ **Maserati Ghibli 1967**

Origin Italy

Engine 4,719 cc, V8

Top speed 165 mph (266 km/h)

Maserati's magnificent four-cam, V8 engine enabled this luxurious coupe to perform like a supercar. The car's perfectly proportioned fastback body was styled by Giorgetto Giugiaro at Ghia of Italy, and the coupe was joined later by an impossibly stylish convertible.

▷ **Ferrari 275GTB 1965**

Origin Italy

Engine 3,286 cc, V12

Top speed 153 mph (246 km/h)

Perfectly proportioned styling by Pininfarina, a five-speed gearbox, and all-independent suspension showed that Ferrari was moving with the times. The six-carburetor versions did 165 mph (266 km/h). The Long-nose Series 2 was available from 1965, and an even faster 275GTB/4 with four-cam engine and many other improvements from 1966.

Body built by Ferrari's regular collaborator, Scaglietti

Long-nose front end introduced in 1965

Spoiler helps to reduce rear end lift at speed

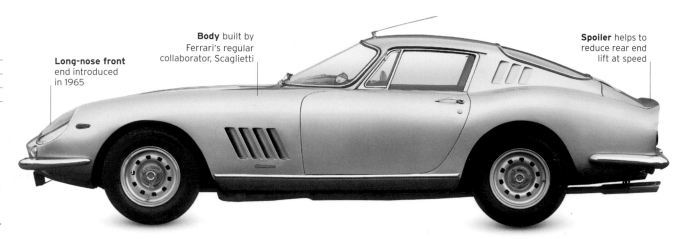

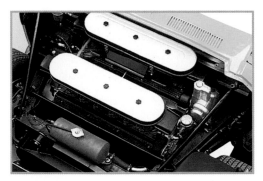

Italian Powerhouse
To allow for a shorter, more nimble wheelbase, the V12 engine was mounted transversely. The gearbox, final drive, and crankcase were all cast in one piece to also save space.

FRONT VIEW

Steel style
Miura had a steel superstructure and steel doors. The front and rear closing panels were made of aluminum alloy. All the production Miuras were fixed-roof coupes, although Bertone made a single Miura Roadster. A few more cars have since been converted.

Fuel filler hidden under the grille

Engine bay louvres allow hot air out

Flared fenders
The Miura SV had wider rear wheels, and the rear fenders were extended outward to suit. The rear lights were also updated, and there was "SV" badging. Under the skin the engine had new carburetors and modified valve timing to liberate an extra 15 bhp, and the last cars had separate gearbox/engine lubrication.

REAR VIEW

Center-lock alloy wheels are standard

Headlamps pop up and there are driving lights inside glass cowls

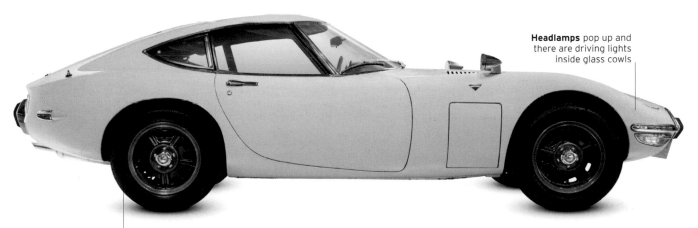

◁ **Toyota 2000GT 1966**

Origin	Japan
Engine	1,988 cc, straight-six
Top speed	128 mph (206 km/h)

A pretty coupe with performance and equipment to match its good looks, this model remained rare (only 337 built) because it was made before Toyota was ready to tackle big export markets. It proved, however, that Japanese designs could now rival the best in the world.

Independent suspension by coil springs all around

Fixed metal top on GT, but GTS had a lift-out roof panel

Pininfarina-styled body made of steel

Low, sloping front possible due to mid-engine layout

▷ **Dino 246 GT 1969**

Origin	Italy
Engine	2,418 cc, V6
Top speed	148 mph (238 km/h)

Ferrari's Porsche 911 competitor, the Dino, was beautiful, fast, and handled superbly. The first 206 was a 2.0 liter, but the 246 of 1969 had 2.4 liters and 195 bhp. Dino was a marque in its own right, so these cars never wore Ferrari badges when new.

Executive Sedans

The styling excesses of the 1950s gave way to a more conservative, more tasteful era in the 1960s. The change was most noticeable in premium sedans, with crisp and well-honed influences from Italian designers taking over from the brash styles pioneered in America. The vehicles were gradually becoming more technically sophisticated, too. Disc brakes, which had been the preserve of racing cars just a few years earlier, were starting to become a standard feature. Live axles and leaf springs were giving way to independent suspension using coil springs. Under the hoods, overhead-cam engines were now common.

Old-fashioned appeal
In contrast to the very modern interior of the smaller P6 model, the P5B offered more traditional appointments with a wooden dashboard, leather trim, and chrome highlights. A picnic tray slid out from under the dash, and hid a toolkit inside.

▷ **Rover 3.5-liter P5B 1967**

Origin	UK
Engine	3,528 cc, V8
Top speed	108 mph (174 km/h)

Rover's successful P5 started with a 3-liter, six-cylinder engine but acquired a smooth, gutsy V8 in 1967. This coupe version still had four doors, but with a lower roofline. More than 20,000 were made by the end of production in 1973.

Rover's first unibody construction

Auxiliary lamps standard on V8 model

Rostyle wheels identify P5B

American power
Rover bought the design for this all-alloy V8 engine from Buick when the General Motors company switched to thin-walled, iron-block engines. Rover fitted twin SU carburetors that were much better-suited to European driving conditions.

Ministerial favorite
The P5B was regularly employed as an official car by UK government ministers. Prime Minister Margaret Thatcher used one long after more modern Rovers were available.

Traditional wooden dashboard

Coupe has a lower, curving roofline

SIDE VIEW

Fins are an American touch

Wing mirrors rise from car body

◁ **Ford Zephyr 6 Mk III 1962**

Origin UK

Engine 2,553 cc, straight-six

Top speed 95 mph (153 km/h)

Ford offered four- and six-cylinder engines in its biggest British sedan. This car came with front disc brakes, an all-synchromesh gearbox, and the option of automatic transmission. With big rear fins and lavish chrome trim, it was the closest the UK got to an American-style car.

All-synchromesh gearbox with column gear lever

Front disc brakes have servo assistance

Styling has much in common with the smaller Vauxhall Victor

Smooth six-cylinder engine

▷ **Vauxhall Cresta PB 1962**

Origin UK

Engine 3,294 cc, straight-six

Top speed 93 mph (150 km/h)

The Cresta was a large, comfortable car from the British branch of General Motors, with more conservative styling than its 1950s' predecessor. Front disc brakes were standard, and from 1965 automatic transmission was available. There was also a conversion to a station wagon by coachbuilder Martin Walter.

Drum rear brakes but front discs are standard

Sedan body less spacious than wagon model

Six-cylinder engine has twin carburetors

◁ **Triumph 2000 1963**

Origin UK

Engine 1,998 cc, straight-six

Top speed 93 mph (150 km/h)

A stylish car, well-liked among business executives of the 1960s, the 2000 featured a smooth, six-cylinder engine, all-around independent suspension, front disc brakes, and attractive Italian styling by Giovanni Michelotti. Later models adopted a 2.5-liter engine, initially with Lucas fuel injection.

Four-wheel independent suspension

Michelotti styling is modern and handsome

Comfortable interior with wood and leather

Twin-cam engines in 2.8-liter and 4.2-liter sizes

▷ **Jaguar XJ6 1968**

Origin UK

Engine 4,235 cc, straight-six

Top speed 124 mph (200 km/h)

Jaguar gambled by replacing its entire range of cars in 1968 with just one model—the XJ6. Widely hailed as the finest sedan in the world at its launch, it offered a superb blend of performance, refinement, ride comfort, and roadholding.

Jaguar E-type

With the ground-breaking Mini at the forefront of the Swinging 60s, lovers of high-performance cars favored the Jaguar E-type. Instantly recognizable and enormously desirable, it was never quite as fast as the public imagined. However, with aerodynamic lines clearly derived from the Le Mans-conquering D-type, it was nevertheless frequently voted the most beautiful car ever designed, and with some justification.

SEEKING TO BUILD on the success of such cars as the XK120, C- and D-type, Jaguar founder, Sir William Lyons, charged his racing department with the creation of the first E1A prototype in the late 1950s. Intended purely for technical evaluation (and scrapped before the public had seen it) it was 1961 before a version went on sale.

The E-type's windcheating shape, 3.8 liter straight-six, and exceptional economic value meant success came quickly. The availability of both coupe and roadster versions served only to magnify sales. Larger engines included a smooth V12, although these later models abandoned the purity of the original design.

SIDE VIEW

Styling
Early versions of the E-type, when adornments were kept to a minimum, displayed the cleanest and sleekest shape of any car in production. Enzo Ferrari, on seeing his first, is said to have called it "the most beautiful car ever made."

Powerful straight-six engine closely related to Le Mans-winning Jaguars of the 1950s

With its long hood and low-slung body, the E-type represented the schoolboy ideal of what a sports car should look like

Glass-covered headlights

Power-assisted disc brakes

Flat-floor design gives limited leg room

FRONT VIEW

REAR VIEW

Jaguar badge
Every bit as recognizable as the E-type itself, Jaguar's badge was both stylish and attractive. The additional big cat logo was clearly intended to convey the speed and lithe muscularity of its cars, which for years were sold under the banner "Grace, Pace, and Space."

SPECIFICATIONS	
Model	Jaguar E-type Series I, 1961-64
Assembly	Coventry, UK
Production	15,490
Construction	Steel unibody
Engine	3,781 cc, straight-six
Power output	265 bhp
Transmission	4-speed manual
Suspension	Front torsion bar, rear coil springs
Brakes	Four-wheel discs
Maximum speed	143 mph (230 km/h)

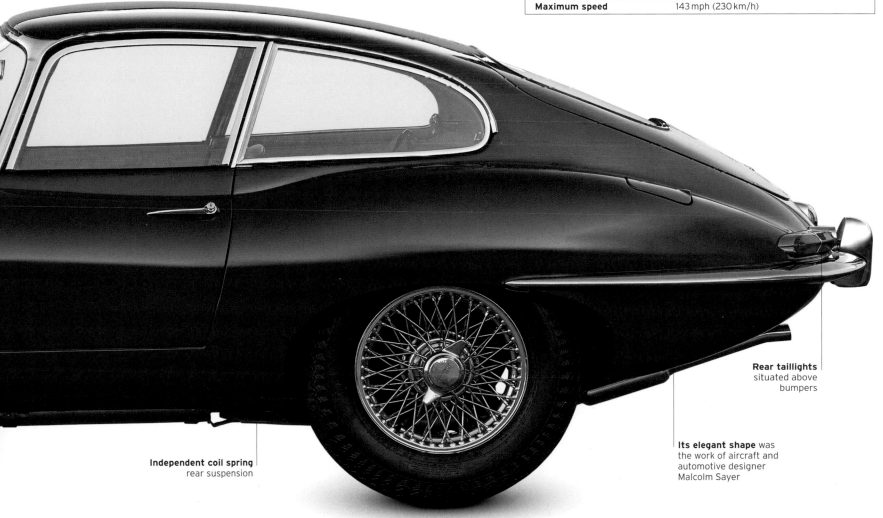

Independent coil spring
rear suspension

Rear taillights situated above bumpers

Its elegant shape was the work of aircraft and automotive designer Malcolm Sayer

ON THE ROAD

It's easy to see why the Jaguar E-type attracted so much attention. With its long, sleek hood and short rear, compact dimensions, and aerodynamic, windcheating shape (not to mention the pleasing rumble of its classic XK straight-six engine), it's hard to believe that the Jaguar debuted as one of the most affordable cars in its class.

In truth it still is. E-type prices have rocketed in recent years, particularly for the earlier cars, but as classics go it is still possible to enjoy smooth E-type motoring for a fraction of what you might pay for a Ferrari of a similar vintage.

Enthusiasts still argue about which design is the best looking—roadster or coupe, two-seater or the later 2+2—but one thing is certain, few cars before or since have ever looked this good.

1. Iconic snarling big-cat badge **2.** Cowled headlamps on early cars for improved aerodynamics **3.** Beautifully slim rear lamp cluster **4.** Unusual triple wipers **5.** Chrome spinners on wire wheels **6.** Refined chrome and leather interior **7.** Slim leather bucket seats **8.** Simple, clear switch gear **9.** Elegantly crafted handbrake lever **10.** Classic "XK" straight-six engine

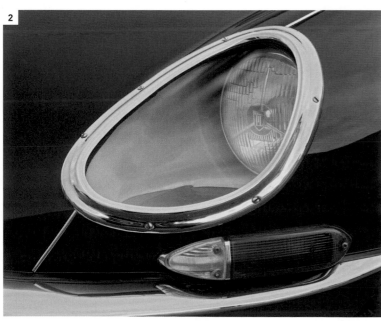

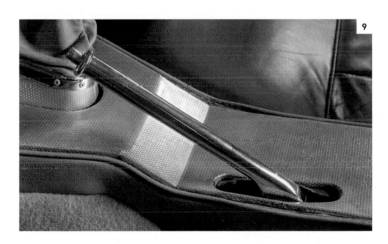

Luxury Sports Cars

In the 1960s, if you wanted the epitome of speed and style, these exotic (and expensive) sports cars provided it. The established Italian firms, Ferrari and Maserati, made the cars everyone aspired to, and by mid-decade they were joined by a third Italian super-sports manufacturer, Lamborghini. American Corvettes were too brash and British Jaguars just too affordable to be considered alternatives by the super-rich. Bentleys too were staid, but the UK countered with the custom-made sporting coupes from Aston Martin. And if none of those appealed, there was the elegance and surefootedness of Mercedes' latest SL—wealthy buyers had plenty of choice.

Driver safety
The SL evolved with the times, and later models incorporated the latest safety features, including a padded steering wheel hub and a collapsible, energy-absorbing steering column. The SL's interior appeared pared back, with its simple painted dashboard. Standard equipment included vinyl seats and a manual gearbox.

▷ **Mercedes-Benz 280SL 1963**

Origin	Germany
Engine	2,778 cc, straight-six
Top speed	124 mph (200 km/h)

The "pagoda roof" 230SL of 1963 was followed by the larger-engined 250SL and 280SL. It's wide track, which aided handling, was the result of sharing running gear with the 1959 Fintail sedan. This car was also the first sports car with "crumple zone" safety technology.

Sophisticated Lichtenheit lamp cluster

Hardtop's raised outer edges lead to "Pagoda roof" nickname

Exterior has lavish but tasteful use of chrome

NJM 1L

Wide track aids handling and grip

SL grows up
The 280SL was more of a touring car than its predecessors. The smoother, seven-bearing engine had a more flexible power delivery, and the revised suspension gave a quieter and more comfortable ride.

"Clap hands" windshield wipers

Rear and front designed as crumple zones

SIDE VIEW

▷ **Ferrari 250 California Spider 1959**

Origin Italy

Engine 2,953 cc, V12

Top speed 145 mph (233 km/h)

One of the most beautiful and desirable Ferraris ever made, the California Spider was a car of film stars–famous owners included James Coburn and Alain Delon. The V12 engine was shared with other Ferrari 250 models and delivered 276 bhp. Disc brakes and radial tires were other features.

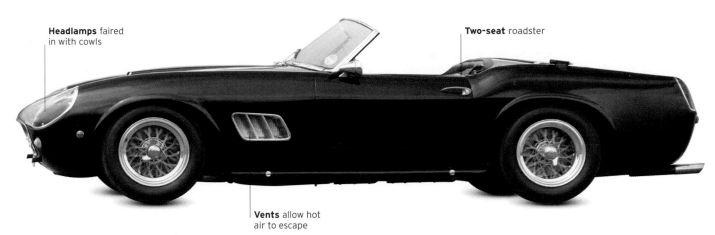

Headlamps faired in with cowls

Two-seat roadster

Vents allow hot air to escape

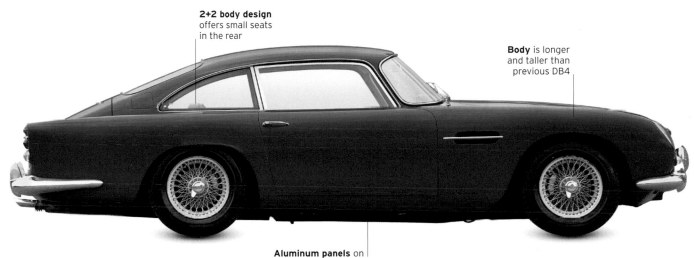

2+2 body design offers small seats in the rear

Body is longer and taller than previous DB4

Aluminum panels on Touring Superleggera tubular body frame

◁ **Aston Martin DB5 1963**

Origin UK

Engine 3,995 cc, straight-six

Top speed 148 mph (238 km/h)

Numerous detail improvements turned the 1958 DB4 into the 1963 DB5, most notably an enlarged 4.0-liter engine. A higher roofline and distinctive cowled headlamps were shared with the last DB4s. The car was made famous by its appearances in James Bond films, starting with *Goldfinger* in 1964.

▷ **Maserati Mistral Spider 1963**

Origin Italy

Engine 3,692 cc, straight-six

Top speed 145 mph (233 km/h)

Maserati fuel-injected its engine to get Jaguar-level performance, and commissioned Frua to design this understated and sophisticated, two-seat body in coupe and open spyder formats. The next generation of Maseratis used V8 engines, making this the last six-cylinder model from Modena until the V6 Merak of 1972.

Aluminum bodywork on early cars, but steel available later

Folding roof concealed under tonneau cover

Conventional live rear axle

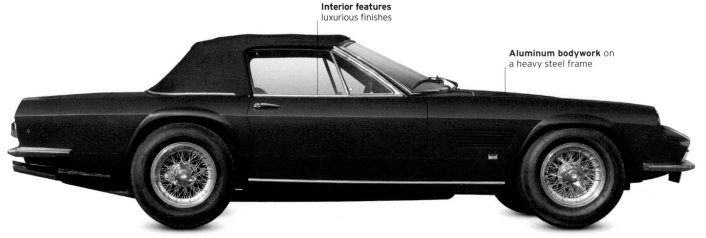

Interior features luxurious finishes

Aluminum bodywork on a heavy steel frame

◁ **Monteverdi 375C 1967**

Origin Switzerland

Engine 6,974 cc, V8

Top speed 150 mph (241 km/h)

Peter Monteverdi was a Swiss prestige car importer who began building cars under his own name in 1967. The 375C was the convertible version, with body by Fissore and Chrysler V8 power. These cars were only ever made in tiny numbers, and production ended in 1977.

Dodge Charger

Although Dodge was already well-established as a manufacturer of cars and trucks, it was its record-breaking achievements on the Bonneville Salt Flats in the 1950s that really got America sitting up and taking notice. Beneath a scorching sun, the company smashed no fewer than 196 speed records in a single year, but it was the 1968 launch of the awesome, V8-engined Dodge Charger that really got things moving for the brand.

BY OFFERING BUYERS of an otherwise standard production car a choice of several powerful V8s including the near-legendary 426 Chrysler Hemi, Dodge dealers found themselves with a fast yet eminently practical machine that appealed to ordinary customers.

Already a street-racing legend with its signature fastback styling, the Charger's role as the General Lee in the TV hit series *Dukes of Hazzard* secured the Dodge's place in pop-culture history. The R/T (Road/Track) version gave Dodge the halo model it needed to succeed in the increasingly competitive muscle market, and spawned the legendary Charger Daytona, which in 1970 became the first car to shatter the 200-mph barrier in a NASCAR race.

SIDE VIEW

Rear seat folds flat on some models, making this particular muscle car a surprisingly practical load carrier

Dynamic styling marks the Charger as something special

Kick-up spoiler appearance at rear

Curved quarter panels at rear

FRONT VIEW

REAR VIEW

Charger badge
The Charger was from an era when Dodge models tended not to carry a corporate emblem, their identity being individually designed for each model; hence the dramatic typography and meaningless graphic motifs on the Charger.

SPECIFICATIONS	
Model	Dodge Charger, 1967-70
Assembly	USA
Production	96,100
Construction	Steel monocoque
Engine	5,211-7,206 cc, V8
Power output	290-375 hp
Transmission	3- or 4-speed manual, 3-speed automatic
Suspension	Front torsion bars, rear leaf springs
Brakes	Drum with optional front discs
Maximum speed	126-150 mph (203-241 km/h)

Some cars feature electroluminescence to light up the interior instrument panel

Launched with a 318 cubic inch V8 (5.2 L) engine it was the availability of even larger engines that turned a slow seller into a surefire hit

Styling
Clean, swept lines, dynamic styling, pillarless window apertures, and a sleek, complex profile gave the semi-fastback Charger a dominating presence, and made a powerful statement about the direction in which Dodge was heading.

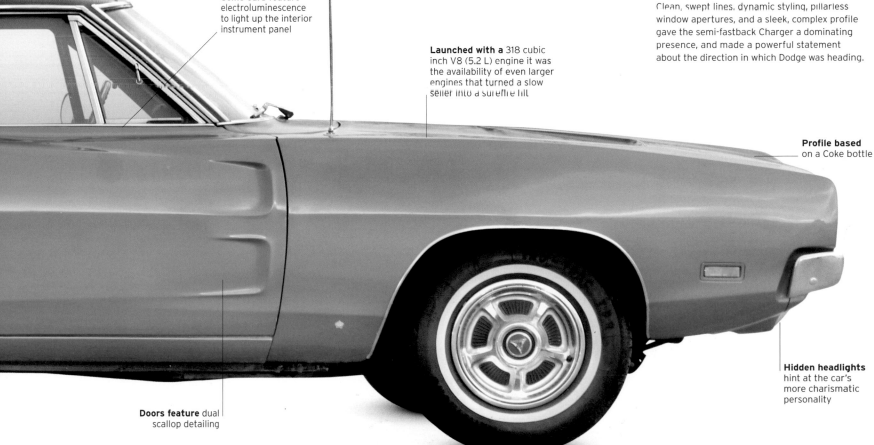

Profile based on a Coke bottle

Hidden headlights hint at the car's more charismatic personality

Doors feature dual scallop detailing

ON THE ROAD

With only modest sales outside North America, it is easy to underestimate the significance of Dodge and to ignore the many highlights of its century-long history.

Huge, fast, and with a brutal personality, for lovers of Americana there is little to beat the appeal of the muscle car. None could rival the handling and technical sophistication of a European thoroughbred, but the US cars were just as fast (at least in a straight line), and still offered quite extraordinary levels of bang for your buck.

Large and lazy V8s drink fuel, but they are durable and relatively easy to maintain. Mammoth sales at the time, and components shared with lesser models, also mean that Charger spares are usually readily obtained from US suppliers.

1. Twin headlamp—uncovered **2.** Retractable plastic headlight covers **3.** Styling details on hood **4.** Sporty hubcaps featuring Dodge logo **5.** Opening quarter windows **6.** Rear roof buttress covered in black vinyl **7.** Ornamented chrome fuel filler cap **8.** Purposeful black and chrome dashboard **9.** Automatic-shifter is center-mounted **10.** Head-restraints are an unusual safety feature for the time

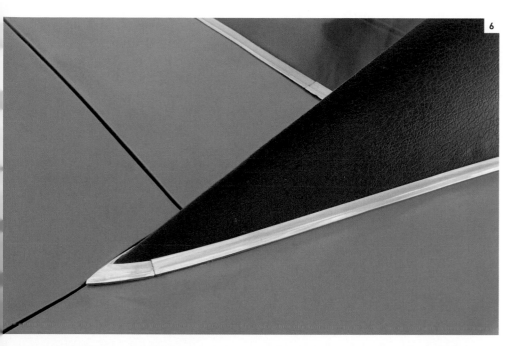

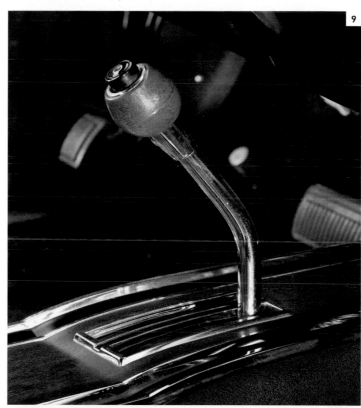

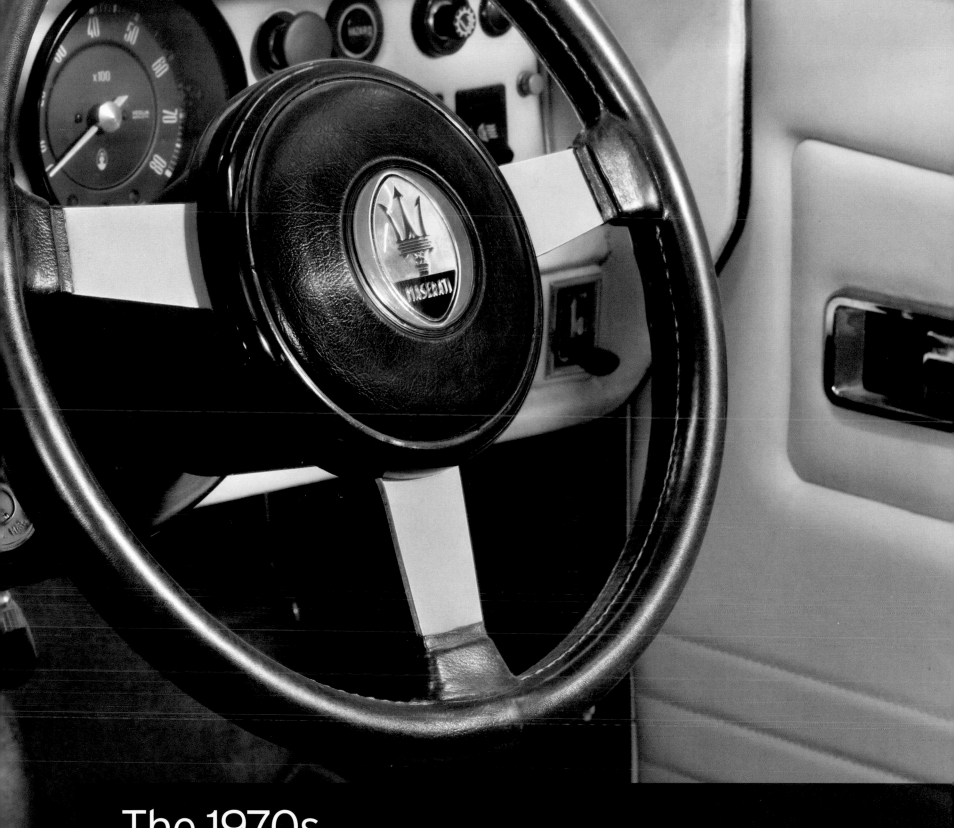

The 1970s
A CLEANER STYLE

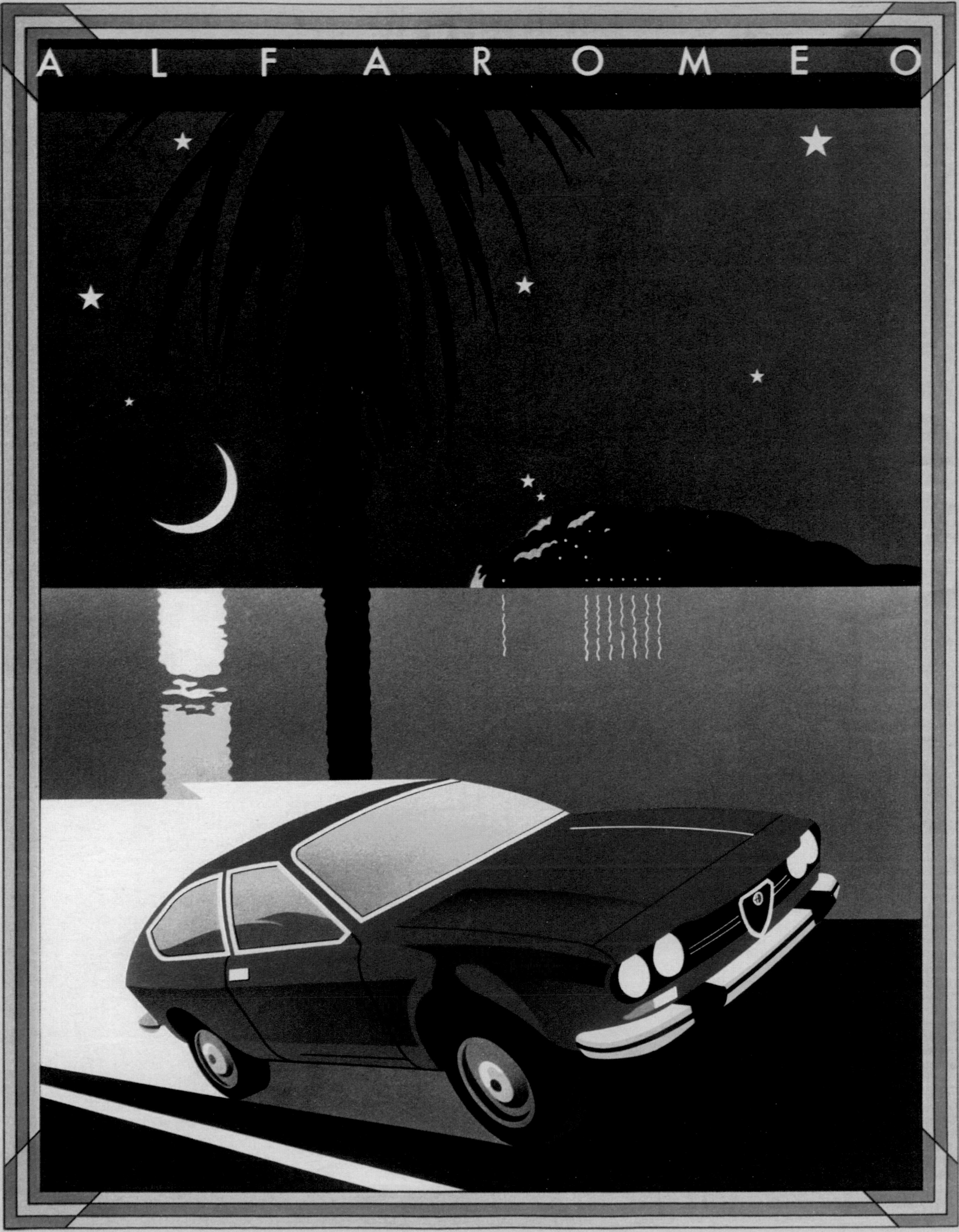
A L F A R O M E O

A CLEANER STYLE

△ **Oil shocks**
Cars line up at a gas station in California during the oil shortage of 1974. Gas prices in the US were much higher than elsewhere in the world.

The 1970s was as turbulent for the car industry as it was for society and the world economy at large. With fuel prices subject to wild fluctuations, manufacturers of fast and powerful cars faced a rocky road. In the US, the muscle-car era ended abruptly, while in Italy Maserati struggled, and its rival Iso vanished entirely. The UK's Jensen went out of business, but Rolls-Royce and Jaguar managed to survive.

However, the early 1970s did see some iconic high-performance, wedge-shaped supercars come to life. For example, the mid-engined Lamborghini Countach and Ferrari Berlinetta Boxer both offered excellent handling and aerodynamism.

Japanese companies such as Toyota, Datsun, Honda, and Mazda produced mass-market cars whose reliability and specifications were revelatory. Europe fought back with design brilliance: the Renault 5 defined the popular supermini breed, while the Volkswagen Golf proved a watershed in versatile family motoring.

Declining air quality in big cities and all over California forced automakers into a new environmental awareness and impelled engineers to strive for lower emissions and improved fuel economy. Meanwhile, Volvo hit on a totally new selling point: safety. Seatbelts, crumple zones, and padded interiors were a prelude to airbags and anti-lock brakes.

While the development of alternative fuels—particularly electricity—was a hot topic, a new generation of quieter and more efficient diesel engines proved the most practical innovation. Turbochargers were soon added to these, just as they had been to gasoline-engined cars, in an effort to boost performance without the need for massive extra cubic capacity.

"I'd sooner die than **imitate** other people ... That's why we had to **work** so **hard**, because we didn't imitate."

SOICHIRO HONDA, FOUNDER OF THE MOTORBIKE AND CAR COMPANY

◁ **UK magazine ad** for Alfa Romeo, 1970s

Key events

▷ **1970** British Leyland launches 4x4 Range Rover and the convertible Triumph Stag.

▷ **1970** Russian firm VAZ builds its first Fiat 124-based Lada car.

▷ **1970** The Citroën SM is built as a collaboration between the French automaker and Italy's Maserati.

▷ **1971** Lamborghini Countach show car is revealed

▷ **1972** The 15,007,034th VW Beetle is built and overtakes the Ford Model T as best-selling car ever.

△ **Mass production**
Assembly line workers apply the finishing touches to rows of 1972 Volkswagen Beetles. By 1973 more than 16 million cars had been produced.

▷ **1972** The Honda Civic and Renault 5 start the market for economical and versatile superminis.

▷ **1973** Ford responds to the worldwide oil crisis with its drastically smaller personal car, the Mustang II.

▷ **1974** The first Volkswagen Golf comes off the Wolfsburg production line; the Golf GTI arrives a year later.

▷ **1975** Jaguar launches its successor to the E-type, the XJ-S grand tourer.

▷ **1976** Jensen Motors declares bankruptcy.

▷ **1978** The front-engined Porsche 928 becomes the only sports car ever to win European Car of the Year.

▷ **1978** Mazda demonstrates its renewed faith in rotary engines with the launch of the RX7 sports car.

Lancia Stratos HF

The winner of the Rally World Championships in 1974, 1975, and 1976, the Lancia Stratos was developed from a striking, fluorescent orange, wedge-shaped concept car designed by Bertone and launched at the Turin Motor Show in 1971. Swapping that model's four-cylinder Lancia engine for Ferrari's Dino V6 made it one of the decade's most charismatic stars, and—in the right hands, at least—an authentically potent weapon when it came to top-level motorsports.

BERTONE'S CONCEPT was the design work of Marcello Gandini who, in a bid to win some business from Lancia, created a machine quite unlike any other.

Very compact, with a low front nose and high tail, the Stratos offered fantastic forward visibility thanks to its unique, deep, crescent-shaped windshield, but almost nothing to the rear. It was light, as little as 1,984 lbs (900 kg), and with more than 500 hp in the most extreme version the 2.4-liter Ferrari engine ensured it was devastatingly quick.

In expert hands the Stratos was also an astonishingly capable rally car, winning three consecutive world championships during the 1970s, so it more than earned its place among the all-time international greats.

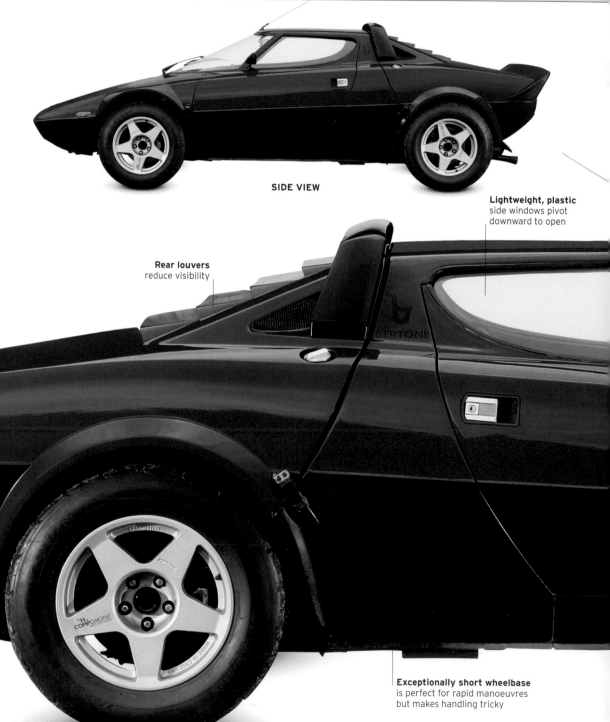

SIDE VIEW

Lightweight, plastic side windows pivot downward to open

Rear louvers reduce visibility

Aerodynamic spoilers grew to vast proportions on some later competition cars

Exceptionally short wheelbase is perfect for rapid manoeuvres but makes handling tricky

FRONT VIEW

REAR VIEW

Stratos badge
This wild, almost psychedelic graphic was
specially created for the car at Bertone's
design studios. It is in stark contract to the
traditional Lancia badge on the stubby hood,
featuring the traditional flag-on-a-lance regalia.

SPECIFICATIONS	
Model	Lancia Stratos HF, 1973-80
Assembly	Turin, Italy
Production	492
Construction	Fiberglass and steel
Engine	2,418 cc, V6
Power output	190 bhp
Transmission	5-speed manual
Suspension	Coil springs front and rear
Brakes	Four-wheel discs
Maximum speed	143 mph (230 km/h)

Deep wraparound windshield
provides superb forward view

Styling
So short as to be almost square when viewed
from above the compact dimensions of the
Stratos HF are purposeful in the extreme. Its
striking, wedge-shaped profile is made possible
by the engine being mounted directly behind
the driver and ahead of the rear axle.

Wedge-shaped design
gives the Stratos a
futuristic appearance

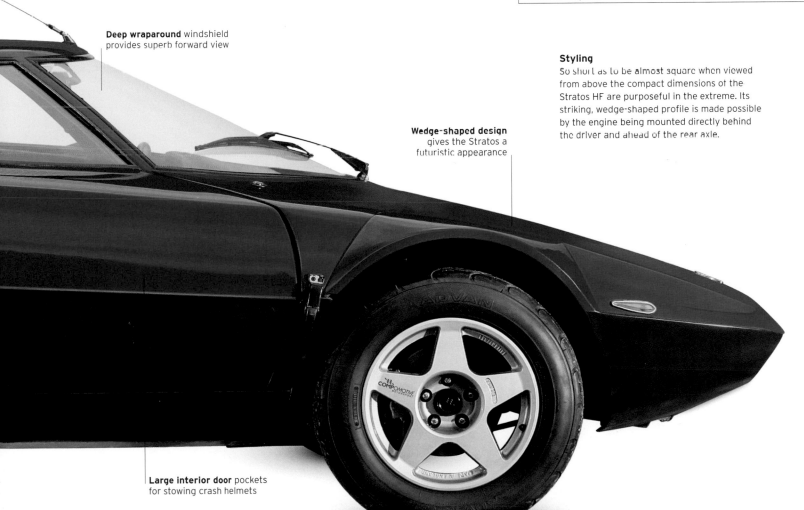

Large interior door pockets
for stowing crash helmets

ON THE ROAD

Offering Corvette levels of performance in something barely larger than the original Honda Civic, the Stratos was an outstanding piece of engineering, even without its impressive record in international motorsports. The fact that many of the parts were shared with other companies in Lancia's parent group, Fiat, did nothing whatsoever to dim its immense attraction. The astonishing Bertone profile gave the Stratos immediate kerb appeal, and Lancia the kind of big draw it had been lacking for years. Prices remained high because it was, and is, an exceptional car. It was hot, frantic, noisy, and somewhat uncomfortable, but it was a genuine milestone for the marque, and decades later, it is still remembered as one of rallying's all-around greats.

1. Lancia badge positioned on hood **2.** Louvered body panels improve engine cooling **3.** Bertone badge and logo **4.** Black louvers shade the rear windshield but restrict vision **5.** Simple speedometer—top speed was 143 mph (230 km/h) **6.** The stark dashboard contrasts against the vivid interior **7.** Conventional handbrake lever, operating on rear wheels **8.** The Stratos' 2.4-liter Ferrari engine

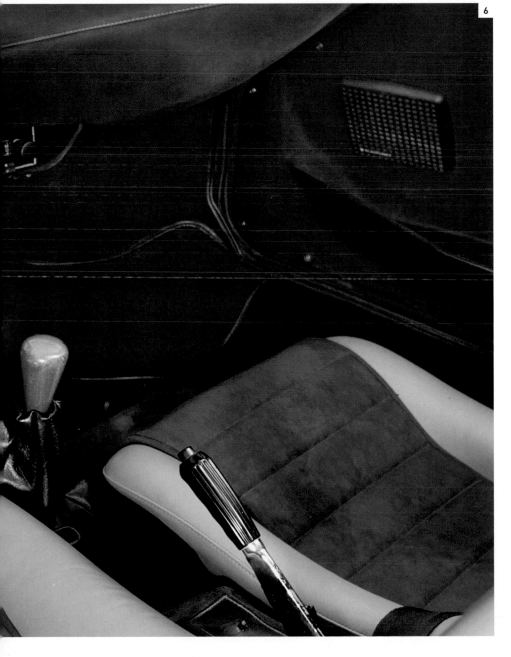

Great Designers
Nuccio Bertone

Arguably the greatest name in the history of car styling, Nuccio Bertone's company was one of the world's longest-lived design brands. Under Nuccio's guidance, the company created pioneering and commercially successful designs for the likes of Alfa Romeo and Lamborghini, applied ideas of genius to concept cars, built a bustling car factory, and discovered and nurtured exceptional talent.

Career highlights

▷ **1912** Giovanni Bertone founds a carriage-making business in Turin

▷ **1920** Bertone expands rapidly, opening a car plant in Turin

▷ **1933** A 19-year-old Nuccio Bertone joins his father's company

▷ **1952** Bertone appears at the Turin Show with two widely admired MG designs

▷ **1953** The first of the aerodynamic Alfa Romeo BAT series stuns the design world

▷ **1959** New factory opens at Grugliasco on the outskirts of Turin

△ **Alfa Romeo Giulietta SZ, 1960**
Premiered at 1960's Geneva Motor Show with lightened bodywork designed by Bertone, the Giulietta SZ was entirely hand-built. Its lightweight speed secured it several racing victories.

▷ **1966** Nuccio invents the supercar form with the Lamborghini Miura

▷ **1967** Marzal is the first of many pioneering Bertone dream cars

▷ **1973** The World Rally Championship-winning Lancia Stratos is launched

▷ **1980** The Fiat Ritmo Cabrio and X1/9 are manufactured and sold under the Bertone brand

▷ **1997** Nuccio dies at age 83

▷ **2014** Bertone files for bankruptcy

EX-WHEELWRIGHT GIOVANNI BERTONE was a pioneer of the Italian design movement, founding his *carrozzeria* (auto shop) in Turin as early as 1912. However, the company's heyday only really began in the 1950s, after Giovanni's son, Giuseppe "Nuccio" Bertone, took over the reins. A talented and instinctive designer, Nuccio instantly saw that the future of coachbuilding lay not in rebodying chassis but in adapting bodywork to fit the new "monocoque" (unibody) platforms manufacturers were adopting. He was also one of the first design managers to realize the impact made by pure "dream car" shapes.

Bursting triumphantly into the postwar era, Nuccio's most striking creation was built for Alfa Romeo in 1953: the Berlina Aerodinamica Tecnica, or BAT. Designed to be as aerodynamically efficient as possible, its bold, swooping shape was reputed to have a drag coefficient of just 0.19—

one of the lowest figures of all time. Nuccio later magnified the batlike form in two further, even more striking BAT designs in 1954 and 1955.

THE AUTOMAKERS' DARLING
It was another Alfa Romeo—the Giulietta Sprint, launched at the 1954 Turin Motor Show—that really cemented the Bertone name or design brilliance. This elegantly simple coupe won Bertone such a reputation that it became the first port of call for a raft of car manufacturers.

In the early 1960s, Bertone created such iconic shapes as the BMW 3200 CS, Iso Grifo, and Fiat Dino, but one car stands out above all: the Lamborghini Miura. The effect the Miura had on car design when launched in 1966 cannot be underestimated: its elegant proportions, striking details, and pioneering mid-engined layout all won instant acclaim.

> "A car is the **product of a feeling**, or rather, a series of feelings."
>
> NUCCIO BERTONE

ALFA ROMEO BAT 9 1955   **POP-UP HEADLIGHT, LAMBORGHINI MIURA 1966**   **CONSOLE, LAMBORGHINI MARZAL 1967**

Nuccio had a knack for hiring brilliant young talent: such great names as Giorgetto Giugiaro, Marcello Gandini, Giovanni Michelotti, and Franco Scaglione all served their apprenticeships at Bertone.

The company was also bold in its pursuit of manufacturing contracts, building cars for Alfa Romeo, Fiat, Volvo, and Opel among others. By 1968 it was assembling 30,000 cars a year. Bertone also became a commercial brand in its own right, badging models under its name, including the X1/9, Ritmo Cabriolet and Freeclimber off-roader.

WICKED CHILDREN

Above and beyond everything else, however, Nuccio always kept a special place in his heart for his pure show cars, which he dubbed his "children", particularly the ones he called his "wicked children" – his controversial dream cars that pushed at the boundaries of the possible.

The late 1960s were inaugurated by 1967's Lamborghini Marzal, a four-seater supercar with enormous, glass-filled gullwing doors, giving full view of the silver leather-clad cabin. No less dramatic was the 1968 arrow-shaped Alfa Romeo Carabo. The fluorescent red nose hinted at red-shift, "light-speed" velocities, while the upward-hinging "scissor" doors anticipated Bertone's seminal Lamborghini Countach by four years.

Bertone's 1970 Lancia Stratos Zero is perhaps the closest that car design has ever come to pure sculpture. Extreme in every way, it was wedge-shaped and ultra-low, with the passengers entering the car via a hinged windscreen and walking in over the front end. The seats were like beds, and the mid-mounted engine lid opened up like a grand piano. The Stratos name would later be revived for Lancia's road and rally car in 1973 – another iconic Bertone shape.

GEOMETRIC APPROACH

More strikingly original concepts followed: the 1974 Lamborghini Bravo with a wraparound windscreen that seemed to be formed of a single pane; the 1978 Lancia Sibilo whose plastic windows morphed into the bodywork, apparently in a single sheet; and the Ferrari Rainbow of 1976, composed almost entirely of angular lines. This geometric approach characterized a generation of Bertone designs.

Unlike almost every other studio, Bertone took pride that its show cars were always fully running vehicles. Even after retirement, Nuccio would check on his designers at weekends, and leave gentle handwritten suggestions on their work.

Nuccio Bertone died in 1997. By then, his company was a colossus employing 1,500 staff. Sadly its fortunes waned and it collapsed into bankruptcy in 2014.

The personal touch
Nuccio Bertone inspects his 1968 concept car for Alfa Romeo, the Carabo. Its dramatic wedge shape would continue to influence car designs until well into the 1970s.

Go-Anywhere Ability

The utilitarian off-road vehicles designed during World War II matured into pickups, station wagons, and SUVs that offered comfort and convenience features such as power steering, coil-spring suspension, and automatic transmission, but still retained that essential go-anywhere capability. They made excellent towing vehicles, too, and with soft springs and good visibility thanks to their lofty driving positions, they won fans—even among drivers who never left the asphalt. Higher standards of trim and additional labor-saving devices such as electric windows and electric mirrors became more common as SUVs increasingly appealed to luxury buyers.

Wagon body provides room for four and lots of luggage space

FRONT VIEW

REAR VIEW

Broader hood
The Range Rover's "clamshell" hood, which took the fender-tops with it when opened, had raised corners at the front to help position the car in low-speed maneuvers.

Easy access
A two-part tailgate, split in the middle, was a key feature; the upper glazed window opened upward, the lower part dropped down. A top-mounted wiper was an unusual–and invaluable–feature.

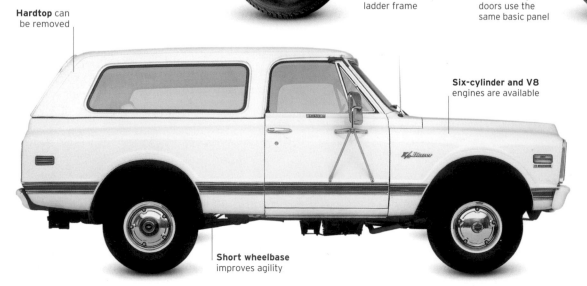

Flat glass reduced build cost

▷ Ford Bronco 1970

Origin	USA
Engine	2,781 cc, straight-six
Top speed	76 mph (122 km/h)

Conceived by the same team who gave Ford the Mustang, the Bronco was a brave early take on the SUV concept but was too small to capture the US market. Second-generation models from 1978 onward were based on the larger F-100 pickup.

Chassis is a simple ladder frame

Left and right doors use the same basic panel

Hardtop can be removed

Six-cylinder and V8 engines are available

◁ Chevrolet Blazer K5 1970

Origin	USA
Engine	5,735 cc, V8
Top speed	98 mph (158 km/h)

The Blazer was a shortened version of Chevrolet's pickup truck, with a full cab added. It was offered in two- or four-wheel-drive models with six- or eight-cylinder engines to compete against the Jeep, Ford Bronco, and International Harvester Scout. GMC sold the same vehicle as the Jimmy.

Short wheelbase improves agility

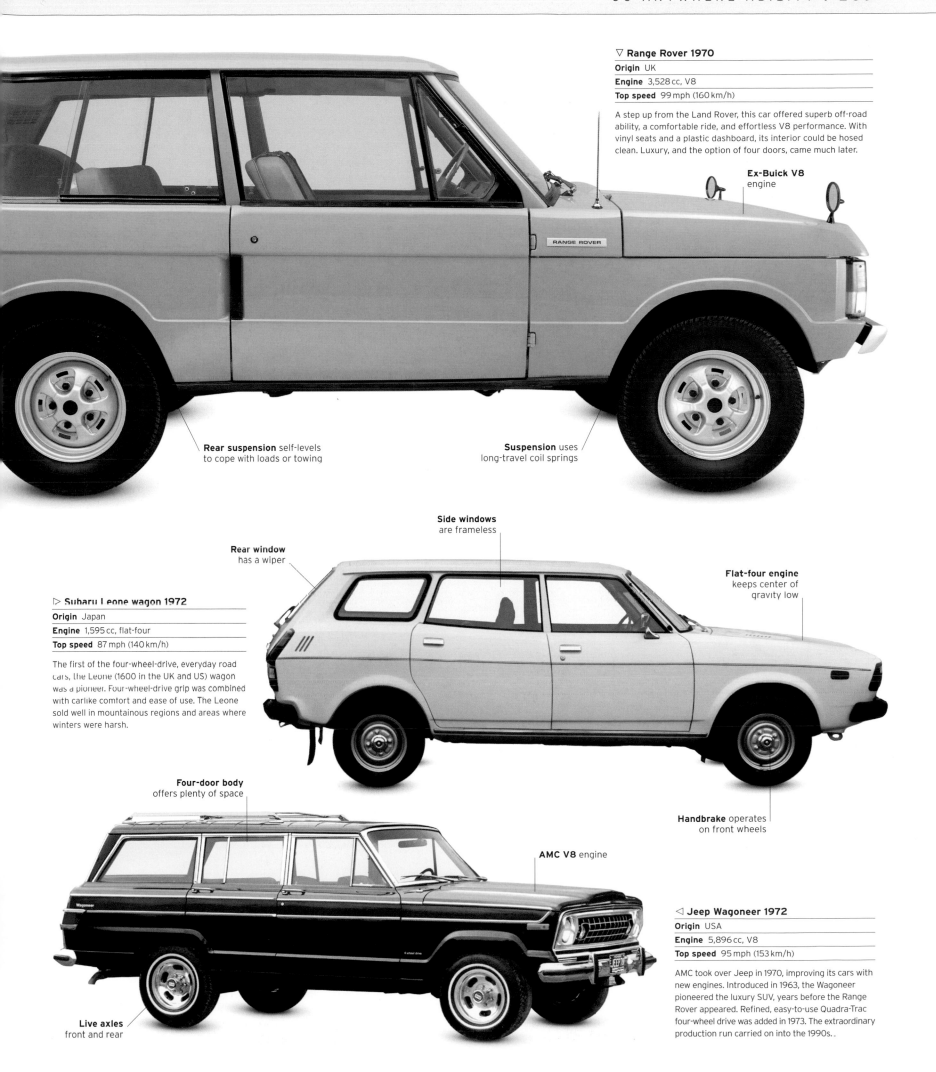

▽ **Range Rover 1970**

Origin	UK
Engine	3,528 cc, V8
Top speed	99 mph (160 km/h)

A step up from the Land Rover, this car offered superb off-road ability, a comfortable ride, and effortless V8 performance. With vinyl seats and a plastic dashboard, its interior could be hosed clean. Luxury, and the option of four doors, came much later.

Ex-Buick V8 engine

Rear suspension self-levels to cope with loads or towing

Suspension uses long-travel coil springs

Side windows are frameless

Rear window has a wiper

Flat-four engine keeps center of gravity low

▷ **Subaru Leone wagon 1972**

Origin	Japan
Engine	1,595 cc, flat-four
Top speed	87 mph (140 km/h)

The first of the four-wheel-drive, everyday road cars, the Leone (1600 in the UK and US) wagon was a pioneer. Four-wheel-drive grip was combined with carlike comfort and ease of use. The Leone sold well in mountainous regions and areas where winters were harsh.

Handbrake operates on front wheels

Four-door body offers plenty of space

AMC V8 engine

◁ **Jeep Wagoneer 1972**

Origin	USA
Engine	5,896 cc, V8
Top speed	95 mph (153 km/h)

AMC took over Jeep in 1970, improving its cars with new engines. Introduced in 1963, the Wagoneer pioneered the luxury SUV, years before the Range Rover appeared. Refined, easy-to-use Quadra-Trac four-wheel drive was added in 1973. The extraordinary production run carried on into the 1990s. .

Live axles front and rear

Motorsports, California Style

In the late 1950s, inventive American motor fanatics created an inexpensive, exhilarating new pastime for themselves—sand-dune racing. Lightweight beach buggies were constructed for the races using the remains of crash-damaged Volkswagen Beetles and a simple fiberglass conversion kit. It was back-to-basics, off-road fun, and four-wheel-drive was not required.

CRESTING THOSE DUNES

Rowdy power from tuned VW engines, and fat tires on extra-wide wheels, were all that was needed to power up sand dunes and fly through the warm air on the other side. Creating a "Baja Bug" was an even more cost-effective way to enjoy the desert

wilderness of the Baja peninsula on the California coast in the late 1960s. The front and rear metal panels of the VW Beetle were cut away, exposing the engine to air and creating an efficient cooling system. The minimum of lightweight plastic body panels were added to accommodate the broad, soft tires, essential for bouncing over soft sand. Plus, the radically modified yet road-legal little car would look pretty cool on the highway after a day spent thrashing the dunes.

A Volkswagen "Baja Bug" tackles the desert sands of Baja California in October 1972, its huge tires enabling it to cut through the sand with ease.

Horace and John Dodge being driven in one of their early cars

Great Marques
The Dodge Story

From respected component manufacturer to automaker to core brand of Fiat Chrysler Automobiles, Dodge has become a fixture in US motoring history that survives and thrives today. Merged into Chrysler as a mid-priced brand, it blossomed in the '60s' muscle car boom, and was the pioneer of the minivan in the '80s.

BROTHERS HORACE AND JOHN Dodge founded a precision engineering company in 1901 that quickly won a reputation for quality, and counted the Olds Motor Vehicle Company and the newly established Ford Motor Company among its customers. The brothers became Ford shareholders too, owning 10 percent of Henry Ford's expanding empire until a disagreement over the running of the company ended up in court. Despite his company's success, Ford denied shareholders a dividend, ostensibly to reinvest in new production facilities but also in part to avoid financing Dodge's development of a car to rival his Model T. The matter was resolved in the brothers' favor after a second, more famous lawsuit in 1919.

Ford's fears of a Dodge rivalry proved well-founded when the Dodge brothers released their first car in 1914. The steel-bodied Model 30 offered a higher-quality and more exclusive alternative to Ford's ubiquitous Model T. Offering 35 bhp, a 12-volt electrical system, and sliding-gear transmission, the Model 30 propelled the Dodge Brothers Company to second in the sales charts behind Ford. The early success was checked however, after both Horace and John Dodge died suddenly within a few months of each other in 1920, and thereafter the company gradually lost ground. In 1925, the Dodge brothers' widows sold the company to the Dillon Read investment bank for $146 million, which

Dodge Polara convertible, 1963
The relatively restrained lines of this midsize model still concealed plenty of Detroit horses, with a choice of powerful V8 engines.

reorganized it and sold it to the Chrysler Corporation in 1928. This placed Dodge's cars between the bargain-basement Plymouths and DeSotos, and the higher-spec Chryslers in the corporation's lineup. By that time, Dodge had become a leading manufacturer of light trucks, and the advent of World War II saw the company build more than a quarter of a million military trucks and WC54 ambulances in both 4×4 and 6×6 versions.

After the war sales slowed for several years, until Chrysler stylist Virgil Exner's Forward Look design and new V8 engines breathed life back into the brand. In the early 1960s, the full-size

Dodges were downsized to become the successful midsize Coronet and fastback Charger, with new full-size Polara and Monaco models added above them. NASCAR success backed up the image of Dodge's muscle cars, led by the Super Bee, which was a more expensive and higher-specification version of Plymouth's Road Runner. Racing demands led to Dodge introducing the low-drag Charger Daytona in 1969, which Plymouth reprised as the Superbird.

As the oil crisis of the 1970s turned American buyers off full-size cars, Dodge adopted the European Chrysler Horizon to form the basis of its Omni

Dodge Coronet, 1959
This large sedan was popular with US Police departments across the country for its robustness and roominess.

"Travel behind it on an **English country lane,** and you get the impression of an **error of scale.** It's as if an **elephant had sat on a Cobra.**"

PERFORMANCE CAR MAGAZINE ON THE DODGE VIPER, NOVEMBER 1993

hatchback, and rebadged Japanese Mitsubishis as the compact Colt and Challenger. Meanwhile, the cash-starved Chrysler Corporation struggled to find the resources to renew its American range, and it took the arrival of a new Chrysler chairman—Lee Iacocca—and several federal loan guarantees to rejuvenate the ailing automaker.

The new era began with the Aries, Dodge's version of the corporate front-wheel-drive K-car, and the Caravan, which beat the Renault Espace to market by a few weeks, establishing a whole new minivan market sector. In the 1990s, Dodge introduced the exciting V10-engined Viper, a new Dodge Ram pickup, and modern "cab forward" styling on its Intrepid, Stratus, and Neon sedans.

Unlike its stablemate Plymouth, Dodge survived the merger of Chrysler and Daimler-Benz in 1998,

and benefited from a new rear-wheel-drive platform that led to stylish new Charger and Challenger models. In 2007, the American private-equity Blackstone Group purchased Chrysler for $7.4 billion, but the financial crisis of 2009 saw Chrysler file for Chapter 11 bankruptcy protection and receive a bailout from the US government. The loan was repaid ahead of time and Chrysler was absorbed by Fiat. Bold, supercharged Hellcat models announced that Dodge's future in the new Fiat Chrysler Automobiles would be as a performance brand.

Dodge Challenger, 1970
A fixture of US car racing, Dodge's muscle car heavyweight was also the four-wheeled star of the hit car chase movie *Vanishing Point*.

CLASSICS OF THE FUTURE

Viper RT/10 Chrysler boss Bob Lutz wanted a modern version of the Shelby Cobra, and he got it in 1989. The hugely positive reaction to the Viper concept car convinced Dodge to put it into production, using a steel tube chassis and composite body panels. To ensure performance, Dodge added a new V10 engine with an alloy block designed by Lamborghini. The Viper was fast and frantic. GTS race cars engineered by Reynard and campaigned by Oreca took three consecutive class wins at the 24 Hours of LeMans.

△ **Dodge Viper RT/10 1992**

Origin	USA
Engine	7,990 cc, V10
Top speed	180 mph (290 km/h)

A '90s' take on the Shelby Cobra, Dodge's roadster packed 400 bhp from a vast V10 engine, designed with input from Lamborghini.

Challenger SRT Hellcat Dodge unveiled its 21st-century Challenger in 2007–a stylish two-door notchback that harked back to the first-generation Challenger, made famous by the film *Vanishing Point* in 1971. The Hellcat specification added a 6.2-liter HEMI V8 with a twin-screw IHI supercharger, driving the rear wheels through a ZF 8-speed automatic transmission. Output was no less than 707 bhp, making it the most powerful muscle car ever.

△ **Dodge Challenger SRT Hellcat 2015**

Origin	USA
Engine	6,166 cc, V8
Top speed	199 mph (320 km/h)

This was a supercharged version of the Challenger SRT8, with a blistering 707 bhp. Its retro-styling evoked the glory days of American muscle cars.

Muscle Cars

American motoring muscle reached its zenith at the start of the 1970s. V8 engines were bigger than ever before, and delivered unprecedented power. The fastest and rarest muscle cars were the specials built for NASCAR racing, such as the aerodynamic Dodge Charger Daytona and Plymouth Road Runner Superbird, but most muscle cars were built for on-street show rather than race-track go. The era of the muscle was soon over, however, thanks to emissions concerns and rising insurance costs. Then came the impact of the oil crisis in 1973. Performance cars would be back, but they would never be quite the same again.

Peak power
"Factory blueprinted to save you money," screamed the ads. The monster 455 cu in V8 was stock for 4-4-2s in 1971, but that was its swan song year. Power output would soon dwindle as emissions controls kicked in and the use of unleaded gasoline demanded lower compression ratios.

V8 engine was the biggest production unit available

Optional disc brakes available

Fiberglass nose cone cuts drag

All engines are V8s

High rear fender with Road Runner decals

◁ **Plymouth Road Runner Superbird 1970**

Origin USA

Engine 7,213 cc, V8

Top speed 130 mph (209 km/h)

A NASCAR racer made road-legal, the Superbird was endorsed by the *Looney Tunes* cartoon character The Road Runner and even had a "meep-meep" horn. Around 1,900 of these winged wonders are believed to have been built. Only 135 of those were fitted with the most powerful 426 Hemi engine.

R/T pack includes tachometer and oil pressure gauge

Exposed fuel tank cap

Magnum V8 engine is Dodge's biggest at the time

▷ **Dodge Challenger R/T 440 1970**

Origin USA

Engine 6,276 cc, V8

Top speed 114 mph (183 km/h)

Dodge's late arrival onto the muscle-car market was a practical hardtop coupe. Electrifying acceleration was assured by a 7.2-liter engine option, which boosted its power from 300 bhp to 385 bhp. This car was made famous by its starring role in the 1971 film *Vanishing Point*.

▽ Oldsmobile 4-4-2 1970

Origin	USA
Engine	7,456 cc, V8
Top speed	120 mph (193 km/h)

The 4-4-2 was launched in 1964; the figures signified a four-barrel carburetor, four-speed gearbox, and dual exhaust pipes. This was a standalone model from 1968-72, although its vast 455 cu in engine became standard in 1970. The same year a 4-4-2 was used as pace car at the Indy 500.

Optional extras
This was already an impressive machine, but new owners could still specify even more extras to enhance the car's performance. Options included upgrades to the gearbox, rear axle, brakes, and steering. A weight-saving fiberglass hood was also available.

Contrasting roof color was an optional extra

Round parking lights in front bumper

FRONT VIEW

Reflectors indicate a growing interest in safety

Hidden power
In marked contrast to the aggressively styled front end, the elegantly sloping rear was more subtle. Only the 4-4-2 badge and twin exhausts gave away the fact that this was a muscle car.

Dual exhausts are part of the 4-4-2's identity

REAR VIEW

Subframe-mounted engine and front suspension

◁ Chevrolet Nova SS 1971

Origin	USA
Engine	5,736 cc, V8
Top speed	107 mph (172 km/h)

At first this model was offered only as a signature performance package, but fitting V8 engines into the car from 1968 made the Nova SS (Super Sport) the fastest of the compacts. Capable of reaching 0-60 mph (96 km/h) in under 6 seconds, its abundant wheelspin and heavy steering only boosted the car's macho appeal.

Front disc brakes standard from 1969

Vents provide outlet for hot air from the engine bay

Hood scoop feeds air to carburetors

▷ Pontiac Firebird Trans Am 1973

Origin	USA
Engine	7,459 cc, V8
Top speed	132 mph (212 km/h)

This model was often distinguished by a huge decal on its hood called the Screaming Chicken. The Trans Am was named after the racing series in which the first-generation Firebirds excelled in the late 1960s, even though the Trans Am's engines were too powerful for it to compete in the series itself.

Safe-T-Track option limited-slip differential

Hindustan Ambassador

With production ceasing in the UK in the late 1950s, the Morris Oxford Series III was reborn almost immediately in India. Renamed the Hindustan Ambassador, it was the first car to be built on the subcontinent (rather than merely assembled), and retained its dominant position as the "King of Indian roads" until the 1980s. The "Amby" remained on sale until May 2014.

WHEN MORRIS MOTORS in the UK switched to manufacturing its new Farina-styled models, tooling for the outgoing Oxford sedan was transferred to West Bengal, India, enabling a modified version of the old car to remain in production. Although undeniably a car from the 1950s, tweaks to the design included a new dashboard and stylish steering wheel.

In a country lacking its own domestic motor industry, few customers objected to this, and, despite the woeful performance of its 1,476 cc, side-valve gasoline engine, sales were good. Subsequent modifications were made, including a new dimpled hood and front grille, and in time the "Amby"'s British origins were forgotten.

Monocoque chassis meant the interior was exceptionally spacious

Cars exported back to the UK had to be equipped with catalytic converters to comply with emissions regulations

FRONT VIEW

REAR VIEW

Ambassador badge
Named after the region where its car plant was based, the Hindustan Ambassador was conceived by six engineers at Hindustan Motors in West Bengal, and soon became the car of choice for well-heeled Indians. With a name that suggested class, it was considered the definitive Indian car.

SPECIFICATIONS	
Model	Hindustan Ambassador, 1958–2014
Assembly	Uttarpara, India
Production	Over 4 million
Construction	Steel monocoque
Engine	1,476–1,817cc, straight-four
Power output	40–75 bhp
Transmission	4- or 5-speed manual
Suspension	Front torsion bars, rear leaf springs
Brakes	Four-wheel drums
Maximum speed	69–90 mph (111–145 km/h)

External hood hinges

Styling
Despite numerous small, cosmetic changes, the basic shape of the car was largely unchanged. Its simple, traditional looks were characteristic of the 1950s, and its spacious and comfortable interior meant it became one of India's best-loved cars.

Deep headlamp cowls

Four-door design and robust construction made the vehicle perfect for use as a taxi on the Kolkata streets

ON THE ROAD

Certainly better loved than the Morris Oxford original ever was, the Ambassador was such a curiosity outside of India that this only enhanced its appeal to would-be buyers. By contemporary standards the car was almost comically old-fashioned, and there was no doubt that in practical terms later models made better cars. But many of the modifications appeared to be no more than cheap compromises, and it was the earlier Ambassadors that looked the most stylish. Owners made allowances for the combination of poor performance and lack of comfort. Perhaps it was enough that this was the first car to be made on the subcontinent, and became a much-revered national icon.

1. Prominent chrome radiator grille replaced on later models **2.** A mascot—a 1950s Morris touch **3.** Optional sun visor—more use in Delhi than the UK **4.** Prominent filler cap **5.** Opening front quarter windows **6.** Minimal rear lights **7.** Ambassador name proudly displayed on trunk lid **8.** Simple but practical door-pull, typical of the design **9.** Bench seats front and rear **10.** Well-worn steering wheel sporting the Hindustan logo **11.** Sparse instrumentation for driver

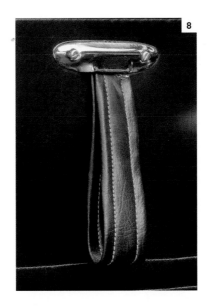

Supercars

In the 1970s, ever larger and more powerful engines provided greater top speeds, while slashing acceleration times. Ferrari was the last of the big three Italian supercar-makers to switch to mid-engined designs: while Lamborghini built the Miura and prepared the Countach, and Maserati offered the Bora and Merak, Ferrari built the Daytona, the last of its traditional front-engine, rear-drive GTs. But that was followed by the flat-12 Berlinetta Boxer, which joined Lamborghini, Maserati, and others in an era of glamour and drama.

Radical engine
So-named due to the punching action of its horizontal pistons, the "Boxer" engine was positioned behind the cockpit. The alloy cylinder heads held two camshafts each, and used composite belts instead of timing chains.

▷ **Ferrari 365 GT4**
Berlinetta Boxer 1973

Origin	Italy
Engine	4,390 cc, flat-12
Top speed	175 mph (281 km/h)

The "BB" broke new ground: this was Ferrari's first super-sports car with a mid-engine configuration and, not only that, it had a new type of engine. Like the F1 and Le Mans cars this was a flat-12, with the gearbox underneath. Just 387 were made.

Radio aerial mounted in windshield

Steel bodywork with alloy panels

Four triple-choke Weber carburetors

Drag efficiency
The Ferrari's mid-engine design gave a more balanced distribution of weight, while the use of a Boxer engine allowed the car to sit closer to the road, resulting in improved aerodynamics and a lower center of gravity.

SIDE VIEW

Five-spoke alloy wheels are standard

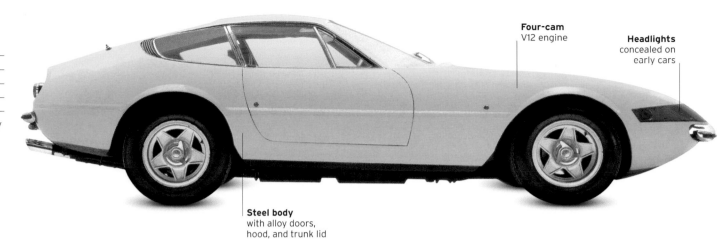

▷ **Ferrari 365GTB/4**

1968 "Daytona"

Origin Italy

Engine 4,390 cc, V12

Top speed 174 mph (280 km/h)

Classically sculpted and outrageously quick, the Daytona was a supercar with a split personality: recalcitrant when dawdling, sublime at speed. It was the last of the great front-engined V12 war horses, for a while, at least. "Daytona" was only ever a 1970s nickname, not an official title.

Four-cam
V12 engine

Headlights
concealed on
early cars

Steel body
with alloy doors,
hood, and trunk lid

Ducktail spoiler
characteristic of
the RS

Thinner glass
and minimal trim

◁ **Porsche 911 Carrera RS 1973**

Origin Germany

Engine 2,687 cc, flat-six

Top speed 149 mph (240 km/h)

Porsche pulled out all the stops to turn the 911 touring car into a road-going racer. Minimal equipment, lightweight trim, and even thinner glass reduced the weight, and the engine was expanded to 2.7 liters and 210 bhp. Buying a Porsche 911 today is a sound classic investment.

Rear wheels wider
than standard 911

NACA ducts feed
cooling air to the
radiators

Mid-mounted
four-cam V12

Dramatic styling
by Marcello Gandini

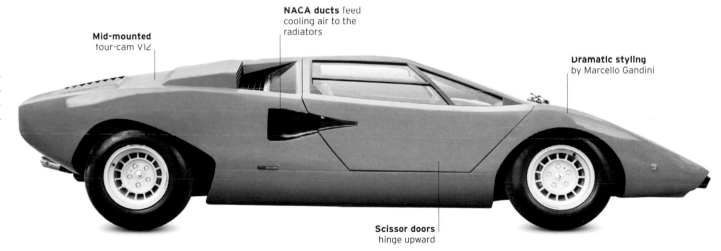

▷ **Lamborghini Countach 1974**

Origin Italy

Engine 3,929–5,167 cc, V12

Top speed 183 mph (294 km/h)

Project 112 was Lamborghini's first mid-engined road car. It had a tubular chassis and a development of the Miura's V12 powerplant—this time mounted longitudinally, with the five-speed gearbox in front and a driveshaft running back through the oil sump to the final drive. This was dramatic, even by Lambo standards.

Scissor doors
hinge upward

Mid-mounted
six-cylinder,
24-valve engine

Body design similar
to the 1972 BMW
Turbo show car

Fiberglass
body work

◁ **BMW M1 1979**

Origin Germany

Engine 3,453 cc, straight-six

Top speed 162 mph (259 km/h)

BMW turned a race-car project into a road-going supercar, with a lusty, mid-mounted six in a sharp suit by Giorgetto Giugiaro (see pp. 264–65), around a Lamborghini-designed chassis. Just 453 were made in four years, with 20 of them built for racing in the short-lived Procar series.

Great Designers
Colin Chapman

One of the great visionaries of the car world, Colin Chapman was a born competitor. To fund his passion for building race-winning cars, he created a string of dazzling Lotus sports cars for road drivers. Chapman was a magician when it came to weight reduction and a master in the art of sharp handling, all of which he employed in his championship-winning constructions.

Career highlights

▷ **1948** Colin Chapman joins the RAF and briefly becomes a pilot before returning to civilian life

▷ **1952** Chapman founds Lotus Engineering, based behind his father's pub in north London, to make sports cars

▷ **1957** The iconic Elite is the world's first-ever fiberglass unibody, and the stripped-down Lotus Seven is produced

▷ **1962** The new Elan defines sports-car qualities for the modern era

▷ **1963** Jim Clark wins Lotus's first F1 title in the unibody F1 car, the Type 25

△ **Lotus Elan, 1967**
The fast, elegant, and lightweight Elan epitomized Chapman's philosophy of lowering weight. With four-wheel independent suspension and rack-pinion steering, the car was also technically advanced.

▷ **1968** Graham Hill takes the F1 crown for Lotus in the 49—the first car to use its engine as a stressed chassis member

▷ **1976** Mid-engined Esprit marks a high point in handling finesse and endures for almost 30 years in production

▷ **1978** The Lotus 79, designed by Chapman, pioneers the use of "ground effect" aerodynamics in F1

▷ **1982** Chapman dies of a heart attack at only 54

COLIN CHAPMAN NEVER CEASED in his single-minded drive to innovate and improve. This determination, combined with a genuine genius, made him a brilliantly intuitive engineer with a passion for racing and an unmatched ability to design championship-winning Grand Prix racing cars.

It all began very humbly in 1947. As an engineering student and part-time car dealer, Anthony Colin Bruce Chapman had been captivated by a trials racing event. Inspired, he turned an old unsold Austin Seven into a trials special, which he registered as a "Lotus." Very soon he switched to racing on tarmac and was so successful in his self-built cars that other racers pleaded with him to build replicas. The experience persuaded him to form Lotus Engineering in 1952.

The same year, Chapman designed his Mk VI, the first Lotus to have its own chassis. His ideology was to make everything as light as possible, and, by combining a lightweight chassis with the latest technological advances in suspension, he successfully distilled the essence of what makes a sports car. 1957's Lotus Seven was perhaps the ultimate expression of this lightness-above-all approach, and the same essential design remains on sale today as the Caterham Seven.

Meanwhile, Chapman became more serious about racing cars. His Mk VIII of 1954 and Mk IX of 1955 were formidable competition machines. Acceptance into the Society of Motor Manufacturers and Traders meant Lotus could now race—and

Lotus Esprit, 1976
The Giugiaro-designed Esprit gained worldwide fame, starring in the James Bond film *The Spy Who Loved Me*. Unlike in the movie, the standard roadgoing Esprit was incapable of converting into a submarine.

win—at prestigious events such as Le Mans, competing first with the Lotus Eleven of 1956. Chapman's compulsion to eliminate unnecessary weight led him to take a revolutionary approach with 1957's Elite, which did away with a chassis completely. It was the first car in the world to have a fiberglass unibody/chassis supporting the mechanicals. This design ultimately proved impractical for road cars, so Chapman innovated again on his 1962 Elan. With its simple backbone chassis and jewel-like, twin-cam engine, it could run rings all around its contemporaries on the road. A seminal car in every way, it was also both profitable and popular, selling more than 11,000.

Such success was partly built on Lotus's Grand Prix wins. The company's first-ever Formula 1 victory came in 1960 with Stirling Moss at the wheel, followed by F1 titles in 1963 and 1965 for Jim Clark, and in 1968 for Graham Hill.

"**A brilliant designer, but his intense desire to win** would sometimes cause him to come too **close to the edge.**"
SIR STIRLING MOSS

LOTUS ELITE 1960

DASH, LOTUS ESPRIT 1976

As racing cars made the switch from front to mid-mounted engines, so Chapman sought to do the same for road cars. The Europa—launched in 1966 as Lotus moved headquarters to Norfolk—was one of the world's first mid-engined road cars and it set new standards in terms of handling.

Lotus was fast outgrowing the days of selling cars for home assembly in kit form. Its design ethos was evolving, too, since Colin Chapman only ever built cars that he wanted to drive, and his tastes were broadening. The 1974 Elite was Lotus's first four-seat luxury sports car, and it marked the company's move toward a new era of mature sophistication and aspiration—it was becoming the British equivalent of Porsche.

TRIUMPH AND TRAGEDY

Then came the Esprit, a superb mid-engined sports car styled by Giorgetto Giugiaro, and once again one of the sharpest-handling cars of its generation. Indeed, the Esprit was a marvel in both concept and execution, ensuring that it would remain in production for another 28 years until 2004.

Disaster struck in 1982 when Chapman suffered a fatal heart attack. In the wake of his death, Lotus sought external investment and took on more consultancy work. General Motors bought Lotus in 1986, beginning a period of rising and falling fortune as it was sold to Bugatti, then on to the Malaysian firm Proton.

However, Chapman's legacy of innovation never left Lotus. The 1996 Elise returned Lotus to its roots. Here was a car whose light weight, stripped-out feel, and innovative technology would truly have made Colin Chapman a contented man.

Racing engines
Graham Hill (center) and Colin Chapman (right) inspect an engine with Cosworth's Mike Costin. The collaboration between the two men brought racetrack success, with Hill scoring a victory for Lotus in 1968.

The Superminis

Small cars made great strides in the 1970s. Hatchback bodies were used almost universally, making little cars more useful and adaptable than they had ever been before. Many manufacturers adopted front-wheel drive, which brought with it improvements in space utilization, allowing for more passenger and luggage space within compact overall dimensions. Front-drive also delivered safe, stable handling that was ideal for mainstream driving. However, some held out against the trend—generally because they were reusing rear-drive platforms left over from previous-generation models that were at least well-suited to pocket-sized performance cars.

▽ **Fiat 127 1971**

Origin Italy

Engine 903 cc, straight-four

Top speed 83 mph (134 km/h)

Fiat had always been adept at making well-packaged, quick, small cars and the 127 proved another such success, with sales of 3.7 million. Early cars had trunks but a hatchback body soon followed. The 1300 Sport option had a 1,300 cc engine and could reach 95 mph (153 km/h).

Circular cabin air vent

Transverse overhead-valve engine

Clamshell hood forms top part of fenders

Short tailgate leaves high loading sill

Rear suspension has transverse leaf spring

Recess in wing instead of conventional door handle

▷ **Renault 5 1972**

Origin France

Engine 956 cc, straight-four

Top speed 86 mph (138 km/h)

The class-defining and perhaps most popular supermini, the Renault 5 offered a clean and modern two-door body, reasonable prices, six engine choices ranging from 782 to 1,397 cc, and all-independent suspension. The hot Alpine/Gordini model and even hotter mid-engined Turbo added speed and glamour to the range.

Longitudinal engines unusual for a front-drive car

Suspension uses torsion bar springs

Early use of polyurethane bumpers

Four-cylinder engine is all-alloy

◁ **Peugeot 104 1972**

Origin France

Engine 954 cc, straight-four

Top speed 84 mph (135 km/h)

Peugeot's first supermini was launched as a fastback four-door, then a hatchback five-door. A shorter three-door 104 Coupe followed later. The all-new engine and independent suspension added to its appeal. Pininfarina designed a "Peugette" roadster based on the 104, but it never reached production.

MacPherson strut front suspension

Front windows have quarter windows

Overhead-cam, water-cooled engine

4-speed manual transmission

▽ **Volkswagen Polo 1975**

Origin Germany

Engine 895 cc, straight-four

Top speed 80 mph (129 km/h)

VW completed its modern revolution with the Polo, which first appeared as the Audi 50 in 1974. It had a new front engine, all-independent suspension, and front-wheel drive, with engines from 0.9 to 1.3 liters. The Polo and its big-brother Golf remain huge sellers for VW today.

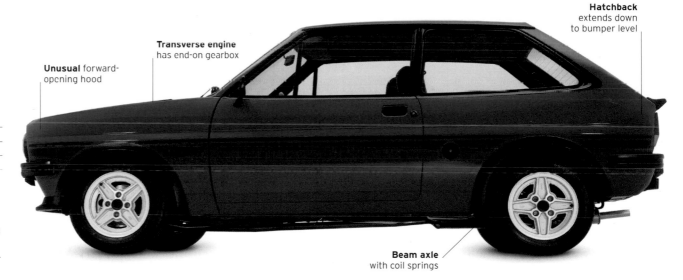

Hatchback extends down to bumper level

Transverse engine has end-on gearbox

Unusual forward-opening hood

▷ **Ford Mk I Fiesta 1976**

Origin Spain

Engine 957 cc, straight-four

Top speed 79 mph (127 km/h)

Ford's first supermini for Europe was basic, with only four gears, but it had engines up to 1,600 cc and was priced competitively. Sales reached 1.75 million by the end of production in 1983. Fiestas were built in Spain, the UK, and at two German factories. This is the XR2 model.

Beam axle with coil springs

Interior trimmed in red tartan cloth

Unusual multi-valve cylinder-head

Deep front air dam denotes 2300HS

Alloy wheels are standard

◁ **Vauxhall Chevette HS 1978**

Origin UK

Engine 2,279 cc, straight-four

Top speed 115 mph (185 km/h)

Most Chevettes were pedestrian 1.3-liter hatchbacks and sedans but Vauxhall made a virtue of the old-fashioned, rear-drive layout by creating a high-performance version with a bigger, 16-valve engine. The 2300HS quickly became a serious competitor in rallies, challenging the might of Ford's Escorts RSs.

British Sports Cars

The classic front-engine, rear-wheel-drive, softtop sports car appeared to be under threat from all directions in the 1970s. New US emissions laws were emasculating engines, affecting those European models that relied on lighter weight and relatively little power. Added to this, safety and insurance concerns mandated ugly, impact-resistant bumpers, and there was even talk of banning convertibles altogether—but the sports car survived, and thrived.

All-British ambience
The driver interface of the TR6 was the epitome of the purposeful British roadster: polished wood dashboard, white-on-black instruments that were easy to read through the three-spoke steering wheel, and stubby gear lever; the predominant matte-black trim cut down on glare.

▷ **Triumph TR6 1970**

Origin	UK
Engine	2,498 cc, straight-six
Top speed	119 mph (192 km/h)

Produced from 1968 until 1976 and similar in shape to the TR5 but with a squared-off front and rear, the TR6 was as muscular as the TR series got. There were some who complained that, like the big Healeys, its power outstripped its poise, but that just made it more fun to drive.

Independent rear suspension with coil springs

Body restyled by Karmann

Round headlights a prominent feature

Tough separate steel chassis

Contoured lines
The side profile was a natural development of the TR4, TR4A, and TR5/TR250, but the TR6's distinctive, cut-off design was styled this time by Karmann of Germany, not Italy's Michelotti.

Six-cylinder engine has Lucas fuel injection

SIDE VIEW

Power under the hood
All TR6s share the same basic 2.5-liter, straight-six engine; for the US—the car's primary market—it came with carburetors and just 105 bhp, but for European markets there was fuel injection and 150 bhp, later detuned to 124 bhp.

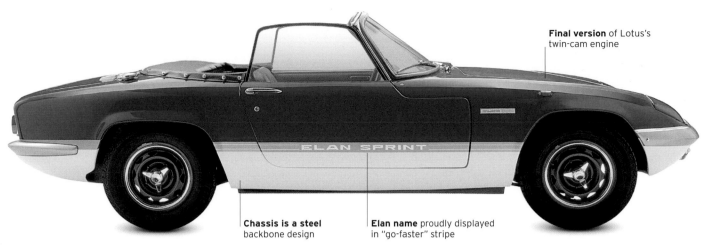

Final version of Lotus's twin-cam engine

◁ **Lotus Elan Sprint 1971**

Origin UK

Engine 1,558 cc, straight-four

Top speed 120 mph (193 km/h)

The fifth, final, and arguably finest incarnation of Colin Chapman's benchmark sports car, the Elan Sprint had 126 bhp from its big-valve, twin-cam engine, a 5-speed transmission, and striking livery. Road manners were excellent thanks to four-wheel independent suspension.

Chassis is a steel backbone design

Elan name proudly displayed in "go-faster" stripe

▷ **Jensen-Healey 1972**

Origin UK

Engine 1,973 cc, straight-four

Top speed 120 mph (193 km/h)

Created by legendary sports-car designer Donald Healey, and built by Jensen, this roadster was the first car to use Lotus's new engine. It was great to drive and light on fuel, but could be temperamental. The short-lived wagon version was called the Jensen GT.

Bodywork is all-steel

Lotus engine has 16 valves

Live rear axle with coils and trailing arms

GT body has tailgate

Front end shared with MGB roadster

◁ **MGB GT 1974**

Origin UK

Engine 1,798 cc, straight-four

Top speed 105 mph (169 km/h)

The MGB GT's fastback body was more slippery than that of the MGB roadster, so the GT had a higher top speed. It was also more practical, with its tailgate opening onto a useful luggage area, and two small rear seats in the cabin.

Impact-resistant polyurethane bumpers introduced in 1974

▷ **TVR 3000S 1978**

Origin UK

Engine 2,994 cc, V6

Top speed 121 mph (195 km/h)

Blackpool sports car-maker TVR produced this convertible after three decades of being in business. An open-top version of the Ford V6-powered 3000M, it had abundant power, was extremely lightweight and very fast, and boasted tight handling.

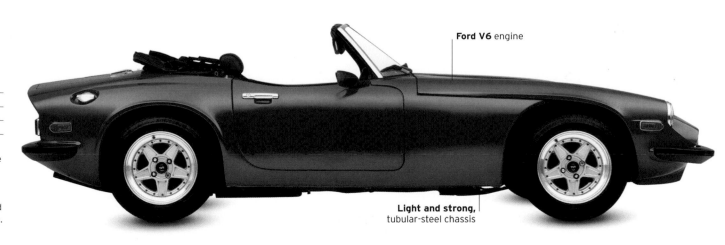

Ford V6 engine

Light and strong, tubular-steel chassis

Early manufacture
of Toyota trucks
in progress

Great Marques
The Toyota Story

Toyota was at the forefront of the Japanese motor industry's move into exports in the 1960s, establishing satellite plants around the world. It became a force in rallying, but its foray into Formula 1 proved unsuccessful. While rocked by quality scares in recent years, it remains the world's largest automaker.

SAKICHI TOYODA INVENTED Japan's first powered weaving loom in 1897, and his son Kiichiro created an automatic loom in 1924. After a visit to the US and Europe in 1929, Kiichiro began experimenting with gasoline-powered engines and in 1933 he established an automotive business within the Toyoda Automatic Loom Works. Although the move was considered risky by some, the Japanese government encouraged Toyoda's diversification as it sought to foster domestic car production during the war with China.

Toyada bought cars from Chevrolet and DeSoto, which were dismantled and examined in detail. The lessons learned went into Toyoda's first vehicles, the A1 car and G1 truck of 1935—soon refined into the AA and GA models, all of them using the 65 bhp, four-cylinder, Model A engine. In 1937, the name Toyota was adopted, and the automotive operation was spun off into a separate company, the Toyota Motor Corporation.

During World War II, Toyota concentrated on truck production and engine research, which continued during the reformation of Japan in the late 1940s. The company then re-entered

Poster advertising
early Toyota Celica

the passenger car market with the Toyopet SA small car in 1947. By 1958, Toyota was exporting its slow but solid Crown sedan to the US. Its next step forward was the development of the Corolla, a compact economy car that boasted a 1077 cc, four-cylinder engine with more power than its competitors, a four-speed transmission when many rivals only offered three ratios, modern strut-type front suspension, and minimal maintenance requirements.

Launched in 1966, it was an immediate success, helping Toyota to exceed export sales of one million vehicles by 1969. Toyota was so successful that the US, UK, and other export markets introduced import tariffs to protect their own motor industries from the new Japanese competition.

Toyota's export sales continued to increase into the 1970s with new generations of Corollas (eventually it became the best-selling car model of all time) and the introduction of the Corona, Carina, and Celica models. All of the cars were reliable and efficient, if less than enthralling to drive. Yet when Toyota chose to build cars for enthusiasts, it could do an incredible job. The rear-drive AE86 Corolla GT of the 1980s was

famed for its handling and punchy, 128 bhp, fuel-injected, in-line four, and the same engine was mounted amidships in the delightful MR2 sports car. But these were all-too-rare highlights in an otherwise more workaday lineup.

Toyota's image was boosted by its World Rally Championship campaigns with the four-wheel-drive Celica GT-Four in the 1990s. The German-based Toyota Team Europe took championship wins in 1990 and 1992 with Carlos Sainz, in 1993 with Juha Kankkunen, and in 1994 with Didier Auriol. But the team was banned from rallying in 1995 for using an illegal air restrictor bypass system. In 1998 Toyota moved into sports car racing, but the newly developed GT-One never lived up to its promise. Formula 1 beckoned next, but that proved to be a similar story. Ten seasons in the sport, at enormous cost to the company, delivered little beyond a pair of second place finishes each for Jarno Trulli and Timo Glock.

But Toyota continued to achieve sales success around the world, and sidestepped

**Toyota Crown
Hardtop Coupe, 1971**
Designed for the 1970s, the Crown followed US styling trends; the power unit was a 2.6-liter straight six.

"The MR2 ... sets **new standards** in a number of areas and it is **enormous fun** to drive."

AUTOCAR MAGAZINE ON THE TOYOTA MR2, MARCH 1985

Toyota MR2, 1984
The Fiat X1/9 had blazed the trail for affordable mid-engined sports cars, but this Toyota was a step up in quality, performance, and handling; optional extras included a T-bar roof and a supercharger.

import restrictions by establishing new production facilities in its biggest markets outside Japan. It introduced the first mass-produced hybrid, the Prius, in 1997 and by 2014 had overtaken Volkswagen and General Motors to become the world's biggest automaker. A series of safety recalls cast doubts on Toyota's quality, but has had negligible impact on sales.

With the challenge from Volkswagen fading as the German company battles slowing sales in China and the fallout from its diesel emissions scandal, Toyota has returned to its place as the biggest automaker in the world and now looks set to remain there for some time.

Toyota Celica, 1971
Here was Japan's answer to Europe's Ford Capri and Opel Manta: a sporty coupe with both mundane and exciting engine options.

CLASSICS OF THE FUTURE

Supra Toyota's flagship performance coupe stepped up a gear in its A80 generation. Under the curvaceous new body was a twin-turbocharged version of the 3-liter, straight-six 2JZ engine, with the turbos acting sequentially for reduced lag. Japanese market cars had 280 PS (a power ceiling laid out in a gentleman's agreement between Japanese automakers) but in Europe the Supra reached 326 bhp and could sprint from 0–60mph (96 km/h) in 4.6 seconds.

△ **Toyota Supra 1992**

Origin	Japan
Engine	2,997cc, straight-six
Top speed	155 mph (250 km/h)

Spectacular in looks and performance, the twin-turbo Supra could deliver supercar speed without the exotic price tag.

GT86 Toyota came up with the concept and Subaru (which Toyota part-owns) supplied the flat-four engine and did the bulk of the development work on this new rear-drive platform. The result was a snug sports coupe with quirky looks and only-just-enough power. However, its handling, the most responsive and adjustable of any car in its price range, made it very fun to drive. It was sold in the US as the Scion FR-S (until that brand was shuttered in 2016) and also built as a Subaru, the BRZ.

△ **Toyota GT86 2012**

Origin	Japan
Engine	1,998 cc, flat-four
Top speed	145 mph (233 km/h)

A Toyota/Subaru joint development that produced a sports coupe with an emphasis on responsive handling.

Mazda Cosmo 110S

Named for an era when the world was caught up in the excitement of the international space race, the diminutive Cosmo 110S was a sophisticated, two-seater coupe designed to sit at the very top of the Mazda range. At its launch in 1967, it was Japan's first rotary-engined production car, the Hiroshima-based company hoping to project an image of itself as daring, forward thinking, innovative, and unconventional.

THE COSMO WAS first seen as a prototype at the 1964 Tokyo Motor Show, after which a limited run was produced for evaluation by both the factory and its dealers. Launched to the public three years later, its most distinctive feature was a unique two-rotor, Wankel rotary engine. Lacking conventional cylinders and with a capacity of under 1.0 liter, its 110 hp meant it was good for around 115 mph (185 km/h).

The cars were built by hand at a rate of one a day, with more than 1,500 leaving the factory before production ceased in 1972. Two of these joined the racing circuit, one taking fourth place in the grueling 84-hour Marathon de la Route at Germany's Nürburgring, and showing the resilience of the unorthodox engine.

SIDE VIEW

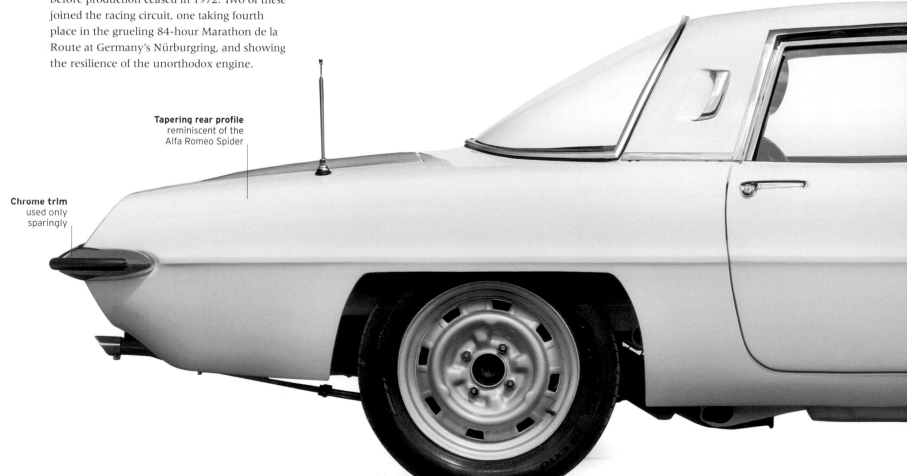

Tapering rear profile reminiscent of the Alfa Romeo Spider

Chrome trim used only sparingly

FRONT VIEW

REAR VIEW

Mazda badge
From 1962–75, the stylized M for Mazda was derived from the name of the company's founder, Jujiro Matsuda, but for many Asian owners it also had an association with Ahura Mazda, the god of wisdom, intelligence, and harmony.

SPECIFICATIONS	
Model	Mazda Cosmos 110S (1967-72)
Assembly	Hiroshima, Japan
Production	1,519
Construction	Steel monocoque
Engine	982 cc, twin-rotor Wankel engine
Power output	110 bhp
Transmission	4-speed manual
Suspension	Front coil springs, rear leaf springs
Brakes	Front discs, rear drums
Maximum speed	115 mph (185 km/h)

Styling
By borrowing stylistic touches from contemporaries such as the Lotus Elite and Ferrari's exceptionally rare 410 Superamerica, Mazda designers produced a car that was fresh, modern, and entirely distinctive—with a dash of space-age exuberance.

The 982 cc rotary engine offered ample performance

Sweeping line above front wheel arch conveyed an impression of speed even when stationary

Lower hood line due to its compact rotary engine

The Cosmo had disc brakes at the front and drum brakes at the rear

ON THE ROAD

Previously a manufacturer of competent but unremarkable family cars, Mazda made a courageous move into new territory with the Cosmo and—like the company's sensational victory decades later at Le Mans in 1991—an explicit declaration of its faith in the value of novel technology.

Fast and undeniably stylish, the Mazda's design has aged beautifully. Its rotary engine offered a driving experience quite unlike any other, with smooth power delivery belying its tiny size. As a demonstration of what a small, forward-looking company could achieve with the will and the right technical know-how, the Cosmo deserved its place in automotive history. It was special in the 1960s and decades later it still is. That it is a true classic is beyond question.

1. Cosmo name reflects the spirit of the age   **2.** Covered headlights give aerodynamic appearance   **3.** Neat detailing on front wings   **4.** Cabin air vent on side of pillar   **5.** Stylized rear light cluster   **6.** Sporty interior with vinyl trim and traditional wooden steering wheel   **7.** Full instrumentation underlines the car's sporting credentials   **8.** Short-throw gear lever for rapid gear changes   **9.** The Cosmo's revolutionary Wankel engine is notably compact

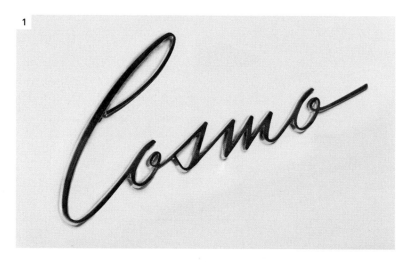

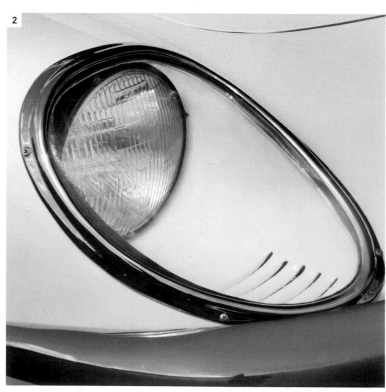

High-Performance Sedans

Premium sedans were offering all sorts of routes to performance and panache. The old-school method was to drop a big, lazy V8 into a medium-sized body. This was the path taken by Mercedes in Germany and Rover in the UK. Other automakers went for smaller motors but added sophistication: fuel injection was one method of improving efficiency, while multivalve cylinder heads would emerge as a common route to better breathing and more power. Another introduction was turbocharging, which hit the mainstream with Saab in 1978 and would soon spread across the motor industry.

▽ **BMW 3.0 CSI 1972**

Origin Germany

Engine 2,985 cc, straight-six

Top speed 130 mph (209 km/h)

BMW lengthened its four-cylinder 2000 C/CS coupe to make space for the "Big Six" engine, and ended up with an all-time classic. Originally it was a 2.8-liter, but this definitive fuel-injected 3.0 CSi came in 1971. It led to the lightweight 3.0 CSL of 1972, which proved effective in touring-car racing.

Independent rear suspension uses semi-trailing arms

Body is a pillarless design

Comfortable interior with cloth trim

Wooden dashboard is well-stocked

Engine has a single overhead cam operating 16 valves

Light alloy wheels are standard

◁ **Triumph Dolomite Sprint 1973**

Origin UK

Engine 1,998 cc, straight-four

Top speed 115 mph (185 km/h)

Triumph built innovative cars with attractive styling on a tight budget. The Dolomite's shape was aging by the early 1970s, but the Sprint gave the car a new lease on life. Its clever 16-valve engine—one of the first in series production—gave it performance to challenge BMW's 2002 series.

Stainless steel bumpers on Series 1 cars

Single windshield wiper

▷ **Citroën CX2400 1974**

Origin France

Engine 2,347 cc, straight-four

Top speed 113 mph (182 km/h)

The Citroën DS's successor combined all its predecessor's innovation with a transverse engine for increased passenger space. Inside, it was as quirky as cars come, with revolving drum instruments and minor controls on pods on either side of the steering wheel. Facelifted in 1985, it stayed in production until 1989.

Big Six
The CSI's superb six-cylinder engine offered an energetic 200 bhp, thanks to Bosch fuel injection; the non-injected CS sister model had 180 bhp. The long-legged nature of the car made it an accomplished long-distance tourer – many were sold as automatics.

Sport and sophistication
The CSI had sports seats and a three-spoke sports steering wheel, and power steering was standard - the car's only concession to driver ease. This was a taut, fine-handling car to relish driving along highways or twisty roads.

Six-cylinder engine
with Bosch fuel injection

Sharply sloping
windshield

Special build
All BMW's six-cylinder coupes were built under contract by German coach builder, Karmann, of Osnabruck. The same basic shell was used for the spectacular CSL racing cars, albeit with aluminium bonnet, bot lid and doors.

FRONT VIEW

Hatchback body
a first for Rover

All-alloy Rover V8
based on a Buick design

◁ **Rover 3500 SD1 1976**

Origin UK

Engine 3,528 cc, V8

Top speed 125 mph (201 km/h)

Despite its advanced looks, luxury features, and excellent dynamics, the SD1 rapidly gained a reputation for poor quality in the 1970s. Racing victory bolstered its image. Upgraded and relaunched as the Vitesse in 1982, it was driven to victory by Andy Rouse in the 1984 British Saloon Car Championship. There were successes in Europe and Australia as well.

Body inspired by the Pininfarina BMC 1800

Scalloped rear profile

Aerodynamic windshield

▷ **Saab 99 Turbo 1977**

Origin Sweden

Engine 1,985 cc, straight-four

Top speed 122 mph (196 km/h)

Developed from the fuel-injected EMS model, the Turbo added a Garrett turbocharger to increase power. A hundred prototypes covered 2.9 million miles (4.7 million km) before Saab was happy with its prodigy. Rare, esoteric, and historically significant, the 99 Turbo is an undisputed classic.

Out and About in a Concept Car

Giorgetto Giugiaro's Italdesign (see pp. 264–265) was the most influential car-design bureau in the world in the 1970s. The Alfa Romeo Alfasud and Volkswagen Golf put a Giugiaro original into the hands of even the humblest motorist.

BRAVE NEW WORLD

The decade saw Italdesign present a seemingly never-ending parade of concept cars that kept its name at the cutting edge of design trends. Cars such as this Maserati-based Medici II, a dart-shaped executive sedan, drew huge motor-show crowds for its novel features, such as its glass roof panels. Mechanically based on the Maserati Quattroporte, with its race-proven,

4.9-liter V8 engine, it was a super-luxurious model with four wide, sumptuous seats—the car, painted a shimmering silver, was just under 6ft (2m) wide. And yet Italdesign's coach-building traditions were merely the latest in Italy's creative heritage. Perhaps that is why the contrasting textures of ancient sites, such as the stunning cathedral square in Milan, were often chosen as locations for publicity shoots that captured the fashionable zeitgeist of the times.

The historic aura of Milan's Piazza Del Duomo is here enjoyed through the open roof of Italdesign's Maserati Medici II, in 1974.

Exotic Sedans and Tourers

Increasingly sophisticated technology made the best sedans and GT cars even better as the 1960s turned into the 1970s. At the top end power usually came from V8 engines, often built in the US, although V6s and V12s were used as well. All of them provided superior performance and refinement, generally with a stirring soundtrack. Independent suspension and disc brakes were standard, and automatic transmission was often available. It was an era of distinctive design, as car makers blended the organic curves of the 1960s with the new sharp edges, wedge shapes, and aerodynamic efficiency.

Body panel seams filled with lead for a seamless finish

Limited rear space despite car's length

Comfortable and stylish leather-trimmed interior

Maserati V6 is an all-alloy unit

Teardrop-shaped enclosures over rear wheels

△ Citroën SM 1970

Origin	France
Engine	2,670 cc, V6
Top speed	137 mph (220 km/h)

Citroën owned Maserati at the time, so the power of this extraordinarily streamlined coupe came from a 90-degree Maserati V6. Typical of Citroën engineering, the suspension was hydropneumatic, and the steering and brakes used high-pressure hydraulics. It looked, and drove, like nothing else on the road at the time.

Interior designed for luxury

▽ De Tomaso Deauville 1970

Origin	Italy
Engine	5,763 cc, V8
Top speed	143 mph (230 km/h)

Though styled by Ghia, the four-door Deauville had a disadvantage because, while it resembled a Jaguar XJ12 (which offered similar performance), it cost twice the price. The Deauville was only ever built in tiny numbers, but remained available into the late 1980s.

Rear end resembles that of Jaguar XJ12

Disc brakes fitted all around

Spectacularly curving rear window

▽ Buick Riviera 1971

Origin	USA
Engine	7,458 cc, V8
Top speed	125 mph (201 km/h)

Buick's status-symbol coupe was given a stunning new look for the 1970s. Its boattail body, made possible by a complex, curved rear window, was inspired by the Corvette Stingray. Despite giving the model a V8 engine, Buick progressively cut back the car's power to conform with evolving emissions regulations.

Headlights pop up as needed

V8 engine offers 250 bhp

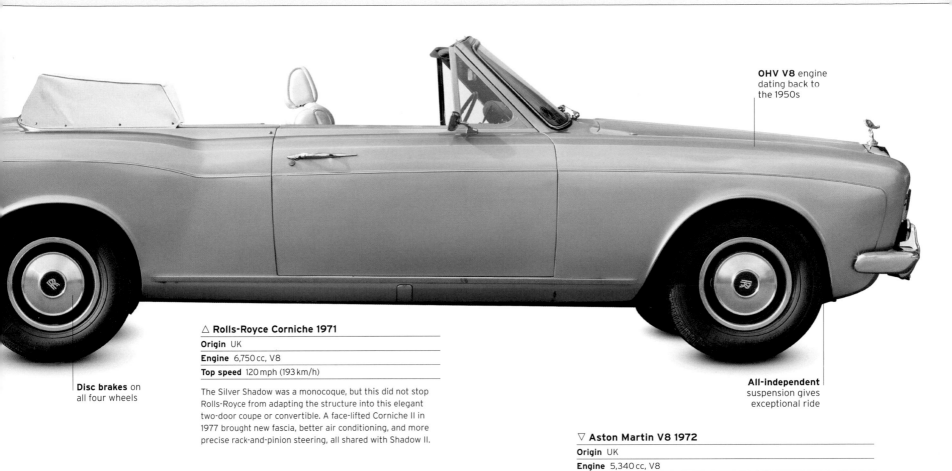

OHV V8 engine dating back to the 1950s

Disc brakes on all four wheels

All-independent suspension gives exceptional ride

△ **Rolls-Royce Corniche 1971**

Origin	UK
Engine	6,750 cc, V8
Top speed	120 mph (193 km/h)

The Silver Shadow was a monocoque, but this did not stop Rolls-Royce from adapting the structure into this elegant two-door coupe or convertible. A face-lifted Corniche II in 1977 brought new fascia, better air conditioning, and more precise rack-and-pinion steering, all shared with Shadow II.

Aluminum body panels

Non-independent rear suspension; a system also known as "solid axle"

Tough platform chassis made from steel box

▽ **Aston Martin V8 1972**

Origin	UK
Engine	5,340 cc, V8
Top speed	162 mph (259 km/h)

The big potent Aston Martin V8 had 282–438 bhp, and was sharply styled by William Towns. A huge success, the car stayed in production for two decades. A high-performance Vantage model was the fastest-accelerating four-seater in the world, while Volante was an elegant convertible version.

Interior offers space for a driver and three passengers

Steel body with a lightweight fiberglass floor

Pop-up headlights

▽ **Ferrari 400GT 1976**

Origin	Italy
Engine	4,823 cc, V12
Top speed	156 mph (251 km/h)

Unlike Ferrari's traditional sports models, the 400 was designed for long-distance cruising, could seat a driver and three passengers, and was its first car with an automatic gearbox. In spite of the fact that Ferrari purists considered the 400 controversial, it sold well.

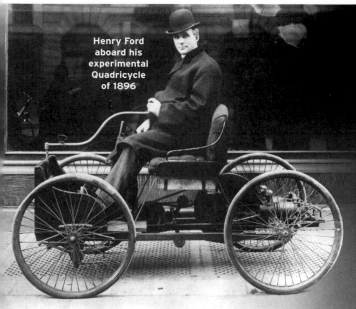

Henry Ford aboard his experimental Quadricycle of 1896

Great Marques
The Ford Story

Henry Ford was the first motor manufacturer to use mass-production techniques, and his Model T was the best-selling car of its era. The company he founded has been one of the world's largest automakers for decades, with an enviable automotive portfolio as broad as any in the industry.

FORD WENT TO WORK AS A MECHANIC in Detroit at the age of 16, and experimented with newfangled gas engines in his spare time. He built his first "horseless carriage" in 1896 and finished a second in 1898. His designs won backing from Detroit businessman, William H. Murphy, who founded the Detroit Automobile Company with Ford as technical chief to build cars. However, the venture made little headway, and was closed in 1901. Ford started again with his Henry Ford Motor Company, but failed to get a complete car ready for production. When his backers brought in the automotive entrepreneur Henry M. Leland as a consultant, Ford left the company, which was then reorganized and became Cadillac.

Ford then founded the Ford Motor Company in June 1903. Here, he was finally able to build a complete production car, the two-cylinder Model A. The four-cylinder Model B and six-cylinder, Model K, which followed were the result of Ford's partner Alexander Malcomson's desire to take the company upmarket. However, Ford wanted to concentrate on low-priced cars instead, and he bought out Malcolmson in 1906 so that he could follow his own path unhindered.

This led to the most successful of his cars, the Model T, in 1908. At $850, the "Tin Lizzie" was more affordable than most cars, yet it offered neat, modern styling, a new four-cylinder engine, and an easy-to-use transmission. It was a roaring success, so much so that Ford was forced to refine the production process to keep up with demand. In 1913, the company pioneered the use of a moving production line, cutting the time taken to build a Model T from over 12 hours to just 93 minutes.

But as much as the Model T had created the foundation for Ford's success, it almost brought the company to its knees. Unable to see that competitors were catching up to and surpassing the Model T, Henry Ford kept it in production until 1927, by which time it was hopelessly outclassed. Ford had nothing to replace it with, and car production had to be halted for six months while a new Model A was prepared.

Ford's son Edsel had been in line to take over the company but he died young, so it was Edsel's son, Henry Ford II, who took control when Ford senior died in 1947. In the postwar period, the company pioneered new market segments with the 1955 Thunderbird and 1964 Mustang,

Anglia a **real** car for your money

Ford Anglia 105E, 1959
With this crisply styled, UK-market Anglia, Ford added driving enjoyment to economy cars, with a four- speed, synchromesh gearbox and a rev-happy engine.

and earned a reputation for good-value cars for the mass-market. In Europe, Ford led sales charts with the Anglia, Cortina, and Escort. But the Blue Oval was not restricted to humdrum family motoring: it instituted a "Total Performance" program in the 1960s, which saw it succeed in every class of motorsports it cared to attempt. Its modern V8s won in IndyCar racing and in NASCAR, the GT40 beat Ferrari at Le Mans, and in Europe the Anglia proved an effective sedan racer while the Escort became the car to beat in rallying. Ford also bankrolled the Cosworth DFV engine,

Ford Thunderbird, 1958
After four years as a relatively compact car, the 1958 T-Bird grew in length, weight, and luxury, as the design became ever more elaborate.

"The MK IV Cortina has all the attributes that sent its predecessors **rocketing to the top of the sales** charts."

MOTOR MAGAZINE, OCTOBER 1976

which became the most successful in the history of Formula 1 and then went on to a turbocharged second career as a CART/IndyCar power unit.

However, Ford's reputation suffered in the 1970s due to the Pinto compact's safety failings, which led to a recall of 1.5 million models, the largest recall in automotive history, up to that time. There were further troubles in the 1980s, as Ford struggled to cope with the effects of the energy crisis. It fought back with aerodynamic

body shapes and won new generations of customers thanks to the design leadership of J Mays and the technical efforts of Richard Parry-Jones.

Ford survived the recession of 2008 without government assistance, though it steadily sold off both Hertz and its stable of luxury brands, including Aston Martin, Jaguar, Land Rover, and Volvo. Today, the company has returned to profitability in the US, and is refocusing on Europe in an attempt to boost its performance and sales there.

Ford Mustang, 1964
Demand was so strong for Ford's "personal" car that sales topped 1 million units in less than two years.

CLASSICS OF THE FUTURE

Racing Puma The Puma coupe was reworked by Ford's rally engineers in Boreham, England with bigger Alcon brakes, wider track, wide aluminum fenders, bucket seats, and extra power. The FRP engine was closely based on the standard 1.7-liter Puma unit, with hotter camshafts and freer-flowing intake and exhaust systems liberating an extra 30 bhp. The high price kept sales down, so only 500 were ultimately made—all by Tickford, which had previously assembled the Sierra RS500.

△ **Ford Racing Puma 1999**

Origin	UK
Engine	1,679 cc, straight four
Top speed	121 mph (195 km/h)

This limited-edition performance version of the curvy Ford coupe had an engagingly lively character and rally car genes.

GT Ford kicked off its GT40 revival with a concept car in 2002, followed by a production GT in 2004. It was more than just a new run of an old car: it had a superplastic-formed aluminum chassis with aluminum body panels, and was noticeably bigger than the old racer. Power came from a 5.4-liter, four-valve version of Ford's Modular V8 engine boosted by a Lysholm screw-type supercharger. Just over 4,000 of this amazing blend of classic style and 21st-century technology were built.

△ **Ford GT 2004**

Origin	USA
Engine	5,409 cc, V8
Top speed	206 mph (332 km/h)

Although it looks just like the 1960's GT40, this was a completely new car, with an alloy chassis and body, and supercharged V8 power.

Hatchbacks

Hatchbacks were the big trend of the 1970s. Within a few years almost all small cars had adopted the front-engine, front-wheel drive layout and the rear hatch body style with three or five doors to add practicality. Fold-flat rear seats provided even more versatility. The seats were often split—one side could be folded but the other left in place for passenger use—extending the adaptability of the hatchback. Hot hatches, such as the Volkswagen Golf GTi, added performance and modern sports car styling but retained most of the practicality. They proved immensely popular around the globe, but were largely limited to cult status in America.

Fuel-saving design
American Motor's chief stylist Richard A. Teague developed the Pacer's aerodynamic design in response to the two fuel crises of the 1970s. The car's slippery shape achieved a relatively low drag efficiency, but its large engine proved thirsty. Nonetheless the car sold well.

▷ **AMC Pacer 1975**

Origin	USA
Engine	3,802 cc, straight-six
Top speed	92 mph (148 km/h)

Advertised as "the first wide small car," the Pacer had the passenger compartment of a sedan, the nose of a European commuter shuttle, and no back end at all. However, it did not offer the economy that drivers expected from a compact car.

Gutterless
roof design

Passenger door
wider than the driver's door

Distinctive
bug-eye headlights

Larger engine
than European and Japanese rivals

Compact and quirky
Designed as a compact car for US drivers more accustomed to the interior space found in full-size models, the Pacer offered room for a driver and three passengers. It was quickly dubbed "The Flying Fishbowl."

Large windows
cause the interior to broil in summer

SIDE VIEW

Transverse
in-line engine

**Hatchback body
style** provides
practicality

▷ **Austin Maxi 1969**

Origin UK

Engine 1,748 cc, straight-four

Top speed 97 mph (156 km/h)

The packaging skills of Alec Issigonis
(see pp. 146-47) shone in the transverse-
engined Maxi, the last car he produced
before retirement. It had hydrolastic
suspension and a five-speed gearbox
(rare then), but its cable operation
proved unreliable. This Maxi sold
well during the 1970s.

**Front and rear
seats** fold back
to form a bed

GTi has matte
black rear
window surround

Transverse four-cylinder
fuel-injected engine

◁ **Volkswagen Golf GTI 1975**

Origin Germany

Engine 1,588 cc, straight-four

Top speed 112 mph (180 km/h)

Developed by Volkswagen engineers
as an off-hours side project, the Golf
GTi proved to be a phenomenal sales
success and set the pattern for
generations of hot hatches to come.
GTi versions have been a core part of
Golf model ranges ever since.

Engine mounted
at an angle

▷ **Renault 14 1976**

Origin France

Engine 1,218 cc, straight-four

Top speed 89 mph (143 km/h)

Renault sold almost a million of this
pear-shaped, five-door hatch. It featured
a transverse canted-over Douvrin engine
with its transmission in the sump, which
it shared with the Peugeot 104 and
Citroën Visa. Spacious and comfortable
to ride in, the car was prone to rust.

Torsion bar
suspension

Aerodynamic
design reduces
wind drag

Impact-resistent
plastic bumpers

◁ **Fiat Strada/Ritmo 1978**

Origin Italy

Engine 1,585 cc, straight-four

Top speed 111 mph (179 km/h)

Fiat was eager to stress that this car
was built by robots. Its geometric
lines led some to suggest it had been
styled by them, too. The car had a
peppy engine and tidy handling, but
protection from rust was feeble.
Abarth's twin-cam performance
versions were reputedly fun to drive.

Quirky Small Cars

Fast can be fun, but these cars demonstrated that there were plenty of other ways to get your motoring kicks. From pint-sized sports cars to the quirkiest of lightweight economy cars, they proved that good things really did come in small packages. And they fit with the mood of the times. After the oil crisis in 1973, when petrol shortages almost led to the reintroduction of rationing, the cost of fuel skyrocketed and even those who could afford higher prices did not want to look wasteful. Suddenly small, efficient cars were all the rage.

Ogle-designed fiberglass body

Interior has four seats

▷ **Reliant Robin 1973**

Origin UK

Engine 848 cc, straight-four

Top speed 80 mph (129 km/h)

This plastic-bodied three-wheeler was designed by Ogle and made by Reliant in Tamworth. It was popular in the UK during the 1970s' fuel crisis. It was thrifty due to its low weight, and in the UK it could be driven on a motorbike license.

Optional rear luggage rack

Rostyle wheels standard but wire options available

◁ **MG Midget Mk III 1969**

Origin UK

Engine 1,275 cc, straight-four

Top speed 95 mph (153 km/h)

The beloved Sprite/Midget was updated for the 1970s with features including rounded rear wheel-arches, a bigger engine, matte black trim, and a better hood. Revisions in 1974 added black bumpers and a Triumph Spitfire engine, and raised the ride height.

Matte black sills visually lower the Midget

Tall wing mirrors offer a good view to the rear

Tiny engine thrives on revs

Glass rear window lifts for access to luggage space

▷ **Honda Z Coupe 1970**

Origin Japan

Engine 598 cc straight two

Top speed 77 mph (124 km/h)

Bigger-engined twin of the Z360, this little coupe followed from the equally tiny N "kei car." Only the larger-engined Zs were sold in the UK and US, but they still produced only 36 bhp. However, while they were not particularly speedy, they were frantic and huge fun.

Rear window lifts for access to luggage

Live rear axle with leaf springs

FRONT VIEW

Single front wheel
Like Reliant's previous three-wheelers, and in contrast to cars such as the Morgan, the Robin had its single wheel at the front. This made the steering and front suspension simpler and lighter.

REAR VIEW

Partly practical
The Robin's fiberglass body had an opening rear window for access to the load space. As the window did not extend very far, items had to be lifted high up to get them into the trunk.

Simple interior
The Robin's dashboard was a fiberglass molding with a speedometer and this combination fuel-and-temperature gauge. Switches were spread across the fascia rather haphazardly.

▷ **Bond Bug 1970**

Origin	UK
Engine	700 cc, straight-four
Top speed	76 mph (122 km/h)

The three-wheeled Bug embodied the spirit of youth, freedom, humor, and optimism with which Britain entered the 1970s. But it cost as much as a Mini, although it was quicker and more exclusive. Fewer than 3,000 people were inspired to buy one.

Canopy lifts for access to interior

700 cc Reliant engine unit

Self-color, fiberglass body

Two tiny seats in the rear

Disc brakes at front

◁ **Suzuki SC100**

Origin	Japan
Engine	970 cc, straight-four
Top speed	89 mph (143 km/h)

Suzuki inserted a bigger four-cylinder engine into the back of its tiny Japanese-market Cervo coupe to make the export-model SC100 in 1978. Not fast, but enormous fun to drive thanks to rear-wheel drive and all-round independent suspension. Today's owners are more enthusiastic about them than ever.

Invasion of the Roadsters

In the 1970s, North America simply couldn't get enough of imported sports cars, and demand especially from the "sunshine states" was a lifeline for many European marques, such as the UK's MG and Triumph, and Italy's Alfa Romeo and Fiat. Roadsters like the MGB and Fiat 124 Spider were exact opposites of the typical American car—their small size, nimble handling, and dainty lines couldn't be found in anything produced locally.

TWO-SEATER FUN

The Triumph Spitfire 1500, which made its debut in 1970, was a very strong seller in the US throughout the following decade. Although it was built in Coventry, England, most of the cars

produced there were left-hand-drive models, and left the factory with export documents taped to their windshields. British Leyland, Triumph's parent company, failed to produce a replacement model for the Spitfire, leaving a gap in the roadster market that was subsequently filled by the Mazda Miata beginning in 1990. The spunky Spitfire, however, has since become a classic car favorite, still offering open-top fun with low running costs.

A large consignment of colorful Triumph Spitfire 1500s–in soft-top and hardtop forms–destined for export to the US, photographed in about 1976.

Mid-Engined Marvels

Sports cars at all levels adopted a race-proven, mid-engined layout in the 1970s. Mounting the motor amidships provided extra cornering agility, greater handling precision, and better traction. Moving the engine behind the passengers also meant the nose could be lower, which helped to improve aerodynamic efficiency and inspired some spectacular, wedge-shaped body designs. Luggage space could be restricted, however, and engine access was often tricky. Mid-engined cars also proved to be noisy, and in some designs the transmissions shifted poorly. But even with small engines and relatively little power, they were the ultimate in driving thrills and drama.

Sleek design
Locating the engine behind the passengers allowed for a low, sloping hood that forced air downward onto the nose and front wheels, improving grip. To provide cooling, conical air inlets were positioned behind the front doors, channeling the air to the engine bay.

▷ **Ferrari 308 GTS 1977**

Origin	Italy
Engine	2,926 cc, V8
Top speed	154 mph (249 km/h)

One of the bestselling Ferraris ever, Pininfarina designed the gorgeous body and Scaglietti built it. The engine and gearbox were both inherited from the 308 GT4. Later cars had four valves per cylinder and Bosch fuel injection.

Cabin seats the driver and one passenger

Fiberglass body panel later replaced by steel

Mid-mounted, four-cam V8

Roof has removable targa top panels

Familiar features
The 308 featured design details from the Dino 246, while a black stripe along the side evoked the 365 GT4's familiar twin-body, shell appearance.

DXI 308

SIDE VIEW

Rear spoiler
fitted to Gran
Finale cars

**SOHC
four**
engine

Roof panel
lifts off

Luggage space
in nose

◁ **Fiat X1/9 1972**

Origin Italy

Engine 1,498 cc, straight-four

Top speed 110 mph (177 km/h)

The X1/9 brought mid-engined sports cars
to the masses. Bertone designed and built
the wedge-shaped body, and Fiat supplied
the mechanical parts. However, from 1982
Bertone took over final assembly and
marketing. The X1/9 remained popular
in Europe and the US right up to 1989.

Seating for two front
passengers next to the driver

Polyurethane
body panels

▷ **Matra-Simca Bagheera 1973**

Origin France

Engine 1,422 cc, straight-four

Top speed 110 mph (177 km/h)

An aerospace company built this
mid-engined coupe using engines and
transmissions from Simca family cars. It had
unusual three-abreast seating and a plastic
body. A facelift of the car undertaken in
1976 affected almost every panel, and
smoothed out the styling. It was replaced by
the Murena, another three-seater, in 1980.

**Buttress body
features** later
gain glass panels

Steel body
styled and built
by Pininfarina

◁ **Lancia Beta Montecarlo 1975**

Origin Italy

Engine 1,756 cc, straight-four

Top speed 118 mph (190 km/h)

Proposed in 1969 as a V6 Fiat but
launched as a four-cylinder Lancia,
this model was reworked in 1978 with
glass panels in the flying buttresses for
better visibility, and the brake servo was
removed. Lancia ultimately developed this
into a successful turbo racing car.

Longitudinal
four-cylinder
engine

Pop-up
headlights

▷ **Lotus Esprit Turbo 1980**

Origin UK

Engine 2,174 cc, straight-four

Top speed 148 mph (238 km/h)

Lotus road cars reached supercar status
when the exotic Giugiaro-styled Esprit
(introduced in 1976) was given a capacity
upgrade and a turbocharger.

Steel backbone
chassis design

Great Marques
The Porsche Story

A galaxy of legendary road and racing cars has carried the Porsche family name since 1948. There is an unbroken lineage from the earliest 356 to the current 911, spiced with countless race successes, although Porsche's non-sports car models have proven even more popular with audiences worldwide.

WHEN IN 1948
Dr. Ferdinand Porsche decided to become a car manufacturer in his own right, Austria's most outstanding automotive engineer already had five decades of car design innovation behind him— including four-wheel drive, superchargers, rear-engined Formula 1 cars, and, of course, the Volkswagen Beetle.

Together with his son Ferry, Porsche created a "weekend sports car," using the chassis of the Beetle but with a lighter, more aerodynamic body and a mildly tuned Volkswagen, flat-four, air-cooled engine. Out of this humble cocktail, the Porsche 356 was born, and one of the world's most exciting and innovative sports car names grew.

The company started production of the model in an old sawmill in Gmünd, Austria in 1948, and the first 52 cars were built entirely by hand. The 356 was agile and fun, but also uncommonly reliable and comfortable. Lightweight with nimble handling, this rear-engined, rear-wheel-drive sports car was available in both hardtop coupe and open configuration.

The first Porsche 356 was sold in the US in 1950 and, with engine power upped from 40 to 60bhp, the little rocket quickly established a cult following for its quick responses. Even today, these early Porsches are highly desired by collectors and enthusiasts worldwide.

In 1953, a sports-racing model called the 550 Spyder established Porsche as a major player in motorsports. Starting in more than 370 races around the European and US circuits between 1953 and 1965, the Spyder outshone the more powerful cars in its class. It was easy to handle on both the road and track, and was extremely

Porsche 550 Spyder
Actor James Dean (right) with Rolf Wutherich in Dean's 550 Spyder; the teen heartthrob would die in the car in a crash in California in September 1955.

flexible. But it hit the spotlight in 1955 when film star James Dean was killed in his 550 in a freak road traffic accident in Cholame, California.

By 1958 the 10,000th Porsche had been built, including the now highly coveted 356 Speedster and the 100bhp Carrera. But when the 911 replaced the 356 in 1963, a new chapter began for Porsche. The technical centerpiece was Porsche's all-new flat-six engine, while the sleek, fastback shape (the work of Ferry's son Butzi) would rapidly turn it into an automotive icon. The Targa version of 1966 offered open-top motoring with a removable roof panel and a fixed rollover bar. The 1973 Carrera RS, with 2.7-liter engine and lightweight construction, was the ultimate incarnation of the original 911.

The company rekindled its relationship with Volkswagen in 1969 when the partners co-designed the mid-engined 914, giving buyers a choice of VW or Porsche engines. Its replacement in 1975 was the Porsche 924—the firm's first front-engined, water-cooled model.

Porsche had originally planned to replace its 911, including the 160mph (258km/h) Turbo, with its impressive 928 in 1977, another front-engined model with a brand-new V8 power unit. The 911 was hugely popular, however, and the never-ending demand kept the model in production with near-constant updates.

Porsche 356 Speedster
Seen on the left alongside a 356 Coupe in 1956, the Speedster had a racy, cut-down windshield that was immediately distinctive.

From 1972, Porsche began offering its engineering research and development skills to outside companies. Its own products also continued to evolve, and in 1982 the 924 became the finessed 944. Faster than its predecessor, the new version included a Porsche-specific engine that could be purchased with or without turbocharging.

In 1990 a radically revamped 911 now offered four-wheel drive—the rear-engined layout, with pronounced rear-weight bias, was a challenge for the uninitiated driver. Three years later, the concept car for a new mid-engined roadster, the Boxster, was unveiled, and a production version joined the range in 1997, shortly after Porsche made its millionth sports car.

An historic era ended in 1998 when the 911's water-cooled engine ended the air-cooled association that stretched back to Ferdinand Porsche's Volkswagen. However, that was nothing compared to the company's radical next

"I couldn't find the sports car I dreamed of, so I decided to build it myself."

DR. FERDINAND PORSCHE

Porsche 911S, 1970
Topping the range of 911s, now all with a longer wheelbase and 2.2-liter engines, was the 180 bhp S model. With lighter handling and increased performance, it had a top speed of 230 mph (370 km/h).

move—the introduction of the Cayenne sport-utility vehicle in 2002. The car was in instant sales smash around the world. In 2009 the Panamera, a powerful new luxury sedan joined the range. Like the Cayenne, it was created in partnership with VW. Yet, destined to appeal to new customers in China, it veered away from Porsche's usual offerings.

The open-cockpit Carrera GT, with a 6-liter, V10 engine, arrived in 2003—a 200 mph (322 km/h) supercar bridging the gap between Porsche's road and race cars. At speeds above 70 mph (113 km/h),

the Carrera GT's automated rear spoiler could be deployed into the air draft to reduce lift by generating stabilizing downforce.

Porsche has become synonymous with sports and race cars alike, winning the 24 hours of Le Mans more than a dozen times (in 1970 with the 917 and later with the 936 and 962 cars), among some 24,000 other race victories worldwide.

CLASSICS OF THE FUTURE

911 Carrera S The purity of the 911 concept has remained undiluted since 1963, although this contemporary model, codenamed the 991, used a third-generation platform with aluminum dominating its construction—its lighter weight offsetting its enlarged proportions. Extremely fast, with up to 430 bhp on tap, it could sprint to 60 mph (96 km/h) in just 3.9 seconds, and was the first car ever with a seven-speed manual gearbox.

△ **Porsche 911 Carrera S 2012**

Origin	Germany
Engine	3,800 cc, flat-six
Top speed	130 mph (209 km/h)

The latest generation of the legendary 911, this is the most powerful non-turbo, rear-wheel-drive model—Porsche engineering purity at its finest.

918 Spyder This mid-engined roadster with plug-in hybrid technology was manufactured between 2013 and 2015, with exactly 918 examples completed. A remarkable machine, thanks to its combination of gasoline V8 engine and lithium-ion batteries, it delivered a combined power output of 887 bhp. The car lapped Germany's 12.8-mile (20.6-km) Nürburgring racetrack at 6 minutes 57 seconds, a world record for a road car.

△ **918 Spyder 2013**

Origin	Germany
Engine	V8/twin electric motors
Top speed	218 mph (350 km/h)

Porsche broke new ground with this carbon-fiber supercar, mixing a Le Mans racing engine with electric motors front and rear.

Stylish Coupes

There was a greater choice of affordable, high-style coupes in this decade than there had ever been before. Some had two doors, some added a rear hatch, and almost all were based to some degree on the engines, transmissions, suspension components, and structural platforms of their bigger-selling sedan brethren. All of them were designed with the same aim in mind: to offer clean-cut style, drama, and elegance that even the best sedans—which inevitably had to make more compromises in the name of practicality—could scarcely hope to match.

Sunroof available on some models

Integrated rear spoiler

▷ **Mazda RX-7 1978**

Origin Japan

Engine 1,146 cc, two-rotor Wankel

Top speed 125 mph (201 km/h)

The RX-7 sold on its clean European looks and the Swiss-watch smoothness of its rotary engine. Mazda was the first to make Felix Wankel's engine actually work and the RX-7 was a desirable and well-built car popular throughout the early 1980s.

Engine has two Japanese Hitachi carburetors

▷ **Datsun 240Z 1969**

Origin Japan

Engine 2,393 cc, straight six-cylinder

Top speed 125 mph (201 km/h)

The 240Z established Japan on the world sports car stage at a time when there was a gaping hole in that sector. It had the looks, performance, handling, and equipment levels. A great value sporting package that outsold all rivals and founded a Z-car dynasty.

"Dustbin lid" wheel trims now rare

All-independent strut-type suspension

Taillights have distinctive circular shape

Fuel-injected four-cylinder engine

◁ **Opel Manta GT/E 1970**

Origin Germany

Engine 1,897 cc, straight-four

Top speed 116 mph (186 km/h)

Despite attractive styling and almost half-a-million made, most Mantas have rusted away: a great shame, as this was a civilized touring car with engines from 1.2 to 1.9 liters. The fuel-injected GT/E was the highest-specification model, although there was a rare turbo version in 1973.

Rotary Power
Instead of pistons in cylinders, the Wankel engine has, in essence, triangular rotating elements inside a figure eight shaped chamber. Because there are no reciprocating parts, the engine revs very smoothly.

Smooth Snout
The RX-7 is a great example of the emerging sports car styling trend—a low, penetrating nose with pop-up headlamps, plastic bumpers, and an air dam to reduce front-end aerodynamic lift at speed.

FRONT VIEW

Impact-resistant plastic bumpers

Alloy wheels are a standard feature

Practical and Purposeful
The RX-7's rear window lifts up for access to the luggage space behind the rear seats. A big rubber spoiler is essential trim for an 70s sports car. There's no exterior brightwork here—everything is either body-colored or black.

REAR VIEW

Rear hatch opens slightly for ventilation

Plexiglass panel covers grille and lights

▷ **Alfa Romeo Junior Zagato 1970**

Origin	Italy
Engine	1,290 cc, straight-four
Top speed	105 mph (169 km/h)

Ercole Spada at Zagato achieved the impossible: he took an Alfa Romeo GT Junior and turned it into something even more arresting to look at. Alloy doors and hood made for minor weight reduction, but it was only fractionally faster than the standard car. The cost held back sales.

Doors made of alloy

Curved rear window lifts for access to luggage space

Front-mounted, water-cooled engine a first for Porsche

◁ **Porsche 924 1976**

Origin	Germany
Engine	1,984 cc, straight-four
Top speed	125 mph (201 km/h)

Purists disapprove of the 924's provenance: originally it was a Volkswagen/Porsche joint venture, and its engine was shared with a Volkswagen van (though with a new Porsche cylinder head). But the front-engined 924 was a best-seller for Porsche and expanded its market beyond the dedicated sporting driver.

The 1980s
ADVANCING TECHNOLOGY

Only those who dare... truly live

ADVANCING TECHNOLOGY

△ **Grand unveiling**
The Jaguar XJ220 prototype car is unveiled at the 1988 British International Motor Show held in Birmingham, UK. It recieved an overwhelmingly positive reception.

Cars from 1980 are recognizably related to those on sale today. In overall concept, the typical car has hardly changed at all, and the electronic systems in modern cars owe a great deal to the technical advances of the 1980s.

Perhaps the most significant development was the introduction of automotive electronics and sensors, which began to appear throughout this period. These triggered a mini revolution in engine management systems, increasing fuel efficiency, and leading to power units that could perform more reliably and consistently. Furthermore, functions that maximized convenience and luxury such as electrically assisted seats and windows could now be incorporated, safe in the knowledge that they would work properly.

Engine systems and transmissions advanced, too. Fuel injection, turbochargers, and four-wheel drive all began the decade as exotic new technologies and ended it as relatively commonplace features. Emissions rates were significantly reduced thanks to the widespread introduction of lead-free fuels and catalytic converters.

Designers were drawn to experiment with new formats for the family car, such as the off-road sport-utility and versatile multipurpose vehicle (SUV and MPV respectively). In the upper echelons, roadgoing supercars finally pushed top speeds beyond 200 mph (322 km/h).

Competent cars from South Korea now fought for a slice of world markets alongside their Japanese, American, and European rivals. Everywhere there was a drive toward increasing standardization as many outwardly different cars began sharing internal platforms to cut the huge investment costs now demanded to turn a simple design into complex reality.

> " Mud, snow, water, woods—you can take a **rented** car **anywhere**. True, you can't always get it back—but that's not your **problem**, is it?"

SATIRIST P.J. O'ROURKE IN HIS 1987 BOOK *REPUBLICAN PARTY REPTILE*

◁ **US magazine ad** for the Ferrari 308 GTB, 1981

Key events

▷ **1980** MG's world-famous Abingdon plant closes down.

▷ **1981** The Audi Quattro is the first car with four-wheel drive and a turbocharged engine.

▷ **1982** TV series *Knight Rider* makes a star of the new Pontiac Firebird, a robot car named KITT.

▷ **1983** Chrysler's Plymouth Voyager/ Dodge Caravan begins the trend for multipurpose vehicles (MPVs).

▷ **1984** Toyota launches its affordable mid-engined sports car, the MR2.

▷ **1984** Jaguar is privatized and floated on the London Stock Exchange.

▷ **1985** General Motors creates Saturn, an all-new marque, to combat Toyota.

▷ **1987** Ford buys a 75 percent stake in Aston Martin.

▷ **1987** Enzo Ferrari unveils the 201 mph (323 km/h) Ferrari F40; he dies the following year.

▷ **1988** Jaguar reveals its sensational XJ220 supercar.

▷ **1989** The M5 edition of the BMW 5 series is acclaimed as the world's best sports sedan.

△ **Mini milestone**
After nearly thirty years since its launch, the five-millionth example of the original Mini is built in 1986. Production ceased in 2000—after 5,387,862 cars.

Renault 5 Turbo

A true pocket-rocket, the 1980 Renault 5 Turbo was clearly related to the company's popular Super Cinq, but in terms of engineering, construction, and performance it was a whole different beast. Intended primarily for rallying, and therefore pitted head to head with cars such as the Lancia Stratos and Audi Quattro, it also became a successful road car with more than 3,500 sold over a four-year period.

WITH SOME RADICAL restyling, Bertone's Marcello Gandini transformed the familiar 5 Turbo into a two-seater with rear-wheel drive. The back half of the cabin was taken up by a fire-breathing, 1397 cc Cléon-Fonte, turbocharged, four-cylinder engine.

With a long and successful history in motorsport, the resulting machine nevertheless proved to be a real landmark car for Renault. As one of the most super superminis ever created, it went on to win the opening round of the 1981 World Rally Championship race, the historic Monte Carlo Rally.

SIDE VIEW

SPECIFICATIONS	
Model	Renault 5 Turbo, 1980–86
Assembly	France and Belgium
Production	3,576
Construction	Aluminum and fiberglass monocoque
Engine	1397 cc, straight-four
Power output	158 bhp (in standard form)
Transmission	5-speed manual
Suspension	Front and rear coil springs
Brakes	Four-wheel discs
Maximum speed	130 mph (209 km/h)

Cars were built by Renault's Alpine subsidiary at its factory in Dieppe, northern France

Renault badge
Intended to highlight the company's quality, design, and engineering, the diamond badge was first introduced in 1925. Initially it included the word "Renault" on a central crossbar, but with increasing brand recognition, this was removed in 1972 to simplify the graphic device.

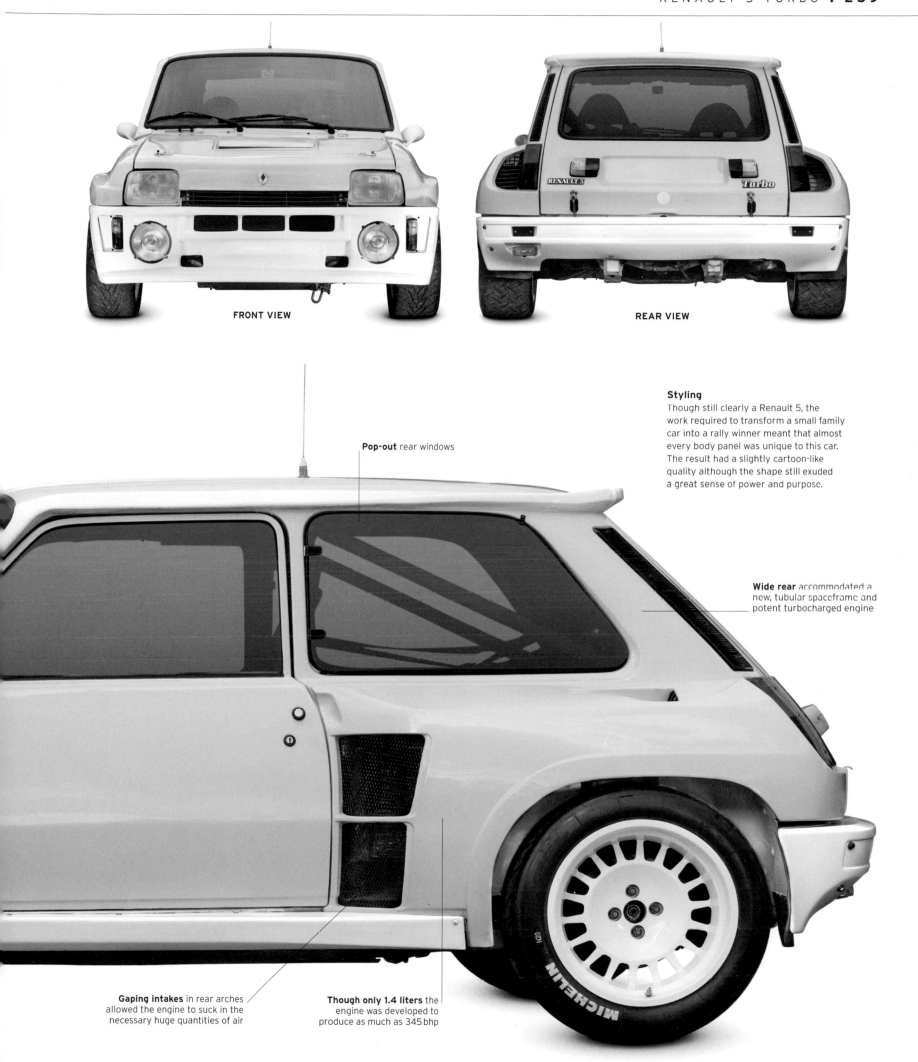

FRONT VIEW

REAR VIEW

Styling
Though still clearly a Renault 5, the
work required to transform a small family
car into a rally winner meant that almost
every body panel was unique to this car.
The result had a slightly cartoon-like
quality although the shape still exuded
a great sense of power and purpose.

Pop-out rear windows

Wide rear accommodated a
new, tubular spaceframe and
potent turbocharged engine

Gaping intakes in rear arches
allowed the engine to suck in the
necessary huge quantities of air

Though only 1.4 liters the
engine was developed to
produce as much as 345 bhp

ON THE ROAD

Something of a golden era for rally car racing, the late-1970s and early '80s saw big names such as Ford, Audi, and Renault spending huge sums of money in a bid to wow spectators and car buyers alike. Renault's challenger looked much like the standard R5 but it was effectively an entirely new car, and one which arguably owed more to the company's pioneering Formula 1 contenders—the first to introduce turbocharging—than to the chic, bestselling supermini. Removing the body revealed the stark, purposeful racing machine it really was. That this could be driven quite legally on normal roads seemed astonishing, but it also explains why such an odd little vehicle commanded so much attention as a modern classic.

1. Rear lights are one of few parts shared with standard R5 **2.** Fog lamps inserted into front skirt—essential for rallying **3.** Air intakes cool the front brakes **4.** Rear mirror encased in impact-resistant plastic **5.** Lightweight alloy wheels **6.** Turbo badge hints at car's performance **7.** Heavily modified dashboard features equipment used in rallying **8.** Complex electrical systems maximize performance **9.** Turbocharged Renault engine

RENAULT 5

Performance 4x4s

Fast cars took a radical new direction in the 1980s. Led by Audi's Quattro, a new generation of performance machines adopted four wheel-drive for the first time, delivering optimum traction and improved handling. The Quattro was soon winning in rallies, where loose-surface traction is vital, and other manufacturers quickly followed suit. Lancia developed a four-wheel-drive version of its Delta HF Turbo and refined it into the definitive Delta Integrale, Ford produced their all-drive Sapphire Cosworth, and there were rally competitors from Peugeot, Toyota, and more—plus a host of all-wheel-drive performance cars dedicated to road use.

Four rings
Audi's four ring logo is a clue to the company's heritage. The rings represent the four German manufacturers that were brought together in the Auto Union group in 1932–Audi, DKW, Horch, and Wanderer. The Audi name had disappeared in the 1930s but was resurrected in 1965.

▷ **Audi Quattro Sport 1983**

Origin Germany

Engine 2,133 cc, straight-five

Top speed 155 mph (250 km/h)

The Quattro changed the way we think about four-wheel drive, and the Quattro Sport tailored it for rallying with a short wheelbase, 300 bhp engine, and a body made of aluminum, fiberglass, and Kevlar. It had all of the charisma, and nearly all the performance, of a Ferrari GTO.

Steeply raked windshield

Alloy five-cylinder engine

Lightweight power
Like the regular Quattro, the Sport had an in-line five-cylinder engine, but it was otherwise very different. The block was made of aluminum alloy, and the alloy head had four valves per cylinder. Road engines had just over 300 bhp—rally cars had 500 bhp.

Short cut
The original Quattro was too big and heavy for rallying, so Audi cut more than 12 in (30 cm) from the wheelbase to make the Quattro Sport lighter and more agile. The reduction in length was most noticeable at the rear side window.

Luxurious, leather-trimmed interior

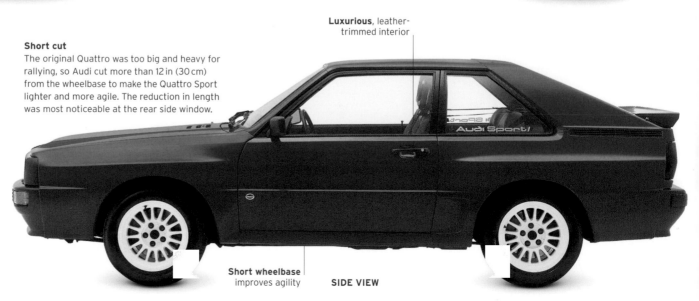

Short wheelbase improves agility

SIDE VIEW

Scroll-type "G-lader" supercharged engine

▷ **Volkswagen Golf Rallye 1989**

Origin Germany/Belgium

Engine 1,763 cc, straight-four

Top speed 130 mph (209 km/h)

Volkswagen also jumped on the all-drive rally-car bandwagon. This supercharged Golf used the company's Syncro four-wheel-drive system, and its boxy wheel arches and rectangular headlamps made it look quite different than a regular Golf Mk 2.

Distinctive box arches and bodykit

Aftermarket body-colored taillamp lenses

Crisp lines contrasted with the "jello mold" styles common at the time

Trunklid spoiler denotes Turbo model

Larger-engined 21s like the Turbo had north-south engine orientation

◁ **Renault Turbo 21 1986**

Origin France

Engine 1,995 cc, straight-four

Top speed 141 mph (228 km/h)

Renault's forgettable repmobile was turned into a dramatic sports car with the addition of a 2-liter turbo engine. Turbo Quadra models added four-wheel drive to tame the wheelspin on the original two-wheel-drive car. However, its questionable build-quality means there are very few survivors.

Body styled by Pininfarina

▷ **Peugeot 405 1987**

Origin France

Engine 1,905 cc, straight-four

Top speed 135 mph (217 km/h)

Peugeot followed up the excellent 205GTI hot hatch with the two-wheel-drive 405Mi16 sport sedan and its rare 405Mi16x4 four-wheel-drive stablemate. The smooth, 16-valve engine produced 158 bhp, and the chassis offered a blend of grip, agility, and ride quality. Sadly, however, the 405 was not built to last.

Four-cylinder engine with four valves per cylinder

Five-spoke alloy wheels standard

Attractive interior with striped, cloth sports seats

All Integrales were left-hand drive

Raised hood makes space for turbocharged, intercooled engine

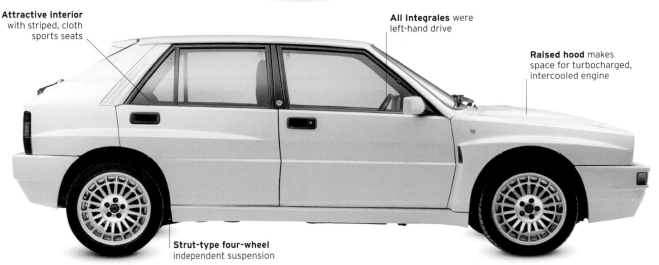

◁ **Lancia Delta Integrale 1987**

Origin Italy

Engine 1,995 cc, straight-four

Top speed 134 mph (215 km/h)

Giugiaro's Delta was very modern for its time, and was European Car of the Year in 1980. The HF Turbo version added extra pace, then Lancia provided four-wheel drive and ultimately a 16-valve head to turn a stylish runabout into the multi-rally-winning Integrale.

Strut-type four-wheel independent suspension

Great Designers
Giorgetto Giugiaro

A colossus in the world of design, Giorgetto Giugiaro is often regarded as the greatest car stylist of all time. A precocious talent, he showed an aptitude for design while still a teenager, and created some of the most beautiful car shapes in history. He also invented the angular "folded paper" design style, made truly remarkable concept cars, and even designed his own pasta.

Career highlights

▷ **1955** Giugiaro takes his first job at the Fiat Special Vehicles Styling Center in Milan

▷ **1959** Nuccio Bertone offers a 20-year-old Giugiaro the position of design chief at his company

▷ **1965** Giugiaro moves over to head up design at Ghia

▷ **1968** Giugiaro sets up his own design company, which will come to be named Italdesign

▷ **1971** Italdesign's first commercial project is completed – the Alfa Romeo Alfasud

△ **Maserati Boomerang, 1971**
The wedge-shaped Boomerang, with its stark, angled body, had a huge impact when first revealed. Elements of its design would be echoed in several Giugiaro designs in the following years.

▷ **1973** The first design for Volkswagen enters production–the VW Passat–followed by the Mk1 VW Golf

▷ **1976** Giugiaro's design for the Lotus Esprit goes into production, while his New York taxi concept invents the MPV form

▷ **1999** Giugiaro is named "Car Designer of the Century" in Las Vegas

▷ **2002** Giugiaro is inaugurated into the Automotive Hall of Fame

▷ **2015** Giugiaro retires after VW acquires full control of the company he founded

BORN INTO A FAMILY of musicians and artists, Giorgetto Giugiaro showed a precocious talent from a very early age, and his first job in Fiat's styling department came when he was just 17 years old. A few short years later, in 1959, he had become the youngest ever head of styling at the design house Bertone. Nuccio Bertone offered Giugiaro the position on the strength of a sketch he had received from the young designer, and which the studio head subsequently sold to Alfa Romeo. That sketch was for the Alfa Romeo 2000; it was the very first production car in Giugiaro's long career as a designer.

His work at Bertone was sensational, and included such greats as the BMW 3200 CS, Alfa Romeo Giulia GT, and Fiat 850 Spider. In 1965, he left Bertone to take the top design job at Ghia, where he styled the De Tomaso Mangusta.

Then in 1968, at only 29, Giugiaro felt confident enough to set up his own consultancy in Turin. This company—eventually named Italdesign—offered not only styling but also provided everything necessary to bring a design to production.

DE TOMASO MANGUSTA 1966

HEADLIGHTS, VW SCIROCCO 1974

This was an era when manufacturers actively courted design houses—and Giugiaro reigned supreme as brand after brand flocked to his studio, attracted by the elegant sense of proportion and crisp lines in his work. He fashioned many of the world's best-selling cars, including the seminal VW Golf of 1974, a clean-cut creation of singular simplicity. His "folded paper" design school produced such iconic vehicles as the VW Scirocco and Audi 80 (1974), Lancia Delta (1979), Fiat Panda (1980), and Fiat Uno (1983).

The tide of production cars continued to flow into the 1990s, with the best-selling Fiat Punto (1993) and widely lauded Lexus GS (1991) being Guigiaro classics. Guigaro also provided designs for Asian companies such as Hyundai, Daewoo, Isuzu, Proton, and China Brilliance.

SUPERCAR SUPERSTAR

The dream of any car designer is to have a supercar design put into production, and Giugiaro achieved this many times over. The Lotus Esprit, Maserati Bora, DeLorean DMC-12, and BMW M1 were all notable for their exceptionally clean lines. The Maserati 3200GT of 1998, meanwhile, adopted a highly original "boomering" taillight design.

Giugiaro's influence as a trendsetter stemmed from his pure concept cars. The first of these was 1968's Manta, a dramatic coupe for the Italian car maker Bizzarrini, followed by such greats as the Alfa Romeo Iguana (1969), VW-Porsche Tapiro (1970), Alfa Romeo Caimano (1971), and VW Cheetah (1971).

Perhaps the most striking dream car that Giugiaro designed was the Maserati Boomerang. Designed in 1971 with an ultra-steep, 15-degree windshield—the most extreme angle possible—the machine pushed at the frontiers of what was acceptable in car design. Other classic supercars followed: the BMW Nazca, Volkswagen W12, and several Bugatti concept cars. Lamborghini also asked him to create a small sports car, the Calà, which came tantalizingly close to production. The only marque with which Giugaro did not enjoy such success was Ferrari—just one of its cars bore his name, the GG50 built in 2005.

PIONEER OF PURPOSE

Giugiaro was a consistent pioneer whose influence is still felt in almost every area of car design today. For example, his 1976 New York taxi and 1978 Lancia Megagamma concept cars anticipated the Multipurpose Vehicle (MPV): a high-roof, one-volume vehicle with an adaptable interior layout.

Giugiaro was always more than just a stylist; aerodynamism numbered among his many interests. The 1980 Medusa, built on the Lancia Beta platform, boasted a drag coefficient figure of just 0.263, making it the most aerodynamic road car ever available at that time.

Bizzarrini Manta, 1968
One of the first independent designs produced by Giugiaro, the Manta was intended to demonstrate what he could do. It had a particularly unusual seating arrangement, with the driver positioned between two passengers.

Giugiaro never shirked from producing outrageous concepts. His 1986 Machimoto combined elements of both cars and motorbikes, and was capable of seating nine passengers astride two rows of seats.

With so many Volkswagen products to the Giugiaro name, it was perhaps unsurprising that VW bought a controlling interest in Italdesign in 2010, with Giugiaro himself remaining in place until his retirement in 2015.

Giugiaro's output was prolific. His work spanned arenas as diverse as menswear, Nikon cameras, Beretta guns, the Pendolino train, watches, and even pasta, but cars were always his first passion, and that was evident in every vehicle he created.

In the office
The models, drawing board, and even the desk lamp display Giugiaro's creativity, which the Italian constantly put to work when creating innovative and exciting new designs.

"I have **designed cars** for every **major company but Honda**, and one day **I will do that.**"
GIORGETTO GIUGIARO, WHO NEVER DID WORK FOR HONDA

Superminis

The small-car template set in the mid-1970s matured in the '80s. Front-wheel drive, a transverse four-cylinder engine with the transmission and final drive on the end, and a hatchback body with three or five doors became the format for the majority of car sales in Europe and beyond, as buyers recognized the practicality and all-around competence of these superminis. Advances in suspension design meant they were fun to drive, too, and car manufacturers followed the lead set by the Volkswagen Golf GTI to insert hot, fuel-injected motors into their shopping cars, making for compact performance machines.

▽ **Austin Mini-Metro 1980**

Origin UK

Engine 998 cc, straight-four

Top speed 84 mph (135 km/h)

Only 21 years after the Mini, in 1980 a new British supermini arrived. The Mini-Metro—later just plain Metro—carried over the old A-series engines dating back to 1953. Well-packaged, it featured a novel, nitrogen gas and hydraulic suspension.

Bumpers and side-moldings with red trim

Disc brakes all around

Large interior space despite small dimensions

Transverse engine with transmission underneath

Two-door version joined by five-door model in 1985

Suspension uses Hydragas units instead of steel springs

▷ **Opel Corsa GSi/GTE 1983**

Origin Spain

Engine 1,598 cc, straight-four

Top speed 117 mph (188 km/h)

The "hot hatch" GSi/GTE joined GM's supermini Corsa/Nova family a bit later than the other 1.0–1.4-liter models and was by far the most stylish looking, and fastest, of the group. Tough, reliable, and good fun, it was built in Spain like Ford's Fiesta.

Fuel-injected single-cam engine

Deep front air dam cuts drag

Alloy wheels standard

Switches on pods either side of the instrument panel

Engine mounted transversely

◁ **Fiat Uno 1983**

Origin Italy

Engine 1,301 cc, straight-four

Top speed 104 mph (167 km/h)

The 127's successor was a great all-around car, and sold 6.5 million by 1994. Giugiaro's Italdesign company designed the Uno with a taller body than other superminis, providing more passenger space. Nimble handling and eager engines added to its popularity.

Torsion beam rear suspension

Factory sunroof
on most models

△ **Peugeot 205 GTi 1984**

Origin France

Engine 1,905 cc, straight-four

Top speed 121 mph (195 km/h)

The sparkling GTi was an impressive derivative of
Peugeot's 2.7-million selling hatchback. Heavy-steering,
but with responsive handling, its fuel-injected engine
provided plenty of power. First introduced with a
1,580 cc engine, this was replaced in 1986 with a larger,
more powerful 1,905 cc unit that produced 130 bhp.

**Aerodynamic
design** saves
fuel costs

▷ **Citroën AX 1988**

Origin France

Engine 954 cc, straight-four

Top speed 83 mph (134 km/h)

Replacing the Visa and LNA models, the
AX was available at first as a three-door,
then as a five-door in 1988. It shared its
running gear with small Peugeots, but had
its own chic styling. Good aerodynamics
made for an economical drive.

Hubcaps feature
AX's geometric
design themes

Back seat can be
removed for more
luggage space

Rear bumper built
into the tailgate

5-speed manual
transmission

◁ **Škoda Favorit 1987**

Origin Czechoslovakia

Engine 1,289 cc, straight-four

Top speed 92 mph (148 km/h)

This was Škoda's first front-engine,
front-wheel drive car, following years of
rear-engined models. Styled by Bertone,
there was just one engine option. The Favorit
became one of Central Europe's most popular
cars, and its success meant many buyers
took the company seriously for the first time.

Front-wheel
drive–a first for Škoda

A New Brand for Bond

The world of top-level espionage never stands still. Maverick MI6 agent, James Bond, may have become inextricably linked with Aston Martins, the DB5 especially, but things changed in the 1970s and '80s. The very latest in British automotive excitement was required, and Lotus stepped into the limelight. Roger Moore, in the James Bond title role, first used an Esprit in the 1977 film *The Spy Who Loved Me*, plunging it into the sea after a spectacular car chase. In the water it transformed into a submarine, its wheels retracting to reveal fins, propellers shooting from the rear, and a periscope rising from the roof.

FOR OUR EYES ONLY

The 1981 Bond film, *For Your Eyes Only*, had a harder edge and more realism than the previous big-screen outings for Ian Fleming's hero. Two turbocharged Lotus Esprits featured in the film—a white model, blown up when Bond was forced to activate the car's self-destruct system, and a copper-colored replacement that came with custom ski racks. The Bond production team made Lotus work hard for its few moments of screen time. But the rewards for the small British sports car company were huge, as its mid-engined, Giugiaro-designed, flagship model was publicized on cinema screens all over the world, with sales figures increasing as a result.

Roger Moore in February 1981 on the set of *For Your Eyes Only*, in which he starred with a pair of Lotus Esprit turbos. The producers chose a copper color for the second car so it would contrast with the snowy landscape.

The Dixi, BMW's first car, a license-built Austin Seven

Great Marques
The BMW Story

Bayerische Motoren Werke (BMW) started life as an aircraft engine manufacturer in Munich, Germany in 1916, before diversifying into automobiles. The company had a burst of glory in the 1930s, but it was only in 1961 that BMW really started its journey to become one of the world's finest manufacturers of sport sedans.

BMW ENTERED THE CAR market in 1929 when it bought the Eisenach-based company that produced the Dixi—an Austin Seven built under license. By 1932 it had developed its own car, and just two years later had designed a six-cylinder engine, installing it in several handsome cars that all featured "twin kidney" grilles. These included the 326 sedan and 327 tourer. The stylish 328 was the sports car of the lineup, and it soon became a force to be reckoned with on the race circuit, racking up more than 100 class wins in 1937.

BMW's Munich factory was heavily bombed by the Allies during World War II due to its production of aircraft engines for the Luftwaffe, and later its Eisenach plant in eastern Germany was seized by the Soviets. At the end of the war, its six-cylinder engine technology was

BMW Isetta (left) and 502, 1955
The 1950s was a rocky decade for BMW; the Isetta bubble car venture made up for losses on the luxury V8-engined range, such as the 502.

appropriated by Bristol in the UK, which used it to launch its own, high-quality sports car.

BMW had to start again from scratch. It began with motorcycles in 1948, and in 1951 launched

a V8 luxury car called the 501, nicknamed the "Baroque Angel" for its shapely contours. The V8 theme continued with the 503 luxury coupe and polished 507 two-seat roadster. But all these cars were unprofitable, and the company searched for a lifeline. It found it in the Isetta three-wheeler. The rights were acquired from Iso in Italy, a BMW motorbike engine was installed, and the tiny, bubble-shaped, economy car went on to sell in the thousands. The slightly larger 600 and 700 models followed, with two-cylinder engines.

Financier Herbert Quandt acquired the struggling firm in 1959, and changed BMW's direction. In

BMW 507, 1955
Surely one of the most beautiful and powerful of all 1950s roadsters, a mere 253 were sold.

"We at BMW do not build cars as consumer objects. We build mobile works of art."

CHRIS BANGLE, FORMER BMW CHIEF DESIGNER AND CREATOR OF THE MARQUE'S "FLAME SURFACING" DESIGN THEME IN THE 1990S

1961, its Neue Klasse 1500 was launched—a sport sedan with a new overhead-camshaft engine aimed at company executives, followed by 1.8- and 2-liter versions. Coupes came next, and then the compact 02 two-door models, before a range of impressive six-cylinder sedans in 1968. Both the 02 and the CSL coupe saw great success in track racing, the CSL tussling memorably with Ford Capris to win the 1973 European Touring Car Championship. The 2002 Tii was the first European production car with a standard turbocharger.

The Neue Klasse was replaced by the 5-Series in 1972—a mid-range executive car that combined safety, comfort, superb handling, and slick styling.

The 5-Series was joined in 1975 by the smaller 3-Series, the larger 7-Series in 1977, and the 6-Series coupe in 1976, in a well-honed range based on rear-wheel drive, and superb four- and six-cylinder engines. The 1979 M1 mid-engined supercar was also impressive, albeit short-lived.

BMW "Neue Klasse," 1961
BMW's flourishing destiny was set by the launch of the lively 1500 in 1961, and its sport sedan descendants, like this 2000 model.

In the 1980s the 3-, 5-, and 7-Series sedans were all replaced by carefully evolved successors, and in 1987 a magnificent V12 engine arrived for the top 7-Series, and the all-new, 8-Series coupe. But the most iconic BMWs of this decade were the M-Sport derivatives. The 1985 M5 and M6 used the M1's 24-valve, 286 bhp, 3.5-liter, straight-six, for sub-7 second, 0-60 mph (96 km/h) acceleration allied to impressive handling in a sophisticated and expensive performance package.

BMW's turbocharged Formula 1 engine powered Brabham driver Nelson Piquet to the World Championship in 1983. The marque also supplied V10 engines to Formula 1's Williams team between 2000 and 2005.

During the 1990s BMW expanded the scope of its core range by developing the Z3/Z4 sports cars, the X-Series of SUVs, and electric and hybrid models for both city driving and long-distance touring. BMW also owns the Mini and Rolls-Royce marques.

CLASSICS OF THE FUTURE

M5 With performance, sounds, and responses often compared to Ferrari supercars, this was regarded as one of the finest sport sedans ever built. When announced, it became the world's fastest production four-door sedan. It was also the most successful M5, with 19,564 sedan, and 1,025 Touring wagons made between 2005 and 2010. Besides the engine, it had new body panels and alloy wheels, a wider track, and an F1-inspired, launch control system so standing starts could be conducted automatically.

△ **BMW M5 2005**

Origin	Germany
Engine	4,999 cc, V10
Top speed	155 mph (250 km/h)

Slick and stylish, the M5 set the benchmark for high-performance sedans, delivering the power figures expected of BMW.

i8 The turbocharged, three-cylinder gasoline engine provides power for long-distance driving and also helps charge the plug-in lithium-ion battery pack so the car can be used in electric mode—with simulated engine noises to alert pedestrians. Carbon-fiber construction and exceptional aerodynamics help limit fuel consumption. The electric motor can be fully recharged in about 3½ hours. Laser headlights are an innovation, while "butterfly" doors are spectacular, and rearview cameras useful.

△ **BMW i8 2014**

Origin	Germany
Engine	1,499 cc, straight-three and electric motor
Top speed	160 mph (258 km/h)

BMW's hybrid supercar can delivers the electric equivalent of 76 mpg (3.0 l/100km). Its rear-mounted, 1.5-liter engine was linked to an electric motor at the front.

Cuban Classics

When Fidel Castro's revolutionaries ousted President Batista from power in 1959, it signaled a rapid departure for most Americans from the island paradise. The US trade embargo subsequently imposed on Cuba meant that the cars they left behind—1940s and 1950s Cadillacs, Buicks, Fords, Chevrolets, and others—were sealed in the world's most bizarre automotive time warp. Pressed into use as taxis, they shared roadspace with mostly Russian cars and vans, imported cheaply from Cuba's supportive communist ally across the Atlantic.

MAKE DO AND MEND

Fuel was no problem for Russian-backed Cuba, so these lumbering old American tanks were able to soldier on in everyday use. Since importing spare parts from the US was forbidden, the cars were kept on the road with makeshift repairs, often using custom-built components or parts recycled from completely different makes of car. Today, these rolling monuments to a bygone age look amazing from afar, although most bear the scars of a hard life when examined up close. Now that relations with the US have thawed, the future for such working classics is uncertain. However, their influence as a symbol is undeniable; they are destined always to be an iconic part of Cuba's heritage, no matter the prevailing political dogma.

Classic 1950s American convertibles line up in the Havana sunshine, with a 1951 Chevrolet nearest the camera just ahead of a 1956 Cadillac.

Very Fast Sedans

Supercar pace with sedan space was yours for the asking, thanks to super sedans with epic engines. The in-house projects, like Mercedes-Benz's mighty 500E and Aston Martin's futuristic Lagonda, were joined by collaborations across big automotive groups—Fiat's luxury car brand Lancia dropped a Ferrari engine into its Thema, while General Motors' sports car maker Lotus reworked the Opel Omega/Vauxhall Carlton with turbo power. All these cars delivered executive-level comfort and the kind of performance big sedans had never offered before—provided you could cope with their spectacular price tags.

Ferrari power
This was the second Lancia after the Stratos to have a Ferrari engine, in this case the Tipo 105L borrowed from the mid-engined Ferrari 308, its 32 valves signaled in the sedan's name.

Unique features
The discreet yellow radiator badge was one of the few visual clues to this Lancia's special status. Another was the custom leather interior, by Italy's upmarket Poltrona Frau.

FRONT VIEW

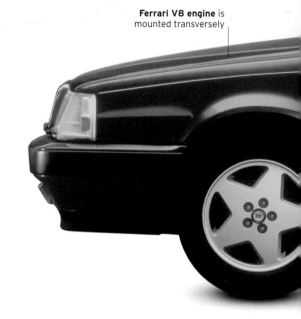

Ferrari V8 engine is mounted transversely

Wedge-shaped body
styled by William Towns

Dashboard has touch switches and digital LED instruments

Engine is a four-cam V8

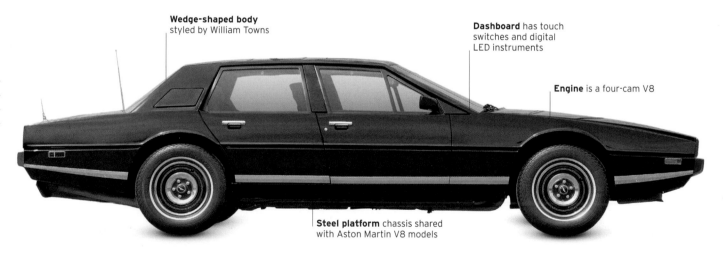

▷ Aston Martin Lagonda 1980

Origin	UK
Engine	5,340 cc, V8
Top speed	143 mph (230 km/h)

A computerized digital dashboard and harsh wedge styling made the Lagonda seem futuristic in the 1970s. Announced in 1976, problems with the futuristic dash meant it was 1980 before for the first customer car was delivered, the model truly coming of age in the 1980s.

Steel platform chassis shared with Aston Martin V8 models

Wooden dashboard features an oval analog clock

Later cars have a fairing over the windshield wipers

Engine is the first twin-turbo V6 in production

◁ Maserati Biturbo 1981

Origin	Italy
Engine	1996cc, V6
Top speed	132mph (212km/h)

To expand the market for his Maserati marque, Alejandro de Tomaso launched this turbocharged, rear-drive sedan. Some thought the styling was too staid, and build quality was spotty, but the motors were punchy and the interiors were a fine blend of Italian wood and leather.

Two- and four-door sedans and a convertible were available

Wood dashboard and optional Italian leather trim

▽ **Lancia Thema 8.32 1987**

Origin Italy

Engine 2,927 cc, V8

Top speed 149 mph (240 km/h)

Trimmed to the highest standard and hugely expensive, the Lancia Thema 8.32 was fitted with a Ferrari engine based on the unit used in the 308GTB/GTS and Mondial but with a cruciform crankshaft and smaller valves. Price, and availability in left-hand drive only, limited its appeal.

Interior has sports seats

Engine has a variable length intake

SHO has Mercury Sable hood and front fenders

▷ **Ford Taurus SHO 1989**

Origin USA

Engine 2,986 cc, V6

Top speed 143 mph (230 km/h)

Yamaha reworked a Ford V6 engine for use in a sports car and limited-run performance sedan, but only the four-door made it to production. The Taurus SHO proved so popular it became a regular production model and survived for two more generations.

Suspension has stiffer springs, dampers, anti-roll bars, and bushings

Rear suspension has a self-leveling system

Six-speed manual transmission

Extended arches cover wider wheels

◁ **Vauxhall Lotus Carlton 1989**

Origin Germany/UK

Engine 3,615 cc, straight-six

Top speed 177 mph (285 km/h)

Sold in mainland Europe as the Opel Lotus Omega, this was a modified version of the standard Carlton sedan. The engine was enlarged, reinforced, and turbocharged with twin Garrett T25 units and a water/air intercooler to give phenomenal performance. Just 950 were built.

Type-1 Beetles leaving the factory, ready for export to Switzerland

Great Marques
The Volkswagen Story

Volkswagen began life with the humble Beetle, Adolf Hitler's vision of a car for the masses. It was a huge success, becoming the best-selling car of its era, and giving VW a foundation from which it grew into Europe's biggest automaking group—before the 2015 diesel emissions scandal rocked it to its core.

MASS PRODUCTION OF VOLKSWAGENS did not begin until after World War II. Allied automakers turned down the chance to take over the company's Wolfsburg factory and the curious little Beetle with its rear-mounted, air-cooled engine, so the British army, in the shape of Major Ivan Hirst, reorganized the war-ravaged production line and secured an order from British forces in Germany for 20,000 cars. Production was soon running at 1,000 cars a month, limited by supplies of raw steel and the availability of factory workers. However, the simplicity, reliability, and low cost of the Type-1, or Beetle, made it the ideal car for a Europe struggling to repair itself in the aftermath of war and by 1955, more than a million Beetles had been built.

VW Beetle 1303, 1970
The Super Beetle was the top-shelf model, with its padded dashboard, curved windshield, and greater luggage space.

The United States was a major export market, and there the Beetle was a cult car, sold on its rule-breaking, anti-establishment image. Advertising agency Doyle Dane Bernbach turned what many Americans saw as the Beetle's weaknesses—small size, four-cylinder engine, and lack of annual styling changes—into selling points in a classic series of advertisements.

Throughout the 1960s, Volkswagen continued to rely on the Beetle and its derivatives, such as the Type-2 camper van, the stylish Karmann Ghia, and the 1500/1600 sedans. Although the final variants were the four-door 411 and 412 of the early 1970s, Beetle sedans were produced in Germany until 1978, and the convertible was built until 1980. Even after production ended in Germany, the Beetle was still being built in good numbers in South America. But alongside its increasingly outdated Beetle-based cars Volkswagen was also

Volkswagen Karmann-Ghia, 1955
Clever reuse of the Volkswagen chassis allowed for derivatives, especially this pretty Italian-designed, German-built coupe.

"If you've wanted to **buy a car** that **sticks out** a little, you **know** what to do."

VOLKSWAGEN CAMPER ADVERTISEMENT, 1968

expanding, acquiring new technology by buying Audi in 1965 and NSU in 1969. These two companies were producing advanced front-wheel-drive cars, and Volkswagen eventually adopted this technology for its front-wheel-drive Golf and Polo hatchbacks, which effectively replaced the Beetle in 1974. They arrived at just the right time, as one oil crisis after another had persuaded buyers, especially those in the US, to switch to smaller cars.

While the Golf had been conceived as a family car, one group of Volkswagen engineers had other ideas. Working in their own time, they developed a hot fuel-injected version of the three-door Golf with motor sports in mind, and then persuaded a reluctant Volkswagen management to put it into production as the Golf GTI. Its groundbreaking success surprised everyone: The GTI remains a legend and staple of the VW lineup today.

Volkswagen established low-cost manufacturing plants in Eastern European countries after the fall of the Berlin Wall in 1989 and was one of the first European companies to set up a joint venture in China. NSU's Wankel-engined Ro80 proved to be an expensive failure, but Audi cemented its place as a premium BMW and Mercedes rival.

Volkswagen 411, 1968
The rear-engined, air-cooled theme reached its limits with this large, four-door family sedan—not a notable success.

Developments such as the novel, narrow-angle five-cylinder VR5 and six-cylinder VR6 engines in the 1990s, and the DSG twin-clutch transmission in 2003, enhanced Volkswagen's reputation for quiet innovation. And while the original Beetle continued to sell well for many years in Brazil and Mexico, Volkswagen introduced a New Beetle, which had nothing in common with the original car except its fashionable retro styling, but which became a successful niche model.

In 2008, Volkswagen became, briefly, the biggest company in the world with a stockmarket value of around $370 billion (€300 billion) thanks to the activities of hedge funds and investments. In 2011, it brokered a merger with Porsche and seemed destined to become the world's largest automaking group—until in 2015 tests in the US showed that it fitted its vehicles with "defeat devices" to circumvent emissions regulations. The revelation has cost Volkswagen billions of dollars, and caused a major rethink in its future model strategy as the company struggled to rebuild its credibility in the wake of the scandal.

CLASSICS OF THE FUTURE

Polo G40 Volkswagen gave its small hatchback a big heart in G40 form, starting with the 1,272 cc four-cylinder engine that delivered 75 bhp. Adding an unusual supercharger with a scroll-shaped element—Volkswagen called it the "G-lader"—delivered 115 bhp and sparkling performance. Just 500 G40 models were made in 1987, but when the Polo was facelifted in 1990, the G40 was made a fixture in the range.

△ **Volkswagen Polo G40 1990**

Origin	Germany
Engine	1,272 cc, straight-four
Top speed	107 mph (172 km/h)

The "G-lader" supercharger transformed the Polo into a pocket-sized performance car. A high price meant that it never sold well, making it a rare collector's car today.

Corrado VR6 This crisp sports coupe had a novel speed-sensitive rear spoiler. Introduced in 1988 with 1.8-liter engines in naturally aspirated and G60 supercharged forms, it came of age when mated with Volkswagen's VR6, a V6 with just 15 degrees between cylinder banks. At the same time, the running gear was upgraded and the Corrado was given wider arches and a humped hood, which greatly improved its looks. It was attractive, smooth, and rapid, but too expensive to sell well.

△ **Volkswagen Corrado VR6 1992**

Origin	Germany
Engine	2,861 cc, V6
Top speed	146 mph (234 km/h)

Volkswagen's front-drive coupe was stylish and well-mannered. Its narrow-angle, V6 engine gave the car smoothness, pace, and a refined soundtrack.

Volkswagen Golf GTi MK I, 1975
Fitting the Golf with a fuel-injected engine, wide wheels, and taut suspension produced the granddaddy of all "hot hatchbacks."

US Compacts

Two oil crises in the 1970s prompted US car buyers to seek more fuel-efficient alternatives to Detroit's vast and profligate land yachts. At first, those newcomers came from Japanese automakers, such as Honda and Toyota, and European brands, such as Volkswagen and BMW, which were already building what Americans considered to be small cars for their own buyers. US automakers hit back with their own compact cars, not always with great success. But they only really got into their stride in the early 1980s, developing new platforms that were the basis for hundreds of thousands of compacts during the decade.

Individual alloy wheels
In keeping with the sporty character that Chrysler wanted the LeBaron to embody, the car came standard with a set of specially designed alloy wheels; they reduced unsprung weight in order to make the handling slightly more nimble.

▷ **Chrysler LeBaron Coupe 1987**

Origin	USA
Engine	2,501 cc, straight-four
Top speed	103 mph (166 km/h)

The first LeBaron of 1982 made the switch to front-wheel drive for Chrysler. This newer model added sophisticated and wind-cheating styling and a luxurious interior. There was a choice of 2.2 and 2.5 engines, and the car was offered as both this coupe model and as a convertible. It was also built in Mexico, where it was called the Chrysler Phantom.

Interior space for four adults

Headlights hidden by retractable metal panels

Grille extends below bumper

Trip computer crunches data on the move

Slim profile
Within its sleek bodywork, the LeBaron remained a very practical car, with comfortable accommodation for four adults on leather-covered seats.

SIDE VIEW

All Eagles have
"4 wheel drive" badges

Galvanized panels and
Ziebart rustproofing
are standard

▷ AMC Eagle 1980

Origin USA

Engine 4,228 cc, straight-six

Top speed 88 mph (142 km/h)

In the late 1970s, AMC filled the
gap between its off-road Jeeps and
its Concord sedan range with
this pioneering, US, four-wheel-drive
crossover. The Ferguson Formula four-
wheel-drive system was completely
automatic. Production ran up to the
Chrysler takeover of AMC in 1987.

Centre differential
with viscous coupling

Independent front suspension
and raised ride height

Body is very similar
to Chevrolet Cavalier

Interior trimmed
in leather

◁ Cadillac Cimarron 1981

Origin USA

Engine 1,835 cc, straight-four

Top speed 100 mph (161 km/h)

In a rush to enter the compact
car market—and to compete with
European and Japanese imports—
General Motors failed to turn its
worldwide J-car platform into a
convincing Cadillac. However,
equipment levels were good—a
4-speed manual transmission and
four-cylinder engine were standard.

Front-wheel drive and
manual transmission

Torsion-beam
rear suspension

▷ Dodge Aries 1981

Origin USA

Engine 2,213 cc, straight-four

Top speed 98 mph (158 km/h)

This spacious, front-wheel-drive sedan
based on Chrysler's K-car platform was
Motor Trend Car of the Year in 1981. It
sold 1 million units in seven years, and
alongside its sister car, the Plymouth
Reliant, it helped to improve Chrysler's
fortunes in the 1980s.

Transverse
four-cylinder engine

Solid beam
rear axle

Interior has
space for two

Four- or six-cylinder
engine is mid-mounted

Plastic outer body
panels

◁ Pontiac Fiero GT 1985

Origin USA

Engine 2,838 cc, V6

Top speed 124 mph (200 km/h)

General Motors astonished the world
with the mid-engined, two-seat
Fiero sports car. With economy-car
roots and a four-cylinder engine in
base models keeping the price low,
it fitted into the GM range below the
Chevrolet Corvette. It sold 370,158
units in five years.

Chevrolet Corvette

One of the most evocative names in the business, after more than 60 years on the road the Corvette is still very much the definitive American sports car. Originally intended as a rival for the UK's Jaguar XK120, it cost almost twice as much as previous Chevrolets and sold slowly at first, only really taking off when V8 engines were added. Since then a process of continual development has kept the Corvette at the very forefront of US motoring.

VERY MUCH THE jewel in the crown for General Motors, and the iconic star of screen and song, the 'Vette was the brainchild of Harley Earl, head of design at the company in the 1950s. Eager to compete with a flood of European imports, he sought to combine a relatively modest, six-cylinder engine with an all-new roadster body made from plastic.

Few buyers were convinced, and most early sales were reportedly to GM's own executives. The turning point came when the company adopted a V8 engine in 1956. Further success seemed assured when Zora Arkus-Duntov began raising the power output, and by 1960 sales were running at 11,000 a year.

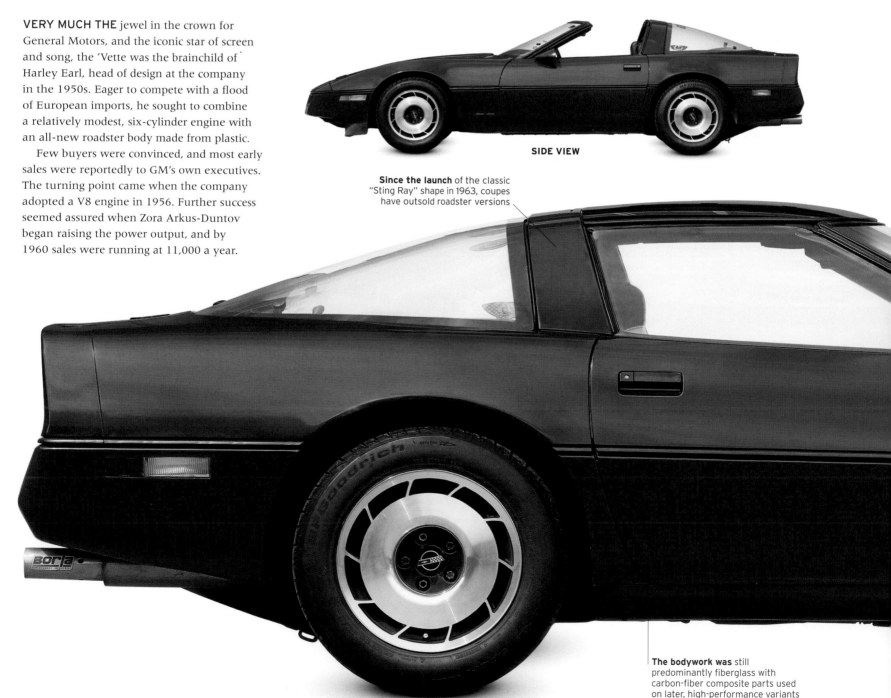

SIDE VIEW

Since the launch of the classic "Sting Ray" shape in 1963, coupes have outsold roadster versions

The bodywork was still predominantly fiberglass with carbon-fiber composite parts used on later, high-performance variants

FRONT VIEW

REAR VIEW

Chevrolet badge

When he introduced it to the world in 1913, company cofounder William C. Durant claimed to have copied the "bow-tie" logo from a design on the wallpaper in a French hotel. This story has since been disputed, and conflicting accounts have emerged, but the new Chevrolet badge proved instantly recognizable to early customers.

SPECIFICATIONS	
Model	Chevrolet Corvette, 1984–96
Assembly	USA
Production	317,700
Construction	Steel monocoque with fiberglass panels
Engine	5,735 cc, V8
Power output	230–330 bhp
Transmission	4- or 6-speed manual; 4-speed automatic
Suspension	Front and rear fiberglass leaf springs
Brakes	Four-wheel discs
Maximum speed	140–180 mph (225–290 km/h)

The immense "clamshell" hood has covered some of the largest engines

Over time the engine has grown from 3.9 liters to 7.0 liters, with racing versions producing as much as 1,300 bhp

Styling

Since the mid-1960s, the classic Corvette shape has continually evolved. By retaining elements such as the paired, round rear lights and vast, sweeping hood, its designers have absorbed stylistic details from rivals such as Ferrari but never lost the distinct appearance and appeal of America's classic sports car.

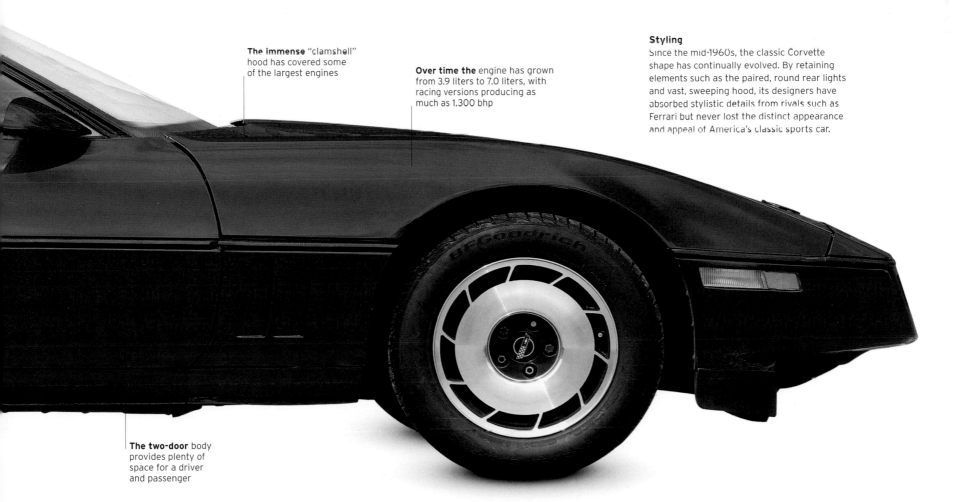

The two-door body provides plenty of space for a driver and passenger

ON THE ROAD

By the mid-1980s, the Corvette had moved into its fourth generation, and would-be buyers were eager to see the first total redesign of the car for nearly 20 years. The 5.7-liter V8 was only slightly more powerful than its predecessor, but in both coupe and roadster form, the new look was clean and fresh. Less curvy than the outgoing car, no one could mistake it for anything but a Corvette and the shape aged extremely well.

By European sports-car standards these were large cars, combining impressive levels of performance and comfort. Those in good condition always found willing buyers, especially rarities such as the 1988 limited edition launched to mark the Corvette's 35 years as an American icon.

1. Pop-up headlamps reduce drag when closed **2.** Stylish lightweight alloy wheels **3.** Fins channel cooling air to brakes **4.** Repeater sidelights set into rear bumper **5.** Corvette badge boldly displayed on rear panel **6.** Dashboard with electronic display **7.** Dual taillamps—a long-standing Corvette feature **8.** Twin pairs of dual exhaust pipes **9.** Interior badge detailing performance statistics **10.** Interior door handles **11.** 5.7–liter V8 engine

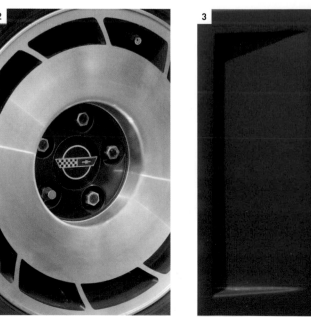

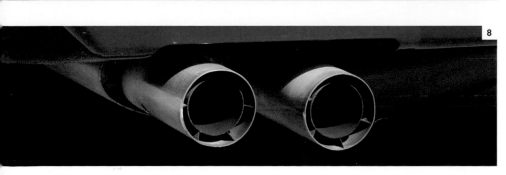

Two-Seat Roadsters

Planned US legislation threatened to outlaw convertibles—which meant almost all sports cars—but the expected new laws were never implemented. By the 1980s, sports cars still in production were antiquated, but a few survived and adopted new engines and running gear to compete with a whole new generation of sports cars aiming to take their place. Most adopted the traditional front-engine, rear-drive layout, but there were mid-engined cars, experiments with front-wheel drive, and even some that eschewed the open roadster body for a compact, fixed-roof shape. It was a renaissance for the sports car.

Engine comes from the BMW 325i

Undertray cuts aerodynamic drag

▷ BMW Z1 1986

Origin Germany

Engine 2,494 cc, straight-six

Top speed 140 mph (225 km/h)

BMW's first two-seat roadster since the 507 of the 1950s had a novel steel platform with plastic outer panels that were easily removable, and drop-down doors. Suspension was from the E30 3 series at the front, with a new multi-link rear. The company sold 8,000 cars.

Fixed seats but adjustable pedals

All-alloy Rover V8 has fuel injection

▷ Marcos Mantula 1984

Origin UK

Engine 3,947 cc, V8

Top speed 150 mph (241 km/h)

The classic Marcos of the 1960s sprang back to life in the 1980s as the Mantula. The biggest change was the adoption of a gutsy Rover V8 engine, which increased power and at the same time reduced overall weight. Later there was a convertible Spyder version.

Rear suspension was independent on later models

Steel tube chassis and fiberglass body

Transverse, mid-mounted engine

Strut-type independent suspension all round

Pop-up headlamps keep nose low

Intake on right-hand side feeds air to engine

◁ Toyota MR2 1984

Origin Japan

Engine 1,587 cc, straight-four

Top speed 120 mph (193 km/h)

The MR2 may not have been the first affordable mid-motor sports car, but it was certainly the best yet. A smooth and revvy 16-valve engine, pin-sharp handling, plus a decent ride and Toyota's usual reliability made the MR2 an irresistibly attractive package.

Tradition updated
BMW front-ends featured twin nostrils, known as "kidneys," from prewar days. For the Z1, the intakes were sunk into the plastic nose, bumper, or air dam molding. Despite the shovel-nose shape, the headlamps were not pop-up units.

FRONT VIEW

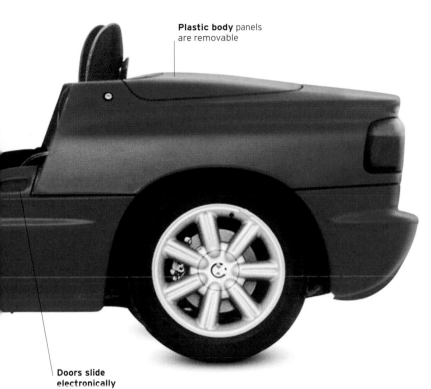

Plastic body panels are removable

Doors slide electronically into bodywork

Driving environment
BMWs became well-known for the carefully considered ergonomics of their interiors, with well-placed controls. The Z1's occupants also benefited from wraparound sports seats that kept them securely in place during hard cornering.

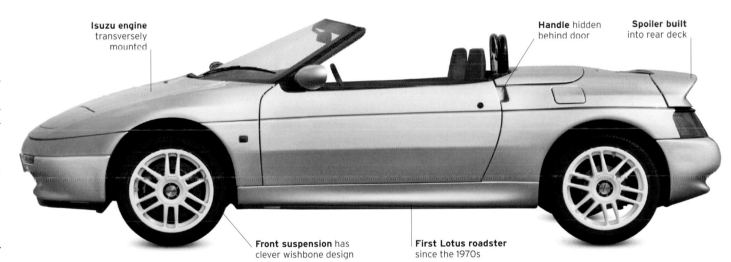

Isuzu engine transversely mounted

Handle hidden behind door

Spoiler built into rear deck

▷ **Lotus Elan 1989**
Origin UK
Engine 1,588 cc, straight-four
Top speed 136 mph (219 km/h)

Lotus's only front-wheel-drive sports car—and the company's first roadster since the 1970s—this short lived Elan was exciting to drive. Styling was by Peter Stevens, who had previously restyled the Esprit. The car's Isuzu-built engine was usually turbocharged, although there was also a rare non-turbo model.

Front suspension has clever wishbone design

First Lotus roadster since the 1970s

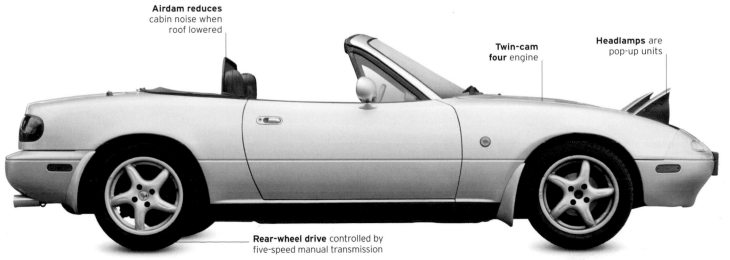

Airdam reduces cabin noise when roof lowered

Twin-cam four engine

Headlamps are pop-up units

◁ **Mazda MX-5 1989**
Origin Japan
Engine 1,597 cc, straight-four
Top speed 114 mph (183 km/h)

Inspired by the 1960s' Lotus Elan, Mazda reintroduced the world to traditional open roadster fun with the MX-5, which was more comfortable and reliable than traditional open roadsters ever were. The car was a huge success and was known as the Miata in the US and the Eunos in Japan.

Rear-wheel drive controlled by five-speed manual transmission

Shaped in Italy

Italian styling houses reached the zenith of their influence in the 1980s, delivering an extra touch of glamour to the premium cars of the era, from the ill-fated DeLorean penned by Giorgetto Giugiaro's Italdesign to the perennial partnership between Ferrari and Pininfarina. Zagato was back too, reviving links with Aston Martin that dated back to the 1960s. But the Italian impact on design went much further than these collaborations, as their stylish and innovative new themes were incorporated into mainstream car designs. Modern, geometric styles and small cars with taller, more spacious passenger compartments were the result.

Gullwing controversy
The DeLorean's gullwing doors were distinctive but not universally loved. There were concerns that users might be trapped inside if the car rolled over, while some found themselves stuck when the mechanisms failed to operate.

FRONT VIEW WITH OPEN DOORS

▷ **DeLorean DMC-12 1981**

Origin	UK
Engine	2,849 cc, V6
Top speed	121 mph (195 km/h)

Intended as a glimpse of the future, the DeLorean became one of the car industry's greatest failures. The cars were unreliable, and sales were never close to the company's wildly optimistic forecasts. However, its iconic status was assured by its appearance in the film *Back to the Future*.

Gullwing doors have fixed windows with opening sections

Brushed stainless steel outer panels

Lotus-style backbone chassis

European power
The DeLorean used a 2.8-liter PRV V6 engine. Originally this unit was designed as a joint venture between Peugeot, Renault, and Volvo. Almost a million of these engines were built between 1974 and 1997.

Stainless steel
The DeLorean's outer body panels were in unpainted stainless steel, supported by a fiberglass underbody and a steel backbone chassis. The stainless steel surface proved susceptible to fingerprints, and was hard to repair other than by replacing whole panels.

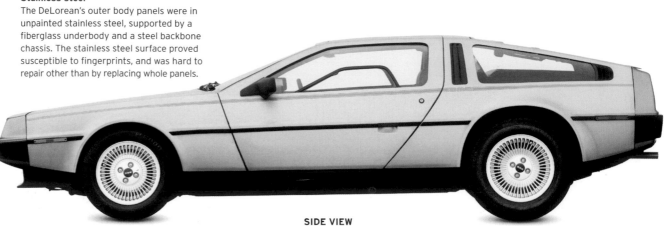

SIDE VIEW

Clamshell hood opens forward

▷ **Isuzu Piazza Turbo 1980**

Origin Japan

Engine 1,996 cc, straight-four

Top speed 127 mph (205 km/h)

General Motors' Japanese partner engaged Giugiaro to style its new coupe. A turbo engine was added in 1984 to make it go as well as it looked, but it handled poorly until Lotus was engaged to redesign the suspension. The Piazza Turbo was supplanted by a new front-drive coupe in 1990.

Live rear axle

Partly hidden lights

Flush glazing reduces wind resistance

Vertical tail always painted black

Front-wheel drive with transverse four-cylinder engine

◁ **Autobianchi Y10 1985**

Origin Italy

Engine 999 cc straight-four

Top speed 114 mph (183 km/h)

Sold as an Autobianchi in Italy and many other markets, and as a Lancia in the UK, the Y10 was small, chic, and very aerodynamically efficient for its era with a drag coefficient of just 0.31. Equipment levels were high, while Turbo and 4WD versions added interest.

Traction control introduced in 1990

Digital instruments with analog option from 1988

Four-wheel independent strut suspension

▷ **Cadillac Allanté 1987**

Origin USA/Italy

Engine 4,087 cc, V8

Top speed 119 mph (192 km/h)

Pininfarina designed the body and built it in Italy. The fully trimmed bodyshells were flown to the US to be united with Cadillac mechanicals. The Allanté was an upmarket convertible aimed at Mercedes' SL, but some potential buyers were put off by its front-wheel-drive layout.

Second rear window behind rear seat

Slim headlamps give nose a penetrating look

◁ **Citroën XM 1989**

Origin France

Engine 2,975 cc, V6

Top speed 143 mph (230 km/h)

The Bertone design was derived from Gandini's Citroën BX concept, with a practical hatchback and long nose. V6 engines were available to ensure the XM had better performance than the old CX, and the hydropneumatic suspension now had sophisticated electronic control.

Floorplan shared with Peugeot 605

Aston Martin DB2 with David Brown (left) and Lord Brabazon

Great Marques
The Aston Martin Story

Founded in a London garage in 1913 by Robert Bamford and Lionel Martin, the sports car adopted part of the name of the famed motoring venue, the Aston Hill Climb, to reinforce its sporting character. Reborn after World War II, Aston Martins became synonymous with high-performance, style, and racing credentials.

AFTER THE PROTOTYPE had been thoroughly tested, including an effortless run on the Aston Clinton hillclimb course, it was registered for road use in 1915. But another seven years would pass before a production car went on sale, long after Robert Bamford had departed the enterprise. The first Aston Martin featured a responsive, 1.5-liter, four-cylinder engine and, although manufacture was laborious, it quickly gained a reputation as a high-quality sports car.

Aston Martins were well suited to the Le Mans 24-hour endurance race, making their debut at the course in 1928. Despite a change of ownership in 1926, a move to Feltham, Middlesex, and an all-new car created by the Bertelli brothers, fans of the marque were already enormously loyal.

After World War II, the firm was bought by industrialist David Brown, and merged with luxury car company Lagonda. The subsequent Aston Martin DB2 featured Aston's capable chassis combined with Lagonda's superb 2.6-liter, six-cylinder engine. Even the rough-and-ready prototypes competed at Le Mans in 1949. However, the marque's future was sealed at the course in 1950, when George Abecassis and Lance Macklin were fifth overall, and won the 3-liter class; Reg Parnell and Charles Brackenbury finished sixth and

Aston Martin DB2/4 convertible coupe
The rare open version of the car pictured outside the Carlton Hotel in Cannes, south of France. The car could accelerate from 0-60 mph (0-96 km/h) in about 10 seconds.

second in class, running like trains. In 1951, DB2s finished third, fifth, seventh, 10th, and 11th—a highly impressive five finishes from five starters.

David Brown was elated, but the achievement was eclipsed in 1959 when the DBR1 team topped the World Sports Car Championship winning the 620-mile (1,000-km) race at the Nürburgring, along with the Le Mans 24 hour.

Following Brown's acquisition of the Tickford coachbuilding company to make Aston Martin bodies, the hand-built cars became ever more beautifully appointed and finished. In 1958, the company turned to Italy, collaborating with design house Carrozzeria Touring on

production of the DB4. The Italian company's elegant, fastback styling and lightweight construction expertise helped build a car that offered an all-new, 3.7-liter, straight-six engine with 240 bhp on tap. This gentlemen's express featured disc brakes, overdrive, and optional automatic transmission, but still had a steely edge—DB4 GTs and the lightweight GT Zagatos made formidable racers on the track.

The car evolved into the DB5 in 1963—sleeker, more powerful, and, from 1964, became world famous as the car of choice for Sean Connery's on-screen role as Ian Fleming's secret agent

Aston Martin DB5
Sean Connery relaxes on set during the making of the James Bond film *Goldfinger* with the Aston Martin DB5 that shot to fame as his villain-defeating steed.

"It must be **placed high** on the list of the **world's most desirable** grand touring cars."

AUTOSPORT MAGAZINE ON THE ASTON MARTIN DB4GT IN JANUARY 1962

Aston Martin Lagonda
The Lagonda, first seen in 1976 and on sale three years later, shocked marque enthusiasts, but with strong demand from the Middle East it kept the company afloat.

James Bond. The 1965 DB6 and 1967 DBS preceded a brand-new V8 engine in 1969. David Brown sold the company in 1972, and it struggled during the 1970s and 80s. The Aston Martin Lagonda of 1976 was controversial with its starched, wedge-shaped profile, but it was popular in the Middle East, and the sales helped keep the company afloat until Ford acquired a share of it in 1987. With Ford's backing, Aston Martin

launched a more affordable, six-cylinder model in 1993. The DB7 was hugely successful, with 5,000 produced up to 2001 (Aston's grand total only reached the 10,000 mark in 1984). Subsequent models, the V12-powered DB9 and DB10, were also profitable. The company gained its first ever purpose-built factory in Warwickshire, England, and in 2005 began production of the all-new V8 Vantage, a distinctive British alternative to the Porsche 911 and Ferrari 360 Modena.

In 2007, Ford sold the company to a Kuwaiti-funded consortium, and Aston Martin returned to top-level motor racing. Victories at Le Mans in the GT1 class in 2007 and 2008 were followed by a fourth overall place finish at the 2009 race with a new LMP1 car. That same year, the V12 Vantage GT made its racing debut at the Nürburgring 24-hour race, grabbing a class victory.

The V12 Vanquish of 2001 was the last of the old-school, upper-crust Astons. New, exclusive models included the V12 Vantage and One-77 supercar in 2009. The company celebrated its centenary in 2013, and in 2015 announced its 800 bhp Vulcan, a rear-wheel drive, track-only, limited-edition monster with all-carbon-fiber construction and a 7-liter, V12 engine. Only 24 were made, at $2.3 million (£2 million) apiece.

CLASSICS OF THE FUTURE

One-77 In the classic car world of the future, this is going to be very hard for collectors to get hold of, as only 77 were made. Launched in 2009, each car was custom-crafted for its owner, with aluminum panels on a carbon-fiber unibody structure. The cost per car was at least $1.5 million (£1.1 million), but then its 700 bhp engine could pretty much guarantee a top speed of 220 mph (354 km/h). Like almost all recent Aston Martins, it was built in Warwickshire, in the UK.

△ **Aston Martin One-77 2009**

Origin UK

Engine 7,312 cc, V12

Top speed 220 mph (354 km/h)

The booming British company went all out for ultimate supercar status by creating a $1.4 million-plus (£1 million) machine only a select few would ever drive.

Rapide Many supercar lovers have to face the practicalities of family life at some point, and so Aston Martin cleverly stretched the DB9 into a four-door sedan while concealing the two rear doors within the dramatic, fastback tail. The full-length, glass sunroof was an unusual touch, arching over the sumptuous interior. Assembly was first contracted out to an Austrian company before returning to the Gaydon headquarters.

△ **Aston Martin Rapide 2010**

Origin UK/Austria

Engine 5,935 cc, V12

Top speed 188 mph (303 km/h)

It might have four doors and be child-friendly, but it was still a sports car at heart; one powered by hydrogen completed the 2010, 24-hour race at the Nürburgring.

Rugged Off-Roaders

Most off-roaders were tough, basic trucks intended for military, agricultural, and emergency service uses, or for hardy outdoor types, but changing attitudes saw them evolve into multipurpose vehicles that had just as much appeal on the road as off it. Truck-type leaf springs were replaced by coils for a more comfortable ride, with no loss of off-road ability, and some vehicles adopted car-like unibody construction to cut weight while also improving refinement and driving dynamics. Demand rocketed as buyers caught on to the idea of tough, practical vehicles that could cope with any situation.

Coil springs give a good ride on- or off-road

Short wheelbase for convertible

△ **Mercedes-Benz G-Wagen 1979**

Origin Germany/Austria

Engine 2,746 cc, straight-six

Top speed 92 mph (148 km/h)

Coil-sprung live axles gave the G-Wagen a smoother ride than its rival Land Rover, and it had axle differential locks for genuine, go-anywhere ability. But a high price and primitive looks limited sales until Mercedes-Benz improved these in 1991, gradually taking the G-wagen upmarket.

▽ **Mitsubishi Pajero/Shogun 1982**

Origin Japan

Engine 2,838 cc, V6

Top speed 96 mph (154 km/h)

Designed as a recreational vehicle rather than a workhorse, the Pajero offered car-like qualities with off-road abilities. Standard equipment was generous, and there was a wide range of engine choices, including a turbo diesel. A long wheelbase was launched to appeal to families.

High roofline gives spacious interior

Steel plate protects engine and transmission

Pickup style rear end

▷ **Jeep Cherokee 1984**

Origin USA

Engine 2,836 cc, V6

Top speed 96 mph (154 km/h)

The XJ-series Cherokee was the first Jeep to have its chassis built on a unibody platform with steel body panels, and was a much more civilized car to drive on the road than its predecessors. As a result, the Jeep stole sales away from the conventional station wagons available at the time.

Early cars have General Motors V6 gasoline engines

Rear-and 4WD models became available in 1985

▷ **Rayton Fissore Magnum 1985**

Origin	Italy
Engine	2,492 cc, V6
Top speed	104 mph (168 km/h)

The Magnum was built by Fissore using a shortened, military, Iveco four-wheel-drive chassis. It had Fiat/VM/Alfa 4- or 6-cylinder engines–or a V8 in the US, where it was sold as a Laforza. A luxury model, the Magnum was designed to compete with the Range Rover.

Gasoline and diesel models available

Suspension and brakes adapted from Iveco trucks

Stereo system mounted in a roof console

▽ **Lamborghini LM002 1986**

Origin	Italy
Engine	5,167 cc, V12
Top speed	125 mph (201 km/h)

Italian supercarmaker Lamborghini opened up a whole new market with the "Rambo Lambo." Power came from a new version of the Countach's huge V12 engine, feeding from six Weber carburetors. Huge, aggressive, and superfast on sand, the vehicle became a favorite among Arab oil sheikhs.

Chassis built from steel tubes

Stylish Conran-designed interior

Steel body with aluminum hood

▷ **Land Rover Discovery 1989**

Origin	UK
Engine	2,495 cc, straight-four
Top speed	107 mph (172 km/h)

Bridging the gap between the standard Land Rover and the luxury Range Rover, the Discovery was superb off-road thanks to its coil-sprung beam axles, locking center differential, and gusty engine. It also had a plush, Conran-designed interior, and won a British Design Council award.

Coil-sprung beam axles front and rear

Great Designers
Robert Opron

The name Robert Opron may not be widely known, even among car enthusiasts, but the extraordinary sweep of his achievements is still greatly admired by those who appreciate the craft of styling. A colourful man with a fondness for brash bow ties, his remarkable designs for Simca, Citroën, and Alfa Romeo are all often voted some of the most beautiful of all time.

Career highlights

▷ **1958** Robert Opron's first job with Simca is to design a car of pure fantasy called the Fulgur

▷ **1964** Opron takes over the job of design chief at Citroën

▷ **1970** In a stellar year, Opron produces his two most respected masterpieces at Citroën: the GS and SM

△ **RENAULT FUEGO 1980**
In a fairly humdrum period for Renault cars, Opron's sleek and glassy Fuego four-seater coupe re-lit the flame of a creative approach.

▷ **1975** Opron's widely-lauded Citroën CX wins the European Car of the Year award. Opron himself moves on to work at Renault

▷ **1980** The new Fuego is launched; it is seen as the best design Opron produced at Renault

▷ **1989** The launch of the extraordinary Alfa Romeo SZ causes widespread controversy

▷ **1991** After his retirement from Fiat, Opron continues to design cars on a freelance basis

▷ **1998** Opron is one of 25 nominees for Car Designer of the Century

ROBERT OPRON WAS always an artist at heart. Born in 1932 and brought up in French colonial Africa, he studied architecture, painting, and sculpture in Paris. On graduation, he dreamt of a career in aviation, and even designed his own plane, but an offer to join the car industry proved too tempting for him. In 1957 Opron secured a position at the French car manufacturer Simca, joining the company's design centre, which was then run by an Italian count called Mario Revelli de Beaumont.

Opron immediately made an impact with one of the most extaordinary dream cars of the 1950s: the Simca Fulgur. A cartoon-like vehicle with a domed roof and jet-age aesthetic, the 1958 show car was sponsored by a children's magazine as a vision of what people might be driving in the year 2000. Opron imagined a glass-cabined car that, with its use of atomic power and a gyroscopic balancing system, may have overestimated the rate of technological progress, but did correctly predict innovations such as radar guidance. Opron's design predated satellite navigation by decades.

A HOME AT CITROËN
In 1961 Opron found himself redundant, as Simca began to be subsumed by Chrysler. He decided to

Simca Fulgar, 1958
Conceived as a vision into the future, predicting cars of the year 2000, the Simca Fulgur is an exemplar of 1950s' bubble-top styling. It never made it into production, sadly.

migrate to Citroën, where he was interviewed by its celebrated design chief, Flaminio Bertoni – the Italian-born creator of Citroën's iconic Traction Avant and DS models. At the interview, Bertoni threw Opron's design portfolio on the floor and declared his work "worthless". Opron felt insulted, said so in forceful terms, and Bertoni responded: "You interest me." He got the job.

In 1964, Bertoni's sudden death left Opron holding the French company's design reins. At Citroën, Opron designed the top-selling Ami estate and, much more significantly, the technologically advanced GS. The super-streamlined GS was an aesthetic triumph and when it launched in 1970, it was unlike any other family car of the time. Opron knew the car had to be aerodynamic to

> "The dolphin, the leopard, the swift, **they each move** at a **speed consistent** with their **environment.**"
> ROBERT OPRON

FRONT LIGHTS, CITROEN SM 1970

ALFA ROMEO SZ 1989-91

make up for its small engine, and when he finished his design the GS gave a better performance with its 1,015 cc engine than most of its larger-engined rivals. It perfectly filled the gap in Citroën's stable between the economical 2CV and the more luxurious DS sedan.

However, Opron's masterpiece was undoubtedly the Citroën SM. Bold and iconoclastic, it was a defiantly French design. It regularly appears in lists of the most significant car designs of the 20th century, and was regarded by many as the best car in the world in the early 1970s, with its enviable combination of haute-couture luxury, Maserati V6 power, and radical design flair. It was, however, a commercial flop: ultimately, a mere 12,920 were made between 1970 and 1975.

A MOVE TO FREELANCE

A much rosier fate awaited the sublime Citroën CX. Despite having the unenviable role of replacing the achingly beautiful and long-lived DS, it met with instant acclaim when it was launched in 1974. Its avant-garde looks and advanced technology (deriving from the SM) promptly won it the European Car of the Year award when it was launched.

Peugeot assumed control of Citroën in 1976, hastening Opron's departure for rival Renault, where he took over the styling department. Renault was a very different, more bureaucratic, kind of employer, and perhaps

Citroën CX, 1982
The distinctive, fastback shape of the Citroën CX made it another triumph of aerodynamism. It is considered by enthusiasts to be the final "true" Citroën, before the company was taken over by Peugeot.

as a result Opron's time at Renault was characterized by a number or lacklustre efforts, the best of these being the Fuego with its dramatically curvaceous rear hatch. The anonymous R9, R11, and R25 are all better off consigned to history.

He left for Fiat in 1986, where the Italian company put him in charge of "advanced studies". His best design in this period was a hastily formulated project for Fiat's latest acquisition, Alfa Romeo. This was to be a fresh flagship car to

boost Alfa's flagging reputation. Project ES30 (Experimental Sportscar 3.0 litres) took just 19 months to develop from first draft to final unveiling at the 1989 Geneva Motor Show. When the covers came off, the gasps were audible: the car that lay underneath utterly polarized opinion. With its flaring body, odd double trio of headlights, and aggressive ridges, the Italian press dubbed it "Il Mostro" – the Monster – but it provoked enough of a reaction at trade shows for Alfa Romeo to put it into production as the SZ.

Opron retired from Fiat in 1991, but continued to design on a freelance basis, including such surprising designs as the Ligier Dué city car. He is still treated as a celebrity when he attends Citroën events today; there is evidence enough to suggest that he should be viewed as such in the wider world, too.

Reviewing the GS
In his trademark bowtie, Robert Opron looks over his design for the Citroën GS at the company's Bureau des Études. Following its launch, the car proved an instant success for Citroen.

Absolute Luxury

Premium cars offered higher levels of comfort, convenience, safety, and performance than ever before. Sophisticated electronics were one of the big developments, with computer controls providing features and benefits that had previously been impossible. Engines were still big V8s—or occasionally V12s—but electronic fuel injection offered more precise control, cutting emissions and fuel consumption while increasing power and flexibility. Antilock braking and traction control added an extra layer of safety, while electric seats and sophisticated air-conditioning systems enhanced the luxury feel. Cars had never been so comfortable.

Interior a luxury
blend of wood
and leather

Upgraded suspension
made for a very
smooth ride

Rear axle
located with a
Panhard rod

Long wheelbase
for extra legroom

Turbocharged
Chrysler V8
engine

Four headlights at
front distinguishes
it from other
Bristols

▷ **Bristol Beaufighter 1980**

Origin UK

Engine 5,900 cc, V8

Top speed 150 mph (241 km/h)

Named after a WWII fighter, the niche-market Beaufighter was based on the 412 and rather bluntly styled by Zagato. With the extra appeal of a turbocharged Chrysler V8 engine and a removable roof panel, it was rapid, classy, and exquisitely built, but fewer than 20 were made.

Aluminum alloy
body panels

Plush interior
with high standard
of equipment

**Shorter, narrower
body**, much lighter
than previous models

V8-6-4 engine cuts
cylinders when power
not needed

Rear-wheel drive
and live rear axle

◁ **Cadillac Fleetwood
Brougham 1980**

Origin USA

Engine 6,037 cc, V8

Top speed 104 mph (167 km/h)

The top of Cadillac's prestige sedan line remained its most conventional car. Although smaller than before, its dimensions were still ample. The V8 was Cadillac's biggest, there was a live rear axle, and luxury trim and power steering came as standard.

▽ Bentley Turbo R 1985

Origin	UK
Engine	6,750 cc, V8
Top speed	143 mph (230 km/h)

Rolls-Royce transformed Bentley's flagging sales by making the cars more distinctive, and the introduction of a turbocharged engine restored the marque's sporting credentials. The R added a reworked suspension so the road manners matched the straight-line urge. It was ultimate luxury with a big kick.

Traditional craftsmanship
The Turbo R may have adopted newfangled engine technology, but inside it was as traditional as ever. Acres of soft leather covered the seats and door trims, while the dashboard was built from fine veneered wood by skilled craftsmen.

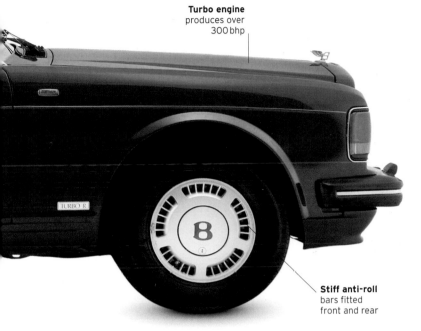

Turbo engine produces over 300 bhp

Stiff anti-roll bars fitted front and rear

Turbo technology
Turbocharging was all the rage in the 1980s, as it offered an efficient route to greater power while retaining reasonable economy when cruising. Underneath was the familiar Rolls-Royce/Bentley pushrod V8, which dated back to 1959.

Elegant pillarless body style

Engine and running gear from S-class sedan

▷ Mercedes-Benz 560 SEC 1985

Origin	Germany
Engine	5,547 cc, V8
Top speed	156 mph (251 km/h)

The 560 SEC was at the top of Mercedes' S-class coupe range. Very expensive when new, it had 300 bhp from its big M117 V8 engine and 6.8-second 0-60 mph (96 km/h) acceleration. Quality, performance, and comfort appealed to well-heeled buyers, and nearly 30,000 were built.

Flared arches and wider tires

Interior has leather trim and wood dash

Electrically operated hood

V12 engine is Jaguar's own

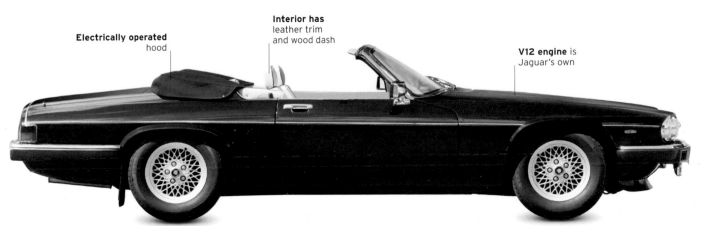

◁ Jaguar XJS 1988

Origin	UK
Engine	5,343 cc, V12
Top speed	150 mph (241 km/h)

XJS began in 1975 as a coupe and later there was a cabriolet with a removable roof panel, but it took until 1988 for Jaguar to introduce a full convertible. It came with an electric hood, antilock brakes, Jaguar's silken V12 engine, and abundant style.

Ferrari Testarossa

Reviving a famous name last used in the 1950s, the 1984 Ferrari Testarossa was a Pininfarina-designed, 12-cylinder two-seater. The early "red heads" had been racing machines, but this was a pure road car—sleek, very fast, and enormously expensive. Like many Ferrari Formula 1 engines of the period, it was powered by a flat or "boxer" engine rather than a more conventional V12. It remained in production until 1996.

FACING RENEWED COMPETITION from Lamborghini, Ferrari was eager to address complaints from customers about its range-topping 512i BB. These issues included a lack of luggage space and an interior that became stiflingly hot in summer, due to the car's mid-mounted engine and front-mounted radiators.

Ferrari's solution was a wider and longer car, with deep intakes ahead of the rear wheels to channel cooling air into the engine. Lacking the curves of its predecessor, the radical new look was controversial, but a spacious and more comfortable interior made it increasingly sought after by collectors.

With its profile raised by a lead role in the *Miami Vice* TV series, Ferrari sold almost 10,000 cars in all, an astonishing total for such an expensive model.

SIDE VIEW

Characteristic color of engine cam covers inspired name Testarossa (red head)

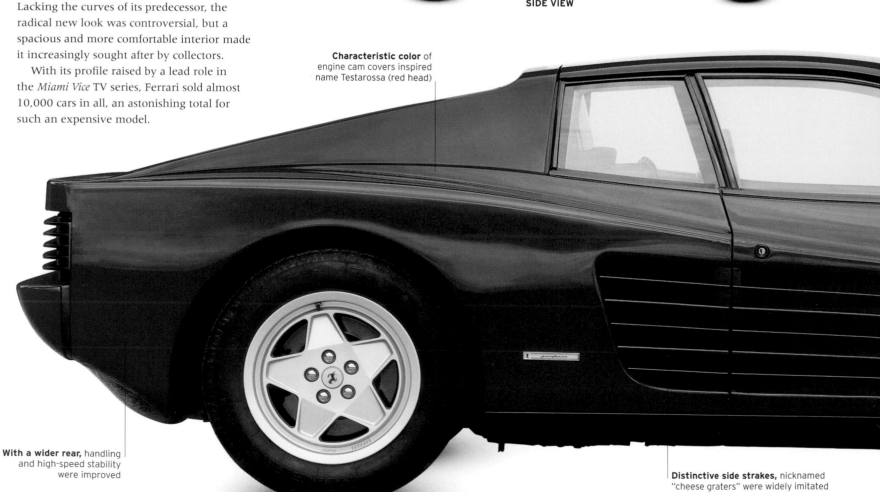

With a wider rear, handling and high-speed stability were improved

Distinctive side strakes, nicknamed "cheese graters" were widely imitated

FRONT VIEW

REAR VIEW

Testarossa badge
A legendary name in Ferrari circles, Testarossa recalls the company's 1957 World Sportscar Championship-winning racer that took Le Mans by storm the following year. Just 34 machines were built and survivors today command the very highest prices on the global auction market.

SPECIFICATIONS	
Model	Ferrari Testarossa, 1984–91
Assembly	Maranello, Italy
Production	7,177
Construction	Tubular steel frame with aluminum panels
Engine	4,943 cc, flat-12
Power output	390 bhp
Transmission	5-speed manual
Suspension	All-around double wishbones with coil
Brakes	Four-wheel discs
Maximum speed	180 mph (290 km/h)

Styling
Pininfarina designers courted controversy by abandoning the strong family look of earlier Ferraris and designing a car much larger than its predecessor. Criticized at the time for pandering to the 1980s' taste for excess, the car is now recognized for what it is—a legitimate Ferrari classic.

4.9-liter, 12-cylinder engine produced up to 440 bhp in later models

Elegant shape more aerodynamic than the Testarossa's closest rival, Lamborghini's Countach

ON THE ROAD

A strong seller when new, the Testarossa was slow to achieve classic status. Now, however, its position seems assured, with values climbing rapidly. Detractors said the car was too large, and that it exemplified the worst of 1980s' tastes. But on the plus side, it had a superb engine, and as supercars go, it was surprisingly practical. Also, with prices for its Berlinetta Boxer (p.210) and Daytona (p.211) predecessors now firmly established in the stratosphere, enthusiasts were increasingly willing to consider more recent cars.

Anyone taking the plunge was unlikely to be disappointed. These cars looked and felt very special indeed, and with later versions capable of almost 200 mph (322 km/h)—what was not to like?

1. Pop-up headlamps (fitted until 1994) **2.** Five-spoke alloys (the company's familiar company trademark) **3.** Side strakes channel air into side-mounted radiators **4.** Ferrari's favorite designer **5.** Ferrari badge proudly displayed **6.** Red cover for a red head **7.** Interior was Ferrari's most comfortable so far **8.** Simple dashboard with just four instruments **9.** Ferrari's familiar gated gear lever. **10.** Red cam covers, hence Testarossa, Italian for "red head"

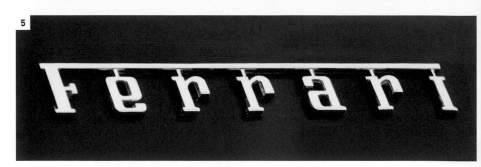

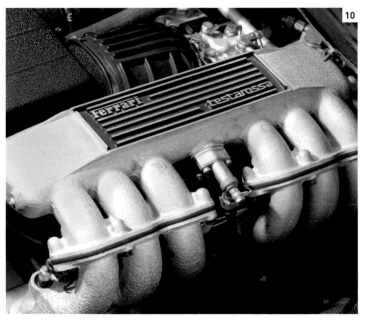

Supercars

Despite the legacy of energy crises and the recessions, there were still plenty of buyers for the most glamorous cars, just as there had always been. Group B rally racing added extra impetus to the creation of truly spectacular performance cars, the new competition category requiring just 200 road-going examples to be built to qualify a car for motorsports. But following a string of high-profile crashes, the class was scrapped, and suddenly these supercars were being bought by collectors in roadgoing trim, rather than stripped out for a life of competition on the race track.

Contoured for aerodynamics
The F40's retractable headlights maintained optimum airflow efficiency by sinking back down into the car's streamlined hood when not in use. The body was made up of 11 panels, variously made from materials such as Kevlar, Nomex, and carbon fiber, and all coated in lightweight red paint.

Roll-down windows
replace the fixed plastic versions of early models

Main headlights
pop up

Ducts feed air to engine and brakes

Front-mounted transmission aids weight distribution

▷ **Ford RS200 1984**

Origin UK

Engine 1,778 cc, straight-four

Top speed 118 mph (190 km/h)

The RS200 was built from scratch for rallying, the 200 in its name reflecting the number of road cars that had to be made to homologate the car in Group B rally racing. Styled by Ghia, built by Reliant, with turbo power from Cosworth, it was an instant classic.

Reliant-built body
with fiberglass panels

Twin turbos and Marelli-Weber fuel injection

Racing-type
transmission betrays motorsport roots

Steel-tube chassis with composite body panels

◁ **Ferrari 288 GTO 1984**

Origin Italy

Engine 2,855 cc, V8

Top speed 189 mph (304 km/h)

Intended as Ferrari's Group B competition car, this limited-edition, high-performance model was consigned to the road when the class was abolished. Based on the 308 GTB, the 288's slightly smaller engine suited competition rules, but its twin turbos took power up to 400 bhp.

▽ Ferrari F40 1987

Origin Italy

Engine 2,936 cc, V8

Top speed 201 mph (323 km/h)

The F40 was the world's fastest production car from 1987 to 1989, and an aggressive response to those who said Ferraris were getting too soft. With twin turbos, 478 bhp, and lightweight composite bodywork, it was created to mark Ferrari's 40th birthday as an automaker.

Rear body comes off in one piece

Huge, built-in rear wing

Keeping its cool

The F40 was covered with air intakes to ventilate its mechanical systems; the two on the nose are called NACA ducts, named after NASA's predecessor—the National Advisory Committee for Aeronautics—and shaped for aerodynamic efficiency.

FRONT VIEW

Maximum downforce

The towering, full-width, aerofoil wing at the back directed airflow to push the tail of the F40 down onto the road or track surface, aiding roadholding. The four round taillights were typically Ferrari.

REAR VIEW

▷ Porsche 959 1986

Origin Germany

Engine 2,994 cc, flat-six

Top speed 190 mph (306 km/h)

Porsche built 200 of these awesome cars to qualify the 959 for Group B rallying. A technical tour de force, it had computer-controlled four-wheel drive, electronic ride height adjustment, and 444 bhp from a twin-turbo engine that was rear-mounted just like a 911.

Turbo, flat-six engine is rear mounted

Bodywork incorporates aluminum, Kevlar, and Nomex

Ducts cool engine

Hood bulge necessary to accommodate carburetors

Bodywork built by Zagato in Milan

◁ Aston Martin V8 Vantage Zagato 1986

Origin UK/Italy

Engine 5,340 cc, V8

Top speed 185 mph (298 km/h)

A revival of the Aston/Zagato partnership begun in the 1960s with the DB4GT Zagato, the Vantage was brutally fast, and expensive. Just 50 coupes were built, on a shortened V8 Vantage platform. They were followed by 25 Zagato Volante convertibles, most with the lower-tune V8 engine.

CLASSIC CAR
RESOURCES

Glossary

2+2
Shorthand for cabin accommodation consisting of two full-size front seats and two small rear seats. The rear seats are unually only suitable for young children or adults on short journeys only.

4x4
Shorthand for four-by-four, or four-wheel drive (4WD). A four-wheel-drive vehicle has power transmitted to every road wheel.

24 Hours of LeMans
A 24-hour endurance motor race, staged annually at Le Mans, France, since 1923. It uses a circuit consisting of public roads that have been cordoned off for the event.

ABS (Anti-lock Braking System)
A braking system that stops the wheels from locking during braking, so the car can be steered away from danger in an emergency.

air dam
A metal or plastic "lip" at the lowest point of the front of a car that improves aerodynamics by keeping moving air from getting underneath, reducing drag and lift.

air filter
A felt or paper component that cleans air of particles before it enters the engine.

air-cooled engine
An engine that circulates air externally to cool hot components, usually asisted by a fan. Internal water-cooling is favored in modern engines.

air suspension
A suspension system that uses inert gas or pumped air to keep the car stable on rough roads or fast corners.

alternator
A small generator that converts the engine's mechanical energy into an electrical current. The electricity it produces charges the battery and powers circuits for lights, electric windows, and radios.

anti-surge baffle
A plate that stops liquids from shifting position inside a reservoir, particularly an oil sump, as a result of the car's movements.

automatic
A clutchless transmission that will automatically select the appropriate gear for the driver.

backbone chassis
A longitudinal, central structure supporting a car's body, drivetrain, and suspension.

BDA engine (Belt-Drive A-type)
A Ford-based competition car engine designed by Cosworth.

beam front axle
A single suspension beam with a wheel on either end, attached to the car's frame by coil or leaf springs.

bearing
Component providing a support between the fixed and moving parts of a machine.

Bertone
An Italian coachbuilder and design consultancy, operating between 1921 and 2014.

bhp (brake horsepower)
Horsepower originally gave a measure of the energy output of steam engines in terms of the equivalent amount of pulling power provided by a draft horse. In cars, "gross" bhp is a measurement of the power output of a standalone engine. "Net" bhp is an engine's output after power has been sapped by ancillary equipment, such as the alternator. Bhp is measured by applying a special brake to the crankshaft.

big end bearing
The larger, lower bearing of the connecting rod that links the pistons to an engine's crankshaft.

block
See **cylinder block**

blown (engine)
A general term for an engine that has its power boosted by a turbocharger or a supercharger.

bore
The usually cylindrical hole within which an engine's piston moves. Also refers to this cavity's diameter.

Brooklands
The world's first purpose-built race circuit, near Weybridge, Surrey, UK, in use from 1909 to 1939.

bubble-top
A car roof that is notably rounded, made from glass, Plexiglass, or metal.

butterfly valve
A disc that pivots along its diameter within a duct, forming a valve that can be opened and closed in order to regulate the flow of air into an engine component, such as a carburetor.

cabriolet
A two-door car, although usually not a sports car, with a fabric-covered removable or folding roof.

camshaft
A rotating shaft featuring cam lobes that open and close the engine's inlet and exhaust valves. It can operate the valves indirectly by pushrod (usually in an overhead-valve engine) or directly (in an overhead-cam engine). Two camshafts per cylinder are used in double-overhead-camshaft engines—one for the inlet valves, and one for the exhaust valves.

carburetor
A device on older engines in which fuel and air are combined, producing a combustible mixture, which is then ignited in the cylinder.

catalytic converter
A device fitted to the exhaust of cars running on unleaded gasoline. It uses a chemical catalyst to stimulate reactions that convert harmful gases into harmless ones.

cc
Short for cubic centimeters, the universal measurement of the volume of an engine's cylinders.

chassis
A load-bearing frame on wheels, which, in all early cars, carried the mechanical parts and to which the body was attached. Most of today's models have a unibody design, and so have no specific chassis unit, but the word survives to denote the drivetrain package.

choke
A carburetor valve that temporarily restricts air flow so that the fuel-air mixture is gasoline-rich and easier to ignite when the engine is cold.

clap-hand windshield wipers
Windshield wipers that fold together in the center of the windshield, and sweep toward the outside edges of the windshield when they are activated.

classic
A car built after January 1, 1940, and more than 25 years old.

close-coupled
A body style of a two-door compact car that places the rear two seats within the wheelbase.

clutch
A device that disconnects the engine from the transmission so that a different gear can be selected.

coachwork
A car's outer, painted body panels—work traditionally executed by a coachbuilder.

coefficient of drag
The result of a complex scientific equation, which proves how aerodynamic a car is, usually expressed as a figure to two decimal places. Drag means the resistance of a body to airflow and low drag means better penetration, less friction, and therefore more efficiency, although sometimes poor dynamic stability. The term is routinely shortened to Cd. The Citroën SM was considered to have an exceptionally low coefficient of drag figure of 0.24, which is better than most modern cars now at 0.30-0.25.

column gearchange
A gear-selector lever mounted on the steering column instead of on the floor.

combustion chamber
The space at the top of an engine's cylinder into which the fuel-air mixture is compressed by the piston when at its high point, and the place where the spark plug is located to initiate combustion.

compression ratio
The ratio between the volume of one cylinder and the combustion chamber when the piston is at the bottom of its stroke, and the volume of the combustion chamber alone when the piston is at the top of its stroke.

compression ring
See **piston ring**

compressor
A device that increases the pressure of a gas by reducing its volume by compression. Used in turbochargers and superchargers to increase the performance of the engine.

connecting rod
A mechanism that connects an engine's piston to the crankshaft—often shortened to con-rod.

copper-brazed engine
An engine found in Crosley cars and constructed from metal sheets, instead of castings, held together by copper alloy soldering techniques.

Cosworth-tuned
An engine modified by Cosworth, a UK-based designer and builder of engines for road and race cars.

coupe
From the French verb *couper*, ("to cut,") this originally referred to a two-door closed car with a lower roof-line. Coupes today tend to have a roofline tapering at the rear.

courtesy light
A small light activated on opening a car door, lighting the car interior, door sill, or ground beneath the car.

crankcase
The lower part of the cylinder block that houses the crankshaft.

crank handle
A hand tool inserted into the front of an engine and used to turn it so that the internal combustion process is activated. Also known, in the UK, as a starting handle.

crank pulley
The main pulley at the end of an engine's crankshaft. It is used to drive ancillary devices, such as the alternator and the water pump.

crankshaft
The main engine shaft that converts the reciprocating (up and down) motion of the pistons into a rotary motion to turn the wheels.

crumple zones
The front and rear sections of a car designed to deform or collapse on severe impact; the energy absorbed prevents damage to the passenger compartment and fuel tank.

cu in (cubic inches)
A former volumetric measurement of cylinder capacity—and therefore engine size—for engines in the US; replaced by the liter from the 1970s.

cylinder
The cylindrical bore in which an engine's pistons move up and down.

cylinder block
The body, usually of cast metal, into which cylinders are bored to carry the pistons in an internal combustion engine, and to which the cylinder head or heads attach.

cylinder head
The upper part of an engine, attached to the top of the cylinder block. It contains the spark plugs that ignite the fuel in the cylinders and usually the valves.

dead axle
An axle that carries a wheel, allowing it to spin freely, but through which no power is transmitted.

differential
A gear set in the drive system of a car that allows an outer wheel to rotate faster than an inner wheel, necessary when turning a corner.

DIN figures
A measure of engine power output defined by Germany's Deutsches Institut für Normung.

direct injection
See **fuel injection**

disc brakes
A braking system in which each wheel hub contains a disc that rotates with the wheel and is gripped by brake pads in order to slow the vehicle.

distributor
A device that routes high voltage from the ignition coil to the spark plugs in the correct firing order.

dohc (double-overhead camshaft)
See **camshaft**

downdraft carburetor
A carburetor in which fuel is fed into a downward current of air.

drag coefficient
See **co-efficient of drag**

drivebelt
A belt that drives various devices in, or attached to, a car's engine, including the alternator.

driveshaft
A revolving shaft that takes power from the engine to the wheels.

drivetrain
The group of mechanical assemblies—engine, transmission, driveshafts, and differentials—that generate and harness power in a car. Today these are collectively know as the "chassis," and can be transplanted into several different models to save on development costs. Sometimes "drivetrain" can refer to the engine and the transmission only.

drophead
A body style featuring a convertible top that folds flat.

drum brake
A braking system, largely supplanted by disc brakes, in which braking shoes are pressed against the inner surface of a drum that is attached to the car's wheel.

dual-circuit brakes
A braking system that has two independent hydraulic circuits to retain braking capability should one circuit fail.

dynamo
An engine-driven generator of electric power in early cars. It has now largely been replaced by the alternator.

entry-level
A car model that is the lowest-priced or features the lowest specifications in a range.

exhaust manifold
A piping system that carries waste exhaust gases from the cylinders to the exhaust pipe.

exhaust port
A passageway in the cylinder head leading from the exhaust valve(s) to the exhaust manifold.

exhaust valve
A valve in the cylinder head that opens at the beginning of the exhaust stroke, allowing the piston to push the exhaust gases out of the cylinder.

eyebrow headlights
A stylistic feature, first seen on the Lamborghini Miura, that gives the impressions of eyebrows or eyelashes framing the headlights.

factory team
A racing team funded by a car manufacturer.

fairing
Any cover or cowling designed to make components that extend outward (of an engine, for example) more aerodynamic.

fastback
A rear roofline profile that tapers to the end of the car's tail, giving it a sportier appearance.

FirePower engine
A sub-brand name for Chrysler's first generation of V8 engines with a hemispherical combustion chamber, made between 1951 and 1955.

firewall
The bodywork sections that form a barrier between the engine and the passenger compartments and that support the windshield.

flat-twin, flat-four, flat-six, flat-twelve
Any engine that has its cylinders and pistons positioned horizontally in two opposed banks. These are sometimes called "boxer" engines because the pistons in opposing pairs of cylinders move toward and away from each other alternately, as if trading punches.

floorpan
A shallow, pressed-metal tray that forms the underside of the car and carries suspension and other drivetrain elements. Clever design has often allowed the same floorpan to be shared by several different models.

fluid flywheel
A now-redundant transmission device allowing the driver to change gear without using a clutch.

flywheel
A heavy circular plate attached to the crankshaft that stores the rotational energy produced by the engine's torque impulses. Releasing this energy between impulses smoothes engine operation.

Formula 1
More formally known as the FIA (Federation Internationale de l'Automobile) Formula One World Championship, this is the premier world series of single-seat motor races. It was inaugurated in 1950.

four-stroke engine
This is the predominant type of car engine today. There are four stages in the power cycle, which occupies two crankshaft rotations: intake, compression, combustion, and exhaust. Each of these is governed by the upward or downward motion or "strokes" of the piston.

four-wheel drive (4WD)
See **4x4**

front-wheel drive
Power is transmitted to the two front wheels of a vehicle only. This

lightens the car, which needs no transmission shafts or trunking to its rear wheels.

fuel injection
A fuel supply system, universal to new cars, which dispenses with a carburetor. Fuel is pumped from the gasoline tank and sprayed by injectors straight into the engine's inlet ports, where it mixes with air before being burned in the cylinder. In diesel and direct-injection gasoline engines, fuel is injected straight into the cylinder, rather than into the inlet port.

Futuramic
The term used by General Motors' Oldsmobile division for the styling of its 1948–50 car range.

gas turbine
A jet-type rotary engine drawing its energy from the continuous burning of a flow of fuel–air mixture, which drives a turbine. Used experimentally in cars, it is too slow-reacting to directly replace the reciprocating engine.

gated shifter
A style of gearbox in which the slots into which the gear selector lever must be pushed are visible. It is usually found in sports or racing cars; other types of car tend to cover it up with a rubber or stitched-leather gaiter.

gear
A toothed or cogged machine part that meshes and rotates with other such parts to transmit torque.

gearbox
The metal case in which the gears and gear-changing mechanism are housed. It is usually joined to the end or the bottom of the engine.

Giugiaro
This can refer to the Italian car stylist Giorgio (often alternatively known as Giorgetto) Giugiaro, or to the design consultancy he started in 1968, which is more formally called Italdesign-Giugiaro. The consultancy was acquired by Volkswagen in 2010.

grand routier
An informal name, more common in English than French, which translates as "grand road traveler." It is often applied to elegant and fast European touring cars.

GT
From the Italian gran turismo, meaning "grand touring," these initials refer to high-performance closed cars.

gullwing doors
Doors that open upward. They are a key feature of the Mercedes-Benz 300SL and the DeLorean DMC-12.

hardtop
A sports, or sporty, car with a rigid roof that is either fixed or removable. A car with a fabric roof is called a soft-top.

hatchback
The tailgate on any non-wagon with a sloped, instead of vertical, tail. It is also a style of car pioneered in four-door form by the Renault 16 of 1965, and in two-door form by the Renault 5 of 1972.

head
See **cylinder head**

heat shield
Rigid or flexible layers of heat-resistant material that protect a car's components or bodywork from excessive engine- or exhaust-generated heat.

homologation
A rigorous testing program that new cars must undergo to ensure they meet construction and usage rules in a territory; only then can they be legally driven on the road. The term is also applied to the rules governing individual motorsport categories. A "homologation special" is, in general, a roadgoing version of a racing car; a minimum number of these must be constructed for it to qualify as a production model.

hood
A hinged covering for a car engine. It can also refer to the folding, canvas-covered top of any convertible car.

horizontally opposed layout
The full technical term for an engine whose cylinders are mounted flat on either side of the crankshaft.

hot hatch
The nickname for a high-performance version of a compact three-door (sometimes five-door) car, exemplified by the Renault 5 Alpine and Volkswagen Golf GTi of 1976.

hot rod
Short for "hot roadster," a US term that originated in the 1930s to

describe any standard car whose engine had been modified for higher performance. After World War II, hot rods were modified production cars used in straight-line speed trials.

hp (horsepower)
See **bhp (brake horsepower)**

Hydramatic transmission
General Motors' own brand of automatic transmission.

hydraulic brakes
A braking system that uses fluid to slow the car down via pressure on the brake pedal.

hydraulic damper
A damper is the proper name for a shock absorber, which dissipates the energy of a car's suspension movement and converts it hydraulically, via internal oil, into quickly dissipated heat.

Hydrolastic suspension
A brand of suspension system featuring fluid-filled rubber displacement units. It was used in cars made by the British Motor Corporation in the 1960s.

Hydropneumatic
Citroën's own brand name for its self-leveling suspension system. Hydraulic fluid from an engine-driven pressure pump transmits the movement of the suspension arms to metal gas springs containing pressurized nitrogen, which absorb bumps and maintain constant ride height. The system has preset ride heights to cope with differing driving conditions. Complex and eccentric, it never became popular.

idle-speed positioner
A device that optimizes the rate at which the engine runs at idle, when the throttle is closed, to maximize fuel efficiency.

ignition coil
An ignition system component that converts the car battery's 12-volt power into the thousands of volts required to ignite the spark plugs.

independent suspension
A suspension system that allows every wheel to move up and down independently of the others. Its advantages are better handling and a more comfortable ride.

Indianapolis 500
An iconic US motor race for single-seat cars, staged annually since 1911 at the oval Indianapolis Motor Speedway.

induction system
The apparatus through which air passes as it enters the engine.

inlet plenum chamber
An air chamber between an engine's throttle body and inlet manifold that beneficially affects the operation of the induction system.

inlet port
The route within a cylinder head through which the fuel-air mixture passes to the inlet valve.

inlet trumpet
A trumpet-shaped engine air intake designed to exploit the effects of wave motion to force more air into the cylinders.

inlet valve
The valve through which fuel is drawn into the engine cylinder.

inline engine
An engine that has its cylinders arranged in a straight line or row; it has been the predominant automotive layout in small cars for decades.

intercooler
A radiator that cools the compressed air from a turbocharger or supercharger before it enters the engine. This increases power and enhances reliability.

IRS (Independent Rear Suspension)
A suspension system in which the rear two wheels are free to move up and down independently of each other.

kei car
A Japanese taxation class for very small cars, which must be no more than 11.15 ft (3.4 m) in length and have an engine of no more than 660 cc to qualify.

knock-off wire wheels
These are wheels consisting of wire spokes between hub and rim that fit on to splined hubs, and are secured in place with, effectively, a large nut. Traditional British sports cars have traditionally had wings on these nuts so that it can be undone (or "knocked off") using a mallet; this system was for years illegal in Germany. Italian cars often had a plain nut that needed a special tool to undo it for wheel removal.

laminated windshield
Fitted to all new cars as a legal requirement for many years, a laminated windshield consists of

two layers of glass with a layer of plastic in between. The screen will not craze all over if hit by a stone, and won't splinter if it breaks.

landaulet-body style
A type of coachwork featuring a folding fabric top above the heads of the rear seat passengers while the front of the car remained closed in with a metal roof. The style, which is now old-fashioned, has often been seen on cars used for formal processions where royalty or political leaders wish to be seen by their subjects or citizens.

leaf spring
Also known as a "cart spring," this is a basic means of suspension noted for its toughness, although not for its supple ride quality. The spring comprises overlaid arcs (or leaves) of steel that are fixed to the underside of the car, forming a shock-absorbing cushion on which the car's axle presses. The heavier the car, the more leaves must be added to the spring.

limited-slip differential
A differential that counteracts the tendency of wheelspin if one driven wheel hits ice or another slippery surface.

limousine
A luxurious sedan, usually with a long or extended wheelbase, with an emphasis on rear-seat comfort. Limousines are sometimes fitted with glass divisions between driver and rear passengers.

live axle
A beam-type axle that contains the shafts that drive the wheels on each end.

MacPherson strut
Named after its inventor, Ford engineer Earl MacPherson, this is a suspension upright comprising a hydraulic damper with a coaxial coil spring. Most often used for front suspensions, it has the advantage of causing little intrusion into the engine bay.

Mille Miglia
A 1,000-mile (1,609-km) road race around Italy on public roads, held 24 times between 1927 and 1957. In 1977, the name was revived for an annual parade of historic cars.

monobloc
An engine design in which the cylinders are cast together as a single unit. This improves the

mechanical rigidity of the engine and the reliability of the sealing.

monocoque
See **unibody construction**

MPV
Shorthand for Multi-Purpose Vehicle or Multi-Passenger Vehicle. The term applies to tall, spacious cars that can carry at least five passengers, and often as many as nine, or versatile combinations of people and cargo as a people hauler.

muscle car
A US standard production car, usually with two doors, featuring a large-capacity, high-performance engine. Many experts consider the 1964 Pontiac GTO the first true muscle car, although the Rambler Rebel was an ancestor in the same spirit.

NACA duct
America's National Advisory Committee for Aeronautics created this distinctively shaped air intake, which can be used to ventilate internal components such as brakes while causing minimal disturbance to external aerodynamics.

NASCAR
The National Association for Stock Car Auto Racing—a US organization that oversees motor racing series and events.

ohc (overhead-camshaft)
See **camshaft**

ohv (overhead valve)
See **overhead-valve engine**

overdrive
A gear ratio for fast cruising that causes the gearbox output shaft to turn faster than the input shaft. This lowers the engine revs for a given vehicle speed, which cuts fuel consumption, but also torque, which restricts overtaking power.

overhead-camshaft
See **camshaft**

overhead-valve engine
An engine in which the inlet and exhaust valves are contained within the cylinder head, and not beside the cylinder, as they are in a side-valve engine.

overrider
A metal or rubber-faced metal upright fitted to a bumper to protect against the bumpers of other cars in a low-speed collision.

over-square engine
An engine in which the cylinder bore measurement is greater than the stroke.

people hauler
A popular term to describe an MPV, particularly one that has at least seven seats.

Pinin Farina/Pininfarina
An Italian coachbuilder and design consultancy founded as Pinin Farina in 1930 by Battista "Pinin" Farina. The company adopted the Pininfarina title in 1961.

piston
The component that moves up and down inside the engine cylinder and which, on the combustion stroke, transfers force from the expanding gas to the crankshaft via a connecting rod.

piston ring
An open-ended ring that fits into a groove in the outer surface of an engine's piston, sealing the combustion chamber. Piston rings also act to cool the piston by transferring heat to the cylinder wall, and regulate oil consumption.

platform
The concealed, but elemental and expensive, basic structure of a modern car. It is the task of car designers to achieve maximum aesthetic diversity from a single platform.

pony car
A genre of car informally named after the Ford Mustang, which was one of the first compact sporty coupes, aimed at the US "baby boomers" of the 1960s, and featured the emblem of a galloping horse. It could be ordered with several high-performance engine options.

powertrain
See **drivetrain**

propshaft
A contraction of "propeller-shaft"; a long shaft that conveys engine torque to the rear axle of a rear-wheel-drive or four-wheel-drive car.

pushrod engine
An engine in which the valves are not operated directly via the camshaft but via intermediate rods. This allows the valves and camshaft to be widely separated.

Q-car
A car with a performance that belies its mundane appearance. The

name derives from the heavily armored but innocuous-looking Q-ships in Britain's Royal Navy in World War I. A Q-car is often called a "Stealth car."

rack-and-pinion steering
A rack and pinion consists of two gears that together convert rotational motion into linear motion. It is the favored system for car steering because it provides good feedback to the driver about the behavior of the wheels, and gives what is often described as "accurate" steering.

radiator
A heat-exchanger used to cool liquids by presenting a large surface area to a flow of air.

razor-edge styling
A car styling trend toward sharp-edged lines that emerged in the UK coachbuilding industry in the late 1930s. It was a reaction to the prevailing preference for rounded, streamlined forms, and instead was used to convey dignity and formality.

rear-wheel drive
Power transmitted to the two rear wheels of a vehicle only.

reciprocating engine
Also known as a piston engine, which converts the up and down (or "reciprocating") motion of pistons to the rotary motion needed by the wheels.

redline
The maximum speed at which an engine is designed to operate without incurring damage. It is usually indicated by a red line on the rev counter dial.

rev
Short for revolutions-per-minute, a measure of engine speed.

roadster
A term that originally described an open car with a single seat to accommodate two or three abreast, but which now applies to any kind of two-seat open sports car.

rocker arm
A pivoted lever, one end of which is raised and lowered by the camshaft, either directly or via a pushrod, while the other end acts on the stem of the engine valve.

rocker panel
The section of a car's bodywork between the front and rear wheel

arches and below the side doors; usually called the "sill" in the UK.

rolling chassis
The frame of an older, separate-chassis car, with all drivetrain components fitted.

rollover bar
A strong metal hoop incorporated into the structure of a car with a folding roof. It is designed to protect the heads and upper torsos of driver and passengers should the vehicle overturn.

Rostyle wheels
A brand of styled pressed metal wheel manufactured by British company Rubery Owen (hence RO-style) made under license from the Motor Wheel Corporation of the US. They resemble cast aluminum or magnesium wheels found on racing and sports cars, but were heavier and much cheaper to make.

rotary engine
Any type of power unit that dispenses with the reciprocal motion of pistons, producing rotary motion directly. The only type ever fitted to production cars was one designed by Dr. Felix Wankel, and the most recent car to feature one was the Mazda RX-8, which appeared in 2001.

running board
A fixed step below the doors on early cars that aided entry and exit in the days when seating positions were high, as in horsedrawn carriages. Running boards began to disappear in the 1930s as cars were built lower.

running gear
The wheels, suspension, steering, and drivetrain of a car.

scavenge oil pump
In a dry sump engine, this additional pump evacuates oil that collects at the bottom of the engine, sending it to a separate oil tank.

sedan
Any type of car with a fixed metal roof.

semi-elliptic springs
Another term for leaf springs.

semi-trailing suspension
An independent suspension assembly for the rear wheels of a car in which each wheel hub is linked to the chassis by a lower

triangular arm that pivots at an acute angle to the vehicle center-line.

servo assisted braking
A braking system that uses a stored vacuum (or "vacuum servo") to magnify the force the driver applies to the brake pedal.

shaft drive
Power delivered from the engine to the wheels by means of rotating shafts.

side-valve engine
A form of engine design in which the valves are placed at the side of the cylinder, rather than within the cylinder head. In an L-head engine, the inlet and exhaust valves are placed together on one side of the cylinder; on a T-head engine they are located on opposite sides.

silencer
A chamber placed along the route of the exhaust pipe and designed to reduce exhaust noise.

six-pot
"Pot" is slang for "cylinder"; a six-pot engine is a six-cylinder unit.

skirts
Metal body panels that partly conceal the wheels to give a sleek styling continuity to body lines. They are usually fitted over the back wheels, and can be detached for wheel changes.

sleeve-valve engine
An engine that has a metal sleeve placed between the piston and cylinder wall. The sleeve oscillates with the motion of the piston and has holes that align with the cylinder's inlet and exhaust ports, facilitating the entry and exit of gases.

slide throttle
A type of throttle featuring a perforated plate that slides across the air inlet to allow more or less air to enter the engine.

sliding gear transmission
An old-fashioned manual gearbox. When in neutral, nothing inside the transmission revolves apart from the main drive gear (attached to the crankshaft) and cluster gear (attached to the wheels). To mesh the gears and apply engine power for motion, the driver presses the clutch and moves the shift handle to slide a gear along the mainshaft mounted above the cluster. The clutch is then released and the

engine power transmitted to the driven wheels. This system has been superseded by constant-mesh, or "synchromesh," gears.

small-block
The smallest V8 engines from Chevrolet and Ford, first produced in the 1950s.

sohc (single overhead-camshaft)
See **camshaft**

solenoid switch
An electronically controlled switch, more properly known as a relay, which allows a low-current electric circuit to control a high-current one. A car's starter motor, for example, requires a high-current circuit.

Spa 24 Hours
An annual endurance motor race held in Spa, Belgium, since 1924.

spark plug
An electrical device, screwed into the engine cylinder head of a gasoline engine, that ignites the fuel in the cylinder.

sports car
A two-seater with a convertible top, low or rakish lines, good roadholding, and above-average speed and acceleration.

spider
A "spider-phaeton" was originally a light horse-drawn cart with two seats and large wheels. Alfa Romeo adopted the name for its two-seat sports cars in 1954, and it is now the standard name for cars of that type, particularly ones that are compact and low with a snug cockpit.

spyder
The German equivalent of a "spider," and most commonly associated with Porsche.

stovebolt
A nickname for a Chevrolet straight-six-cylinder engine, coined because the fastener securing the valve cover, lifter cover, and timing cover resembles the bolt found on wood-burning stoves.

straight engine
See **inline engine**

subcompact
A North American term that originated in the 1970s to describe domestically produced rivals to the Volkswagen Beetle, such as the Ford Pinto and the Chevrolet Vega. The latter were smaller than the

Ford Falcon and the Chevrolet Corvair, which at the time were termed as "compacts" by Detroit manufacturing standards.

subframe
A self-contained structure, additional to the chassis, that is designed to carry specific components such as the engine or suspension.

suicide doors
A slang term for passenger doors that are hinged at the rear. Before the time when seatbelts were universally fitted, such doors could be hazardous if a passenger fell from a moving car. They were also, in early motoring times, prone to flying open when on the move and being forced back by the air stream, dragging the occupant out as they struggled to slam them shut.

sump
An oil reservoir at the bottom of an engine. A "dry sump" is usually fitted to a racing car or sports car engine that is likely to be subjected to high cornering, braking, and acceleration forces. In a conventional "wet sump," these forces can cause oil to surge, uncovering the oil pick-up pipe, which can result in engine damage. In a dry sump system, a scavenge pump removes oil as it falls into the sump, pumping it to a separate oil tank.

supercar
A very expensive, high-performance sports car. The first supercar is widely recognized to have been the Mercedes-Benz 300SL of 1954, but the term later came to describe a mid-engined two-seater as exemplified by the Lamborghini Miura of 1966.

supercharger
An engine-driven compressor that forces air into the inlet system, thereby increasing the amount of fuel-air mixture entering the cylinders, and hence the torque and power.

supermini
A market term for a small hatchback car with a four-cylinder engine, as exemplified by the Renault 5 of 1972.

suspension
A system that cushions the car's structure (and occupants) from the motion of the wheels as they traverse uneven road surfaces.

SUV
Stands for Sport-Utility Vehicle, a high-riding car with four-wheel drive intended for consumer rather than industrial use.

swash plate
A plate attached at an angle to a rotating shaft that is used to convert the shaft's rotational motion into reciprocal motion at pushrods lying parallel to the shaft axis.

swing axle suspension
An early type of independent rear suspension consisting of two half-axles pivoted at the rear differential. The wheels remain perpendicular to the axles at all times. The system improved ride comfort but could lead to alarming handling in high-speed maneuvers, and has not been used for several decades.

synchromesh gearbox
A gearbox in which gear wheels are in constant mesh. All-synchromesh gearboxes are universal in modern road cars.

tappet
A valvetrain component that makes sliding contact with the camshaft lobe, converting the cam's profile into the reciprocating motion of the valve.

Targa Florio
An open-road race through the mountains of Sicily, staged between 1906 and 1973, and since revived as a classic car event.

throttle
A device that controls the amount of air flowing into the engine.

torque
The twisting force produced by the engine.

torsion-bar
A suspension part that acts as a spring when twisted by the wheel's movements.

traction control
Electronic equipment, relying on sensors, that reduces wheelspin and, therefore, improves adhesion to the road.

trafficator
A direction indicator device, common in cars until the mid 1950s, consisting of a semaphore arm containing a small light that sticks out of the side of a car to show which way the driver intends to turn. They were replaced by vastly more effective flashing indicator lights on permanent view on a car's bodywork.

transaxle
The term for an assembly that combines the gearbox and differential components in a single casing.

transmission
All the components of a car's drivetrain, although often it refers to the gearbox alone.

transmission tunnel
The raised section running lengthwise along the centerline of the cabin of a car with a front engine and rear- or four-wheel drive. It houses the propshaft.

transverse engine
An engine that is mounted with its crankshaft axis across the car, rather than parallel to its centerline.

tuned
A term to describe an engine that has been modified for added performance.

turbocharger
A device fitted between an engine's inlet and exhaust systems that uses the exhaust gases to drive a turbine. This in turn drives a compressor that forces air into the intake system, boosting engine power when the car is under hard acceleration.

turning circle
The diameter of the circle described by a car's outer front wheel when turning with its steering at full-lock.

twin-cam
See **camshaft**

two-stroke engine
An engine with pistons that move up once and down once (performing two "strokes") in the combustion cycle.

two-wheel drive
Transmission to the front two or rear two wheels only, in contrast to four-wheel drive.

undertray
A cover with a flat or shaped surface that bolts to the underside of a car to create better aerodynamics or protect components from damage.

unibody construction
A car structure, now almost universal, in which the car body bears all the structural loads. It is, effectively, the chassis and the body combined in one strong unit.

unblown
An engine without a supercharger or turbocharger, properly termed "normally aspirated."

V4, V6, V8, V10, V12, V16
The designations for engines designed with their cylinders arranged in a V-formation for compactness. The numbers relate to the number of cylinders in each engine.

vacuum advance
A mechanism that enables the distributor to adjust spark timing according to engine load.

valvetrain
The parts of the engine that control the operation of the valves.

wagon
A square-backed car that is adapted to carry cargo, with a load bay accessed by a fifth door or tailgate, or else twin hinged doors. The term was originally coined for a utility vehicle used for running errands on large country estates. In the US, it is called a station wagon.

water-cooling
A system that uses circulating water to cool engine components. It is the predominant cooling system in modern engines, although some use an air-cooling system.

waterfall grille
A curved radiator shroud as a styling feature on the exterior nose of an older car, whose bright metal slats and cascading shape give the impression of a waterfall rushing over the car's metal prow. They give the impression of being aerodynamic, although frequently they are not.

wet-liner
A cylinder liner that is in direct contact with the engine's liquid coolant.

wheelbase
The exact distance between the axes of the front and rear wheels.

whitewall tires
Tires featuring a decorative ring of white rubber on their sidewalls. It was a popular styling fad, particularly in the US, from the late 1930s to the early 1960s.

wishbone suspension
An independent suspension system that uses two wishbone-shaped arms to link each wheel hub to the chassis.

works driver
A racing driver employed by a car manufacturer to drive for its team, as opposed to an independent "privateer."

Ziebart rust-proofing
A proprietary brand of rust-proofing material, added to cars in private ownership to stop the build-up of rust. It is named after its inventor, ex-mechanic Kurt Ziebart.

Directory

The best way to experience classic cars is to own them, and when time, space, and means allow, it's possible to build up a personal collection. To see the widest range, however, including the rarest and most sought-after models, visiting a museum or collection is definitely worthwhile. There are a huge number around the world, large and small, with some displaying broad selections, and others instead specializing in specific marques or vehicle types. In addition to seeing fascinating cars, museums and collections can be an excellent source of advice and information for your own cars, or those you hope to own.

UK

Bo'ness Motor Museum
Bridgeness Road, Bo'ness,
Scotland
EH51 9JR
www.motor-museum.bo-ness.org.uk

Brooklands Museum
Brooklands Road, Weybridge,
Surrey, KT13 0QN
www.brooklandsmuseum.com

**CM Booth Collection of
Historic Vehicles**
63 High Street, Rolvenden, Cranbrook,
Kent, TN17 4LP
www.morganmuseum.org.uk

Cotswold Motoring Museum
The Old Mill, Sherborne
St, Bourton-on-the-Water, GL54 2BY
www.cotswoldmotoringmuseum.co.uk

Coventry Transport Museum
Millennium Place, Hales Street,
Coventry, CV1 1JD
www.transport-museum.com

Donington Grand Prix Collection
Castle Donington,
Derby, DE74 2RP
www.donington-park.co.uk

**Haynes International
Motor Museum**
Sparkford, Yeovil,
Somerset, BA22 7LH
www.haynesmotormuseum.com

Lakeland Motor Museum
Old Blue Mill, Backbarrow,
Ulverston,
LA12 8TA
www.lakelandmotormuseum.co.uk

Llangollen Motor Museum
Pentrefelin Mill, Pentrefelin,
Llangollen, LL20 8EE
www.llangollenmotormuseum.co.uk

London Motor Museum
3 Nestles Avenue, Heys,
Middlesex, UB3 4SB
www.longonmotormuseum.co.uk

**The British Motor
Heritage Museum**
Banbury Road,
Gaydon, CV35 0BJ
www.britishmotormuseum.co.uk

The National Motor Museum
John Montagu Building,
Beaulieu, Hampshire, SO42 7ZN
www.beaulieu.co.uk

Europe

Rolls-Royce Museum
Gütle 11a, 6850 Dornbirn,
Austria
www.rolls-royce-museum.at

Autoworld
Jubelpark 11, 1000 Brussels,
Belgium
www.autoworld.be

Mahy Motor Museum
3 Rue Ema, 7900 Leuze-en-Hainaut,
Belgium
www.fiaheritagemuseums.com/
125-mahy-motor-musem.html

**Ferdinand Budicki Automobile
Museum**
Zavrtnica 7, 10000 Zagreb,
Croatia
www.otk-ferdinandbudicki.hr

**Cyprus Historic and Classic
Motor Museum**
Epimitheos Street, 3056, Limassol,
Cyprus
www.cyprusmotormuseum.com.cy

Skoda Auto Museum
Tr. Václava Klementa 294,
29360 Mladá Boleslav, Czech Republic
museum.skoda-auto.com

Mobilia Finland
Kisaranta, Gustav Third Road 75,
36270 Kangasala,
Finland
www.mobilia.fi/welcome-mobilia

Cite de l'Automotivle
15 Rue de l'Épée, 68 100 Mulhouse,
France
www.citedelautomobile.com

Le Conservatoire Citroën
Case Courrier AN 081, Bd Andre Citroën,
BP 13, 93601 Aulnay-sous-Bois Cedex,
France
www.citroen.fr/univers-citroen/citroen-
heritage/conservatoire-citroen.html

**Le Musee des 24 Heures-Circuit
de la Sarthe**
9 Place Luigi Chineti,
72100 Le Mans, France
musee24h.sarthe.com

**Musee Automobile Reims
Campagne**
84 Avenue Georges Clemancequ,
51100 Reims, France
www.musee-automobile-reims-champagne.
com

Musee de l'Aventure Peugeot
Carrefour de l'Europe,
25600 Sochaux, France
www.museepeugeot.com

The Renault Museum
27 Rue des Abondances,
92100 Boulogne Billancourt, Paris,
France
www.boulognebillancourt.com

Audi Museum
Ettinger Straße, 85057 Ingolstadt,
Germany
www.audi.com/corporate/de/
unternehmen/historie.html

**August Horch
Museum Zwickau**
Audistraße 7, 08058 Zwickau,
Germany
www.horch-museum.de

**Autostadt
(Volkswagen Museum)**
Stadtbrücke, 38440 Wolfsburg,
Germany
www.autostadt.de

BMW Museum
Am Olympiapark 1, 80809 München,
Gebäudeöffnung,
Germany
www.bmw-welt.com

Mercedes-Benz Museum
Mercedesstraße 100, 70372 Stuttgart,
Germany
www.mercedes-benz.com/en/
mercedes-benz/classic/museum/

The Porsche Museum
Porscheplatz 1,
70435 Stuttgart-Zuffenhausen,
Germany
www.porsche.com/museum/en

Hellenic Motor Museum
Ioulianou 33, Athina 104 33,
Greece
www.hellenicmotormuseum.gr

**Kilgarvan Motor
Museum**
Slaheny, Co. Kerry,
Ireland
www.kilgarvanmotormuseum.com

Museo Ferrari
Via Dino Ferrari, 43, 41053
Maranello (MO),
Italy
www.museomaranello.ferrari.com

HENRY FORD MUSEUM, USA

TOYOTA COMMEMORATIVE MUSEUM, JAPAN

Museo Lamborghini
Via Modena 12, 40019 Sant'Agata,
Bologna, BO,
Italy
www.lamborghini.com

Museo Mille Miglia
Viale della Bornata, 123,
25135 S. Eufemia, Brescia,
Italy
www.1000miglia.it

Museo Nazionale dell'Automobile
Corso Unita d'Italia, 40,
10126 Turin, Italy
www.museoauto.it

Museo Storico Alfa Romeo
Viale Alfa Romeo, 20020 Arese (MI),
Italy
www.museoalfaromeo.com

Louwman Museum
Leidsestraatweg 57, 2954 BB Den Haag,
The Netherlands
www.louwmanmuseum.nl

Retro Auto Museum Moscow
Ul. Rogozhskiy Val, 9/2, Moscow,
Russia, 109544
www.auto-retro-museum.ru

Automobile Museum of Barcelona
Via Augusta, 182, 08021 Barcelona,
Spain
www.anticcar.com

Saab Car Museum
Åkerssjövägen 18, 461 55 Trollhättan,
Sweden
saabmuseum.com

Volvo Museum
Arendal Skans, 405 08 Goteborg,
Sweden
www.volvomuseum.com

Swiss Museum of Transport
Lidostrasse 5, 6006 Lucerne,
Switzerland
www.verkehrshaus.ch

**Tofas Müseum of Cars and Anatolian
Carriages**
Fabrika Skans, 16030 Yıldırım,
Turkey
www.tofasanadoluarabalarimuzesi.com/

North America
The Canadian Automotive Museum,
99 Simcoe Sreet South, Oshawa,
Ontario L1H 4G7,
Canada
www.canadianautomotivemuseum.com

America's Car Museum
2702 East D St.
Tacoma, WA 98421
United States
www.americascarmuseum.org

America On Wheels
5 North Front St.
Allentown, PA 18102
United States
www.americaonwheels.org

Crawford Auto-Aviation Museum
10825 East Blvd.
Cleveland, OH 44106,
United States
www.wrhs.org/research/crawford

General Motors Heritage Center
6400 Center Dr.
Sterling Heights, MI 48312
United States
www.gmheritagecenter.com

Henry Ford Museum
20900 Oakwood Blvd.
Dearborn, MI 48124-5029
United States
www.thehenryford.org

Mullin Automotive Museum
1421 Emerson Ave.
Oxnard, CA 93033
United States
www.mullinautomotivemuseum.com

National Automobile Museum
10 Lake St.
Reno, NV 89501
United States
www.automuseum.org

Northeast Classic Car Museum
24 Rexford St.
Norwich, NY 13815
United States
www.classiccarmuseum.org

Simeone Automotive Museum
6825 Norwitch Dr.
Philadelphia, PA 19153
United States
www.simeonemuseum.org

Tampa Bay Automobile Museum
3301 Gateway Centre Blvd.
Pinellas Park, FL 33782
United States
www.tbauto.org

**The Indianapolis Motor Speedway
Hall of Fame Museum**
4790 West 16th St.
Indianapolis, IN 46222
United States
www.indianapolismotorspeedway.com

The Lane Motor Museum
702 Murfreesboro Pike
Nashville, TN 37210
United States
www.lanemotormuseum.org

Rest of the World
Museo Juan Manuel Fangio
Calle 18, Centro, 7620 Balcarce,
Buenos Aires,
Argentina
www.museofangio.com

National Motor Museum
Shannon Street, Birdwood,
South Australia 5234,
Australia
www.nationalmotormuseum.com.au

Shanghai Auto Museum
7565 Boyuan Road, Anting
Shanghai,
China
www.shautocity.com/english/jcbl.htm

The Grand Prix Museum
431 Rua Luis Gonzaga Gomes,
Macau, China
www.macau.com/en/
Grand-Prix-Museum-2-22-152.html

Honda Collection Hall
321-3597 Tochigi Prefecture,
Haga District, Motegi,
Hiyama, 120–1,
Japan
world.honda.com/collection-hall

Toyota Automobile Museum
41-100 Yokomichi, Nagakute City,
Aichi Prefecture 480-1118,
Japan
http://www.toyota.co.jp/Museum/english/

**Toyota Commemorative Museum
of Industry and Technology**
1-35, Noritake Shinmachi 4-chome,
Nishi-ku, Nagoya 451-0051,
Japan
www.tcmit.org/english

**Museum of Transport
and Technology**
805 Great North Road & Meola Road,
Western Springs,
Auckland 1022,
New Zealand
www.motat.org.nz

Southward Car Museum
Otaihanga Road, Paraparaumu 5254,
PO Box 611,
New Zealand
www.southwardcarmuseum.co.nz

**Franschhoek Motor
Museum**
PO Box 435, Franschhoek, 7690,
South Africa
www.fmm.co.za

**Al Ain Classis Car
Museum**
Ain Al Faida Complex,
Al Ain City
Emirate of Abu Dhabi,
United Arab Emirates
www.alainclassiccarsmuseum.net

**Emirates National
Automobile Museum**
Hameen Road, AlBhastra, Abu Dhabi,
United Arab Emirates
www.enam.ae

HAYNES INTERNATIONAL MOTOR MUSEUM, UK

MUSEO FERRARI, ITALY

Index

Page numbers in **bold** indicate main entries.

Acknowledgments

Dorling Kindersley would like to thank Editor-in-Chief, Giles Chapman, for his invaluable support in making this book.

In addition, Dorling Kindersley would like to extend thanks to Alvise-Marco Seno, Press Office, ZED Srl, Milan, Spain.

The publisher would like to thank the following people for their assistance in making the book: Steve Crozier at Butterfly Creative Solutions; Sanjay Chauhan for design help and Tina Jindal, Nishtha Kapil, Antara Moitra, Riji Raju, and Isha Sharma for editorial support at DK India; Joanna Chisholm for proofreading; and Vanessa Bird for preparing the index.

The publisher would also like to thank the following museums, companies, and individuals for their generosity in allowing Dorling Kindersley access to their cars for photography:

Avantgarde Cars
Tamworth, Staffordshire, B78 3QS
www.avantgardecars.co.uk

Benz Bavarian Ltd
Duffield, Derby, DE56 4FQ
www.benzbavarian.com

Terry Bone MGs
North Chailey, Sussex,
www.terrybone.co.uk

David Chapman
Upton-upon-Severn, Worcestershire

Coys
Richmond, London, TW9 2LL
www.coys.co.uk

DK Engineering
Chorleywood, Hertfordshire, WD3 6EA
www.dkeng.co.uk

Patrick Donlan
Calne, Wiltshire

Steve Dyer
Warrington, Cheshire

Robert Gardner
Knowle, West Midlands

Jeremy Gibson
Weare, Somerset

Group B Motorsport
Queensferry, Flintshire, CH5 2TB
www.groupbmotorsport.com

Haynes International Motor Museum
Sparkford, Somerset, BA22 7LH
www.haynesmotormuseum.com

Heritage Transport Museum
Bilaspur-Taoru Road, Gurgaon, Haryana, 122105, India

Jaguar Heritage
Coventry, West Midlands

Joe Mason
Worcester, Worcestershire

Olly Melliard
Shepshed, Leicestershire

Rawles Motorsport
Upper Froyle, Hampshire, GU34 4JR
www.rawlesmotorsport.co.uk

Robin Stainer
Bampton, Oxfordshire

Volkswagen UK Ltd
Milton Keynes, Bucks, MK14 5AN
www.volkswagen.co.uk

Picture Credits
The publisher would like to thank the following for their kind permission to reproduce their photographs:

(Key: a-above; b-below/bottom; c-center; f-far; l-left; r-right; t-top)

The Advertising Archives: 14, 20c, 70–71, 200, 228c, 256; **AF Fotografie:** 206tl, 206–207; **akg-images:** ullstein bild 52tl, 201cr, Jacques Boissay 178–179, Collection Dupondt 40bl, Interfoto / Friedrich 137cr, Interfoto / Friedrich Rauch 271c, Mondadori Portfolio 28clb, 86tl, 172cla, TT News Agency 270tl; **Alamy Stock Photo:** William Arthur 17bc, Bob Masters Classic Car Images 183ca, Ed Buziak 38b, Buzz Pictures 159cr, Car Collection 279cb, CPC Collection 69tr, culture-images GmbH 265tl, Ian Dagnall 310bl, Drive Images 67br, 159br, 271cr, Goddard Automotive 86bc, 251c, 257cla, Martyn Goddard 8, Stanley Hare 139b, Heritage Image Partnership Ltd. 88tl, Heritage Images 223bc, Stuart Hickling 122–123bc, imageBROKER 40ca, Interfoto 64, 250cla, Bo Jansson 208c, Keystone Pictures USA 137clb, Bob Kreisel 201cla, Lordprice Collection 136, Chris Mattison 277br, MF1 collection 185cb, Motoring Picture Library 21tl, 38–39t, 39tc, 39cra, 59cr, 151tl, 206cl, 207tl, 251cr, nawson 222cr, Christopher Nicholson 311bl, pbpgalleries 77tl, 166tl, Pictorial Press Ltd. 67bl, Shaun Pillai 87br, PNC Collection 249cra, Prisma Bildagentur AG 296tl, Matthew Richardson 222cl, 276cb, Rolling Stock 123br, Mark Scheuern 133cr, Phil Talbot 53cr, 89tl, 89tr, 248c, jonathan tennant 87cr, Tolbert Photo 152tl, Uber Bilder 279t, 292cr, 293br, Steve Vidler 310br, Vintage Archives 65ca, Chris Wilson 280tl, Tom Wood 182–183bc, Robert Zuber 101tr; **Art Tech Picture Agency:** 17c, 23cb, 69cb, 85crb, 85b, 109cb, 131cb, 139cb, 208b, 224–225t, 225b, 227b, 252b, 263b, 266–267t, 274b, 279b, 284b, 287t, 287cb, 290b, 291c, 294c, 295cb, 301cb; **Aston Martin Lagonda Limited:** 289cr; **© Bentley Motors :** 20bl, 21br; **BMW AG:** 146tl; **© Fiat Chrysler Automobiles N.V:** 29br, 100cr, 112–113; **Corbis:** Bettmann 15tc, 65cr, Walter Bibikow / JAI 80tl, Philippe Body / Hemis 216tl, Car Culture 33tl, 91t, Martyn Goddard 58–59bc, 59ca, Phillip A. Harrington 100tl, 101br, Vittoriano Rastelli 264tl, Transtock 48bc, Xu Xiaolin 302–303; **DERDEHMEL:** 108b; **Dorling Kindersley:** Matthew Ward / Willem van Aalst 92c, 92crb, 92b, Deepak Aggarwal. Courtesy of Heritage Transport Museum, Taoru 98cb, 216–217 (all other photos), 218 219 (all photos), ames Mann. Courtesy of National Motor Museum Beaulieu 49cra, Andrew Cluett 6br, 11br, Andy Crawford / Anthony Posner. Hendon Way Motors 72tr, 72c, 72bl, Andy Crawford / Julian Aubanel 106 (All), Matthew Ward / D. Baughan 235b, Benz Bavarian Ltd. 5br, 11bl, 62–63, James Mann / National Motor Museum Beaulieu 151cra, Terry Bone 4br, 10bl, 12–13, Matthew Ward / Brian Burgess 226 (All), James Mann / Tim Colbert 120–121ca, 121tl, 121tr, 121cra, Andy Crawford / Phillip Collier 227t, Matthew Ward / Geoff Cook 90–91b, Andy Crawford / Roy Craig 243ca, Andy Crawford / "57th Heaven" Steve West's 1957 Buick Roadmaster 99tl, Andy Crawford / "57th Heaven" Steve West's 1957 Buick Roadmaster 1c, 99tr, 99cra, Andy Crawford / Courtesy of Classic Restorations 177tr, Andy Crawford / Mr PGK Lloyd 174tr, 174crb, Andy Crawford / Nick O'Hara 61tc, Andy Crawford / Neil Crozier 161b, Matthew Ward / Barrie Cunliffe 161cb, Matthew Ward / Mike Farrington 164 (All), Matthew Ward / Alexander Fyshe 184clb, James Mann / Peter Harris 221cb, Harvey Stanley 9br, Haynes International Motor Museum 61cb, Heritage Motoring Club of India 99crb, Jaguar Heritage 9bl, 10br, Matthew Ward / Jeff Hine 22c, 22crb, 22b, James Mann. Courtesy of National Motor Museum Beaulieu 48–49t, Matthew Ward / Kevin Kay 252cb, Andy Crawford / Claude Kearley 176c, Dave King / Tallahassee Car Museum 121cb, 215cb, James Mann 44–45 (all other photos), 46–47 (all photos), James Mann / Haynes International Motor Museum 165t, James Mann / National Motor Museum 125tl, James Mann, courtesy of Harvey Stanley 7br, 296–297 (all other photos), 298–299 (all photos), James Mann, courtesy of Robin Stainer 166–167 (all other photos), 168–169 (all photos), James Mann, courtesy of Steve Dyer 102–103 (all other photos), 104–105 (all photos), James Mann, courtesy of Will Ianson 202–203 (all other photos), 204–205 (all photos), James Mann. Courtesy of A. Coldwell 126–127 (all other photos), 128–129 (all photos), James Mann. Courtesy of Andrew Cluett 140–141 (all other photos), 142–143 (all photos), James Mann. Courtesy of David Chapman 152–153 (all other photos), 154–155 (all photos), James Mann. Courtesy of Olly Melliard 258–259 (all other photos), 260–261 (all photos), James Mann. Courtesy of Patrick Donlan 116–117 (all other photos), 118–119 (all photos), James Mann. Courtesy of Richard Edwards 230–231 (all other photos),
232–233 (all other photos), James Mann. Courtesy of Robert Gardner 280–281 (all other photos), 282–283 (all photos), James Mann. Haynes International Motor Museum 134–135, 194–195 (all other photos), 196–197 (all photos), 213cr, Joe Mason 244t, 245tc, 245tr, 245ca, Matthew Ward / David Selby 30c, Matthew Ward / Garry Darby, American 50's Car Hire 79tl, 79cra, Matthew Ward / Gary Darby / American 50's Hire 79tr, Matthew Ward / L. Kavanagh 30cla, 30ca, 31tr, 31ca, Matthew Ward / on loan from Le Tout Petit Musée / Nick Thompson, director Sussex 2CV Ltd. 36tr, 36c, 36br, Matthew Ward / Tony Paton 31c, Andy Crawford / David Maughan 262 (All), Olly Melliard 7bl, James Mann / John Mould 49cb, James Mann, Haynes International Motor Museum 254–255, Matthew Ward / Colin Nolson 177b, Gary Ombler, courtesy of Benz Bavarian Ltd 80–81 (all other photos), 82–83 (all photos), Gary Ombler. Courtesy of Terry Bone 24–25 (all other photos), 26–27 (all photos), Gary Ombler. Jaguar Heritage 188–189 (all other photos), 190–191 (all photos), Andy Crawford / Privately Owned 184ca, 185tl, 185tc, 185cr, Matthew Ward / Cared for and cruised in by Mark Phillips 214tr, 214–215ca, 215tr, 215cra, Anthony Posner, Hendon Way Motors 220 (All), Matthew Ward / Terry Powell 238b, T. Powell 160tc, 161tr, 161cr, Matthew Ward / David Pratt 242 (All), James Mann. Courtesy of Chris Routledge 239t, Matthew Ward / John Skelton 114b, Andy Crawford / Desmond Small 239c, Matthew Ward / Irene Turner 252–253ca, 253tl, 253tr, 253cra, Matthew Ward / Roger Wait 215br, Matthew Ward / Chris Day 175b, Matthew Ward / Courtesy of Classic Restorations 176ca, Matthew Ward / Derek E.J. Fisher and Citroen 238cla, Matthew Ward / Dream Cars 6bl, Matthew Ward / Geoff Mitchell, Farnborough, England 98b, Matthew Ward / Mr PGK Lloyd 174c, Matthew Ward / Nick O'Hara 60cla, 60ca, 61ca, Matthew Ward / owner Mr P.G.K. Lloyd 174b, Matthew Ward / Panhard PL17 owned by Anthony T C Bond, Oxfordshire, editor of "Panoramique" (Panhard Club newsletter) 156 (All), Matthew Ward / Peggie Pollard 175t, Matthew Ward / Richard Tyzack's historic Rally Alpine 175cb, Matthew Ward / Skoda UK 79b, Matthew Ward / Steve Gamage 171b, E.J. Warrilow saved this car from the scrapyard in 1974; restored by the owner in 1990, maintaining all original panels and mechanics; winner of many concourse trophies 84 (All), Andy Crawford / L&C BMW, Tunbridge Wells 221b, Andy Crawford / Janet and Roger Westcott 150tr, 150c, 150b, James Mann / Chris Williams 286 (All); **Dr. Ing. h.c. F. Porsche AG, Germany:** © 2016 Dr. Ing. h.c. F.Porsche AG 250tl (Ferry Porsche), 250–251, 251br, 56tl, 57br; **Dreamstime.com:** Irinapiven 109b; **Ford Motor Company:** 241cr, 241br; **Henry Ford Museum & Greenfield Village:** From the Collections of The Henry Ford 100cl; **Getty Images:** Apic / Hulton Archive 240tl, Alain Benainous / Gamma-Rapho 132cr, Auger Benjamin 287b, Bettmann 32tl, 33tr, Bloomberg 93cb, Car Culture 265cr, CBS Photo Archive 194tl, The Enthusiastic Network 116tl, 212–213bc, BERTRAND GUAY / AFP 39cb, Keith Hamshere / Moviepix 268–269, Heritage Images 20, 58tl, 101tl, 162–163, 223tl, 223tr, Klemantaski Collection 182cr, Mondadori Portfolio 28–29bc, 89cb, 264br, National Motor Museum / Heritage Images 40tl, National Geographic / Michael E. Long 210–211, Leon Neal / AFP 147tr, Paul Popper / Popperfoto 148tl, Popperfoto 222tl, Willy Rizzo / Paris Match 172–173bc, LAPI / Roger Viollet 34–35, Roger Viollet 102tl, Rainer W. Schlegelmilch 88clb, 172tl, 236–237, Victor Sokolowicz 311br, ullstein bild 40–41, 52ca, Eric Vandeville / Gamma-Rapho 182tl, 182bl, WIN-Initiative 272–273; **Image created by Simon GP Geoghegan:** 19cb; **LAT Photographic:** 209c, 224b, 267b; **Giles Chapman Library:** 16c, 16bc, 28tl, 32cr, 33bc, 36c, 39b, 42–43, 52bc, 53cl, 54b, 55b, 66bl, 69ca, 76cr, 94–95, 110bc, 114ca, 115c, 122tl, 122bl, 144–145, 149bl, 149br, 157t, 158tl, 158cl, 158bc, 159cl, 159bc, 209b, 224ca, 224c, 228–229bc, 230tl, 240–241bc, 243cb, 244b, 246–247, 249cb, 263ca, 263cb, 266cla, 266c, 266b, 267c, 270c, 270bc, 274tr, 274ca, 274–275t, 275c, 276tl, 277cr, 277bc, 278 (All), 279ca, 284–285t, 285tr, 285cra, 287c, 288tl, 290cl, 291t, 291b, 292cl, 294b; **Louwman Museum-The Hague:** 19b, 23tr, 55c, 125br, 157b, 214cb; **magiccarpics.co.uk:** 20–21bc, 29cr, 32cl, 41c, 54c, 56bl, 57tr, 58cr, 58bl, 59br, 60b, 66c, 67cr, 86c, 87cl, 88br, 96tl, 96c, 96bl, 97cl, 97cr, 97br, 111cr, 111br, 122ca, 123c, 132bc, 133c, 133br, 146cl, 149cr, 173c, 183br, 188tl, 202tl, 212cr, 212bl, 213br, 229cr, 234b, 235cb, 240cr, 240bl, 253b, 257br, 275b, 277cla, 289cl, 293tl, 293c, Giulietta Berlina 75crb, John Colley 18tr, 18c, 18clb, 18br, 68tr, 68c, 68b, 74–75t, 75tr, 75cra, 208cla, 208ca, 209t, 225c, 263t, 294–295ca, 295tr, 295cra, Richard Dredge 74c, 75bl, 108–109t, 109tr, 109cr, 245crb, 248tr, 248b, Robert George 16cla, 16ca, 17ca, 138tr, 138c, 138crb, 138bc, 186 (All); **James Mann:** 19ca, 49br, 274cb, 300b; **Mary Evans Picture Library:** Interfoto 126tl, 276cr; **MAUTO – Museo Nazionale dell'Automobile collection (Torino):** 131b; **Malcolm McKay:** 125cra; **Morgan Motor Company Ltd.:** 96–97bc; **© British Motor Industry Heritage Trust:** 24tl, 44tl, 110tl, 110cra, 111cl, 111bc, 140tl, 146cr, 147bc, 148bl; **Motoring Picture Library / National Motor Museum:** 19t, 37tc, 37cb, 214b; **Newspress Ltd.; .:** Alfa Romeo 173br, Aston Martin 289br, Bentley 21tr, BMW 271br, Citroën 41cr, 41br, Jaguar 123cr, Maserati 183cr, Mercedes-Benz 53br; **Reinhard Lintelmann Photography (Germany):** 125clb; **Renault (UK):** 258tl; **Rex by Shutterstock:** 147tl, 264cl, Everett / Shutterstock 288bc, Magic Car Pics 15br, 148cr, 207tc, 207tr, 265tr, 293tr, 300cb, Magic Car Pics / Shutterstock 172bl, 173cr, National Motor Museum / Shutterstock 56br, Shutterstock 29ca, 29bc; **Science Photo Library:** Library of Congress 212tl; **© Aaron Severson:** 233br; **SuperStock:** Heritage 288cla; **Matteo Tessarow:** 157cb; **TopFoto.co.uk:** Fine Art Images / HIP 50–51, Roger-Viollet 61b; **Toyota UK:** 229br, Toyota Heritage Images 228tl, 228bl, 229cla; **Martijn van Well:** 292tl; **Volvo Car Group:** 66tl; **ZED Milano Srl:** 76tl, 76cl, 77tr, 77b

All other images © Dorling Kindersley
For further information see: www.dkimages.com